The B
Series ed

Derel

The Message of
the Trinity

The Bible Speaks Today: Bible Themes series

The Message of the Living God
His glory, his people, his world
Peter Lewis

The Message of the Resurrection
Christ is risen!
Paul Beasley-Murray

The Message of the Cross
Wisdom unsearchable, love indestructible
Derek Tidball

The Message of Salvation
By God's grace, for God's glory
Philip Graham Ryken

The Message of Creation
Encountering the Lord of the universe
David Wilkinson

The Message of Heaven and Hell
Grace and destiny
Bruce Milne

The Message of Mission
The glory of Christ in all time and space
Howard Peskett and Vinoth Ramachandra

The Message of Prayer
Approaching the throne of grace
Tim Chester

The Message of the Trinity
Life in God
Brian Edgar

The Message of the Trinity

Life in God

Brian Edgar

*Director of Theology and Public Policy,
Australian Evangelical Alliance*

Inter-Varsity Press

INTER-VARSITY PRESS
38 De Montfort Street, Leicester LE1 7GP, England
Email: ivp@uccf.org.uk
Website: www.ivpbooks.com

First published 2004

British Library Cataloguing in Publication Data
A catalogue record for this book is available from the British Library.

ISBN 1-84474-048-X

Set in Stempel Garamond
Typeset in Great Britain by CRB Associates, Reepham, Norfolk
Printed and bound in Great Britain by Creative Print and Design (Wales), Ebbw Vale

Inter-Varsity Press is the publishing division of the Universities and Colleges Christian Fellowship (formerly the Inter-Varsity Fellowship), a student movement linking Christian Unions in universities and colleges throughout Great Britain, and a member movement of the International Fellowship of Evangelical Students. For more information about local and national activities write to UCCF, 38 De Montfort Street, Leicester LE1 7GP, email us at email@uccf.org.uk or visit the UCCF website at www.uccf.org.uk.

*Dedicated to my parents
Gerald and Marguerite
with love and appreciation
2 Corinthians 13:14*

Contents

BST The Bible Speaks Today

GENERAL PREFACE

THE BIBLE SPEAKS TODAY describes three series of expositions, based on the books of the Old and New Testaments, and on Bible themes that run through the whole of Scripture. Each series is characterized by a threefold ideal:

- to expound the biblical text with accuracy
- to relate it to contemporary life, and
- to be readable.

These books are, therefore, not 'commentaries', for the commentary seeks rather to elucidate the text than to apply it, and tends to be a work rather of reference than of literature. Nor, on the other hand, do they contain the kinds of 'sermons' that attempt to be contemporary and readable without taking Scripture seriously enough. The contributors to *The Bible Speaks Today* series are all united in their convictions that God still speaks through what he has spoken, and that nothing is more necessary for the life, health and growth of Christians than that they should hear what the Spirit is saying to them through his ancient – yet ever modern – Word.

ALEC MOTYER
JOHN STOTT
DEREK TIDBALL
Series editors

Preface

It is a very great privilege to be asked to write a book about the Holy Trinity. The process of writing it has been one of the finest spiritual exercises possible. The time that I have spent on this manuscript has been very precious and not solitary at all, for I have been very aware of the presence and the love of God the Father, the Son and the Spirit. If the secret to writing a good book is having a good topic then I have been fortunate indeed, for there is no greater subject for human thought than the nature and the life of God.

All those who derive some benefit from this book should be aware of the contribution which has been made by Barbara, my wife and friend. Her part extends far beyond being gracious about my absences and preoccupation with writing, and includes making a very real contribution to the content of the book itself through what she has helped me to learn about God through her own life, prayer and love. There is no doubt that writing about the relationships of Father, Son and Spirit is influenced by one's own experience of family and relationships, so I am also indebted to my whole family, especially my parents, Gerald and Marguerite, to whom I have dedicated this book, and my wonderful daughters, Karly and Tara. I have learnt much from them all.

For the most part this has been a spare time activity, mainly written while I was lecturer and Academic Dean at the Bible College of Victoria. I would like to thank my colleagues on the faculty who helped provide a very fine environment for this pursuit. The students also played their part, perhaps unknowingly, as they were the first recipients of parts of the book which I presented in various lectures and chapels.

My thanks go to Dr Derek Tidball, Bible Themes Series Editor, and Dr Philip Duce, Theological Books Editor of Inter-Varsity Press, not only for the invitation to write on the Trinity but also for their careful advice and the very positive influence they had on content and style. Every reader should be grateful for their involvement!

I trust that the readers will gain benefit from this book and especially that they might find from this exposition of Scripture a deeper understanding of the grace of the Lord Jesus Christ, the love of God and the fellowship of the Holy Spirit.

Abbreviations

AV	The Authorized (King James) Version of the Bible, 1611
ET	English Translation
LXX	The Septuagint (a Greek translation of the Old Testament)
NEB	The New English Bible (1961)
NIV	The New International Version of the Bible (1978)
NRSV	The New Revised Standard Version of the Bible (1989)
RSV	The Revised Standard Version of the Bible (1952)
TEV	Today's English Version (The Good News Bible, 1976)
TNIV	Today's New International Version of the Bible (2002)

Bibliography

Adam, Peter, *Living the Trinity* (Grove Books, 1982).

Allen, Leslie C., *Ezekiel 20 – 48*, Word Biblical Commentary (Word, 1990).

Aquinas, Thomas, *Summa Theologica*, Part 3, Question 34 (Christian Classics, 1981).

Athanasius, 'Against the Arians', in P. Schaff and H. Wace (eds.), *The Nicene and Post-Nicene Fathers of the Christian Church*, Vol. 4 (Eerdmans, 1978).

Augustine, 'On the Holy Trinity', in P. Schaff and H. Wace (eds.), *The Nicene and Post-Nicene Fathers of the Christian Church*, Vol. 3 (Eerdmans, 1978).

Barclay, William, *The Letter to the Corinthians* (Westminster, 1975).

Barnett, Paul, *The Message of 2 Corinthians*, The Bible Speaks Today (Inter-Varsity Press, 1988).

Barrett, C. K., *The Holy Spirit in the Gospel Tradition* (SPCK, 1958).

———, *1 Corinthians*, Black's New Testament Commentary Series (Adam and Charles Black, 1968).

———, *The Acts of the Apostles*, International Critical Commentary, Vol. 1 (T. and T. Clark, 1994).

Barth, Karl, *Church Dogmatics*, eds. G. W. Bromiley and T. F. Torrance (T. and T. Clark, 1936), Vol. I, Part 1.

———, *Church Dogmatics*, eds. G. W. Bromiley and T. F. Torrance (T. and T. Clark, 1956), Vol. I, Part 2.

———, *Church Dogmatics*, eds. G. W. Bromiley and T. F. Torrance (T. and T. Clark, 1956), Vol. IV, Part 1.

Barth, Markus, *Ephesians 1 – 3*, Anchor Bible Commentary (Doubleday, 1974).

———, *Ephesians 4 – 6*, Anchor Bible Commentary (Doubleday, 1974).

Bauckham, Richard, *Jude, 2 Peter*, Word Biblical Commentary (Word, 1983).

————, *Jude and the Relatives of Jesus in the Early Church* (T. and T. Clark, 1990).

Best, Ernest, *Ephesians*, International Critical Commentary (T. and T. Clark, 1998).

Blomberg, Craig, *1 Corinthians* (Zondervan, 1994).

Bock, Darrell L., *Luke 1:1 – 9:50*, Baker Exegetical Commentary on the New Testament (Baker, 1994).

Boff, Leonard, *Trinity and Society* (Orbis, 1986).

Bosch, David, *Transforming Mission* (Orbis, 1991).

Brown, R. E., *The Gospel according to John XIII – XXI*, Anchor Bible Commentary (Doubleday, 1970).

————, *The Birth of the Messiah* (Image Doubleday, 1979).

Bruce, F. F., *The Epistle of Paul to the Romans* (Eerdmans, 1963).

————, *Commentary on Galatians* (Eerdmans, 1982).

————, *The Acts of the Apostles* (Apollos/Eerdmans, 1990).

Buckley, James I. and David S. Yeago, *Knowing the Triune God* (Eerdmans, 2001).

Calvin, John, *Institutes of the Christian Religion* (Eerdmans, 1989).

Carson, D. A., *Showing the Spirit* (Baker, 1987).

Clements, R. E., *Deuteronomy* (Journal for the Study of the Old Testament, 1989).

Cochrane, Charles Norris, *Christianity and Classical Culture: A Study of Thought and Action from Augustus to Augustine* (Oxford University Press, 1940).

Craigie, P. C., *The Book of Deuteronomy*, New International Commentary on the Old Testament (Eerdmans, 1976).

Cranfield, C. E. B., *The Epistle to the Romans*, Vol. 1, International Critical Commentary (T. and T. Clark, 1975).

Cunningham, David S., *These Three are One* (Blackwell, 1998).

Davies, W. D. and D. C. Allison, *The Gospel According to Matthew*, International Critical Commentary (T. and T. Clark, 1988).

Davis, Stephen, Daniel Kendall and Gerald O'Collins (eds.), *The Trinity: An Interdisciplinary Symposium on the Trinity* (Oxford University Press, 2000).

Dubay, Thomas, *The Evidential Power of Beauty* (Ignatius, 1999).

Dunn, J. D. G., *Christology in the Making* (SCM, 1980).

————, *Romans 9 – 16*, Word Biblical Commentary (Word, 1988).

————, *The Theology of Paul the Apostle* (Eerdmans, 1998).

English, Donald, *The Message of Mark*, The Bible Speaks Today (Inter-Varsity Press, 1992).

Erickson, Millard J., *Making Sense of the Trinity: Three Crucial Questions* (Baker, 2000).

Fairweather, I. C. M. and J. I. H. McDonald, *The Quest for Christian Ethics* (Handsel Press, 1984).

Fee, Gordon, *God's Empowering Presence* (Hendrikson, 1994).

Fiddes, Paul, *Participating in God* (Darton, Longman and Todd, 2000).

Fitzmyer, Joseph, *Romans*, Anchor Bible Commentary (Doubleday, 1993).

——, *The Acts of the Apostles*, Anchor Bible Commentary (Doubleday, 1997).

France, R. T., *The Gospel of Mark*, The New International Greek Testament Commentary (Eerdmans/Paternoster, 2002).

Furnish, Victor Paul, *II Corinthians*, Anchor Bible Commentary (Doubleday, 1984).

Giles, Kevin, *The Trinity and Subordination* (Inter-Varsity Press, 2001).

Greenberg, Moshe, *Ezekiel 21 – 37*, Anchor Bible Commentary (Doubleday 1997).

Gregory of Nazianzen, 'Orations', in P. Schaff and H. Wace (eds.), *The Nicene and Post-Nicene Fathers of the Christian Church*, Vol. 7 (Eerdmans, 1978).

Guelich, Robert A., *Mark 1 – 8:26*, Word Biblical Commentary (Word, 1989).

Gunton, Colin, *The One, the Three and the Many* (Cambridge University Press, 1993).

——, *The Promise of Trinitarian Theology* (T. and T. Clark, 2001).

Hafeman, Scott J., *2 Corinthians*, The NIV Application Commentary (Zondervan, 2000).

Heim, S. Mark, *The Depth of the Riches: A Trinitarian Theology of Religious Ends* (Eerdmans, 2001).

Heron, Alistair, (ed.), *The Forgotten Trinity* (British Council of Churches, 1991).

Hilary of Poitiers, 'On the Trinity', in W. Sanday (ed.), *The Nicene and Post-Nicene Fathers of the Christian Church*, Vol. 9 (Eerdmans, 1979).

Hill, David, *Matthew* (Marshall, Morgan and Scott, 1972).

Hodgson, Leonard, *The Doctrine of the Trinity* (Nisbet, 1951).

Jenson, Robert, *The Triune Identity* (Fortress, 1987).

Jüngel, Eberhard, *The Doctrine of the Trinity: God's Being is in Becoming* (Eerdmans, 1976).

Kaiser, Christopher, 'The Discernment of the Trinity', in *The Scottish Journal of Theology*, 28 (1975), No. 5, 457.

Käsemann, Ernest, *Commentary on Romans* (SCM, 1980).

Keck, Leander, 'The Spirit and the Dove', in *New Testament Studies* 17 (1970–71).

Keener, Craig, *IVP Bible Background Commentary* (Inter-Varsity Press, 1993).

15

Kelly, Anthony, *The Trinity of Love: A Theology of the Christian God* (Michael Glazier, 1989).

Kistemaker, S. J., *Exposition of the Acts of the Apostles*, New Testament Commentary (Baker, 1990).

——, *1 Corinthians*, New Testament Commentary (Baker, 1993).

——, *James, Epistles of John, Peter and Jude*, New Testament Commentary (Baker, 1995).

Köstenberger, Andreas and Peter O'Brien, *Salvation to the Ends of the Earth* (Apollos, 2001).

Kruse, Colin, *John*, Tyndale New Testament Commentaries (Inter-Varsity Press, 2003).

——, *2 Corinthians*, Tyndale New Testament Commentaries (Inter-Varsity Press, 1987).

Küng, Hans, *On Being a Christian* (Collins, 1977).

LaCugna, Catherine Mowbray, *God For Us: the Trinity and the Christian Life* (HarperSanFrancisco, 1973).

Lloyd-Jones, D. Martyn, *The Basis of Christian Unity* (IVF, 1962).

Lonergan, Bernard, *The Way to Nicea: The Dialectical Development of Trinitarian Theology* (Darton, Longman and Todd, 1976).

Longenecker, Richard N., *New Testament Social Ethics for Today* (Eerdmans, 1984).

——, *Galatians*, Word Biblical Commentary (Word, 1990).

Lossky, V., *Orthodox Theology* (St Vladimir's Press, 1978).

Lucas, Dick and Christopher Green, *The Message of 2 Peter and Jude*, The Bible Speaks Today (Inter-Varsity Press, 1995).

Luther, Martin, *A Commentary on St Paul's Epistle to the Galatians* (James Clark, 1972).

——, *Commentary on Romans* (Kregel, 1976).

Marcus, J., *Mark 1 – 8*, Anchor Bible Commentary (Doubleday, 2000).

Marshall, I. H., *The Gospel of Luke: A Commentary on the Greek Text* (Paternoster, 1978).

Martin, Ralph P., *2 Corinthians*, Word Biblical Commentary (Word, 1986).

Mascall, E. L., *The Triune God* (Churchman Publishing, 1986).

Mayes, A. D. H., *Deuteronomy*, New Century Bible Commentary (Eerdmans, 1982).

McGrath, Alister, *Understanding the Trinity* (Kingsway, 1987).

McKane, William, *Proverbs* (SCM, 1970).

McKnight, Scot, *A Light among the Gentiles* (Fortress, 1991).

——, *Galatians*, NIV Application Commentary (Zondervan, 1995).

Miller, Patrick D., *Deuteronomy* (John Knox, 1990).

Mitton, C. Leslie, *Ephesians*, New Century Bible Commentary (Eerdmans, 1981).

Moltmann, Jürgen, *The Trinity and the Kingdom of God* (SCM, 1981).

———, *The Way of Jesus Christ* (SCM, 1990).

———, *History and the Triune God* (SCM, 1991).

Moo, Douglas, *The Epistle to the Romans*, New International Commentary on the New Testament (Eerdmans, 1996).

Morris, Leon, *Luke*, Tyndale New Testament Commentaries (Inter-Varsity Press, 1974).

———, *The Epistle to the Romans* (Eerdmans, 1988).

———, *Matthew*, Tyndale New Testament Commentaries (Inter-Varsity Press, 1992).

Murphy, R. E., *Proverbs* (Nelson, 1998).

Newbigin, Lesslie, *The Open Secret* (Eerdmans, 1978; rev. edn 1995).

Nolland, John, *Luke 1 – 9:20*, Word Biblical Commentary (Word, 1989).

O'Collins, Gerald, *The Tripersonal God: Understanding and Interpreting the Trinity* (Paulist, 1999).

Olson, Roger and Christopher Hall, *The Trinity* (Eerdmans, 2002).

Owen, John, *The Works of John Owen*, Vol. 2 (Banner of Truth, 1966).

Pannenberg, Wolfhart, *Jesus – God and Man* (SCM, 1968).

———, *Systematic Theology*, 3 Vols (Eerdmans, 1991).

Payne, D. F., *Deuteronomy*, Daily Bible Study Series (Westminster, 1985).

Peters, Ted, *God as Trinity* (Westminster, 1993).

Pinnock, C. H., *Reason Enough* (Inter-Varsity Press, 1980).

Piper, John, *Desiring God: Meditations of a Christian Hedonist* (Multnomah, 1986).

Powell, Samuel M., *Participating in God: Creation and Trinity* (Fortress, 2003).

Prior, D., *The Message of 1 Corinthians*, The Bible Speaks Today (Inter-Varsity Press, 1985).

Pritchard, J. B., *Ancient Near Eastern Texts* (Princeton University Press, 1969).

Ramsey, Michael, *Holy Spirit: A Biblical Study* (SPCK, 1977).

Rolle, Richard, 'The Amending of Life' in D. Jeffrey (ed.), *The Law of Love: English Spirituality in the Age of Wyclif* (Eerdmans, 1988).

———, 'The Law of Love', in D. Jeffrey (ed.), *The Law of Love: English Spirituality in the Age of Wyclif* (Eerdmans, 1988).

Rusch, William, *The Trinitarian Controversy, Sources of Early Christian Thought* (Fortress, 1980).

17

Sanders, E. P., *Paul and Palestinian Judaism* (Fortress, 1977).

Schaberg, Jane, *The Father, the Son and the Holy Spirit* (Scholars Press, 1982).

Schnackenberg, R., *The Gospel According to John*, Vol. 3 (Crossroads, 1982).

Schwöbel, Christoph (ed.), *Trinitarian Theology Today: Essays on Divine Being and Action* (T. and T. Clark, 1995).

Sherlock, Charles, *God on the Inside* (Acorn, 1991).

Smith, J. B., *Embracing the Love of God* (HarperCollins, 1995).

Smith, Robert H., *Matthew* (Augsburg, 1982).

Snodgrass, Kyle, *Ephesians* (Zondervan, 1996).

Stott, John R. W., *The Message of Acts*, The Bible Speaks Today (Inter-Varsity Press, 1990).

———, *The Message of Romans*, The Bible Speaks Today (Inter-Varsity Press, 1994).

Taylor, J. V., *The Go-Between God* (SCM, 1972).

Thielicke, Helmut, *The Evangelical Faith* (Eerdmans, 1984).

Thomas, D. W., *Documents of Old Testament Times* (Harper and Row, 1961).

Thompson, John, *Modern Trinitarian Perspectives* (Oxford University Press, 1994).

Thurmer, John, *A Detection of the Trinity* (Paternoster, 1984).

Toon, Peter, *Our Triune God: A Biblical Portrayal of the Trinity* (Victor/Bridgepoint, 1996).

Toon, Peter and James D. Spiceland, *One God in Trinity* (Cornerstone, 1980).

Torrance, Alan J., *Persons in Communion: Trinitarian Description and Human Participation* (T. and T. Clark, 1996).

Torrance, James B., *Worship, Community and the Triune God of Grace* (Paternoster, 1996).

Torrance, Thomas F., *The Christian Doctrine of God: One God in Three Persons* (T. and T. Clark, 1996).

Turner, Kathryn, *Jesus, Humanity and the Trinity* (T. and T. Clark, 2001).

Vanhoozer, Kevin J. (ed.), *The Trinity in a Pluralistic Age* (Eerdmans, 1997).

Wainwright, Arthur W., *The Trinity in the New Testament* (SPCK, 1975).

Weinandy, Thomas G., *The Father's Spirit of Sonship: Reconceiving the Trinity* (T. and T. Clark, 1995).

Welch, Claude, *The Trinity in Contemporary Theology* (SCM, 1953).

White, James R., *The Forgotten Trinity: Recovering the Heart of Christian Belief* (Bethany House, 1998).

Witherington III, Ben, *Grace in Galatia* (T. and T. Clark, 1998).

Wright, N. T., *The Climax of the Covenant: Christ and the Law in Pauline Theology* (T. and T. Clark, 1991).

———, *The Lord and his Prayer* (SPCK, 1996).

———, 'Born of a Virgin', in N. T. Wright and M. J. Borg, *The Meaning of Jesus: Two Visions* (HarperCollins, 1998), 175–178.

Ziesler, J., *Paul's Letter to the Romans* (SCM, 1987).

Zizioulas, John D., *Being as Communion: Studies in Personhood and the Church* (St Vladimir's Press, 1985).

Introduction

At the outset let me clearly state the conviction which pervades this book, that the Christian doctrine of God as Trinity is fundamentally simple, thoroughly practical, theologically central and totally biblical. It is not, as sometimes suggested, an abstract or philosophical construction with an unusual perspective on mathematics which makes three equal to one! It is not a doctrine which is incomprehensible in presentation, irrelevant in practice, unnecessary theologically or unbiblical in form. It is in fact the distinctive Christian doctrine and essential for Christian life and discipleship. My aim is to show that the doctrine of the Trinity means that God can be known intimately and personally as Father, Son and Holy Spirit. Although the term 'Trinity' does not itself appear in the Bible, it is a thoroughly biblical doctrine. The word itself comes from the Latin *trinitas* which connects three (*tres*) with one (*unus*), but the idea precedes the word. The early Christians could not avoid the idea of God as Father, Son and Spirit as they reflected on the events surrounding the person of Jesus Christ and their own experience of him as Lord. Consequently, the doctrine of the Trinity is not found or proved in a single verse of Scripture alone, for it permeates the thinking and the writing of the early church. It is something found in the whole testimony of Scripture concerning the story of salvation and is an unavoidable implication of the revelation of God in Jesus Christ through the power of the Holy Spirit.

1. The doctrine of the Trinity is comprehensible

Unfortunately, the doctrine of the Trinity has developed a reputation as a belief which is difficult to understand. This is not helped by the use of mathematical terms (as though the aim was to explain 'three in one and one in three') or philosophical terms such as those prevalent in the fourth century (such as 'person', *hypostasis, ousia* and 'essence'). This is not to say that such terms are completely unhelpful, however. When a crisis emerged in the third and fourth centuries regarding how to reconcile belief in one God with the worship of Christ, the Fathers of the church realized that such questions 'cannot be answered in purely biblical language, because the questions are about the meaning of biblical language itself'.[1] The introduction of non-biblical terminology and thought forms offered new and creative opportunities for exploring the nature of God, but it also introduced risks. The increasingly philosophical and speculative nature of trinitarian discourse led away from biblical simplicity and the comprehensibility of the doctrine of the Trinity suffered as a result. The early Fathers often said that the only difference between the Father and the Son is that the Father is the Father and the Son is the Son. In other words, one cannot really define the distinctive character of Father, Son and Spirit. This is illustrated in Augustine of Hippo's well-known and oft-quoted comment on the persons of the Trinity, 'When the question is asked "What three?" human language labors altogether under great poverty of speech. The answer, however, is given, "Three persons" not that it might be spoken but that it might not be left unspoken.'[2] This kind of agnosticism about the characteristics of the three persons of the Trinity means that the attributes of God are inevitably discussed in terms of the divine oneness and the implications of the three persons for understanding the divine nature are minimized. The aim of this book is to show that God can indeed be known as Trinity, as Father, Son and Spirit, through reading and prayerful reflection upon the Scriptures.

2. The doctrine of the Trinity is logical

Is the doctrine of the Trinity logical? Yes, but logic alone does not enable the Trinity to be understood. It is more a matter of faith. Many are convinced that the Trinity is comprehended when it is expressed in reasonable, logical terms and one common attempt to explain it logically is to utilize the analogy of someone who is simultaneously a father, a son and a husband. Despite the superficial attractiveness of this, it really isn't very helpful. For example, I have those three roles or relationships, but it is always essentially the same me who has them, because when it is all boiled down, I exist in one way and in one way only. I am not like Father, Son and Spirit

---

[1] R. P. C. Hanson, *The Search for the Christian Doctrine of God* (T. and T. Clark, 1988), xx–xxii, cited in C. A. Hall, *Learning Theology with the Church Fathers* (IVP, 2002), 55.
[2] Augustine, *Trinity*, 5.9.

who interact and relate together. I am just me. And the whole point, of course, is that God is *not* like you or me. We have to admit that we really cannot imagine what it means to exist in that way, but that does not mean that the idea is illogical. Just as it is impossible for a rock to imagine what it is like to exist as a person, so it is impossible for us to really imagine what it means for God to exist in more than the one way in which we do. But the fact that we cannot imagine it is no reason to say that there *cannot* be another form of existence which is different from our own. The problem lies with our imagination rather than with the concept. We have at least one advantage over the rock which cannot conceive of being human because we human beings can at least *conceive* of the idea of God, even if we cannot actually *imagine* what this means. This is not unusual; there are many things we can conceive of which are difficult to imagine. For example, I am not sure that I can really imagine a million of anything. When I try it seems pretty much the same as when I imagine ten million, even though there is a considerable difference between them. It is possible for us to *conceive* of the difference without being able to *imagine* it. We can conceive of God as Father, Son and Spirit, even if we cannot imagine what it would be like for God to live in that way. It is not foolish to believe in, think of, or worship a God we cannot fully understand. There is a tremendous *mystery* involved in worshipping God, but no irrationality.

3. The doctrine of the Trinity is practical

The most influential figure of the Enlightenment, Immanuel Kant (1724–1804), argued that 'the doctrine of the Trinity provides nothing, absolutely nothing, of practical value, even if one claims to understand it; still less when one is convinced that it far surpasses our understanding ... [it] offers absolutely no guidance for conduct.'[3] A little later, in the face of the severe criticism of both reason and Scripture as foundations for theology, the father of modern liberal theology, Friedrich Schleiermacher (1768–1834), chose to base his theology in human religious experience. Consequently he found little use for the Trinity and relegated it to a mere fourteen pages – a kind of postscript to his otherwise lengthy (751-page) description of *The Christian Faith*.[4] These twin accusations of impracticality and irrelevance led many into what is essentially a

[3] Cited in Hall, *Theology with the Church Fathers*, 53.
[4] Friedrich Schleiermacher, *The Christian Faith*, ed. H. R. Macintosh and J. S. Stewart, 2nd edn (T. and T. Clark, 1976), 738–751.

unitarian understanding of God, and the effects of this are still felt today.

One example of this is the common attitude that worship is best understood simply as something that people do for God. When understood in that way the responsibility of worshippers is to offer praise, thanksgiving, prayers and the thoughts and desires of one's heart to God in gratitude for his grace. Worship is, therefore, what we do before God. But as James Torrance shows, this is insufficiently trinitarian[5] and is even human-centred to the point that worship becomes a *work* rather than a *grace*. It is unitarian because pastor, priest and people are on one side, offering worship to God who is on the other side, hearing the prayer and receiving the worship. Trinitarian worship is the gift of participating through the Spirit in the incarnate Son's communion with the Father. Trinitarian worship means having God come onto our side and lift us up. Worship is fellowship (or participating or sharing) in the life of God.[6] The Trinity provides 'a participatory understanding of worship and prayer'.[7] Worship, therefore, is properly centred upon God not only as the object of worship but also as the leader and the inspirer of worship. This takes nothing away from the act of offering praise and thanksgiving, but rather than focusing on what *we* can do for God the emphasis falls on the work of Christ and the life of the blessed Trinity. That is, on the Son who takes us into the Father's presence through his sacrifice and intercession and on the Spirit who is the enabler and the inspiration of worship. In this way worship becomes an act of grace rather than a work that we do. Worship understood as a work with a stress on *our* faith, *our* worship, or even *my* worship and *my* commitment, cannot bring one into the presence of God any more than good deeds can bring one to salvation. None of this rules out the human element of response in worship; the problem is that it has become the pre-eminent, and often the only, theme in much contemporary worship. The Fathers of the Reformation referred to this as 'legal worship', born out of an obligation in which worship depends upon what we do and upon *our* enthusiasm, commitment and action, rather than 'evangelical worship' which is the outcome of the grace of God shown in Christ Jesus through the Holy Spirit. The unitarian way of worship ultimately engenders great weariness, while trinitarian worship is led by Jesus Christ (Heb. 8:1–2) and emphasizes grace before gratitude. This one example shows how the doctrine of the Trinity

---

[5] 'This view of worship is in practice unitarian.' J. B. Torrance, *Worship*, 7.
[6] Gal. 4:6; Heb. 2:11; 10:10, 14.
[7] J. B. Torrance, *Worship*, 9.

is a practical, grace-filled doctrine which will take us into the heart and life of God.

4. The doctrine of the Trinity is foundational

In recent years there has been a resurgence of interest in the doctrine of the Trinity. This is due largely to the influence of Karl Barth (1886–1968), who in 1932 began his magisterial series of *Church Dogmatics* with a volume on 'The Doctrine of the Word of God', which showed that 'the doctrine of the Trinity itself belongs to the very basis of the Christian faith and constitutes the fundamental grammar of dogmatic theology'.[8] Just as grammar provides the rules for putting together the various elements of language, so the doctrine of the Trinity provides the basic structure and the ground rules for all theological reflection. Any doctrine which is not trinitarian in character is not Christian. In the time prior to Barth the doctrine had languished as a result of the spread of liberal theology based on the work of Schleiermacher. Barth believed that 'in any continuation along this line I can see only the plain destruction of Protestant theology and the Protestant church'.[9] In a brilliant exposition of the Trinity Barth showed the way in which it could revitalize theological thinking. He tied the doctrine of the Trinity to the theology of God's self-revelation. Revelation occurs precisely and only because God is Trinity. God's nature as Father, Son and Spirit is identical to his nature as God the revealer, God the revelation and God the revealing. Revelation is the revealing of God-self and a direct implication of being Trinity.

Soon Barth was not alone in promoting the cause of the Trinity, although others often took a different approach to exactly how this doctrine should be understood. For example, in 1944 British author Leonard Hodgson advocated a much more 'social' view of the Trinity – one which stresses the threeness more than Barth did[10] – and in 1952 American Claude Welch critiqued both Barth and Hodgson,[11] while over a considerable period of time influential German Catholic theologian Karl Rahner promoted a closer relationship between the doctrines of Trinity and salvation.[12]

[8] This is the editors' description of G. W. Bromiley's English translation of Karl Barth, *Church Dogmatics*, eds. G. W. Bromiley and T. F. Torrance (T. and T. Clark, 1936), Vol. 1, Part 1, ix.

[9] Barth, *Dogmatics*, xiii.

[10] Hodgson, *Doctrine of the Trinity*.

[11] Claude Welch, *The Trinity in Contemporary Thought* (SCM, 1953).

[12] Karl Rahner, *The Trinity* (Herder and Herder, 1970).

Although trinitarian theology is now firmly entrenched in contemporary theological thought, this has not occurred without
dissenting voices. Classic liberal, pluralist, radical feminist and
process approaches to theology have all had difficulty with it.

(a) In *God as Spirit* Geoffrey Lampe attempted to recast the
doctrine of God in non-trinitarian terms. He claimed that attempts
to understand the sense in which Jesus is alive today are more
confused than helped by a doctrine of the Trinity with what he
considered to be an outmoded metaphysic involving the descent to
earth of the divine second 'person' of the Trinity. He argued that
traditional trinitarian language inevitably leads to tritheism and
diminishes the divinity of Christ, while incarnational Christology
(an essential aspect of trinitarian thought) means the abandonment
of monotheism and makes Jesus' humanity questionable. The Holy
Spirit as a member of the Trinity, he says, is too often an afterthought and ill-defined.[13]

(b) A few years later prominent philosopher of religion John
Hick argued, in the context of dialogue between religions, that the
doctrine of the Trinity was merely an intellectual construction
which belonged to Western Christianity and which should be
discarded.[14]

(c) Meanwhile, certain forms of feminist theology were arguing
that the doctrine of the Trinity, as a foundational part of oppressive,
patriarchal theology, had to be rejected. 'Feminist theology must
create a new textual base, a new canon ... Feminist theology cannot
be done from the existing base of the Christian Bible.'[15] Without the
Scriptures as a foundation the doctrine of the Trinity vanishes.

(d) Process theology redefined God's nature in dynamic and
relational terms with a stress on God's closeness or immanence.
God does not stand apart from the world but is connected with it, so
that it can be said that the world is God's body and that God is the
soul of the world. This involvement means that God's nature is
dynamic and undergoing change as the universe develops. Despite
the attempt of some like Norman Pittenger to relate this to the
doctrine of the Trinity, it is clear that it is not intrinsic to the concept
of God in process thought.[16]

In the latter half of the twentieth century theology threatened to
split into numerous, minimally related theologies (Asian, a/theology,

[13] G. W. H. Lampe, *God as Spirit: The Bampton Lectures 1976* (SCM, 1977), 33,
228.
[14] John Hick, *God Has Many Names* (Westminster, 1982), 124.
[15] Rosemary Ruether, *Womanguides: Readings Towards a Feminist Theology*
(Beacon, 1985), ix.
[16] N. Pittenger, *The Divine Triunity* (United Church Press, 1977).

black, evangelical, feminist, liberal, liberation, pentecostal, political, process, postmodern and post-just-about-everything) and if one doctrine has provided anything approaching an integrating focus it has been the doctrine of the Trinity.[17] This is not to say, of course, that there is complete agreement, but a vital and refreshing dialogue is taking place. The notion that the doctrine of the Trinity is obsolete has been put in abeyance and it has been widely agreed that the doctrine of the Trinity can provide a solid foundation for theological thinking. Of course, not everything that is called 'trinitarian' is biblical or even helpful, but properly understood the doctrine of the Trinity is as essential for theology as bones are for a body. The uniqueness of Christianity emerges entirely from it and without it everything which is truly Christian disappears.

5. The doctrine of the Trinity is essential

The doctrine of the Trinity is essential not only in the sense of being important, but also in the sense that it describes the essence, the *inner* life of God who lives uniquely and perfectly as Father, Son and Holy Spirit as well as the *external*, salvific work of God who sent Jesus in the power of the Spirit to redeem the world. These two dimensions, the 'inner life' and the 'outer work', represent the eternal and temporal nature of God and are often referred to as the 'essential' and the 'economic'[18] aspects of the Trinity. Together they remind us that God has not merely appeared to us in a trinitarian fashion in order to save the world while actually being internally different. God is trinitarian in essence. This means that we can have confidence that the God who is revealed to us really is the God of salvation and the God of love.

It is important to hold these two dimensions together. Allowing the economic and temporal aspect to become dominant eventually

---

[17] Often using the work of Karl Barth and Karl Rahner, scholars such as Jürgen Moltmann, Eberhard Jüngel, Wolfhart Pannenberg, Christoph Schwöbel, Miroslav Volf, Leonardo Boff, John Zizioulas, Robert Jenson, Ted Peters, Stan Grenz, John Thompson, Colin Gunton, Thomas F. Torrance and many others have brought about a resurgence of trinitarian theology.

[18] The 'economic' Trinity has reference to 'saving' but not to money (!) except through a very indirect analogy – that to speak of the 'economy' of a nation is a way of describing how the financial system 'works', while the 'economy' of salvation is the way God works in the world as Father, Son and Spirit. The early Fathers of the church referred to God's acts for us in space and time through the ministry of Jesus and the Spirit as the divine economy (*oikonomia* = 'economy' or 'working') of salvation. This was derived from Paul and his calling to preach the gospel and 'make plain to everyone the administration [*oikonomia*] of this mystery, which for ages past was kept hidden in God, who created all things' (Eph. 3:9).

leads to modalism.[19] That is, the various works of salvation are distributed to the three persons, so creation becomes solely the work of the Father, redemption is the work of the Son alone and sanctification the specific work of the Spirit. For example, Christian Schwarz's otherwise useful approach to identifying and developing spiritual gifts creates a 'trinitarian' structure which tends to divide the work and the persons of the Trinity. It begins with the threefold revelation of God (in creation, at Calvary and at Pentecost) and each is related to three ways we can experience God (as Creator, as Jesus and as Spirit) and each of these is related to one of three authorities (science, Scripture and experience), to one of three dimensions of life (body, soul and spirit), to one of three characteristics of ministry (wisdom, commitment and power) and to one of three sets of spiritual gifts.[20] Schwarz's stated aim that everyone should personally integrate the three areas does not overcome the fact that the work of God is divided up. Only Jesus (and not the Creator or the Spirit) is associated with redemption, Scripture, the soul, commitment and certain gifts, and it is only the Spirit who is associated with power, experience and so forth. But this is not the way that Scripture operates. The gifts, for example, are not divided into categories so that their characteristics are determined by only one or other of the three persons of the Trinity. Schwarz has a completely 'economic' approach which distributes the functions and lacks a sense of the 'essential' nature and internal relationships of God.

On the other hand, understanding the Trinity solely in terms of the 'essential' Trinity is no better. To focus on the inner life of God without due reference to the work of salvation can lead to very speculative theology. 'From the fourth century onwards', notes Alistair Heron, 'the doctrine of the Trinity was in grave danger of taking off into the air, of becoming a mystic formula concerning the inner life of God which could and did increasingly detach itself – especially in the west – from the history of Christ and the Spirit at work in human life.'[21] Some of the most creative advances in recent times have come from the exploration of the inner life of God, but it is also a most speculative area of thought and some have built theological enterprises on top of dubious foundations which are insufficiently related to the work of salvation.

Raimundo Pannikar uses the doctrine of the Trinity as a point of

[19] The idea that there really is only one divine nature which appears in three 'modes' of being.

[20] Thirty gifts are placed in groups of ten associated with the Creator, Jesus and the Spirit. Christian Schwarz, *The Three Colours of Ministry: a trinitarian approach to identifying and developing your spiritual gifts* (ChurchSmart Resources, 2001).

[21] Alistair Heron, *The Holy Spirit* (Westminster, 1983), 172.

meeting for all the world's religions. He interprets the Father as transcendent truth and thus to be equated with the *Brahman* of Hinduism and the *Tao* of Taoism, while Christ is understood as the link between the infinite and the finite and thus a mediator akin to the Buddhist *Tathagata*, the Muslim *Allah* and the Hindu *Isavar*. He does not identify the Trinity in terms of a biblical picture of God or the historical nature of the Son, rather he interprets the Trinity in terms of non-Christian concepts.[22] Sallie McFague understands all theology as metaphorical and Scripture is thus understood to be composed of a number of testimonies to the transforming power of God expressed in terms of their own time. In examining the Trinity she uses the models of mother, lover and friend as replacements for Father Son and Spirit. The more traditional, biblical form of Trinity is thus replaced with a less ontological and more metaphorical conception.[23] Jürgen Moltmann's undoubtedly creative and evocative exploration of the Trinity is nonetheless biblically problematic at a number of points. He describes God as being only properly triune through participation in history and, although not polytheist, his emphasis on there being three discrete subjects or centres of activity means that he develops a divine plurality that makes unity difficult. He sees the cross as decisive for the Trinity but makes Christ's suffering an inner, divine experience of God to the point where there is perhaps a loss of divine freedom and sovereignty.[24]

In biblical terms the doctrine of the Trinity cannot be separated from the salvation of the world and any so-called trinitarian theology which neglects that dimension of thought will go astray.

6. The doctrine of the Trinity is structural

The doctrine of the Trinity is not only foundational in the sense that it describes the nature of God, it is also structural in the sense that it provides a biblical pattern or model for the development of all other doctrines.

(a) The diversity and unity of the Trinity is a model for our thinking about the unity (John 17:20) and the community (1 Cor. 12:4–7) of the *church*. To say that God is triune is to say that God lives in community. The church reflects this truth and can never be authentically Christian if it is either autocratic and authoritarian or uncaring and unconnected. The church should reflect the life of the

[22] R. Pannikar, *The Trinity and World Religions* (The Christian Literature Society, 1970).

[23] S. McFague, *Metaphorical Theology* (SCM, 1983).

[24] Moltmann, *Trinity*.

Trinity as a loving community of equal yet different and related persons in mutual submission.[25]

(b) The Trinity is the source of *mission* because the sending of the church into the world is a continuation of the Father's love which led to a sending of the Son and the Spirit. Trinitarian love (not fear, obligation or duty) is what lies at the heart of Christian mission (Matt. 28:19).[26]

(c) The doctrine of *humanity* depends upon the doctrine of the Trinity and without it our understanding of humanity would be deficient. Historian W. E. H. Lecky showed that the idea of the sanctity of human life in Western society developed as a result of the Christian doctrine of God as Trinity. It affirmed the value of persons, showed that to be human is to be personally related to a personal God, and ultimately led to the establishment of a vastly higher standard of care for all people, whether slaves, gladiators, infants, the ill and dying or foreigners.[27] In expounding the doctrine of the Trinity, Augustine (AD 354–430) used the idea of relationship in such a new way that it stressed the reality, the personality and the value of the individual in sharp contrast to the common idea of the day that the real person was an impersonal, inner 'spark'. Charles Norris Cochrane spoke of this as 'the discovery of personality'.[28] Ultimately this transformed society's attitude to the value of people. Everyone was important, everyone had value and everyone existed in relationship with others and with God.

(d) The Trinity is also the Christian's paradigm for *social and political life*. The community and equality of the trinitarian persons shows us the mode of God's reign as king and ultimately counteracts political authoritarianism and tyranny. Lesslie Newbigin says that the Christian understanding of God 'shaped the barbarian tribes of the western extension of Asia into a cultural entity that we call "Europe" – it was this way of thinking that shaped public discourse'.[29] Conversely, Colin Gunton finds the source of many of today's problems in a defective view of the Trinity. The more the modern Western church stressed the monarchy (or the oneness) rather than the triunity of God, the more God was perceived as a 'transcendent and apparently oppressive single deity'. This led to a

[25] Giles, *Trinity*.

[26] Newbigin, *Open Secret*.

[27] See W. E. H. Lecky, *History of European Morals from Augustine to Charlemagne*, 11th edn, Vol. II (Longmans, Green and Co., 1894). Also see K. Tanner, *Jesus, Humanity and the Trinity* (T. and T. Clark, 2001).

[28] Cochrane, *Christianity and Classical Culture*, chapter 11 referring especially to chapters 9, 10 and 15 of Augustine's *On the Trinity*.

[29] Lesslie Newbigin, 'The Trinity as Public Truth', in Vanhoozer *Trinity*, 3.

lack of relatedness between people and God until the most extreme form of modernism became completely secular and abandoned God. He also argues that 'in both the failed experiments of modern totalitarian régimes and the insidious homogeneity of consumer culture there is a tendency to submerge the many in the one'.[30] In searching for a more communal and personally related church and society the great need for our world today is for Christian theology to present a gospel of God as Trinity which not only converts individuals but also provides a new foundation for public dialogue. The aim is to transform society by demonstrating that the world does not operate by impersonal processes; showing that the human person is not just a sophisticated machine or a biological organism; proving that relationships are real, important and achievable; and persuading people that through Christ and the Spirit there is meaning and purpose in life.

(e) The doctrine of the Trinity also enables us to think properly about the physical *nature of the world* in which we live. The world is neither merely mechanical nor biologically determinist. Its existence is contingent upon God who created it, who sustains it and who will ultimately transform it. The doctrine of the Trinity tells us that the same God who has created the world has entered into it in Christ, lives within it through the Spirit and will redeem it. In God the world has a future. The Trinity accounts for the diversity, richness and openness of the world.

(f) The Trinity offers *hope* and a new vision to a fragmented world. That is, it also helps us understand the evil, injustice and suffering of the world. The suffering of the Son on the cross, forsaken by the Father, is perhaps the most challenging dimension of trinitarian theology, yet it is also the richest and most positive statement about the way God has dealt with sin and suffering.[31] Through Christ and the Spirit God knows, understands and deals with sin and suffering.

The doctrine of the Trinity is not only needed for an understanding of God, it is essential for the whole structure of theology.

7. The doctrine of the Trinity is biblical

The doctrine of the Trinity is grounded firmly in the revelation of God recorded in Scripture. However, everyone reads and interprets the Bible from one or another point of view and in broad historical terms there have been two main approaches to the process of

[30] Gunton, *The One*, 38, 210–211.
[31] Moltmann, *Trinity*, and *The Crucified God* (Hodder and Stoughton, 1974); Boff, *Trinity*.

discerning the Trinity in Scripture. For much of the history of the church the Scriptures were read from the point of view of faith as sacred documents which contained the word and the wisdom of God. For a long time, and for many people, this meant reading the Scriptures from the perspective of trinitarian theology as it was expressed in the creeds and councils of the third and fourth centuries. The doctrine of the Trinity was seen as a universal and timeless truth about God. Subsequently, a second and more critical study of the Scriptures began with the Renaissance and was developed through the time of the Reformation and the Enlightenment. This reading of Scripture 'from below' rather than 'from above' meant beginning with a high degree of scepticism and treating the Bible as a very human book grounded in a specific set of historical contexts. This study revealed a process of historical development, observed variations in approach between books of the Bible and concluded that many trinitarian statements were a result of the importation of foreign concepts. No longer was everyone convinced that trinitarian thinking was be found in the various writings of the New Testament, and so some denied that it was an essential Christian belief while others proceeded to develop theologies of Trinity out of philosophical concepts independently of the biblical narrative. Neither approach is entirely satisfactory.

(a) With regard to the more traditional approach it is necessary to reject any suggestion that the doctrine of the Trinity is best understood in terms of the philosophical categories and terminology of the fourth and fifth centuries (person, essence, *hypostasis*, eternal generation, procession, *ousia* and so forth) rather than the New Testament presentation of the Father's sending of the Son to redeem the world and the coming of the Spirit in fullness upon his people. Yet the traditional approach does rightly make the point that the Trinity is best discerned from the standpoint of faith.

(b) With regard to the post-Enlightenment approach this study of the Trinity adopts many of the analytical, literary, historical and grammatical tools of modern scholarship while rejecting the scepticism which always assumes that the doctrine of the Trinity is a development of the later church and difficult (or impossible) to discern in the New Testament. It is, in fact, impossible to eliminate the trinitarian thinking which permeates, for example, Corinthians, Ephesians, John's Gospel and Romans. Although not always self-consciously formulated, it is 'one of the clearest inferences to be drawn from Scripture'.[32] This conclusion is not based upon slender evidence for, as Wolfhart Pannenberg comments, 'the starting point

[32] P. E. Hughes, *The Second Epistle to the Corinthians* (Eerdmans, 1962), 488–489.

for this teaching is not simply in a three-membered formula but in all that the NT has to say about the relation of the Son to the Father on the one side and to the Spirit on the other.'[33]

The method I have followed, therefore, is to commence with two of the clearest trinitarian statements in the New Testament. Chapter 1 is an exposition of the trinitarian formula of 2 Corinthians 13:14, and this is followed in chapter 2 by an examination of one of the most sustained trinitarian discourses (Eph. 1:1–14). Having begun with that which is explicit in the New Testament, it is easier to perceive that which is implicit in the Old Testament. Chapters 3 to 5 are an examination of some of the most relevant Old Testament material (the Shema of Deut. 6:4–9; the concept of wisdom in Prov. 8:22–31 and the Spirit of God in Ezek. 37:1–14). This is followed by an exploration of the most significant moments in the life and ministry of the Lord Jesus: incarnation (Luke 1:26–56); baptism (Mark 1:1–14); mission (Matt. 12:22–32); his teaching (John 14:15–31) and the Great Commission (Matt. 28:16–20). The final section examines the experience of the Trinity in the life of the early church from the Day of Pentecost (Acts 2:1–47) to the final Day of the Lord (Jude 20–21). It examines the experience of the believer (Rom. 8:1–17); the life of the community (1 Cor. 12:1–11) and the nature of Christian security (Gal. 3:26 – 4:7) and unity (Eph. 4:1–16). Together, I trust that they will faithfully expound the biblical doctrine of the Trinity in all its glory.

> Now to him who is able to do immeasurably more than all we ask or imagine, according to his power that is at work within us, to him be glory in the church and in Christ Jesus throughout all generations, for ever and ever! Amen.
>
> (Eph. 3:20–21)

---

[33] Pannenberg, *Systematic Theology*, Vol. 1, 268–269.

Part 1
The Trinity of love

2 Corinthians 13:14
1. The God of grace, love and fellowship

What is the best-known verse in the Bible? On occasion I have asked this of church congregations where I have been preaching and also of classes at the theological college where I teach. A number of likely possibilities are usually put forward, but none of them get my vote. Not even John 3:16 which is probably the most quoted verse in evangelical churches, or Psalm 23 which is a favourite in many traditions, or the Lord's Prayer – or at least the first verse of it – which is familiar among many, including nominal Christians who remember being taught 'to say their prayers'. I think that 'the grace' or 'the benediction' – *May the grace of the Lord Jesus Christ, and the love of God, and the fellowship of the Holy Spirit be with you all* – probably wins out as the best-known verse of all. It has been said at the beginning, within, and at the end of services of worship around the world and has become familiar to Christians down the ages, across the world and to people in every tradition of the church – even when they cannot identify it as a verse from the Bible![1]

Although no other Pauline statement has had the historically significant role of this verse, it is not the only trinitarian statement which can be found in Paul's writings, let alone the Scriptures as a whole. Paul frequently spoke in a triple form when discussing specific aspects of the Christian life. When discussing *prayer* he urged the Romans to join him in prayer 'to God', 'by our Lord Jesus Christ', and 'by the love of the Spirit'. In the ministry of *gifts* he

---

[1] Some English versions have these words of Paul as verse 13, following the versification introduced into Greek and English versions in the 1550s. Others, however, have 'All the saints send their greetings' as verse 13 instead of verse 12b, and the benediction becomes verse 14.

35

called on the Corinthians to recognize the role of 'Spirit', 'Lord' and 'God'. When considering *election* he reminded the Thessalonians to be aware of the way 'God chose' people by the 'work of the Spirit' to 'share in the glory of our Lord Jesus Christ'. And when considering the extent of *salvation* he argued in his letter to the Ephesians that through Christ Jesus all 'have access to the Father by one Spirit'.[2] Paul relates every part of the Christian life to the Trinity and then, in this benediction, in three succinct phrases he sums it all up in the single most important trinitarian statement of the Christian faith.

Each of the three phrases in Paul's trinitarian benediction connects an attribute of God with one member of the Trinity. They are then put in an order which reflects the experience of the believer: that is, it is through encounter with the *grace of Christ* that we come to know *God's love* and thus participate in divine life and *fellowship through the Spirit*. Of course grace is not exclusive to Christ but also comes from the Father, and love is not restricted to the Father as it is also an attribute of Christ, and fellowship is not only found in the Spirit but also in Christ.[3] Yet the connections are made very appropriately as they describe the distinctive and primary work of each person of the Trinity. A proper understanding of them deepens our relationship with God. It is a problem today that many Christians do not think or speak in terms of the Trinity. This affects their actual experience of God. Worship, prayer and personal discipleship, as well as the community life and mission of the church, will be enriched as Christians relate to God as Father, Son and Spirit rather than only as 'God' or 'Lord'.

1. The grace of the Lord Jesus Christ

The first of the three phrases of the benediction refers to *the grace of the Lord Jesus Christ*. In the original Greek the benediction has no verb and consequently it can be interpreted either as a prayer that the grace of the Lord Jesus Christ *may* be with you all or as a declaration asserting simply that the grace of the Lord Jesus Christ *is* with you all. It is also possible, and probably best, to combine both and understand it as a prayer[4] which expresses a confidence that it will be fulfilled by God. Indeed, it is only possible to fulfil the instructions found in the preceding verses (*put things in order, listen to my appeal, agree with one another*) and in the letter as a whole by the power of the grace which comes from God in Christ Jesus. In all

[2] Rom. 15:30; 1 Cor. 12:4–6; Eph. 2:18; 2 Thess. 2:13–14.
[3] See 2 Cor. 1:12; 5:14; 2:17; 5:17; 13:5.
[4] As it is in other blessings and farewells; see Rom. 15:5, 13; 1 Thess. 3:11–13; 5:23.

three parts of the benediction the emphasis falls upon *God* and what he does, an emphasis which belongs in every Christian's life and discipleship.

a. Experiencing the grace of God

How do we understand the word 'grace'? What lies behind this word which appears 155 times in the New Testament, including 100 times in Paul? Grace (*charis*) is one of a series of words derived from a Greek root (*char*) which in contemporary Greek literature referred to things which produce well-being, such as 'kindness', 'beauty', 'thanks' and 'favour'. The Greek-speaking Jews who translated the Old Testament some time before the birth of Christ thought *charis* was an appropriate word to translate the help given by someone in a superior position who comes to the aid of a weaker person. This is the kind of life-saving help given to starving people by Pharaoh's prime minister Joseph, the generous and undeserved honour offered by King Saul to the shepherd boy David and the rescue sought by widowed Ruth in her time of need.[5] In the New Testament the word is used in a distinctive way to describe very specifically that power or favour which flows from God to people to enable them to believe and be saved. Paul makes this word central to his theology and fills it with a meaning that cannot be divorced from the salvation brought to humanity by Jesus Christ. Grace is the totally undeserved and yet freely given gift from God by which we are saved. This grace is personal, it comes from Jesus and touches people and changes lives. It is grace which welcomes the prodigal son home, which grants even the latest-coming workers a full day's pay and which forgives not seven times but seventy times seven.[6] Into a world in which there is no such thing as a free lunch, where everyone expects – and hopes – to get what they deserve, comes the almost incomprehensibly free gift of God, offered unconditionally to all.

We note, firstly, the *means* by which this grace works. God's grace works in our lives by creating faith. As Paul expressed it, 'it is by grace you have been saved ... through faith' (Eph. 2:5, 8). Many people consider this to be one of the most profound statements of the Christian faith. In my own journey of faith I still recall vividly the moment of sudden illumination which took place when I was a teenager as I read and then reread this passage. Although brought up from childhood within faith I still needed to understand, as all

[5] Gen. 47:25; 1 Sam. 16:22; Ruth 2:2.
[6] Luke 15:11–32; Matt. 20:1–16; Matt. 18:22.

Christians do, the assurance and peace involved in knowing the difference between being saved 'by grace' and being saved 'through faith'. Saved 'by grace' says clearly that salvation depends upon God's action in Christ and therefore rests securely in him. Saved 'through faith' says that the means God uses to achieve this salvation is the faith of the believer. It is important, however, not to turn this gift of faith into a human achievement, as though I am saved by *my* faith which *I* create and have in Jesus. As Paul said, 'this [faith is] not from yourselves, it is the gift of God' (Eph. 2:8). Self-generated and sustained attempts at faithfulness are futile. Self-salvation is not possible.

Secondly, we must note the *richness* of this grace. In Ephesians it is variously described as being 'rich', 'lavish', 'incomparable' and 'unsearchable'.[7] The Lord Jesus described it as being like a hidden treasure or a unique pearl of inestimable value for which the wise man or woman would give absolutely anything and everything. On the one hand, this great gift of God is given freely, it is the kind of love which is undeserved and unexpected. It is not for sale and it cannot be bought or demanded. It can only be accepted with gratefulness and praise. On the other hand, although grace is free it is not cheap. It is very costly, for it seeks a response which involves the whole of our lives. But it is a gift well worth receiving and the renunciation of those things which are contrary to a life with Christ is no real loss. Martyred missionary Jim Elliot's well known saying is certainly true, that 'he is no fool who gives away what he cannot keep to gain what he cannot lose'. But even then, in that act of commitment which every Christian makes, we must remember that it is God who is at work in us and that the emphasis lies upon what God does rather than upon what we can do. Every Christian is called to give witness to this, but as we do it is helpful to remember that we are not God's lawyers, arguing well for him, but God's witnesses, simply telling what grace has done.

Thirdly, it is necessary to understand the *comprehensiveness* of grace for the whole of life: it expresses the totality and completeness of salvation for the whole person at all times and in every circumstance. Nothing in the Christian life is outside the orbit of God's grace. The whole person in every dimension of his or her life and being – physical, emotional, spiritual and mental – is saved by the grace of Jesus Christ. Everything is permeated by God's grace and the Christian life not only begins with grace but must continue with it for, as Paul discovered in the midst of weaknesses, hardships, persecutions and calamities of all kinds, grace alone is sufficient for

[7] Eph. 1:7–8; 2:7; 3:8.

everything.[8] As John Newton's well-known hymn concludes, ''Tis grace hath brought us safe thus far, and grace will lead us home.' This does not mean that life will always be easy. Indeed, it is not always easy even to speak of God's grace to those who suffer. Yet time and time again in such situations there has been tremendous evidence of the grace of God – sometimes healing, sometimes simply encouraging or strengthening one who suffers, but showing clearly that every situation is open to the gracious working of our loving God. When people wonder why bad things happen to good people they often blame God. An equally significant but less frequently asked question is why good things should happen to bad people. The answer is grace, and God's nature is best understood as being expressed in grace, and especially in *the grace of the Lord Jesus Christ*.

b. Knowing the Lord Jesus Christ

Paul links grace so intimately and exclusively with Christ that it may be said that Christ *is* grace. He began his first letter to the Corinthians with this point when he thanked God for his grace 'given you in Christ Jesus' (1 Cor. 1:4). He expanded on this theme in the second letter, reminding his readers that the grace that comes to us from Jesus is preceded by an incarnation that was itself a profound act of gracious self-humiliation and sacrifice: 'For you know the grace of our Lord Jesus Christ, that though he was rich, yet for your sakes he became poor, so that you through his poverty might become rich' (2 Cor. 8:9). One cannot overestimate the significance of this amazing fact. In the first place, it reveals to us the true character of God, showing that the eternal, infinite, almighty Creator of the universe was willing to leave aside divine glory and participate in the world that he made. In the second place, it shows that Christianity is unique for it defines the nature of God by reference to one historical, temporal person – Jesus Christ. It is not surprising that some of those who lived at the time of the ministry and death of Jesus of Nazareth felt that it was either a scandalous blasphemy or utter foolishness to identify in any way at all the eternal God with this one specific human being. [9] Yet this is precisely the intention of this first phrase of Paul's benediction and it must be admitted that it would be an absurd idea were it not for the fact that its origin lies in the heart and will of God rather than human imagination. It is the incarnation which lies at the heart of

[8] See 2 Cor. 6:1–9; 12:9.
[9] John 19:1–16; 1 Cor. 1:19.

trinitarian Christianity, and this clearly distinguishes Christianity from any and every other theistic belief and thus makes it impossible to assert that 'all religions are the same' or that 'they all worship the same God'.

The particular, historical person of Jesus of Nazareth is described by faith as the *Lord Jesus Christ*, a name which is, in each of its three parts, a trinitarian name. First, while the term *Lord* (*kyrios*) can be used in a non-religious sense, it can also be much more than merely a deferential title like 'sir'. *Kyrios* was commonly said by Jews in place of the name of God (Yahweh), which was too sacred to pronounce. In the Gospels *kyrios* was used to designate God as well as the masters of slaves and owners of property, and its ambiguity allows the hearers to make their own interpretation.[10] But for Paul, when it is applied to Christ it is clearly an attribution of divine nature which requires spiritual insight, for 'no one can say, "Jesus is Lord," except by the Holy Spirit'.[11] It has trinitarian significance in that it identifies the human *Jesus* with the eternal *God* through the working of the divine *Spirit*. Secondly, the early Christians made no distinction between the baptism of believers in the name of *Jesus* (meaning 'saviour') and baptism in the name of the Father and the Son and the Holy Spirit.[12] Properly understood, the name Jesus implies everything that is contained in the latter, for Jesus is the true revelation of God. Thirdly, the addition of the title *Christ* also has a trinitarian dimension. *Christos* is the Greek version of the Hebrew 'messiah' (lit. 'anointed one'), which refers to the one expected to fulfil the Jewish eschatological expectation that God would one day come and rescue his people. The baptism of Jesus shows him to be the anointed one, the messiah, as the Spirit descends and Jesus is declared to be the one sent by the Father.[13] In other words, as Basil of Caesarea (*c*.330–79) said, 'To name Christ is to confess the whole trinity.'[14]

To call God Trinity is to assert that God lives eternally as Father, Son and Spirit, not as three Gods and not merely as one God with three names. God is the Father, the originator of all things, the transcendent Creator and Lord of the universe, and also the Son, the incarnate, historical participant in human life, and finally the ever-present Spirit of life and love. In Jesus Christ we have a window to

[10] E.g. Matt. 1:20; 10:24; Luke 1:66; 19:34.

[11] 1 Cor. 12:3. Also see Rom. 10:9; Phil. 2:11.

[12] Acts 8:12; 10:48; Matt. 28:19.

[13] Dan. 9:25, 26; John 8:26, 28; Heb. 8; John 18:36; Rev. 17:14; Acts 10:38; Luke 4:16–19; Isa. 61:1–2.

[14] *On the Holy Spirit*, in P. Schaff and H. Wace (eds.), *The Nicene and Post-Nicene Fathers of the Christian Church* (Eerdmans, 1978), 12, 116.

God that allows us to see and understand something of this amazing divine nature, and he is himself truly, fully God. The astonishing nature of this is accentuated by the fact that this revelation of God in Jesus culminates in his death. While it is a death which is tragic, brought about by human sin, it is also, in the wisdom of God, a death not without purpose. In other words, *the grace of our Lord Jesus Christ* is not something only to be connected with his life, but also *especially* with his death and with God's purposes. Call it what you will, the epitome of grace, the hallmark of the gospel, the defining characteristic of God's nature, the high point of salvation, the greatest truth known to the world – but in any words it is the fact that God's greatest gift of grace comes to us through the death of Jesus Christ. The salvation of the world and the rescue of those alienated from God takes place 'by [God's] grace as a gift, through the redemption that is in Christ Jesus, whom God put forward as a sacrifice of atonement by his blood, effective through faith'.[15] Sometimes this connection with the sacrifice of Christ is made memorable by treating the word as an acronym: God's Riches At Christ's Expense.

The extraordinary truth of this atonement should keep on surprising us, for it is a challenge to every human way of looking at things. There was a church which was undertaking a refurbishment of the interior of their building including the artwork they had. It was all done beautifully and everyone was very pleased – except that some were shocked at a crucifix which showed a twisted body and Christ clearly in physical and spiritual agony. It disturbed them so much that they asked for it to be removed. When they were asked why they responded, 'We wanted a lovely Christ.' Although it may at times disturb us, we will find in the death of Christ the greatest truth: that the grace of God comes through our Lord Jesus Christ who died precisely so that we do not have to.

2. The love of God

The grace that is shown in Jesus Christ reveals the great love God has for the world. Put simply, God loves you, Jesus proves it! In this way, the theology of the second phrase of Paul's benediction in which he prays for *the love of God* flows on seamlessly from the first part of the prayer for *the grace of the Lord Jesus Christ*. By putting together these two phrases about grace and love, Paul has taken a significant step towards creating what will be the definitive trinitarian statement of Christian faith. A comparison of the words

[15] Rom. 3:24 (NRSV); also see 5:15–21; Eph. 2:7; 1 Cor. 1:18–31.

of this benediction with the parallel words at the end of his first letter to the Corinthians shows how this came about. At the end of 1 Corinthians Paul sought the blessing of the 'the grace of the Lord Jesus', but in that situation he followed it with a reference to his own love for them, saying, '*my love* to all of you in Christ Jesus' (1 Cor. 16:23–24). He probably added these words in order to reassure the Corinthians that he still felt warmly towards them, because he had to say some critical words to them concerning their attitudes and behaviour.[16] Now, however, instead of praying '*my* love to all of you', he substitutes a prayer that the *love of God* would be with them all. To be loved by Paul or any other believer is a great thing, but to be loved by God means to be strengthened and empowered. With this change to his benediction the more theologically and fundamentally significant love of God is added to the grace of the Lord Jesus Christ, and he thus creates a binitarian statement which is ready for a trinitarian conclusion.

In the meantime though, in this second phrase, at the centre of the benediction, and also at the centre of the Christian doctrine of God, is this statement of the love of God. This love, expressed in Christ, is the heart of the gospel and the foundation of all human love (2 Cor. 5:14). It is unique, profound and powerful. To know God is to be in love; where there is no God there is no love. Hinduism has *karma*, Islam has law, Buddhism has the eightfold path and secularism has self-improvement, but it is only Christianity which dares to say that we find our salvation and the meaning of life in God's unconditional love. Love is the answer to the most fundamental questions of human existence. Without love nothing else really makes sense.

There are so many things one could say about the love of God[17] because it is so central to the gospel, but the following four characteristics are perhaps some of the most fundamental and necessary.

a. God's love is eternal

Very simply, love is eternal because love is the very nature of God. As the apostle John says, 'Love comes from God ... God is love' (1 John 4:7–8). In the same way Paul is able to remind the Corinthians that 'love never fails' (1 Cor. 13:8). Augustine of Hippo (AD 354–430), the North African theologian whose work was to have a profound influence on the church of subsequent generations, reflected on this and sought to explain how it was that

[16] 1 Cor. 3:1; 4:7–8; 5:1; 6:1; 9:1–3.

[17] Paul prays that the Corinthians would know the love *of God* rather than the love *of the Father*, but when Paul's theology is taken as a whole it is clear that this love comes from none other than God the Father of Jesus Christ (2 Cor. 1:3; 11:31).

love constituted the inner life of God through the mutual relationships of Father, Son and Spirit. He said that the Father is the divine Lover, Jesus is the Beloved and the Holy Spirit is the love which exists between them. The great advantage of this is that it helps us see that love does nothing less than constitute the very nature of the Trinity by defining the inner relationships of God. Unfortunately, however, to describe the Spirit in a somewhat impersonal way as the bond of love does not seem to do justice to the biblical material, which speaks of the Spirit in very personal terms as one who actually loves.[18] Nonetheless, the point is made that love flows from the very nature and being of God as Trinity. Love requires a relationship, it does not exist just on its own. It must be expressed by someone and received by another. Love simply could not exist if God was a solitary, undifferentiated being rather than the dynamic, loving community of Father, Son and Spirit. Love existed even before the world was created, for God is eternally a community of mutual love between Father, Son and Spirit. God did not need the world in order to be able to love: the eternal, almighty God *is* love.

b. God's love is powerful

The most fundamental characteristic of this eternal love of God is that it seeks the good of the other. It is the opposite of any and all selfish, self-centred attitudes. These are sin and the basis of all sinful actions. Love reaches out to the other and is grounded in the inner-trinitarian life of God, whose creative, outgoing love overflowed from the divine community and created the universe. This love then reached out to embrace and redeem humanity through the incarnation. It continues to be inclusive, in that God now calls us to share in the fulfilment of his purposes, by living a life of love in which we reach out to others.

> You have heard that it was said, 'Love your neighbor and hate your enemy.' But I tell you, love your enemies and pray for those who persecute you, that you may be children of your Father in heaven. He causes his sun to rise on the evil and the good, and sends rain on the righteous and the unrighteous. If you love those who love you, what reward will you get? Are not even the tax collectors doing that? And if you greet only your own people, what are you doing more than others? Do not even pagans do that? Be perfect, therefore, as your heavenly Father is perfect.
>
> (Matt. 5:43–48)

[18] See Rom. 8:26–27; 1 Cor. 2:10, 11; 3:16; 2 Cor. 3:6; Gal. 5:18; Eph. 4:30.

Love is truly godly love when it is reaching out to one who does not, or is not able to, love in return. Love of those who love us is what anyone can do. Christian love is that love which reaches out to the other, to the one who is different, to the unlovely and especially to the enemy. Love is made perfect in this. The implications of this obviously extend into every area of life from personal attitudes through family relationships to social structures, political actions and global concerns.

This distinguishes Christian love from that more natural, common feeling of one person for another which is also referred to as 'love'. Romantic love can be a wonderful thing and certainly has at least three elements which can be compared to, and differentiated from, Christian love. First, romantic love is strongly focused on another. This is also true of God's love, but whereas romantic love is exclusive in its attachment, God's love is all-encompassing and open to all. Secondly, romantic love can, like the love of God, bring about change. While romantic love can bring about significant change in one's personal life (and perhaps one's perception of the world), it is Christ's love which really changes the world and it continues to do so because it is an open, inclusive love. Thirdly, romantic love has an intensity or emotional charge which can be quite appropriately related to the relationship between God and his people. As the American theologian of revival Jonathan Edwards said, 'If persons have the true light of heaven let into their souls, it is not a light without heat.' The difference is that, although God's love involves emotion, it is not *based* on a feeling but on a chosen course of action. Love exists most particularly where it is offered towards those for whom one feels least: one's enemies.[19] Love is based on nothing less than the cross of Jesus Christ, which is the ultimate revelation of God's love. As the apostle John wrote, 'this is love ... that [God] loved us and sent his Son as an atoning sacrifice for our sins' (1 John 4:10).

c. God's love is constant

It is a universal truth that everyone wants and needs to be loved. It is an unfortunate and even tragic fact, however, that many people do not feel loved. When that is the case then it is inevitable that what will drive them is the search to *gain* love rather than any commit-ment to *show* love. This ought not to be surprising, for the truth is that we can only really love when we have been loved and so for some the focus falls on persuading others to love us. Insecurity

[19] Matt. 5:43–48; Rom. 5:10.

about being loved lies behind many attempts to become lovable by being attractive in looks or successful in business, sport or education, but the reality is that God makes us lovable by loving us in Christ. To know the love of God is to be able to discover the true self. Paul Tournier spoke out of his own experience when he said, 'I am convinced that nine out of ten persons seeing a psychiatrist do not need one. They need somebody who will love them with God's love … and they will get well.'[20]

However, natural human insecurities make it hard for us to appreciate the love of God properly. It stands in impossible contradiction to our own poor love with which we are all too closely acquainted. Consequently, even Christians of some years' standing can find it hard to allow this love to permeate their lives. As Peter Van Breeman says, 'It is fairly easy to believe in God's love in general, but it is very difficult to believe in God's love for me personally.'[21] Our trust in God's love is hindered by the awareness of our own sinful life and the conviction that sin renders us worthless, not only in our own eyes and before others, but especially in the sight of a holy God. There is no doubt that this comes about partly because of the general human tendency to value people according to their 'goodness' and partly as a result of specifically Christian teaching on the way in which God hates sin. But the doctrine of sin must never stand alone. At the same time one must always take into account the great, unchanging love of God which overcomes sin's power and effects. The English Puritan John Owen spoke eloquently on this: 'The love of God in itself is the eternal purpose and act of his will. This is no more changeable than God himself: if it were no flesh could be saved; but it changeth not, and we are not consumed. What then? Loves he his people in their sinning? Yes; his people, – not their sinning.' Owen went on to show that God may change in the way he deals with people; at particular times he might rebuke or chasten, but he never changes in his fundamental attitude towards us: 'Woe, woe it would be to us, should he change in his love, or take away his kindness from us!' We may change in our love for God, it may ebb and flow, we may lose our first love and then grow again, or be 'as unstable as water', but this is not how God is. 'What poor creatures are we! How unlike the Lord and his love!'[22] Thank God!

It would be a grave mistake to assume that all the changes in a Christian's life come about as the result of his or her response to God's love. The whole point of God's love is that by grace '*God* is

---

[20] Cited in J. B. Smith, *Embracing the Love of God*, 146.
[21] Peter Van Breeman, *As Bread that is Broken* (Dimension, 1974), 15.
[22] Owen, *The Works*, 31–32.

at work in us his wonders to perform', and this point must be made first. The writer to the Hebrews put it this way: 'May the God of peace ... equip you with everything good for doing his will, and may he work in us what is pleasing to him, through Jesus Christ, to whom be glory for ever and ever. Amen' (Heb. 13:20–21). God is at work in us through Jesus Christ.

Anthony de Mello tells a story about the need for love that one worried person had.

> I was a neurotic for years. I was anxious and depressed and selfish. And everyone kept telling me to change. And everyone kept telling me how neurotic I was. And I resented them, and I agreed with them, and I wanted to change, but I just couldn't bring myself to change, no matter how hard I tried. What hurt me most was that my best friend also kept telling me how neurotic I was. He too kept insisting that I change. And I agreed with him too. But I felt so powerless and trapped. Then one day he said to me, 'Don't change. Stay as you are. It really doesn't matter whether you change or not. I love you just as you are; I cannot help loving you.' Those words sounded like music to my ears: 'Don't change. Don't change. I love you.' And I relaxed. And I came alive. And, oh wonderful marvel, I changed![23]

It is not the case that we must change to be accepted by God, but rather that we can change because we have been accepted by God. Of course, this does not mean that we do not have a part to play in love – we too can become lovers.

d. God's love is personal

Love is essentially a relationship which can only exist in God because God is Trinity, a community of love, and because this is so fundamental the concept of the Trinity becomes the foundation and structure for all Christian thinking. But this amazing fact, that God is Father, Son and Spirit, should not be reduced to a series of doctrines about grace, salvation, love and the world. 'Trinity' is not so much a concept as a name for God: the Blessed Trinity. It is true to say that 'Christianity is not essentially a philosophy of love but a love affair.'[24]

In love affairs, of course, love must be shown by both partners. When Paul refers in his benediction to the *love of God* there is no

[23] A. de Mello, *Song of the Bird* (Gujarat Sahitya Prakash Anand, 1981), 83–84.
[24] Brennan Manning, *The Ragamuffin Gospel* (Multnomah, 1990), 214.

doubt that the 'of' should be understood in the first instance as a subjective genitive referring to 'the love which *comes from* God'. But this is not ultimately separable from the objective genitive 'the love which Christians *have for* God' in return. From grammatical, theological and pastoral points of view it is important to keep these concepts together. Paul's benedictory prayer not only asks that God's love would be with us, but it also calls for our love in response. Similarly, John's statement 'God is love' has as its logical implication 'God loves *you*'. God calls to us in love and seeks our love in return, and the goal of our life is nothing other than to live in love with God for ever. As G.K. Chesterton said, 'Love means to love that which is unlovable, or it's no virtue at all; Forgiving means to pardon that which is unpardonable, or it's no virtue at all; And to hope means hoping when all things are hopeless, or it's no virtue at all.'[25]

3. The fellowship of the Holy Spirit

Just as grace is the most characteristic quality of the Lord Jesus and love is the distinctive nature of God the Father, so this benediction nominates 'fellowship' or 'communion' as the most characteristic attribute of the Holy Spirit. The addition of this phrase makes this particular benediction unique among all the greetings and benedictions in Paul's letters. On some occasions he will commence or conclude a letter with 'The grace of the Lord Jesus Christ be with you', but the more usual form of prayer in these situations tends to be binitarian in form, for example, 'Grace and peace to you from God our Father and the Lord Jesus Christ.'[26] In this particular case, however, he adds a third and final phrase in which he prays that *the fellowship of the Holy Spirit* would be with them. What is this fellowship of the Spirit?

a. The Spirit creates fellowship

To have *koinōnia* ('fellowship' or 'communion') means to share in something together. In everyday use it described the partnership of the disciples Simon, James and John by which they shared (or 'had shares in') a boat and a fishing business (Luke 5:10). In the more specifically Christian sense it can be understood to refer to three interlocking relationships. First, it refers to the nature of the inner life of God. As with 'the grace of the Lord Jesus Christ' and 'the

---

[25] G. K. Chesterton, *Heretics* (John Lane Company, 1905).
[26] 2 Cor. 1:2; also see Rom. 1:7; 1 Cor. 1:3; Phil. 1:2.

love of God', the reference to 'the fellowship of the Holy Spirit' is primarily a statement about the way in which God exists – that is, God exists as a community or fellowship of grace and love. Secondly, it refers to the fellowship which Christians share with God through the presence of the Holy Spirit, and finally, it refers to the fellowship which Christians share with one another through the mediating presence of the Holy Spirit. In every way then, it is the role of the Spirit to unite and bring fellowship.

As John V. Taylor points out, the benediction does not refer to 'the power of the Holy Spirit', or 'the light of the Holy Spirit', or 'the purity of the Holy Spirit'; it says 'the communion', the in-between-ness, of the Holy Spirit.[27] The fellowship that we experience in the church is the result of this gift of awareness which the Spirit brings, which opens our eyes to one another and enables us to see as we never saw before. The Holy Spirit, says Taylor, is 'the invisible third-party' who stands between us and the other, making us mutually aware. Supremely and primarily he opens our eyes to Christ. But he also opens our eyes to the brother or sister in Christ, to the fellow man or woman in need and to the heartbreaking brutality and the equally heartbreaking beauty of the world. The Spirit is 'the go-between God'.

b. The Spirit gives life

A graffitist scrawled on the wall, 'Life is a hereditary disease of which we all die.' Without a share in the life of God this is indeed the fate of all of us. The life-giving nature of the Holy Spirit is expressed in the Nicene creed, one of the great ecumenical statements of the church, which proclaims the Holy Spirit to be 'the Lord, the giver of life'.[28] To be given life is a great gift, but what we are given is actually fellowship ('a share') in God's own life. It is astonishing to think that the life of God should extend to include people, but this is exactly what happens. The various writers of the New Testament express this differently: Paul stresses union with Christ's death and resurrection and our participation in the Spirit; John focuses on fellowship with the life of the incarnate Son; and Peter speaks of participation 'in the divine nature'.[29] All of them

[27] Taylor, Go-Between God, 17.
[28] Sometimes known as the Niceno-Constantinopolitan creed, this is the form of the creed finalized at the Council of Chalcedon (AD 451). Apparently based on an early baptismal creed from Jerusalem, it was understood to represent the earlier work of the Councils of Nicea (325) and Constantinople (381). Today it is almost universally recognized as a foundation statement of faith.
[29] Rom. 6 and 8; John 6:53–57; 2 Pet. 1:4.

stress the participation of the believer in the life of God and so Paul's addition of *the fellowship of the Holy Spirit* to his benediction is no insignificant afterthought, for it is only through this fellowship that we have life eternal – a life which is a shared life, communion with God.

In human terms it is hard for us to imagine what it means to share in the life of God, because even when we are very close to someone else – sharing their every experience, their joys and griefs – we are still living externally to them, experiencing our own life rather than theirs. But through the presence of the Holy Spirit we are able actually to share in God's life. This is eternal life and a life without eternity is unworthy of the name of life. When thinking of the first of the phrases of this benediction one is inevitably reminded of the words of John Newton's well known hymn, 'Amazing grace! How sweet the sound / That saved a wretch like me!' When reflecting on the second phrase of the benediction Charles Wesley's equally well known hymn which proclaims 'Amazing love! How can it be? / That thou my God shouldst die for me?' is likely to come to mind. Perhaps we also need a hymn that sings of the equally *'amazing communion'* which God shares with his children! It is indeed amazing and it is often neglected. Perhaps we too readily identify the fellowship of the Holy Spirit with the human dimension of that relationship which, while it is a profound communion in itself, is likely to be marred by dissension or some other less-than-perfect characteristic. However, we should not allow this to divert us from the great fact of fellowship in God, the fact that our primary calling in life is nothing other than to be available to God, to meet God, to know God and, by sharing in the fellowship of the Holy Spirit, to live in God for ever.

c. The Spirit builds community

The Spirit is God who is on our side, in our lives, guiding the believer and enabling us to see Jesus Christ as Lord. The possibility of faith in Christ is not a human one, it is a special, inward act of God through the Spirit: an act of grace, love and communion. Consequently, we become aware of the Holy Spirit rather differently from the way we become aware of Jesus Christ. The Spirit is not discerned as an external manifestation but is experienced *inwardly* as the means by which we come to know God. As we grow in faith, hope and love we are more able to discern the prompting of the Spirit, but even then it can sometimes be hard to distinguish the leading of the Holy Spirit from the desires of our own spirit (Rom. 8:15–16). When this occurs we should remember

49

that the focus is upon the *fellowship* of the Holy Spirit, that is, it is primarily *in community* that the Spirit works and we actually distort our relationship with God if we believe that the primary focus of the Spirit's work is with *me*. We must not exclude others from the process of listening for the Spirit. The role of the community is critical and yet, under the influence of the general atmosphere of modern society, it is easy to fall into a ruinous and unbiblical individualism when we look for guidance or interpret the Scriptures. It is an act of great grace that God sends his Spirit to build community in our world. Through the Spirit God has joined us to join us to each other.

It is important to balance the presence of the Spirit in the life of the individual and the life of the community. On the one hand, there are dangers in perceiving the presence of the Spirit *only in the individual*. There are those who behave like the Montanists of the early church, a group founded by Montanus, a converted pagan priest (*c.* AD 155), who claimed to be possessed by the Holy Spirit and thus able to prophesy authoritatively. Montanus was joined by others who also believed that they alone had received special revelations of the Spirit which gave them unique knowledge and truth. Consequently they separated from the rest of the church. They perceived the Spirit leading them irrespective of what others said or did and it led to fragmentation, division and disunity. The Montanist movement brought what could have been of great use to the church, an enthusiasm for the work of the Spirit, a strong eschatological expectation and a commitment to morality, but it fell into extremism and an intolerance of other believers. This cannot be the work of the Spirit who calls us together as one body in Christ. The Montanists mistook their own extremism and enthusiasm for the presence of the Spirit. This can also happen today.

On the other hand, there are dangers in identifying the inspiration of the Spirit with *the life of the community* in such a way that it is thought that the community, the institution of the church, can do no wrong. In the medieval period this led to a form of Christendom in which the working of the Spirit was identified with the institution of the church. The church became dominant and controlled all areas of life, for it was assumed that whatever it did was the will of God whether that included war or torture or enforced conversion. Today another situation has emerged as it becomes clear that there has been considerable abuse of position and power within the church in the sexual abuse of children, women and those in dependent relationships. Certainly the individuals who perpetrated these abuses must bear much of the responsibility, but what has allowed individual sin to turn into large-scale tragedy is the fact that many refused to believe that such things could happen within the church. Others could not see that they had a responsibility to act decisively to bring these actions to an end, and still others participated in cover-ups to protect the guilty. Clearly, many found it hard to believe that there could be such sin inside the church. These things do not arise from the will of God or the working of the Spirit but from the sinful failings of human beings. It must be accepted that the church can be affected by evil, that there is no-one who is without sin. No institution or person is perfect and we will always need the prophetic, inspired individual to speak to the church. However, even the individual who speaks in this way is not apart from or separate from the church. There is no believer who is not a part of the community of God. In every aspect of Christian discipleship we need *the communion of the Holy Spirit* – it is in the community that the Spirit works.

The benediction concludes with the prayer that God's grace, love and fellowship will *be with you all*. While Paul may only have had the Corinthian community in mind when he wrote about the 'you', the benediction has long since been recognized as a summary of the gospel which is appropriate for much wider use, especially as the final blessing in services of worship. In that context it should always be more than just a way of announcing the end of the service. We cannot do any better than to let this trinitarian prayer sum up our worship and become the theology at the foundation of our Christian lives. It would mean that our relationship with God was a dynamic, personal relationship of love, made possible by the grace of Jesus Christ and mediated by the fellowship of the Holy Spirit. That would indeed be a blessing – to us and to the world.

51

Ephesians 1:1–14
2. A trinitarian blessing

There are only about 2,500 words in Paul's letter to the Ephesians: less than one would normally hear in a single sermon, enough for an extended feature in a magazine and a little more than one third of the number in this chapter. It can easily be read in less than twenty minutes, but of all the writings of the New Testament this letter (which may originate from a sermon outline) has had an influence on Christian theology and spirituality which can only be matched by the much longer letter to the Romans and perhaps the Gospel of John. In it Paul outlines the practical relevance, the theological significance and the fundamental centrality of the doctrine of the Trinity.

It is possible to appreciate the continuing relevance of this teaching when we understand something of the original recipients of this letter. Paul's colleague, Tychicus, was to deliver it when he was on his way from Rome (where Paul was imprisoned) to Colosse, and it is likely that it was intended for a number of churches and not just for Christians at Ephesus.[1] Unlike Paul's other letters this one has almost no reference to any specific individual or situation and some early manuscripts do not even have the words 'in Ephesus' as part of the original letter. The widely known suggestion that this was done so that any destination could be included later is unlikely to be correct, however, as the manuscripts without the name of the destination do not leave a gap where another name could be inserted. It does seem possible, though, that Paul was writing a letter aimed at presenting the fundamentals of the faith to people he had not met, and so we should probably assume it was initially intended for churches in the region around Colosse and Ephesus. If we understand Paul's intentions in this light then it is

[1] See Eph. 6:21–22; Col. 4:7–9.

easy to see that, of all Paul's letters, this one has the most direct relevance for *all* believers, including those of us reading it today. Paul has expounded for twenty-first-century Christians as much as for first-century believers the idea and the implications of the doctrine of the Trinity.

1. God's triune nature is expressed in worship

There is an intimate connection between worship and theology. It has been said, 'Let me hear you pray and see you worship and I will know your theology.' This is certainly the case with Paul – his theology of the triune God emerges in the context of praise and worship. He begins by exclaiming *Praise be to the God and Father of our Lord Jesus Christ!* and proceeds to offer worship in a long sentence which blesses God for all he has done as Father, Son and Holy Spirit.[2] At some points it is difficult to establish the precise relationship of the numerous clauses, but this does not mean that it is a haphazard conglomeration of words. Commentators have frequently noted the distinctive literary style of the passage with repeated forms, a rhythmic language and a structure that could perhaps be derived from a hymn, a creed or a liturgy. Whenever Paul expresses himself in worship or adoration his style of language changes and becomes more complex, emphatic and majestic. In this extended blessing Paul clearly indicates his intention specifically to praise the magnificence of the divine Trinity by a triple repetition of an exclamation of praise to God's glorious grace (vv. 6, 12, 14). This phrase marks the conclusion of each of the sections dealing with Father, Son and Holy Spirit and marks this blessing very emphatically and intentionally as a trinitarian blessing. His most significant theological reflection on the nature of God emerges out of worship and thus Paul eloquently demonstrates that the doctrine of the Trinity is not, as some people think, only a rational or philosophical construct involving unusual mathematics in which three can be made to equal one. But while this doctrine is rational and does provide the foundation for a profound philosophical examination of God in relation to the world, the language of Trinity is *primarily* an expression of faith and worship. The single word 'God' is simply not enough to express the fullness of the biblical testimony concerning God, who has related to the world as Father, Son and Spirit and who lives in threefold community.

Because God is a trinitarian community of love, worship is not

[2] Also see 2:15–17; 3:14–21.

merely an action in which an individual treats God as an object of intellectual reflection or distant adoration. It is, in fact, an action through which the believer enters into the life of God. It is a personal relationship with God the Father mediated by Christ and inspired by the Spirit. In this way worship and Trinity go together. Consequently, it is important that Christian worship should always reflect the trinitarian nature of God. We would do well to listen to Paul and reflect on the way his understanding of God's interaction with the world is expressed in trinitarian fashion, with each member of the Trinity united in purpose and yet differentiated in action. It can be summarized in the following way.

(a) The first dimension of this divine activity is that we are blessed by God the Father, who is described as the source and origin of all spiritual blessings. He chooses those who are called to be holy and blameless and predestines them to be adopted as his children.

(b) The second dimension of this work of salvation takes place in Christ, who is the means by which all these blessings occur. This point is made emphatically and repeatedly: our blessings are given 'in Christ', we are chosen 'in him', adopted 'through Jesus Christ', his grace is given 'in the One he loves', and so on. Obviously this is a theme of which Paul never tires![3]

(c) Even the third dimension of the salvific activity of God – the sealing with the promised Holy Spirit – takes place in Christ. This sealing is a guarantee of the perpetual presence of the Holy Spirit in the life of the believer as a promise of the final, future redemption of those who are God's possession.

In these three majestic, grace-filled, divine movements Paul outlines all that God has done in bringing salvation to the world: God has acted to bring all things in heaven and on earth together under one head, even Christ (1:10). God's plan has individual, communal and even cosmic dimensions. All the various elements of this theology should be present in our worship as much as in Paul's. The outsider who comes into worship knowing nothing about God should be able to deduce something of God's trinitarian nature from the worship that is offered. And the regular worshipper should be constantly led, like Paul, into acts of praise that continually extol the glory of Father, Son and Spirit. The language we use for God, the content of every service of worship and the form of our personal devotion should all reflect the distinctives of each member of the Trinity as well as their divine unity.

[3] Eph. 1:1, 3–4, 6–7, 9, 11, 13, 23.

2. God's purposes are revealed by the Father

Paul's hymn of praise is offered in the form of a typically Jewish extended blessing or *bĕrākâ*. Literally, the word *blessing* means 'well spoken of' and as it became specifically associated with religious practice it was used both for God's *grace* in provision and deliverance (e.g. 'God has blessed us') and for his people's *gratitude* and praise in response (e.g. 'Bless the Lord, O my soul'). In a Jewish blessing the reasons for praising God often follow immediately, as in 'Praise be to the LORD, who rescued you from the hand of the Egyptians and of Pharaoh' (Exod. 18:10). In the present case the cause of Paul's blessing of God is the recognition that God *has already blessed us in the heavenly realms*. It might seem that blessings which are in heavenly realms are rather remote from us here and now, but this is far from the truth. Paul means that the Father's blessings are such that we are to consider ourselves as *already* present with God and Christ in the heavenly realms. Through Christ we are raised to sit with God in heaven (1:20; 2:6). As the Father's blessings are poured out on us, they draw us towards God and actually unite us with him in glory. This should produce in the believer two important attitudes: gratefulness to God for what he has done and confidence in the security and safety we have by being with him.

a. The Father's character

Paul blesses God as the *Father* of the Lord Jesus Christ and in so doing expresses a distinctively Christian attitude towards God. In the Old Testament 'Father' is rarely used in relation to God (just fifteen times), and God is never blessed as Father. God is sometimes described as Father of all, but more often (though still not frequently) specifically as the Father of Israel or as the King of Israel.[4] The term is used to illustrate God's care and his right to respect and obedience, but it is not used to express an individual's relationship with God. Any designation of God as Father continues to be rare in Judaism through to the time of Christ. Synagogue worship of the first century, with which the early Christians would have been familiar, did include prayers such as, 'Cause us to return, our Father, to your Torah …' and, 'Our Father, Our King … be gracious to us and teach us.'[5] This points to a degree of continuity between Jewish and Christian understandings of God as Father, but

[4] Deut. 32:6; Mal. 2:10; Jer. 3:19; Ps. 89:26; Isa. 63:16.
[5] R. Webber (ed.), *The Complete Library of Christian Worship*, Vol. 1 (Hendrikson, 1993), 142–143.

God is known primarily as 'Father in heaven' with the 'in heaven' indicating a certain distance between worshipper and deity.

One should not underestimate the radically different approach to the Fatherhood of God in Christian thought, in which Fatherhood is not incidental, or one name among many, but is the most fundamental description of the nature of God. There are several important implications which arise from this. First, Paul's use of Father, Son and Spirit to describe God indicates that God is not to be defined primarily in abstract philosophical terms as an omnipotent, omnipresent, infinite or eternal being. God may be described in those ways, but only after he is revealed and known as Father, Son and Spirit. Christianity is not primarily a philosophy to be learnt intellectually, but faith in a personal God who is known to us through Jesus and the Spirit.

Secondly, Paul is clear that God is Father solely because he is *the Father of our Lord Jesus Christ.*[6] The designation 'Father' must be understood as a reference to God being *specifically* the Father of Jesus Christ rather than as a reference *generally* to the Father-like nature of God by which he is Father of all people. God is not described here as Father because he is Father of all. He is described as Father only because he is the Father *of Jesus Christ.* In other words, God is primarily defined in terms of the divine inner life and relationships between Father and Son. Consequently, while trinitarian descriptions of God which operate in terms of divine *action* – such as Creator, Redeemer and Sustainer – may be used in association with the trinitarian description of God according to the divine *inner nature*, none can replace the most fundamental Christian description of God as Father, Son and Spirit.

The third implication is the recognition that it is possible for believers to see God as Father *only* as they come into relationship with the Son, Jesus Christ. What is particularly excluded here is any thought that there is any way to know or relate to God as Father other than through the Son who has made him known. As believers come into relationship with Jesus, then God becomes their Father as well. To know Jesus as brother, Saviour and Lord means to know God as Father.

b. The Father's plan

Paul's very long single-sentence blessing reaches its climax in verses 9 and 10, in which the Father reveals *the mystery of his will ... when the times reach their fulfilment.* At the time Paul wrote, the word

[6] Cf. 2 Cor. 1:3, 4; 1 Pet. 1:3–12.

'mystery' had religious overtones as it was a concept widely used in pagan cults and philosophies. It was also used to translate an Old Testament concept referring to God's hidden purposes. *Mystērion* was used, for example, to translate an Aramaic word in Daniel referring to the content of Nebuchadnezzar's dream which disturbed him but which was incomprehensible to him (Dan. 2:18, 19, 27). God revealed the meaning of this mystery to Daniel, who praised God for revealing 'deep and hidden things' (Dan. 2:30, 22). Paul now uses 'mystery' to refer to God's purposes which have been hidden for long ages past but are now *made known* by the Spirit in Christ.

This cosmic plan has a distinctly personal dimension to it: that God revealed his pleasure *to us*. It is almost incomprehensible that God should reveal this mystery to us. This knowledge comes as an amazing privilege. In Colossians we find Paul expressing this awareness with wonder: 'The mystery that has been kept hidden for ages and generations ... is now disclosed to God's people. To them God has chosen to make known ... the glorious riches of this mystery, which is Christ in you, the hope of glory' (1:26–27).

In Romans 16:25 Paul speaks about 'the mystery hidden for long ages past, but now revealed' and points out the divine intention which lies behind this: it is done 'by the command of the eternal God, so that all the Gentiles might come to faith and obedience'. This mystery which has been revealed, which is the revelation of God as Father and the summation of all things in his Son, Jesus Christ, is a gift of pure grace and all believers, like Paul, have a responsibility to work and pray that others may know the hope to which they have been called.

In Ephesians 1:10 Paul describes the mystery which is revealed as *anakephalaiōsis* – a word which only occurs twice in the New Testament. It has the sense of 'bringing things together', so that it can be translated 'that he might gather together in one all things in Christ', or 'to unite all things in him'.[7] It is also possible to take the basic meaning as relating to the 'head' (*kephalē*) under which all things are brought, and so it can be expressed as bringing all things 'together under one head'. Recent scholarship prefers to think of it as referring to the 'main point', 'summary' or perhaps 'heading' in the sense that everything is 'summed up in Christ'. In *The Message* Eugene H. Peterson puts it as 'a long-range plan in which everything would be brought together and summed up in him'. This summation is not just a summary in the sense of a condensation such as one might have in a brief chapter summary of a textbook.

---

[7] As in, respectively, the AV and RSV editions.

Ernest Best suggests that it sums up more as an architect's plan sums up a building – it summarizes it *and* determines its shape.[8] The only other New Testament occurrence of this expression is in Romans, where Paul says that all the commandments of the law 'are summed up in this one command: "Love your neighbour as yourself."' If we draw a parallel here we might say that just as Romans 13:9 shows that all that is true, meaningful and significant for human discipleship in the myriad principles and commandments of the law is expressed in one single command, so Ephesians 1:10 shows how all of God's truth, goodness and purpose that is found throughout the various elements and dimensions of the universe is summed up in the person of Jesus Christ. However it is put, it is clear that it refers to nothing short of cosmic reunification in Christ. All things point to Christ – he is the focal point of the whole of creation – and Paul urges people to bring their lives into conformity with God's divine plan so that Christ is central in everything they do.

3. God's love is shown in Jesus

Paul's description of the salvation brought about by Jesus contains three pictures of God's grace which reveal the extent of divine love and the way in which God relates to the believer: God chooses as the sovereign God, adopts as a caring Father and redeems as the gracious Lord.

a. Chosen by the sovereign God

The first dimension of God's choice is that it is sovereign. Paul says that *he (the Father) chose us in him (Christ) before the creation of the world* (v. 4). This provides a great assurance that the believer will not be lost, because our salvation fundamentally depends upon his choice rather than ours. Before we chose God, he chose us. To say or sing something like 'Lord, I choose to follow you', or 'Jesus, I will never let you go', is perhaps a good way to express one's personal commitment but it can be misleading if it is not also understood that these are relatively unimportant statements compared with the Pauline reminder that *he chose us*. The certainty of this is emphasized by the fact that the believer is *marked with a seal, the promised Holy Spirit, who is a deposit guaranteeing our inheritance* (vv. 13–14). It is important to avoid any suggestion that our salvation depends upon our own choosing or our own ability

---

[8] Best, *Ephesians*, 142.

or strength. The focus is clearly upon God's choosing and his election and there is no basis either for boasting in our own strength or for fearing our weakness. What is appropriate is humble gratitude combined with a great confidence that God will keep us safe.

The second dimension of God's choice is that it is loving: God's choosing took place *before the creation of the world*, but one can only understand this in a theological way because time is itself a part of God's creation and it makes no real sense, temporally speaking, to talk about 'a time before time'. 'Where', then, does this election take place? It is important to locate this eternal election as being, as Paul says, *in Christ* and *in love*. God's choosing is grounded in his own free will rather than in temporal circumstances, as though it was a response either to sin or to some human merit. As Ernest Best points out, God is not just like a chess player who responds to the moves of his opponent.[9] God is better understood as a loving Father whose love precedes that of his children and who anticipates and addresses our needs before we are even aware of them. The Christological dimension of divine election certainly means that it is not an arbitrary decree of God which takes place in isolation from God's action in the world. Far from it. All of God's purposes are permeated with the character of Jesus. So for Paul it is the same thing to say that God's choosing is done 'in Christ' and 'in love'. God's choosing is not accidental, or a lucky event, or random, or forced. God chooses out of love.

The third dimension of God's choosing is that it leads to holiness. God chose us *to be holy and blameless in his sight*. There are two reciprocal dimensions of being holy: it can be understood as (a) a status given by God, and (b) a moral obligation for believers to fulfil. These should not be opposed, but in Ephesians generally the emphasis is upon the holiness of God which is *given* to believers through the work of Christ (1:13; 2:21; 3:5). There is no doubt that we have a responsibility to live a life of love and to avoid any kind of impurity, because these are improper for God's holy people, but before holiness is a way of living it is a status or position which is given to us. The instruction to live in love avoiding impurity is not because this *makes* us holy, but because these things are improper for those who *are* God's holy people. In this blessing in particular the focus is upon the praise of God for the blessings he has given, rather than upon the moral obligations of the believer. The emphasis is on living out what we already have in Christ, rather than upon achieving a holiness of our own.

[9] Ibid., 120.

b. Adopted by the caring Father

The significance of spiritual adoption can be seen in the context of the prevailing Roman legal background in which adoption frequently took place when well-to-do but childless citizens wanted an heir to look after their property in their declining years. Those adopted were usually older and were often servants or slaves. The emperor Claudius adopted Nero so that he could succeed him and inherit the throne. Adoption took place via a legal ceremony involving a symbolic payment to the relinquishing relatives. The result was that the adopted child lost all rights and responsibilities in his former family – for example, all debts were cancelled – and received the same legal rights as any natural child in the adopting family. The complete change of status and the full inheritance rights of the adopted child obviously parallel the change which believers undergo as they are adopted into God's family. No longer are they merely *creatures* in God's world, they are *children* in God's family with rights to inherit the kingdom, and the Holy Spirit is a *deposit guaranteeing our inheritance* until the time of final redemption occurs.

God does not adopt because he is like a wealthy Roman citizen who needs an heir. The decision to adopt is done in accordance with an act of the *will* which is based in God's love and his own desire rather than any need (1:5). It is a conscious, deliberate decision to act for the sake of those who are without a home, a family or a Father. Love begins with an act of grace and it is offered even to those who may be enemies. Indeed, the essence of love is not that one simply loves those who are like oneself, but that one loves those who are different (Matt. 5:44–48). Through adoption God becomes the Father of a large family and this family derives its name from its Father (3:14). Sharing a common family name involves a sense of belonging and a degree of responsibility to those with whom one shares the name. It should be for us a precious mark of belonging and a guarantee that we will belong to this family for ever. Friends, colleagues, associates and others may come and go, but family should be for ever.

But what precisely is this name that believers have taken on? Paul does not actually say what it is, but this could be because there is a play on the words involved: Father is *patēr*, while family is *patria*. Is it that we are simply 'the Father's family'? Or perhaps there is a reference here to the fact that the first believers were baptized into the name of Jesus Christ and thus the early disciples became known as Christians (Acts 2:38; 11:26). This would firmly associate the name with the redemption Paul has been outlining. Those who bear his name are the redeemed who belong to him, who owe allegiance to him, who share in the privileges and joys of being his family and who, through the Spirit, share in and reveal his character to the world. Whichever is meant, the effect is the same for the believer: we belong to God's family for ever.

While it is obvious that adoption means a lot for the one who is adopted, it also means something for the adopting parents involved and this adoption clearly means something for God too. The decision to adopt is made not only in accord with the will of God, but also *in accordance with his pleasure* (v. 5). It is something of pleasure to God, something he delights in doing because it is an action which is consistent with, and which contributes to, the inner life of God. This must be expressed carefully, to avoid making God's life dependent upon external circumstances – but the notion of an unchanging, passionless God is a view more in tune with a philosophical view of monotheism rather than with the dynamic, relational, trinitarian understanding of God who is essentially love expressed in the incarnate Jesus Christ. In God's case the choice to adopt is made with full knowledge of the joy and the pain involved. God shares in the various pains and sufferings as well as the joys and blessings which his adopted children experience and while it is impossible to know the full significance of these for God, the fact that he chose to bring them into being in the created world means that we should not fail to attribute significance to them for God's life. It is not too much to say that without them the life of God would, in some sense, have been different, because this is all implied in the fact that God chose to enter and experience the world through the incarnate Son. To say that without these events God would have been missing something is not to say that God would have been deficient, for he is the one who determined that these things should come about. They are not forced on him. Nor do these things change his character. In fact, it is precisely because he is a God whose undying, constant love is for the good of the other that he undergoes the most profound and incomprehensible experiences, including the alienation of the Son from the Father for the sake of his children (Mark 15:34). *To the praise of his glorious grace!*

c. Redeemed by the gracious Lord

With the move from adoption to redemption Paul now shifts the focus from the eternal to the temporal. He turns from the act of choosing which takes place before the creation of the world, and from the eternal predestination of those to be adopted as God's sons, towards the very much more temporal and historic act of redemption: *in him we have redemption through his blood, the forgiveness of sins* (v. 7). Describing salvation as an act of redemption means using the picture of a slave or prisoner of war who needs to be liberated from captivity by the payment of a ransom.[10] Just as the prisoner of war needs to be liberated from his captors, so we need to be liberated from bondage to law and death – and this liberation comes through the forgiveness of sins.[11] This should lead to (a) *thankfulness and praise* for being saved from captivity and death; (b) *awe and wonder* at the price that God was willing to pay to achieve this; (c) *a new understanding* of the value that should be attached to human life given that God has redeemed us in this way; and (d) a wholehearted *commitment* to serve him – in recognition of the fact that the believer is not merely saved 'from' sin but also redeemed 'for' life.

The forgiveness of sins is done *in accordance with the riches of God's grace.*[12] Redemption is costly and cannot be achieved other than *through his blood*. Athanasius[13] was probably one of the first Fathers of the church to discuss the reason for God's forgiveness being so costly, especially when it seems that ordinary people are able to forgive those who have sinned against them without any need for someone to die. In the parable of the prodigal son, for example, the father does not require a death in order to demonstrate his love for his wayward son.[14] All that has to happen is that he should return home. Is God lesser than the father in the parable because he requires a death? Why can God not simply call for sinners to be repentant? Could he not do that, and thus not need the incarnation or the cross? For Athanasius this could *not* be so, because the problem of sin is not only that we have offended God but also that in doing so we have seriously damaged our human nature. The dominant problem is not simply *disobedience*, but the fact that sin also brings spiritual *corruption* and death. These are not external to us, but are 'essential' in that our very essence as humans is damaged. As Athanasius graphically put it, our very being is 'unravelling' or 'disintegrating'. Repentance and forgiveness are important to a Christian, for it is necessary that our status should be changed from guilty to innocent. Forgiveness of sins can only take place *through his blood*; that is, Christ dies to absorb the

[10] Exod. 6:6; Deut. 7:8.
[11] Rom. 6:23; 7:6; Gal. 2:19; Eph. 1:7; cf. John 8:34; Rom. 6:17; Titus 2:14.
[12] Eph. 1:7; cf. 2:5: 'it is by grace you have been saved'.
[13] Bishop of Alexandria (c. 296–373), opponent of the Arians (who denied the true divinity of Christ) and author of one of the most notable books on the work of Christ, *On the Incarnation of the Word*.
[14] Luke 15:11–32 – it should perhaps be known as the parable of the loving father.

consequences of human sin and to pay the penalty (or 'the wages', Rom. 6:23) of sin. In this way the individual is declared righteous. Athanasius, however, points out that it is not only our *status* but also our *nature* that needs changing. In the incarnation Christ takes on human nature and lives and dies perfectly, so when we are in Christ we participate in his perfect, divine nature (2 Pet. 1:4). Or, as Paul says in Ephesians, we are brought together in one body with Christ as the head and we are 'summed up' in him. Our natures as well as our attitudes are changed as we share in the life of God. This means that in Christ we do not just behave as new people, we *are* new people. Our calling as Christians is not to make ourselves new people by the way we live. We must live in a manner which is in accordance with who we already are.

Redemption is thus a present reality for believers: it is something *we have*. And of course it is bound up with Jesus, for it is *in him* that it takes place.[15] Believers cannot achieve redemption other than by fellowship with him and, as we have seen, this is only possible *through his blood*. The ransom price is the death of Christ (Rom. 3:24–25). We may understand this as a great gift which is necessary to enable our lives to be transformed, but there remains a great mystery: that God should die. At this point all human understanding of the nature of God reaches breaking point. The inconceivable has happened and it is of profound significance for the doctrine of the Trinity. But it is only in the Trinity that it becomes possible even to think that God in Christ has come to know death in its fullness.

We might say that God has known death 'from the inside'. Whatever you and I know about death, the obvious fact is that we only know of it 'from the outside'. It is something we know about, have read about, perhaps have seen and may have come close to ourselves. But we have not experienced it 'from the inside'. It is only when we finally stop living that we will experience it from the inside. And even when that occurs the believer will, *in accordance with the riches of God's grace*, only experience physical death as a transition to a resurrected life. The believer will not experience the full horror of death as ultimate separation and alienation from God precisely because the ransom price has been paid for us and the believer thereby is liberated from death.[16] Christ has died and there is a sense in which 'in Christ' God died. A statement such as this requires clarification and some shrink from any suggestion that in Christ 'God died', but it is just as important not to say too little

---

[15] Eph. 1:7; cf. Titus 2:13–14: 'Jesus Christ, who gave himself for us to redeem us from all wickedness and to purify for himself a people that are his very own, eager to do what is good.'

[16] Eph. 4:18; cf. Mark 15:34; 1 Cor. 15:54–57.

about the implications of the death of Christ as to say too much. One certainly cannot imply that God is dead, or that God no longer exists, for God lives eternally. But that truth, in turn, should not be taken as implying that this death of Christ was a mere nothing, a charade, or only a physical – and not a profoundly spiritual – experience, or that it was only related to Christ's human nature and not the divine dimension of his life. Perhaps it is best to say that in the death of Christ God *knows* death without dying, yet knows it fully, from the inside. In the alienation of the beloved Son from the loving Father, God knows death in all its horror. And he does so in order that we will not.

4. God's promises are guaranteed by the Spirit

Paul now directly addresses the role of the Holy Spirit in the life of the Christian believer and his teaching stands, at one and the same time, in perfect *continuity* and profound *contrast* with Old Testament teaching on the presence of the Spirit in the lives of God's people. First, whereas the Spirit had formerly been primarily understood in terms of power, with a close association with God's work in creation, now the Spirit is clearly seen as personal in nature and as undertaking a work of new creation.[17] Secondly, the Spirit had previously been the inspiration and strength of Israel's leaders, but that enabling is now available to all believers and comes as an internal and continuous presence rather than as a more external and somewhat sporadic empowerment which was typical of the Old Testament.[18] Thirdly, under the old covenant the Spirit of God was often associated with the expectation of the coming Messiah, but now that Jesus has come the Spirit is known specifically as the Spirit of Jesus Christ.[19] In this way the New Testament confirms and completes the teaching of the Old Testament regarding the Holy Spirit. In the present age believers are incomparably blessed by the constant, empowering presence of the Spirit.

The close connection between Jesus and the Spirit is seen in the way Paul says believers are known as belonging to Christ by being marked by the Spirit: *when you believed, you were marked in him with a seal, the promised Holy Spirit.* Some have understood this phrase as implying that there is a temporal sequence, beginning with 'when you believed' and followed at a later time by 'being marked with the Spirit'. But *grammatically* it is better to take the 'when you believed' as an action which occurs at the same time as the sealing.

[17] Gen. 1:2; 2:7; Ezek. 37:8; cf. John 3:5; 2 Cor. 5:17.
[18] Num. 11:25; Judg. 14:6; 1 Sam. 16:13; Ps. 51:11; cf. Acts 2, 10, 19; Eph. 1:17.
[19] Isa. 32:15; Jer. 31:31; Joel 2:28; cf. Acts 16:7; Phil. 1:19.

Gordon Fee says that 'the two verbs have nothing to do with separate and distinct experiences of faith'.[20] And *theologically* the close connection of believing with sealing is essential, as both believing *in Christ* and being sealed *in him* are only possible through the working of the Spirit.[21] Even though specific aspects of God's work may be attributed to the various persons of the Trinity, the essential unity of God means that it is not possible for a believer to share in the life of just *part* of God. The presence of God is not divisible into three and being in Christ cannot be separated from being in the Spirit.

At the time Paul wrote, to be marked with a seal meant a number of things. First, a seal was used to denote *possession*. It was a distinctive mark made by, or on behalf of, a particular person – perhaps someone who has just purchased goods, cattle or even a slave – and it was used to indicate ownership (Rev. 7:3–8; 9:4). The presence of a seal on goods at a market was evidence of possession and they could be taken by their rightful owner at any time. The presence of the Holy Spirit in the life of the believer is a mark of God's ownership, a proof of his intention finally and fully to redeem the believer. Secondly, a seal could be used as evidence of the *authenticity* of a document or as a mark of approval. Similarly, the Holy Spirit is evidence of the genuineness of the believer's incorporation into Christ. Finally, a seal was used as *protection* from external forces, and it was used when a tomb or a jail cell was sealed (Matt. 27:66; Rev. 20:3). So, too, it is by the Spirit that the believer is protected from the powers of evil (Eph. 6:10–18). In dealing with evil it is not our strength that is important but that of the Spirit.

Evidence of the presence of the Spirit is found in two principal effects in the life of the believer, known as the *gifts* and the *fruit* of the Spirit. The Spirit brings gifts of ministry and service to build up the church in every way (1 Cor. 12:1 – 14:39). The gifts include apostleship, prophecy, teaching, service, giving, healing, the working of miracles and other diverse spiritual abilities, all of which are essential in order to build up the church. The Spirit also brings certain personal qualities known as the fruit of the Spirit, which are described as love, joy, peace, patience, kindness, goodness, faithfulness, gentleness and self-control. These transform the character and personality of the believer (Gal. 5:22–23). Together the church corporately and the individual believer need both the fruit and the gifts of the Spirit. Yet they work in different ways. While all of the fruit of the Spirit are available to every Christian, the gifts are

---

[20] Fee, *God's Empowering Presence*, 670.
[21] 1 Cor. 12:3; 2 Cor. 3:17.

distributed more specifically and each person serves the Lord with a different gift or gifts. It is important to understand this difference. On the one hand, while all the fruit are for all believers it would be arrogant to believe that any one believer had all the gifts. There is a corporate dimension which means that Christians need one another. On the other hand, it is equally unhelpful for a believer to think that the specificity of the gifts means that it is legitimate to assume, for example, that patience is not one of his or her gifts. All believers are meant to grow in grace and ought not to excuse themselves from any aspect of this.

Both the fruit and the gifts are the implications of the presence of the Spirit in the Christian's life, but while the gifts are invaluable the greatest evidence of the presence of the Holy Spirit in the life of the believer is love (1 Cor. 13). Paul's prayer is that his readers would 'know this love that surpasses knowledge – that you may be filled to the measure of all the fullness of God' (Eph. 3:14–21). It is hard to comprehend the full significance of what Paul says and words struggle to express a love which is so profound that it is beyond knowing. The unknown author of the twelfth-century writing *The Cloud of Unknowing*, when contemplating the nature of God, said, 'He [God] cannot be comprehended by our intellect or any man's – or any angel's for that matter. For both we and they are created beings. But only to our intellect is he incomprehensible: *not to our love.*' He advises his readers not to think that spirituality is fundamentally an activity of the mind. Minds will take us a long way and will help us understand the nature of God as Trinity, but as we penetrate into the life of God we find that God is essentially a God of love, and love is best known and responded to not by mind but by love. The deepest part of God 'may well be loved, but not thought'.[22] We never dispense with thought or theological or devotional reflection on the word of God, but, as Paul says, love will go beyond the highest achievements of human thought and take us into the presence of God.

[22] C. Wolters (trans.) (Penguin, 1978), 4–6.

Part 2
The Trinity in the Old Testament

Deuteronomy 6:4–9
3. The Lord our God is one

'Hey, God is number one!' While it might not catch all the nuances of *Hear, O Israel: The LORD our God, the LORD is one*, this more catchy translation certainly encapsulates the main thrust of what was meant: God is meant to be top of the list. Seventeen-year-old Rachel wrote to her cousin, 'If you had to make a list of the top 5 things most important to you, what would you put? Here's mine, (1) God, (2) Family, (3) Friends, (4) My future, (5) Myself.' For Rachel, as for the author of Deuteronomy and for many others, God was number one and everything else secondary. In this way a young, contemporary teenager shares in the ancient faith of Israel. The context and the difficulties faced, however, are very different: the Israelites were confronting the problem of entering God's Promised (but still occupied) Land, while Rachel was dealing with being a Christian teenager in a pluralist and commercialized society. But the answer to these issues was the same for both: whatever happens, keep remembering to put God as number one. As it turned out, Israel was far from perfect but by God's grace some always remained faithful. Rachel was not perfect either, but nonetheless she grew in grace and love. Her remarkable journal and her letters show that she understood what it meant to put God first in everything. She exhibited a deep spiritual life and wrote about her faith, her awareness of the fragility of life and the strength of God. Soon after, Rachel became one of fifteen victims in a tragic massacre at Columbine High School. Her attacker asked, 'Do you believe in God?' She responded, 'You know I do,' whereupon he said, 'Then go be with him,' and shot her. Earlier, Rachel had faced difficulties because of her faith and wrote, 'I am not going to apologize for speaking the name of Jesus, I am not going to justify my faith to them, and I am not going to hide the light that God has put me into. If I have to sacrifice everything ... I will. I will take it. If my friends have to become my enemies for me to be with my best friend Jesus, then that's fine with me.'[1]

This call to put God first is commonly known as the Shema.[2] Faithful Jews recite these words twice each day and it is probably the text which is most definitive of Jewish faith.[3] It consists of two important and connected statements. The first is a call to make God number one in life: *Hear, O Israel: The LORD our God, the LORD is one*. The second is the equally significant and well known 'Great Commandment': *Love the LORD your God with all your heart and with all your soul and with all your strength*. It is no coincidence at all that these two statements about the *oneness* and the *love* of God are found together. Theologically they are a unity and together they provide a foundation not only for the *unity* but also for the *community* of the divine Trinity. They are actually bound together grammatically by an imperative construction: first, *hear* ... and secondly, *love* ... R. W. L. Moberly prefers to translate them with a causal connection: 'The LORD our God, the LORD is one, *so* love the LORD your God ...'[4]

What is it about the oneness of God that means that we should love him? And how does this provide a foundation for a doctrine of the Trinity? A brief answer to this is that it is only love which can unite that which is separate, alienated or fragmented, and remake it as it was intended to be: one, whole, united entity with complete integrity and harmony. Love unites and makes the lover and the beloved as one. This is a oneness with unity in diversity, rich community and dynamic relationship, and the God of the Shema will ultimately be revealed as the loving, relational Trinity.

1. The Shema

The call to *hear* is not merely an instruction to pay attention; it has the sense of expecting a response and could be 'Take heed ...', or 'Obey this ...', or even 'Get hold of this ...'[5] It follows the

---

[1] Beth Nimmo and Darrell Scott, *Rachel's Tears* (Thomas Nelson, 2000), 92, 96–97.

[2] The Shema is Deut. 6:4–9, although it is often associated with 11:13–21 and Num. 15:37–41. The name is taken from the first Hebrew word, meaning 'hear'.

[3] For a history of the Shema see S. McBride, *Interpretation – A Journal of Bible and Theology* Vol. 27 (Union Theological Seminary, 1973), 274ff.

[4] This reflects a slight nuance in the grammar. See R. W. L. Moberly, 'Towards an Interpretation of the Shema', in C. Seitz and K. Greene-McCreight (eds.), *Essays in Honor of Brevard S. Childs* (Eerdmans, 1999), 125–126.

[5] The initial call, *Hear, O Israel*, marks the start of a new, major section of text and is a common rhetorical device indicating a statement of special wisdom and significance. See Deut. 5:1; 9:1; 20:3; 27:9; Prov. 1:8; 4:1; 8:32.

most fundamental principles of the law expressed in the Ten Commandments and precedes the various specific statutes and ordinances in which they result. The Shema is thus presented as a summary of the whole law of God.[6] As Jesus was to say later, all the Law and the Prophets hang on this verse (Matt. 22:40). Only in the broadest sense can the content of Deuteronomy be called law: it is teaching and exhortation and the aim is to persuade rather than command, to encourage rather than force.[7] This is seen in the fact that the opening statement is not a demand but simply a statement of faith that God is one, and also in the way the 'command' which follows requires a genuine willingness to follow it, or else it becomes a pointless exercise.

The Shema is profoundly important for understanding God. R. E. Clements says that we must regard it 'as the fullest and most significant of all the theological turning-points in the concept of deity which the Old Testament brings to our attention'.[8] It is important that both parts of the Shema are taken together rather than separately, because only then can it be seen to emphasize both the transcendent sovereignty of God and his loving personal nature. It is this which makes God different from all other gods and creatures. One cannot overestimate the importance of the concept of love for understanding the Old Testament doctrine of God.

It is precisely because God has a loving nature that he establishes a covenant with the children of Israel. The words of the Shema are the basis of this relationship between Israel and *the LORD our God*,[9] and it requires a response from them in the form of love, not merely obedience or servitude. 'The operative principle within the relationship is that of love; God moved first toward his people in love and

---

[6] There are echoes of it throughout the various the commandments. See Deut. 6:12–15; 7:8–10; 8:11; 9:1; 10:12–13; 13:2–5; 18:9; 26:16–17.

[7] Mayes, *Deuteronomy*, 58.

[8] Clements, *Deuteronomy*, 53.

[9] English translations of the Old Testament frequently use 'LORD' to represent the Hebrew name for God, which can be transliterated as either 'JHVH' or 'YHWH' and is sometimes known as the Tetragrammaton. This name for God was revealed to Moses and means 'I am who I am', or 'I will be who I will be' (Exod. 3:14). It points to the fact that God is all-powerful and is not subject to any external control. There is uncertainty about the precise pronunciation of this name, because at the time Hebrew did not include vowels in its written form, and respect for the divine nature meant that when reading the name of God in Scripture they preferred to say 'Lord' (*adonai*) instead. Even today orthodox Jews will not say the name of God and prefer to write 'G-d' for 'God'. English translations follow suit and often use 'LORD' for the divine name. Capitalization is used to distinguish it from 'Lord', which is used to translate *adonai*. With vowels supplied the divine name becomes either Jehovah or Yahweh.

they must respond to him in love.'[10] This means that the covenant is not just a one-off event. It is an ongoing, living relationship in which each person and every generation makes a loving commitment to God. The Israelites are reminded of this in the annual covenant renewal ceremony.

a. The Lord our God is one

What Israel was to 'hear' and pay attention to was the fact that God is 'one'. What is the meaning of this? In English this word has a number of different uses. There is 'one' in the singular mathematical sense ('one apple, not two or three'); there is 'one' in the sense of 'special' or 'chosen' ('Barb is the one for me' – she is not the only female, but she is the one I love); there is 'one' in the sense of being united and undivided ('we are at one on this particular matter'); and it can also be used in the sense of the most powerful or most important one ('look after number one', or 'Formula One racing'). Hebrew has a similar situation. There are two main translations:[11]

- *The LORD is our God, the Lord alone.*
- *The LORD our God, the LORD is one.*

These are not necessarily alternative translations. Patrick Miller concludes that 'the ambiguity of meaning is irresolvable; the task for interpretation is to try to understand the meaning and implications of both translations.'[12] Moreover, any examination of the theological implications of the oneness of God is not exhausted by simply determining the original meaning. Although the way it was originally interpreted is obviously exegetically important, the way it was subsequently used in Jewish and Christian contexts is theologically important. Altogether five meanings of 'one' have been attributed to this phrase. It is possible to say that God is:

- the *only* Lord   (Worship no one else)
- the *universal* ruler   (Yahweh is Lord of all)
- the *unique* God   (There is no other God)
- *undivided* holiness   (Yahweh is consistent in character)
- the *unity* of the cosmos   (Yahweh is the foundation of everything)

[10] Craigie, *Deuteronomy*, 37.
[11] There are a number of variations on these. The first is the NRSV and the second is the NIV.
[12] Miller, *Deuteronomy*, 99.

In all these ways, *the LORD our God, the LORD is one*. Our task is now to explain the significance of each of these.

1. God is the only Lord

The declaration *the LORD our God, the LORD is one* is made because there was a real danger that the prosperity of the Promised Land would lead the children of Israel to forget Yahweh. The land they were about to claim was a rich land 'flowing with milk and honey' which would provide much for them, 'houses filled with all kinds of good things you did not provide, wells you did not dig, and vineyards and olive groves you did not plant – [so] *when you eat and are satisfied, be careful that you do not forget the LORD*' (6:3, 10–12). The greatest danger that the children of Israel faced was of being seduced by material things which could make them forget that *the LORD is our God, the Lord alone*. The primary meaning, then, is that Yahweh is the only one to be worshipped, followed, obeyed and loved. The emphasis is not primarily on the unity of God but on the unity and solidarity of Israel's allegiance and commitment to Yahweh. The rhetorical question which lies behind the Shema is not, 'Who is God?' but rather, 'Who is *our* God?' The answer is, 'Our God is *Yahweh alone*' (see also 4:19–20).

There is a great lesson in this for us. While the level of commitment which God calls for is well demonstrated by the account of Rachel's courage, a more common and insidious temptation is still the materialism, consumerism and comfort referred to by the Shema itself. Far more people are in danger of a slow spiritual suicide at their own hands, brought on by a surfeit of materialism, than they are of having their faith tested at the point of a gun. Spiritually, it is easier to survive adversity than prosperity. Materialism tempts us to worship the *creation* rather than the *Creator*. But this is just as foolish today as it was when the Jews were tempted to worship wooden idols and the gods they believed they represented. While it would be unusual today for anyone to attribute wealth to the work of idols or of gods such as Baal, many are still capable of worshipping both material things themselves and the more secular 'gods' which they believe provide them. Some, for example, worship money and are convinced that the stock market holds the keys to wealth. Some attribute material success to an ethic of hard work and efficiency, while others prefer to credit a particular form of political and economic government, and still others simply believe in luck or good fortune. The belief that these things actually control life or are the real means for achieving satisfaction is a complete delusion, yet the temptation to substitute these things for faith in God is powerful – not least because some of

73

them are not intrinsically wrong. However, 'the good is the enemy of the best'. The best is complete allegiance to God. The church needs to speak constantly to today's materialist and consumerist idolatry – not only to those outside the church but also to those within. One test of whether possessions, secular success or any other worldly good has become an idol is to ask whether it is possible to give it away. If we can give something away then we control it. What we cannot give away controls us. The Shema comes as a reminder that nothing should control us except God. The absolute centre of our life should be God and God alone.

2. God is the universal ruler

Yahweh is the only Lord for the children of Israel because he is, in fact, the *only Lord*; he is the *universal* ruler who should be worshipped by *everyone*. Only Israel was called into covenant relationship with God but eventually, as Zechariah prophesied, 'The LORD will be king over the whole earth. On that day there will be *one LORD* [the same phrase as in the Shema], and his name the *only* name' (Zech. 14:9, italics mine). In other words, the Shema not only declares that Yahweh is Israel's only Lord but it also provides a foundation for asserting that he is the *world's* Lord as well. The notion of the universal Lordship of Yahweh flies in the face of the polytheism of the surrounding nations. It is a declaration that the other 'gods', characters, personalities, ideas, values and beliefs to which people bow down are false gods, not worthy to be compared to Yahweh. Once again, this is a necessary lesson for today: just as the pagan polytheism of that time was countered by an assertion of the complete sovereignty of Yahweh, so the pluralism and relativism of today needs to be countered by a reassertion of God's complete Lordship. Unfortunately there is today a reluctance to give complete allegiance to any one thing or any one person. Contemporary culture revels in the acceptance of many truths and values – sometimes even those which are contradictory – just as traditional paganism revels in a multiplicity of gods. Pluralism excludes only the notion that there is such a thing as a single, coherent, universal meaning to life. Everything and anything can be accepted as valid and personally, experientially true on the sole condition that one does not believe *any* of it to be absolutely, universally or really true.

Many Christians have, unfortunately, adopted this position and relativize faith as a purely personal experience, as subjective truth valid only for those who experience it, and not as something objectively true with relevance for all. Other belief systems (or even non-systems) are seen as equally valid. Sometimes those who are not completely comfortable with this form of radical pluralism modify their acceptance of many (often contradictory) perspectives with a claim such as 'it doesn't matter, we all worship the same God'. However, such attempts to find an underlying unity in the face of radical pluralism achieve little. It is intellectual suicide to attempt to find unity and consistency while ignoring the profound differences and contradictions present in the varied approaches to the concept of 'god'. In contrast to both Ancient Near Eastern paganism and postmodern pluralism the Shema declares the *universal* Lordship of God.

3. Yahweh is the unique God

The more one stresses the universality of Yahweh's Lordship, the less room there is for other gods. Logic leads inexorably from the universal Lordship of Christ to the belief that the other gods are not actually gods at all and that Yahweh is the *unique* God. This deuteronomic claim represents a significant, even radical theological development. The Ancient Near East was used to the idea of multiple gods with some being dominant, but the Shema challenged this when it asserted that Yahweh was the one, single, unique God and not merely one among many. Yahweh is not the head of a pantheon like Baal of the Canaanites, or Amon-Re in Egypt, or Marduk in Babylon. Yahweh is not merely the best God but is the *one and only* God. The other gods are no gods at all. In technical terms this is monotheism (belief in one God) as distinct from henotheism (the worship of one among many gods). Other gods only 'exist' as projections or fantasies. They are as impotent and as unreal as the god Baal, who was called upon by his prophets to send down fire from heaven but was unable to put in an appearance at the contest especially designed to demonstrate his power (1 Kgs 18:16–39). However fantastically powerful these conceptions of god were, in reality they were nothing at all. The prophet Isaiah spoke scathingly of the stupidity of those who worship an idol made of wood: not only have they fashioned it themselves, but they themselves prove its spiritual impotence by using some of the same wood on their fire to warm themselves. Where is the sense of either worshipping part of the created world or of creating gods out of it (Isa. 44:9–20)? The idolater, says Isaiah, does not stop to ask, 'Shall I bow down to a block of wood?' or to say, 'Is not this thing in my right hand a lie?' The Old Testament doctrine of God is at its highest point when all other 'gods' fade into such insignificance that Yahweh alone is God.

The significance of this should not be lost on us today. It is not helpful to see God as locked in a titanic conflict with an evil force comparable in power and strength. It is possible for Christians to attribute far too great a power to evil and spiritual forces. One cannot deny the reality of sin and evil, of course, and Christians must be aware of the dangers of the evil one,[13] but this must be balanced by the truth that God is unique, all-powerful and omnipotent, and that evil is limited in scope and power and is already defeated through the cross and resurrection of Jesus. Evil must be seen for what it is: a temporary aberration with power which lessens as God is exalted and which will one day cease to exist as God becomes all in all.

4. God is undivided holiness
In Hebrew there are two words for 'one'. The word used in the Shema refers primarily to the kind of organic unity which implies an undivided inner nature. Yahweh can only be trusted to keep his word and be utterly faithful to his people if he is completely undivided in nature and if his character does not contain ambiguities, conflicts or uncertainties. Someone who is consistent in character will, for instance, behave with the same propriety and honesty when unobserved as when under scrutiny. Such an individual is a person of integrity, whole, sound and complete, just as an integer is a whole (rather than a fractional) number. God is perfectly and completely whole and undivided. This is the basis for God's holiness.

God's holiness refers to his essential life, his unique way of being. It means being 'separated' or 'set apart' and it sums up everything about the divine character and nature. It is what differentiates Yahweh from all other 'gods'. Yahweh's people are called to be holy, that is, 'set apart' for Yahweh, to follow his way of life and no other. This means being obedient to his commands and so holiness takes on a moral dimension. Sometimes Hebrew monotheism is referred to as 'ethical monotheism', indicating that the distinctive ethical standards to which Yahweh called his people could only emerge out of a divine character which held to consistent values. A divided god (or any divided person for that matter) will be morally unpredictable. Yahweh is constant. Is it important, then, that Yahweh is one? Absolutely! Without this, life is fragmented, divided and morally uncertain.

5. God is the unity of the cosmos
The fifth and final meaning of divine oneness is that ultimately God is the unity of the whole cosmos. Everything is centred on him and

---

[13] 'Your enemy the devil prowls around like a roaring lion looking for someone to devour' (1 Pet. 5:8).

is held together by his power. He is the sustainer of the universe, the 'ground of being', the 'go-between God' who links all things, the glue of the universe, the unity of the world. This is not something seen explicitly in the Shema's reference to God as one, but it is an inevitable deduction which finds its completion in the person of Jesus Christ. This unity is seen in the doctrine of *creation*, in which Christ is the focus of unity. As Paul wrote to the Colossians, Christ is 'the image of the invisible God, the firstborn over all creation ... all things have been created through him and for him ... and in him all things hold together' (Col. 1:15–17). It is also seen in the language of *redemption*: atonement means 'to make at one'; reconciliation is to bring back together those who have been separated; 'salvation' has the sense of making something whole; re-creation is a restoration of that which has been broken. In short, in both creation and salvation Jesus Christ is seen as the unity of all things. This truth has been eloquently addressed by Athanasius who is well known for teaching about Jesus as the answer to the 'unravelling' of human nature and the 'disintegration' of the world,[14] and more colloquially by some Christian engineers who have been known to describe a particularly important engine part as 'the Jesus nut' because without it everything falls apart!

2. The Great Commandment

The unity which is found in Jesus is not some abstract philosophical concept. The monotheism of the Shema must be interpreted in the light of God's desire to enter into a relationship of love. It is a unity based on love. This is why the Shema consists of two phrases concerning the *oneness* and the *love* of God. Theologically these concepts belong together, and together they provide a foundation for the *unity* and the *community* of the divine nature. When the Old Testament doctrine of God is interpreted in the light of God's love then it can be seen to provide a foundation for the doctrine of the Trinity. This is something that can only be seen in retrospect, from the perspective of the New Testament, but it is no less significant for that. When it is seen in that way, New Testament trinitarianism can be seen to be a development of Old Testament monotheism. Of course it is such an unexpected and radical development that orthodox Judaism does not think that the Christian doctrine of God can continue to be described as monotheistic. They believe that trinitarian thought goes beyond the boundaries of monotheism. Significantly, some Christian theologians agree with them and

[14] See Athanasius, *On the Incarnation* (St Vladimir's Seminary Press, 1975), chs. 4–6.

prefer to see trinitarian theology as standing in contrast with monotheism[15] and not as a subspecies of monotheism.[16] One of the most influential trinitarian theologians of the last century, Karl Barth, objected strongly to any theology of God which arose independently of the doctrine of the Trinity. Those who argue this way are right, as the doctrine of the Trinity is *the* doctrine which makes Christianity unique and priority must be given to New Testament revelation. Nonetheless, there remains a unity between the monotheistic doctrine of God as found in the Shema and the trinitarian theology of the New Testament. Trinitarianism can be understood to be an explication of monotheism because Jewish monotheism is grounded in an understanding of the love of God. The love dimension of the Old Testament doctrine of God provides a foundation for the doctrine of the Trinity.

a. The heart of the matter

Love is the foundation of both Jesus' teaching and the Christian doctrine of God. Jesus combined the deuteronomic instruction to *love the* LORD *your God with all your heart and with all your soul and with all your strength* with the levitical command to 'love your neighbour as yourself' and made them a summary of the whole law: 'All the Law and the Prophets hang on these two commandments.'[17] Love becomes an indispensable quality of life for the believer precisely because it is the essential dynamic of the divine life. Christians are to *live* in love because God *is* love. Love is not just a good idea, a useful expediency or a noble virtue, it is a participation in the life of God. Christian love is not derived from self-will, personal strength or any human ability. 'God's love has been poured out into our hearts through the Holy Spirit, who has been given to us' (Rom. 5:5).

Christians have become so familiar with the instruction to love God with heart, soul and strength that there is a danger of overlooking the astounding significance of this command. It was an amazing statement then and it is still so today. D. F. Payne, with considerable understatement, notes that love was 'not the usual emotion towards a deity in the ancient near east'.[18] And even today few people would assume that such a position of unparalleled power, authority and majesty would immediately issue in a call to love. It is more likely that the well known saying, 'Power corrupts

[15] Moltmann, *Trinity*, 1–20.
[16] Peters, *God as Trinity*, 39.
[17] Lev. 19:18; Matt. 22:31–40.
[18] Payne, *Deuteronomy*, 48.

78

and absolute power corrupts absolutely,' would spring to mind. In a celebrated scene from the film *The Third Man* Orson Welles's character, Harry Lime, looks down from a giant ferris wheel and comments that the people are so small and so many that they are therefore as worthless as ants, and that killing them would be no crime. God looks at us from a position of transcendent power and might, yet this does not lead to such a ruthless attitude. He values and loves each and every person. So what is the appropriate attitude to have towards God? Respect is appropriate; obedience is right; a sense of awe is inevitable; but love is what God wants. The heart of the matter is love.

The love which the Shema calls for tells us that Yahweh, the God of love, is supremely personal. God is powerful, but our prayer is not just, 'May the Force be with you,' as it is in the *Star Wars* films. This 'prayer' recognizes a force greater than oneself, but a force cannot love as Yahweh does. Love unites, reconciles and brings things together. Love overcomes divisions and makes people at one with God and each other. While the message of the Shema strongly affirms the personal, loving nature of God it is unable to go further and define the inner nature of God.[19] There is a need for a further revelation under a new covenant. In the Old Testament God calls for love from his people and is himself described as caring for them, being gracious towards them and constantly protecting them. He is, moreover, described as a God abounding in an endless love (Exod. 34:6). But this love is specifically a covenant love, that is, a corporate love almost exclusively directed at the nation collectively, rather than at individuals (Deut. 7:9). On those rare occasions when love is referred to individuals it is usually those who represent the nation.[20] This does not mean that God's love did not at that time extend to individuals, but it does imply what is stated clearly elsewhere, that there is a need for a new covenant in which God's covenant law becomes internalized, more personal and more related to the inner being. This was prophesied by Jeremiah: 'This is the covenant ... I will put my law in their minds and write it on their hearts ... they will all know me' (Jer. 31:33–34). God's inner life, the fully personal internal reality of the divine nature, can only be known through that divine self-revelation and interpersonal communion which takes place in Jesus Christ. Only a fully trinitarian model of God can provide a complete theology of love in which the ultimate reality is the dynamic loving community of Father, Son and Spirit. The monotheism of the Shema points us in that direction but needs

---

[19] Lossky, *Orthodox Theology*, 29.
[20] Such as the kings David (2 Sam. 12:24) and Solomon (Neh. 13:26).

completion through the incarnation of the Word and the presence of the Spirit.

b. The extent of love

Love in the deuteronomic sense is not simply an emotion, it is something which can be commanded. Indeed, it cannot really be separated from the idea of obedience. The two concepts are virtually synonymous.[21] Nonetheless, for the Shema to speak of love rather than obedience says something about the character with which the believer is to follow Yahweh. The laws are to be followed spontaneously, willingly and joyously, not merely as the dutiful fulfilment of an obligation. Strong feelings of love and joy cannot be eliminated from this.

Love is to be given with all one's *heart* and *soul* and *strength*. In Hebrew thought *soul* refers to the principle of life itself, while *heart* refers in a general way to the quality of the life of the person including the emotional and mental dimensions. *Strength* refers to spiritual and moral power. When Jesus quoted this passage he added the Greek word for 'mind' because the Hebrew 'heart' includes an intellectual dimension which is not denoted by a reference to 'heart' in Greek. The main point, however, does not lie in a precise delineation of the three (or four) aspects of human life. Rather, together they are intended to emphasize the total commitment of the whole person. It would be wrong to exclude any dimension of our lives from being filled with love for God. Love for God must involve our total being. Today we might talk about the totality of head, heart and hand. Unfortunately, some people and certain parts of the church tend to stress one more than another. Some are better at focusing on the heart (feeling and experience), some believe the head (doctrine and teaching) is more important, and others think that the hand (strength and action) is what really counts. Lyman Frank Baum's *The Wonderful Wizard of Oz* can be used to illustrate the need for the church to hold together these three dimensions of life. As Dorothy follows the yellow-brick road looking for the Wizard to show her the way home she is joined by others who hope that the Wizard can give them what they need. The Tin Man wants to feel and love and so he wishes, 'If I only had a heart.' The Scarecrow made of straw wants to be able to think and wishes, 'If I only had a brain,' and the Lion wants to be able to act bravely without fear and so his wish is to find courage. On their journey they discover that they need each other to overcome the difficulties

---

[21] See Deut. 10:12; 11:1, 13, 22.

they face. They cannot do without each other. Head, heart and hand are all essential. The Tin Man learns that, in fact, he can love; the Scarecrow can think and the Lion is brave. And, interestingly, because of this they, like Dorothy, are ultimately able to find 'home'. The church is 'at home' when it loves with its mind, its heart and all its strength.

Deuteronomy is known as 'the book of the covenant', and love is the basis of the life of the covenant community. It was most appropriate when the levitical command 'and love your neighbour as yourself' was added to the command to love God,[22] because this simply makes clear what Deuteronomy is doing: providing laws which issue out of love for the benefit of the whole community. The book of Deuteronomy is really a commentary on the instruction to *love the LORD our God*. It shows that one loves God by loving other people.

Love should not be seen simply as an individual feeling. It is a way of life for a community and without love there can be no community, only individuals. If British Prime Minister Margaret Thatcher's much criticized declaration, 'There's no such thing as society. There are individual men and women and there are families,'[23] had actually been, '*Without love* there's no such thing as society . . .' then she would have been right. Love turns a group of individuals into a community. Again it is possible at this point to see the connection between love and the oneness of God. God's unity brings community and without it all is fragmented. Erich Fromm called love 'the only sane and satisfactory answer to the problem of human existence'.[24] It is harmony, integration and oneness compared with separate, disunited existence. It is a harmony of parts, a diversity of separate notes working together to make a single chord. Modern Western society does not exhibit in any clear way the principles for community life as described in Deuteronomy. It offers many substitutes to a life of active, thoughtful, caring love. There has been no better description of the disintegration of love in Western society than Aldous Huxley's futuristic *Brave New World*.[25] It was written seventy years ago and, while he was not intending to write scientific prophecy, he was remarkably prescient. Huxley described a world that sought to destroy love and community by substituting a more trivial 'happiness' ('Everybody's happy now') involving the immediate satisfaction of all desires ('Never put off till tomorrow the fun you can have today') in order

[22] By Jesus in Matthew 22:37 and Mark 12:31, and by the scribe in Luke 10:27.
[23] Margaret Thatcher, talking to *Woman's Own* magazine, 3 October 1987.
[24] Erich Fromm, *The Art of Loving* (Allen and Unwin, 1957), 21.
[25] Aldous Huxley, *Brave New World* (Penguin, 1971).

to avoid any recognition of deeper needs. It is a world of constant involvement in one another ('everybody belongs to everyone else') without any depth. It is pure superficiality. There is constant sexual activity without real relationship, a determined passivity through various drugs ('I drink to my annihilation'), and nothing has any intrinsic value. Everything becomes an object of consumption. The situation today is not exactly as the novel describes, but it is uncomfortably close in many respects. In contrast to this, the Shema presents the ideal of a wholehearted, total love of God with heart, soul and strength as the only basis for a society. Israel is to follow Yahweh's commands for the good of their community. They are to keep the commandments 'so that you may enjoy long life' and 'so that it may go well with you' (6:2, 3, 18). The same is true for the world today.

c. The future of the covenant

The latter part of the Shema deals with four things that the children of Israel should do in order to ensure that these important truths remain a priority for the community.

(a) First, they were told to *impress them on your children* (6:7a). It is important that the whole community learn to live according to those commands which reflect the love of God. Children may learn this partially through formal instruction, but the love of God and neighbour is primarily learnt actively through the example of parents and others in the community. Israel learnt about Yahweh's love by being rescued from captivity and from knowing his care and protection.

(b) They were told to *talk about them when you sit at home and when you walk along the road, when you lie down and when you get up* (6:7b). That is, the law of love and the commands of God are to be remembered and retold constantly. Giving continual testimony to the love of God ensures that the whole community is built up and encouraged.

(c) Then they were instructed to *tie them as symbols on your hands and bind them on your foreheads. Write them on the doorframes of your houses and on your gates* (6:8–9). It is still Jewish custom to do this. The Shema is written on small scrolls and placed in containers called phylacteries,[26] which are strapped to the arms and the forehead during prayer. There is also another container called a *mězûzâ* which is set into the doorposts of houses. Although this is done literally, the point is symbolic: they are to keep these

---

[26] Named from the Greek word meaning 'to guard' (also see Matt. 23:5).

things in mind always. They are to remember God and his laws always, for they affect all parts of daily life. Christians would do well to heed this advice and remember that God is part of everything that happens in their homes and is present wherever they go. A useful symbol of this is the use made of the Bible. Literally and metaphorically, where do we keep the word of God? Do we keep God and the words of eternal life close to us? Dag Hammarskjøld bemoaned the fact that for many people, 'On the bookshelf of life, God is a useful work of reference, always at hand but seldom consulted.'[27] Do we keep the Bible, as many people do, by our bedside? Good. Do we keep it in the living room? Better. But perhaps you do the fourth thing the Shema says we should do?[28]

(d) They were instructed to keep the words of God *upon your hearts* (6:6b). This is best of all!

While the deuteronomic covenant is not the same as the new covenant established by the death and resurrection of Christ, there is a continuity between them. It is possible to contrast the two, but it is also misleading to exaggerate the differences. The deuteronomic covenant is sometimes seen as being a matter of external obedience to law, while the new covenant is a matter of the heart. But the Shema indicates that the older covenant was always meant to be as much a matter of the heart as a matter of formal obedience: *these commandments that I give you today are to be upon your hearts.* When Jeremiah prophesied concerning the new covenant there was clearly a stronger emphasis on the internalization of the covenant for each and every individual, but this does not stand in contradiction to the deuteronomic covenant in any way. ' "This is the covenant that I will make with the house of Israel after that time," declares the LORD. "I will put my law in their minds and write it on their hearts ... No longer will a man teach his neighbour, or a man his brother, saying, 'Know the LORD,' because they will all know me, from the least of them to the greatest" ' (Jer. 31:33–44). This heart-based element of the new covenant is a logical, though not inevitable, development of the Shema.

The Shema prepares God's people for God's greatest action: the incarnation, life, ministry, death and resurrection of Jesus. In the events surrounding Jesus the life of God as Trinity is revealed. In this triunity there is the fullest expression of the unity of love. It leads to a final unity of believers with God in Christ through the Holy Spirit. It is impossible to know God except through Jesus Christ. We cannot even know ourselves except through Jesus Christ. In

[27] Dag Hammarskjøld, *Markings* (Alfred A. Knopf, 1964), 10.
[28] This fourth instruction is actually listed first in the Shema, but it is a result of all the rest and so I have treated it last.

83

1 Corinthians 8:6 Paul appears to expound Deuteronomy 6:4 in a manner that is only possible after the more complete revelation of God in Christ. 'For us', he says, 'there is but one God,' and every Jew would agree with that. But then God is explained in terms of 'the Father, from whom all things came and for whom we live; and ... one Lord, Jesus Christ, through whom all things came and through whom we live'. In other words, Paul has redefined the Shema Christologically. He has taken the doctrine of the one and only God and applied it to Jesus and the Father. There is no division between them, only the loving unity of the Trinity.

Proverbs 8:22–31
4. The wisdom of God

There is an English proverb about the biblical book of Proverbs which says, 'Solomon made a book of proverbs, but a book of proverbs never made a Solomon.' The point it makes is that wisdom arises from experiencing life rather than simply reading about it. The wisdom found in the book of Proverbs agrees with that assessment, though with two provisos. The first is that wisdom particularly comes from one's experience of God, and the second is that, although experience is essential, the one who listens carefully to the wisdom of Proverbs can find guidance, grace and life (1:5, 8–9; 4:10). *Listen to my instruction and be wise* (8:33) says the voice of Wisdom herself in one of the poems found in that Hebrew collection of sayings, proverbs and poems, and it is the best advice one can get: 'Wisdom is supreme; therefore get wisdom. Though it cost all you have, get understanding' (4:7). But where is wisdom to be found? The answer is that 'the LORD gives wisdom, and from his mouth come knowledge and understanding' (2:6). Wisdom comes from God.

Of course, there have always been those who consider listening to the voice of God to be a sign of madness rather than wisdom. St Anthony, the third-century ascetic desert Father, noted this when he said, 'A time is coming when people will go mad, and when they meet someone who is not mad, they will turn to him and say, "You are out of your mind," just because he is not like them.'[1] The wisdom which comes from God is often in conflict with the so-called wisdom of the world and those who turn to God seem to be radically out of step. Sometimes the approach to life which seeks the wisdom of God is treated by others with amusement or condescension, while

---

[1] *Sayings of the Desert Fathers*, Anthony, 25 (*Patrologia Graeca* 65, 84), cited in O. Clément, *The Roots of Christian Mysticism* (New City Press, 1982), 16.

at other times it is so countercultural that it is perceived as a threat or an offence to the common way of life. Political totalitarianism of both the far right and the far left has insisted on trying to control how people think and behave and has despised any idea of the wisdom of God. Extreme religious fundamentalism of various kinds has sought to ensure that religious activity is legally restricted to only one form or, in some places, to a limited number of 'traditional' forms. In this way religion itself has been used to try to exclude the ways of God from the world. Aggressive forms of secularism have aimed at creating a strict dichotomy of private belief and public action by rigorously eliminating religious principles and conduct from the marketplace, the school and the public arena. And radical pluralism – a view which goes beyond merely recognizing a plurality of views and itself becomes an ideology – has insisted that all points of view are to be accepted as equally right and valid, with the only exception being that any suggestion that a particular view can be said to be either the truth or in error is itself not be tolerated. These views, along with sheer contempt and indifference at times, have considered deference to the wisdom of God as foolish. Nonetheless, this should not blind us to the fact that there are many searching for true wisdom who will readily accept the way of the Lord if they are given the opportunity to do so. Indeed, the reason for the strong words of the biblical writers contrasting wisdom and foolishness is that they make very clear both the possibility of deciding for the wisdom of God and the importance of the decision.

The wisdom of the book of Proverbs is found mainly, but not solely, in the form of proverbs. The most common and fundamental style of proverb in English is the one-line maxim such as, 'A bird in the hand is worth two in the bush', or 'A stitch in time saves nine.' But in Hebrew the basic form is a two-line parallelism where the second line is slightly different in wording but synonymous in meaning. For example, 'Honest scales and balances are from the LORD; all the weights in the bag are of his making.'[2] A common alternative form is where the second line contrasts with the first, as in 'A fool's talk brings a rod to his back, but the lips of the wise protect them.'[3] There are also expanded[4] and comparative[5] styles and four-, six- and eight-line versions.[6] In addition to the proverbs there are a number of wisdom poems such as those extolling the value of wives of noble character (31:10–31) and the benefits of

[2] Prov. 16:11; also see 16:18, 30, 32.
[3] Prov. 14:3; also see 11:17, 19, 24.
[4] Prov. 10:18–21.
[5] Prov. 25:25, 26; 26:1.
[6] Prov. 23:15–16, 19–21, 22–25.

listening to the voice of Wisdom, who is presented in the form of a woman (1:20–33; 8:1 – 9:6). The image of Wisdom as a woman is presented in such a striking and dramatic fashion that both Jewish and Christian interpretations have considered the possibility of the woman being something more than a mere literary device. The implications of this for the doctrine of the Trinity have to be seriously considered, but only in the context of the overall teaching of the book of Proverbs concerning wisdom.

1. Wisdom for living

The first appearance of the woman Wisdom occurs very early in Proverbs. It comes after the prologue (1:1–7) and a series of encouragements for people to listen (1:8–19). Wisdom is presented as a woman calling aloud in the street and the public square to warn those who do not fear the Lord (1:20–33). This initial presentation is followed later by another in 8:1 – 9:6. This second account begins with the writer directing the readers' attention to Wisdom, who cries out to be heard *on the heights* and *where the paths meet* and *beside the gates leading into the city, at the entrances* (8:1–3). These places are noteworthy for they are the places where people gather, where markets are established and business is done. Even today, outside the gates of Middle Eastern cities there are stalls and markets with people waiting and talking and doing business. This is where one needs God's wisdom. Wisdom's teaching is not some esoteric knowledge far removed from the everyday affairs of life. Far from it. God's wisdom is about how to live. As William McKane says, wisdom 'operates where the competition is fiercest, not so much the competition of other orators as men's preoccupations with those things which they take more seriously than listening to speeches – earning their living, making bargains, getting wealth, transacting local politics, settling disputes and other less gracious enjoyments. It is against all this that Wisdom has to compete.'[7] I know a philosopher who sets up some chairs in a public mall with a sign, 'Would you like to talk to a philosopher?' He then sits and spends his time discussing the issues which are on people's minds. This is where wisdom is really needed, at the point where people have serious questions about life.

In dealing with all of life's questions there is a 'worldly wisdom' or 'common sense' which seeks conformity with the ways of the world. The wisdom of Proverbs, however, seeks conformity with the eternal will of God in whom true wisdom is found. As the

[7] McKane, *Proverbs*, 345.

recorder of Proverbs says, 'The fear of the LORD is the beginning of wisdom' (Prov. 9:10; Ps. 111:10). Wisdom, in the sense in which it is proclaimed by the woman, is more than intellectual knowledge.[8] It is theologically based and strongly moral and practical in nature. It means 'being skillful and successful in one's relationships and responsibilities. It involves observing and following the Creator's principles of order in the moral universe.'[9] The wisdom of the book of Proverbs involves having a certain character, engaging in particular types of conduct and seeing certain consequences.

(a) *Character*: the character of the one that is wise can be described very simply. On the one hand, they understand what is right, just and fair in dealing with other people (1:3; 2:9). On the other hand, they understand, trust and honour God (2:5; 3:5, 9). These two dimensions go hand in hand; the one who honours God will do what is right, while the one who acts justly is honouring God. Those who are wise are not necessarily those with the greatest knowledge about the world, as wisdom has more to do with the character of a person than with intellect. Intelligence and wisdom should not be confused. While both are gifts of God, it is far better to seek wisdom through the development of character than intellectual recognition through the learning of facts and theories.

(b) *Conduct*: the wise person does good and not evil, is gentle and not violent, is honest, truthful and hardworking, faithful in relationships and acts prudently and with discretion.[10] Such people's behaviour is orientated towards whatever is good for themselves, their family and neighbours and society as a whole. Wisdom, in the biblical sense, is practical, active and involved rather than abstract or theoretical. Wise people are always generously and helpfully involved in the lives of others.

(c) *Consequences*: there are consequences from this sort of behaviour for the wise person and others. The wise person is guarded and protected from harm, saved from sin, blessed with good relationships and prosperity, health and nourishment. They are people in favour with others and with a good reputation. They are safe and secure, are guided by God, at peace with others, they

[8] There are various types of wisdom literature, including Job, Ecclesiastes and Proverbs. But some psalms (e.g. 37; 127) and parts of other books (e.g. 2 Sam. 12:1–4; Judg. 14:12–20) also contain elements of wisdom literature and there is also apocryphal wisdom literature such as Ecclesiasticus, the Wisdom of Solomon and the Sayings of the Fathers.

[9] R. B. Zuck, 'A Theology of Proverbs', in R. B. Zuck (ed.), *Learning from the Sages* (Baker, 1995), 99.

[10] Prov. 3:27; 4:26; 3:31; 6:17, 35; 6:6–11, 32; 1:4; 2:11.

enjoy long life and have a hope for the future.[11] They are also a joy to their parents and a blessing to others.[12] These are the normal results of acting wisely and the reason is obvious: those who are kind to others enjoy good relationships; the honest develop a good reputation; it is likely that those who are hardworking will prosper; and the faithful will have loving husbands or wives. It must be stressed, though, that while these are the normal results of a wise person's conduct there is no unconditional guarantee that the wise person will never suffer from accidents, family breakdowns, economic misfortune, untrue rumours, illness, the evil that others do or even, at times, the consequences of his or her own foolishness.

Because of the lack of a guarantee that goodness will bring an immediate reward, many people, including children, sometimes wonder why they should be bothered with 'being good'. Life can sometimes seem unfair when those who have clearly behaved badly gain an advantage or are rewarded in some way for their behaviour. There are two responses to this. The first is that in the end, God will do what is right and everyone will receive their appropriate reward,[13] and the second is that God desires that we do what is right and refrain from evil not because of any reward but simply because it is good for us as well as for others. In being kind and generous, gentle and caring we not only help others but we develop our own character and become more like the person God wants us to be. Even if our acts of kindness produce no other good effect in this world, they still contribute to the transformation of our lives. I remember being told, when young, that 'goodness is its own reward'. This is a valuable principle for all to live by. Right behaviour is not to be done only if by it we gain some other advantage in life or have something done for us in return. God calls us to be obedient because he wants the very best for us. It is a distorted view of God which conceives of him as some kind of eternal killjoy sitting in heaven making up rules and demands so as to test our obedience and to take all the fun out of life. It is not like that at all, yet too many people think of him in those terms. The principles of life which the wisdom literature puts forward are not to be obeyed just because God will be upset if they are not. They are part and parcel of a rich and rewarding life and being wise means living a good life. Wisdom and goodness are completely intertwined. It is as true to say that a person's wisdom emerges from his or her goodness as to say that goodness is what is taught by wisdom.

[11] Prov. 2:8, 12; 3:23; 2:16, 20; 5:18–19; 6:1; 16:20; 3:8; 3:4; 8:35; 1:33; 3:22; 6:22; 3:17; 3:16; 4:10; 23:18.

[12] Prov. 10:1; 15:20; 13:12; 15:4; 10:11; 13:14.

[13] Matt. 6:46; 16:27; Luke 6:23; Eph. 6:8; Rev. 22:12.

THE MESSAGE OF THE TRINITY

Wisdom and goodness together lead to a deeply satisfying and happy life.

2. Wisdom and Yahweh

Proverbs 8 contains the most extended description of Wisdom as a woman. Wisdom when presented in this way obviously has a very special place in God's world. She existed before creation, speaks for Yahweh and lives with him (8:22; 9:10). She is even described as *rejoicing always in his presence* (v. 30). Wisdom has a unique intimacy with Yahweh. How should this be understood? What did the writer intend by his presentation of Wisdom in this way? The matter has been complicated by the fact that, historically, there have been a number of approaches. Some of them have implications for the Christian doctrine of the Trinity.

a. Wisdom as a goddess

One approach is to suggest that Wisdom should be understood as a goddess living alongside Yahweh in the same way that there were female gods who lived alongside male deities in other Ancient Near Eastern religions. There were various goddesses including Egypt's Isis and Ma'at, the Akkadian Ishtar and the Canaanite Asherah. This suggestion is, however, most unlikely given the firm Hebrew repudiation of polytheism in general and the commitment of the author of Proverbs to the knowledge of Yahweh and the covenant made with Israel which demanded that there be 'no other gods before me' (2:5, 17; Deut. 5:7). Even if the idea of a female deity, Wisdom, was co-opted and modified by the author of this passage[14] (an idea which cannot be repudiated but about which there is considerable doubt), the meaning must be determined within the context of Yahweh's relationship with Israel and the world. There is no suggestion in Proverbs of Israel's monotheism being compromised or of the Lordship of Yahweh being challenged by the presence of Wisdom, who was actually *possessed* (or 'brought forth', 8:22) by Yahweh himself. Altogether, the idea of Wisdom as a goddess is a most unlikely possibility.

b. Wisdom as a personification

What seems much more likely is that the presentation of Wisdom as a woman should be interpreted, initially at least, as a simple

[14] As per C. R. Fontaine, 'The Personification of Wisdom', in James L. Mays (ed.), *Harper's Bible Commentary* (HarperSanFrancisco, 1988), 501–503.

personification – that is, as a literary device. This is not unique. It was not unusual for various Ancient Near Eastern religions to personify the attributes of their deity. Moreover, elsewhere in the Old Testament there are various forms of personification. Mountains and hills are able to sing and skip, while the seas can look and flee. Trees clap their hands, the earth trembles, a city is comforted like a person and a nation is described as a virgin. Concepts such as death, righteousness, peace and foolishness can be presented as though they were people.[15] Indeed, the idea of presenting wisdom as something more than an abstract concept can also be found in Job 28. In that situation wisdom is presented as though it was a great treasure like gold or sapphires. People search for it, but in the end the point is made that wisdom is not found in the ground and cannot be bought from a trader. On the contrary, one can only say that wisdom is found in 'the fear of the Lord' (Job 28:28).

The literary technique of Proverbs goes further and actually personifies Wisdom[16] as a woman able to speak for herself.[17] This poetic form of expression allows the concept of wisdom to be communicated with all the drama of a play and the emphasis which comes from direct speech. It reaffirms the teaching found elsewhere in Proverbs, including such ideas that truth and righteousness are to be sought and wickedness avoided (8:6–7), that being wise is a treasure to be valued (v. 11), that the Lord dislikes pride and arrogance (v. 13), that kings reign at God's discretion (v. 15), and that justice and righteousness lead to prosperity (v. 21). All of this is typical wisdom teaching. It is important for those who love the Lord (v. 17).

c. Wisdom as a divine revelation

While the personification of Wisdom in 8:1–21 presents nothing which is out of the ordinary, verses 22–31 introduce new and challenging dimensions to the understanding of Wisdom, her relationship to Yahweh and Yahweh's relationship to the world. The material presented in these verses makes it difficult to interpret Wisdom purely in terms of the literary technique of personification. The way the woman Wisdom is presented here extends the understanding of God in a way which other personifications do not and deals with Wisdom herself and her relationship to God. The

[15] Isa. 55:12; Pss. 96:11–12; 114:3–7; Isa. 40:2; Amos 5:2; Hos. 13:14; Ps. 85:9–13; Prov. 9:13.
[16] As in 3:13–20; 4:5–9.
[17] Prov. 1:20–33; 8:1 – 9:6. The personification of Wisdom is also found in some extrabiblical literature such as Sirach 1:1–30; 24:1–34; 51:1–27.

teaching content of the poem about the woman Wisdom is different from usual wisdom literature in at least five ways.

(a) *Wisdom's origin*: Wisdom proclaims that *the LORD brought me forth as the first of his works, before his deeds of old* (8:22). An exact translation of what the Lord did is difficult. 'Created' or 'brought forth' are possible but so are 'begat', 'acquired' or 'possessed', but whatever the translation the meaning of verses 22–29 as a whole is quite clear: Wisdom pre-existed anything else except God. Wisdom was present *from the beginning, before the world began* (v. 23) and was already there *when he set the heavens in place* (v. 27). This unusual aspect of the poem is not found elsewhere and does not seem necessary as a part of typical wisdom teaching. Its purpose is not immediately clear.

(b) *Wisdom's name*: the relationship between Wisdom and Yahweh develops in verse 30 where, although the translation does not make it easy to see, there are two references to 'I am' which recall the two 'I AM WHO I AM' statements of Exodus 3:14. Roland Murphy concludes that 'there can hardly be any doubt that v. 30 alludes to that passage'.[18] He also comments that this is particularly noteworthy given the general tendency in Proverbs to avoid the verb 'to be' in favour of juxtaposition or simple comparison. In short, Wisdom is not only present with Yahweh but comes close to taking Yahweh's name. This, of course, can simply be explained by the fact that Wisdom is a personification of one of Yahweh's attributes. Nonetheless, it is unusual to relate Wisdom to the 'I AM' when the 'I AM' is also present.

(c) *Wisdom's work*: what is wisdom doing at creation? Unfortunately, once again there are translation difficulties, although *then I was the craftsman at his side* (v. 30) is likely. Others, however, suggest that rather than a crafts(wo)man working, the picture is of a child playing delightedly in the presence of Yahweh.[19] Either way, Wisdom is closely associated with God at the point of creation. If the image is of a craftswoman creating, then Wisdom is actually sharing in the work of creation – something which is usually ascribed to Yahweh alone. If the image of a child playing is the right one, then the stress falls more on the intimacy shared between child and parent and the enjoyment they experience. In either case Wisdom clearly holds a unique role, beyond that of anything in creation.

(d) *Wisdom's place*: Wisdom's work (whether craft or play) is done in close association with Yahweh. Wisdom is *at his side* and *in*

---

[18] Murphy, *Proverbs*, 53.
[19] See Murphy, 48.

his presence (v. 30). Wisdom is not Yahweh, but nor is Wisdom separated very far from Yahweh. They have a common purpose, a common location, she shares in his work and is uniquely close to God.

(e) *Wisdom's delight*: Wisdom's delight is a double one, rejoicing in God, *filled with delight day after day, rejoicing always in his presence* (v. 30), while at the same time *rejoicing in his whole world and delighting in mankind* (v. 31). Wisdom, who is so closely related to Yahweh, is also found involved with humanity and rejoicing in the whole world.

In this description of Wisdom the focus has moved beyond the normal practical wisdom teaching concerning the value of a life lived in accord with the principles of justice, prudence, kindness and discipline. The focus is no longer on what Wisdom teaches but on the origin and the person of Wisdom herself and her relationship with Yahweh. Wisdom has become a divine being with a unique role in creation and a special place beside God. Each aspect of a personification is meant to teach some lesson. What does this teach? The answers to this question have been many and varied within both Jewish and Christian theology. We have already seen that the personification was so vivid for some that it seemed to suggest that Wisdom was a goddess living alongside Yahweh. Even if that option is ruled out it does not prevent other interpretations emerging. There are passages in the New Testament which appear to interpret Wisdom in terms of the pre-existent Christ, and the early Fathers of the church certainly did not hesitate to identify Wisdom in this way. They attributed trinitarian significance to the image of Wisdom. Nor were they alone in interpreting Wisdom in terms of divine life, because even before that there were certain forms of Jewish theology which understood Wisdom to be a divine being.

During the intertestamental period the interpretation of Wisdom was influenced by the fact that Hebrew and Greek cultures interacted to an extent which had not happened previously. Amongst other things, this led to two new sets of associations. First, the Hebrew notion of wisdom entered into dialogue with the Greek philosophical understanding of it. Secondly, the *Wisdom* of God developed a strong association with the concept of the *Word* of God. Wisdom and Word (and indeed Spirit as well) were very flexible words with a wide range of meaning. They were all used as bridging words for expressing the relationship between God and the world and were all, at various times, personified and used as representations of divinity. Three brief examples of the Jewish literature of this period illustrates these connections.

The Wisdom of Solomon: this was written in Greek but drew on both Hebrew and Greek sources and concepts. It described Wisdom in terms similar to those used for the Word (or *logos*). That is, Wisdom is described as being pre-existent, the angel of creation, the divine power at work in the world, the spirit that pervades all things, and even God's 'throne-partner'.

1 Enoch: Enoch personified Wisdom as appearing on earth but then returning to angelic life in the following terms: 'Then wisdom went out to dwell with the children of the people, but she found no dwelling-place. So wisdom returned to her place and she settled permanently among the angels' (42:1–2, NEB).

The Book of Baruch: in this book Jeremiah's scribe is depicted as addressing the Jewish exiles, and the Torah (the Old Testament 'Law') is described in this way: 'Thereupon wisdom appeared on earth and lived among men' (3:37, NEB). This appears to be related to the prologue of the Gospel of John which says, 'The Word [*logos*] became flesh and made his dwelling among us' (John 1:14).

There is no doubt that the description of Wisdom as a woman should be interpreted as a literary device. It is the personification of one of God's attributes and it is done to reinforce dramatically the general teaching of Proverbs. However, it extends the boundaries of the genre and not only provides new teaching but also shifts the emphasis away from what is taught *about wisdom* onto the person of *Wisdom herself* and *her relationship with Yahweh and the world*. Wisdom has become a divine being with a unique role in creation and a special place beside God.

3. Wisdom and Christ

The ideas implied in the concept of Wisdom personified were taken up in the New Testament to facilitate a deeper reflection on the nature of God. The image provided the categories of thought and the terminology which helped the early Christians understand the origin of Christ and his unique relationship to God. What was metaphorical in Proverbs became realized in the one whose origin is with God the Father and who is in dynamic, intimate and constant relationship with him. The identification of Jesus with Wisdom and the subsequent development of that idea in early Christian thought did not simply involve the adoption of the Jewish literary technique of personification. It went beyond that and became part of the foundation for a genuinely new under-standing of the nature of God as Trinity, a teaching so radical that it had to be differentiated from Jewish monotheism. It developed in the following three ways.

a. Christ is Wisdom, the revelation of God

From his earliest days Jesus was associated with wisdom from God.
Luke reports that 'the child grew and became strong; he was filled
with wisdom, and the grace of God was upon him' (Luke 2:40, 52).
Later, in the time of his ministry, many people asked, 'Where did
this man get this wisdom and these miraculous powers?' (Matt.
13:54; see also Mark 6:2). Jesus himself made several comments
which seem to connect his life and ministry with that of Wisdom.
When he was criticized for feasting and associating with known
sinners, he defended his own actions by reference to the actions of
the personified woman Wisdom, saying, 'wisdom is proved right by
her actions' (Matt. 11:16–19; Luke 7:31–35). He also made reference
to Wisdom as presented in the intertestamental book of Sirach,
which closes with wisdom calling out to those thirsting for knowledge, 'Acquire wisdom for yourselves without money. Put your
neck under her yoke, and let your souls receive instruction; it is to
be found close by.' By using similar words Jesus put himself in the
place of Wisdom, calling out to those who were weary and
burdened, 'Take my yoke upon you and learn from me' (Matt.
11:29). An allusion such as this is open to a number of interpretations. It could be argued that it is nothing more than a case of Jesus
refashioning either a common saying or the words of Sirach for his
own use. Or it could mean that Jesus wanted to identify himself
with Wisdom personified, the one able to reveal the deepest wisdom
of God. Given the rest of Jesus' teaching, the latter is likely.

The message of Proverbs is that 'Wisdom is supreme; therefore
get wisdom. Though it cost all you have, get understanding' (4:7–8),
and Jesus spoke of the cost of gaining the wisdom of the kingdom of
God. A wise person would be like a merchant who sold all he had to
obtain a particularly precious pearl (Matt. 13:45). Jesus proclaimed a
wisdom which came from God, but a wisdom hidden from the wise
and learned while revealed to his little children (Matt. 11:25). The
claim was that his was a unique wisdom with no parallel, which
could not be known in the usual manner by the wise and learned.
Wisdom personified in Proverbs said that there would be those who
would not be able to know this wisdom of God: 'Then they will call
to me but I will not answer; they will look for me but will not find
me' (Prov. 1:28). Jesus said he spoke in parables because of those
people who, 'Though seeing, they do not see; though hearing, they
do not hear or understand ... For this people's heart has become
calloused; they hardly hear with their ears, and they have closed
their eyes' (Matt. 13:13). His wisdom could only be known by those
who were children of God, which could only come about through

union with Christ. He knew the deep things of God because of his own special relationship with the Father: 'no-one knows the Father except the Son.' Only through Jesus can this true wisdom be known by anyone (Matt. 11:25–30; Sirach 51:23–27).

Jesus' possibly ambiguous allusions to his relationship with Wisdom gave impetus to the early church's identification of Christ with Wisdom. This went beyond the idea that he stood in the tradition of wise men like Solomon and led to the idea that Christ not only *possessed* wisdom but *was* wisdom (1 Cor. 1:24). For the apostle Paul Christ is wisdom personified and perfected, he is the one 'who has become for us wisdom from God – that is, our righteousness, holiness and redemption' (1 Cor. 1:30). By saying that Christ *is* the wisdom of God (1 Cor. 1:24), he is not only building upon the teaching of Proverbs, he is also identifying Christ with an attribute of God and making Christ indivisible from the divine nature. To take on Christ is to take on God's wisdom and to take on the life of God. The teaching that Christ would live with the believer (John 15:4–6) is far more than, and yet connected with, the teaching of Proverbs concerning the one who feared the Lord, that 'wisdom will enter your heart' (Prov. 2:10). Without wisdom and without Christ there is death (Prov. 1:25–26; John 11:26), while in having wisdom and in having Christ there is the knowledge of God (Prov. 2:5; John 17:26).

To sum up, there is in Christ a fulfilment of the theology hinted at in Proverbs which involves a significant development in the understanding of God and which provides a foundation for the doctrine of the Trinity. The woman Wisdom, as presented in Proverbs, is the wisdom of God personified in literary form, while the Christ of the New Testament is the Wisdom of God personified in historical, physical form. The idea of the woman Wisdom began as a literary construction but was amplified to the point where its teaching about Wisdom herself and her relationship to Yahweh was of such an order that it seemed to challenge the boundaries of its own form. The questions and the issues raised in Proverbs about Wisdom in relation to God could not be answered until the time of Christ. That which was hinted at in Proverbs is revealed in Christ. A mere personification has become an actual incarnation, and in Christ the Wisdom of God is revealed fully and is really present.

b. Christ is Wisdom and Word, the Creator of the world

Of particular interest in the development of the theology of Christ and Wisdom is the way it seems that the apostle John drew on

Proverbs for inspiration concerning the origin and the pre-existence of Christ. The poem in Proverbs has Wisdom saying,

> The LORD brought me forth as the first of his works,
>   before his deeds of old;
> I was appointed from eternity,
>   from the beginning, before the world began ...
> I was there when he set the heavens in place,
>   when he marked out the horizon on the face of the deep,
> when he established the clouds above
>   and fixed securely the fountains of the deep,
> when he gave the sea its boundary
>   so that the waters would not overstep his command,
> and when he marked out the foundations of the earth.
>   Then I was the craftsman at his side.
>
>   (8:22-30)

When John began his Gospel with words echoing the ideas found in the poem of Proverbs 8 he did as the intertestamental writers had done before him and related the concept of the Word of God to the Wisdom of God.

> In the beginning was the Word, and the Word was with God, and the Word was God. He was with God in the beginning.
>   Through him all things were made; without him nothing was made that has been made ...
>   The Word became flesh and made his dwelling among us ... the one and only Son who came from the Father.'
>
>   (John 1:1-3, 14)

Both the Wisdom of Proverbs and the Word of John's Gospel were present with God at the beginning, from eternity, before the creation of the world. They are both identified as being present with God and both had their origin in God. Wisdom was the 'first of his works' while the Word 'came from the Father'. Wisdom was present at creation as craftswoman while the Word was the one through whom all things were made. In Proverbs, 'By wisdom the LORD laid the earth's foundations' (3:19), while in John it is said, 'Through him all things were made; without him nothing was made that has been made' (John 1:3). Both Wisdom and Word were known in the form of human flesh: Wisdom was a woman and the Word became a man. The poem of Proverbs 8 is an anticipation of the doctrine of the incarnation as described in John 1, and thus an anticipation of the doctrine of the Trinity. The fact that it can only

97

be seen clearly in retrospect, after the time of Christ, does not diminish its significance.

A similar point is made in Colossians 1:15–17 when it is said of Christ that he is 'the image of the invisible God, the firstborn over all creation. For in him all things were created: things in heaven and on earth, visible and invisible, whether thrones or powers or rulers or authorities; all things have been created through him and for him. He is before all things, and in him all things hold together.' Here Paul is employing terms for the person of Christ which previously were reserved for divine Wisdom. Moreover, in Hebrews 1:2–3 the writer says that God 'has spoken to us by his Son', that is, by Christ the one 'appointed heir of all things, and through whom also he made the universe. The Son is the radiance of God's glory and the exact representation of his being, sustaining all things by his powerful word.' Once again the imagery is derived from the teaching of Proverbs 8 concerning Wisdom, where she is the one who is 'created' or 'begotten' before creation, who is from all eternity, who is at the side of Yahweh, who helps create the universe and who is the one involved with people and the world (Prov. 8:22–31). Similarly, in the intertestamental Wisdom of Solomon the writer says Wisdom is 'an exhalation from the power of God, a pure effluence from the glory of the Almighty ... an effulgence of eternal light, an unblemished mirror of his goodness'.[20]

The connection of Christ with Wisdom and the creation of the world is important but often overlooked. The role of Christ in salvation can tend to overshadow his work in creation. Often it is the case that those who are more zealous in proclaiming the work of Christ in redemption are less likely to reflect on the work of Christ in creation. And the stress on salvation from the effects and the power of sin tends to lead to somewhat negative views of creation as fallen and distorted. This is perhaps understandable and to some extent defensible, as Scripture itself gives greater prominence to the theology of salvation. However, redemption includes within it the idea of the redemption of the whole of creation, not only that of people (Rom. 8:19–21). The teaching of Proverbs concerning Wisdom and creation helps us to see the world in very positive terms, not simply as fallen, and shows something of God's appreciation of the world that he has made. Proverbs shows that God creates through Wisdom and in doing so it demonstrates the delight that he took in this work and in the world. It says of Wisdom, 'I was the craftsman at his side. I was filled with delight

[20] Translation of the Wisdom of Solomon 7:25–26 by David Winston, *The Wisdom of Solomon* (Doubleday, 1979).

day after day, rejoicing always in his presence, rejoicing in his whole world and delighting in mankind' (Prov. 8:30–31). And if God loves and delights in the world, then so should we.

God's delight in creation as described in Proverbs is reflected in the creation narrative of Genesis 1 – 2. The process of creation as described there is often spoken of as a creation in six days, as though only the six days were important. But 'the six days of creation' should really be 'the seven days of creation' – or, at least, the six days should not be spoken of without reference to the seventh because it was the seventh day that was declared the special day, the holy day (Gen. 2:3). The day on which God apparently did 'nothing' is actually the high point of creation. On that day God 'rested'. We should not think that he was resting because he was completely worn out after six exhausting days of work, but rather that on that day he took time to rest 'in' the creation that he had made. On that day he appreciated it. It is as though he stood back and looked at all he had made which he declared to be 'good', and enjoyed it. Wisdom declares that creation and humanity are worthy of 'rejoicing' and 'delight'. God is not an eternal fidget who has to make and make and make without stopping to contemplate the beauty and magnificence of his world and his people. Those who are unable to stop and reflect on such beauty should remember Wisdom's delight and seek to imitate it.

(c) Christ is Wisdom, the truth of the cross

Perhaps the most significant development of the theology of Wisdom as related to the person of Christ takes place in the way Paul uses it to introduce into the life of God the fact of the death of Christ and a divine 'wisdom' which involves his crucifixion. This was a radically new understanding of the nature of God, because it not only challenged Jewish monotheism but also presented a picture of a God who suffered in Christ. This appeared to be nothing other than foolishness to unbelievers. In 1 Corinthians Paul declares that while Jews demanded 'miraculous signs' and Greeks looked for 'wisdom', 'we preach Christ crucified: a stumbling block to Jews and foolishness to Gentiles, but to those whom God has called, both Jews and Greeks, Christ the power of God and the wisdom of God' (1 Cor. 1:18–24).

In Christ the wisdom of God is shown to be different from any human wisdom. This is consistent with the message of Proverbs in which the ones who resist God's wisdom are shown to be fools. Those who hold to their own opinions and who scorn the words of the wise (Prov. 12:15; 18:2; 23:9) are actually on the way to ruin and disaster (Prov. 10:8, 10). Paul shows how, contrary to human reasoning, God uses weakness to overcome strength, foolishness to shame the wise, and the lowly and humble to nullify pride and ambition (1 Cor. 1:27–31). His message was nothing but Christ and God's power through him (1 Cor. 2:1, 5). This was 'God's wisdom, a mystery that has been hidden and that God destined for glory before time began' (1 Cor. 2:7). It could not be understood by rulers and leaders and could only be learnt from the Spirit (1 Cor. 2:6, 13). He concludes his discussion of the contrary nature of human and divine wisdom by tying possession of this wisdom to life with Christ and Christ to God by reminding his readers who accept the wisdom of God that 'you are of Christ, and Christ is of God' (1 Cor. 3:23).

Paul uses the idea of Wisdom personified as one part of his overall teaching about God and his relationship to the world. He extends the implications beyond that of Proverbs and even beyond the teaching of Christ, for he uses it to introduce the ultimate wisdom – that God in Christ died for the world. Consequently, his theology of God has to become a theology which will later be known as trinitarian. It cannot be contained within traditional Jewish monotheism. The doctrine of the Trinity as it unfolds in Paul and the New Testament generally teaches a wisdom which becomes ever more scandalous to human reason and religious sensibilities. The doctrine of the Trinity is an account not only of a God who is Father, Son and Spirit, but also of a God who embraces within the divine life the death of the Son. The completely contrary nature of human and divine wisdom means that each seems as foolishness to the other.

The introduction to this chapter made reference to the ascetic Anthony who warned that those who spoke the wisdom of God would be called mad, and it seems appropriate to conclude with a similar observation that human wisdom is no more able to understand the wisdom of God today than it was in the first century. The German philosopher Friedrich Nietzsche (1844–1900) wrote a parable about a madman who, like Wisdom in Proverbs 8, cried out in the marketplace with a message about God.[21] In what is generally considered to be one of philosophy's more prescient statements, Nietzsche, himself an atheist, clearly foresaw in the late nineteenth century the way in which modern Western culture would remove God from its centre. He wrote far ahead of his time for 'the very few. Perhaps none of them is living yet' who could

[21] Friedrich Nietzsche, *The Gay Science* (1887), 125, cited in R. G. Smith, *Secular Christianity* (Harper and Row, 1966), pp. 161–163.

understand the far-reaching significance of a philosophy in which the self has to replace God. In his parable, the madman lit a lantern at noon and called out continually, 'I am looking for God,' but those who heard him only laughed and scorned him, 'Has God got lost like a child? Or gone away on a voyage?' But the madman cried out, 'Where has God gone? I will tell you. We have slain him – you and I. We are all his murderers. Can't you hear the sound of the gravediggers as they bury God?' The madman continued, 'How could we do this? How could we drink up the sea or wipe out the whole horizon? And how shall we console ourselves? What water can make us clean? Is not the greatness of this deed too great for us? Must we not ourselves become gods?' For Nietzsche the only alternative to God was for people to become 'supermen' and take his place. But which is the real madness?

Nietzsche was fully aware of the profound implications for a society which removed God from its centre. In his parable the hearers were shocked at the words of the madman, who then threw his lantern on the ground. 'I come too early,' he said. 'It is not yet my time. This monstrous event is still on the way.' Nietzsche foresaw 'the death of God' in modern society and was a forerunner of postmodern theorists such as Michel Foucault. Although his philosophy is ultimately critical of traditional faith and morality, he rightly perceives the significance of whether the life of an individual or a society is lived according to human or divine wisdom. Nietzsche, along with many others, preferred human wisdom, the 'wisdom' which Proverbs describes as foolishness and a path to destruction (2:18, 22; 8:36). It contrasts with the advice given in perhaps the most well known proverb of all, 'Trust in the LORD with all your heart and lean not on your own understanding; in all your ways acknowledge him, and he will make your paths straight' (Prov. 3:5). Nietzsche's parable is a sober reminder of the way people can 'murder' God through their attitudes and behaviour. Through immorality, wilful unbelief, inattention, selfishness, pride and arrogance, carelessness and neglect, individuals and societies can become alienated from God and true wisdom. Christians, like Wisdom, must call out in the marketplace, and also in the school, the local council, the media, the neigbourhood and the workplace, that those who keep the ways of the Lord are blessed and those who listen to his instruction are wise (Prov. 8:33).

Even Christians are not immune from misunderstanding the wisdom of God and sometimes replacing it with a message which appears to be more practical, realistic, logical, conventional, or safer or (particularly) easier or more pleasant. Human wisdom inevitably returns to these themes while divine wisdom takes a different route.

In Nietzsche's parable the madman went into several churches and sang a requiem to God. Led out and questioned, he replied, 'What are the churches, if not the tombs and selpulchres of God?' One does not have to be as negative as Nietzsche was to accept that it is possible for churches and for Christians to replace divine wisdom with human wisdom at times. Every one of us must be careful that we do not form the wisdom of God in a way that suits us. Dietrich Bonhoeffer put it this way: 'If it is I who say where God will be, I will always find there a God who in some way corresponds to me, is agreeable to me, fits in with my nature. But if it is God who says where He will be, that place is the cross of Christ.'[22] The Wisdom of God spoken about in Proverbs 8 is revealed in fullness in the person of Jesus Christ, 'the power and the wisdom of God'.

---

[22] Dietrich Bonhoeffer, *Meditating on the Word* (Cowley Publications, 1986), cited in A. C. Thisleton, *Interpreting God and the Postmodern Self* (T. and T. Clark, 1995), 22.

Ezekiel 37:1–14
5. The Spirit of God

When Ezekiel the priest was thirty years old, the Spirit of the Lord came to him as he sat by the Kebar River in the land of the Babylonians. And what an incredible experience it was! As he said later, 'the heavens were opened and I saw visions of God' (Ezek. 1:1–3). Mysterious living creatures appeared to him and he saw strange wheels whirling about, angelic figures, the dead brought to life, and he was transported in his visions to Jerusalem and the temple.[1] All this came about because, in his words, 'the Spirit lifted me up between earth and heaven'. The Spirit of God raised him up to go where God wanted him to be, to see what God wanted him to see and to hear the message God had for him.[2] This young man experienced what many people search for: spectacular visions which were unmistakably from God, dramatic experiences which changed his life and new revelations which gave him insight into God's intentions for the world. But those who yearn to have the kind of spiritual experience which Ezekiel had would do well to consider the cost. There is no guarantee that the message will not be shocking and it may well come with a great responsibility which makes great demands on one's life. This was Ezekiel's lot, but he was ready to respond – although it took him seven days to recover from hearing the message (3:15). He became a spiritual watchman for the exiles, proclaiming the coming of the Lord. For all of us, as much as for Ezekiel, the best measure of one's true spirituality is not the intensity of ecstasy but the level of obedience to the Spirit of the Lord.

Ezekiel was born in 622 BC,[3] the year the lost Book of the Law was rediscovered, which immediately strengthened the religious

[1] Ezek. 1:4–28; 8:1–18; 10:1–22; 37.
[2] Ezek. 2:2; 3:12, 14, 24; 8:3; 10:15; 11:1, 5; 43:5.
[3] According to Ezek. 1:1 on the likely assumption that it was 'the thirtieth year' of his life.

reforms being undertaken by King Josiah (2 Kgs 22). At this time Judah was a vassal state of Assyria and had been so for a hundred years, but now Assryia was weakening, raising the possibility of greater independence. In 609 BC, when Ezekiel was thirteen years old, the Egyptian Pharaoh Neco sent an army northward to help Assyria against Babylon and the Judean army confronted them, only to be defeated and come under Egyptian control (2 Kgs 23:29–37), until Babylon, under Nebuchadnezzar, finally dominated the region and Judah became vassal to Babylon. But Babylon was no more preferable as master than Egypt or Assyria, so King Jehoiakim rebelled. The rebellion failed again, however, and he was killed. Jehoiachin succeeded him but soon had to surrender to Nebuchadnezzar, who plundered Jerusalem and deported ten thousand leading people to Babylon (2 Kgs 24:14), including the twenty-five-year-old priest, Ezekiel. And so it was that Ezekiel unhappily found himself 'among the exiles by the Kebar River' in Mesopotamia where, five years later, he spectacularly experienced God (Ezek. 1:1).

Ezekiel's experience of God did not involve just a single vision which came and went. It was something which dominated his life for years as God revealed to him a series of messages for the exiles, which he spoke and enacted among a community struggling to find meaning for their life. Ezekiel was sent to preach to them. This did not require 'going' in a geographic sense because it was his own people to whom he was to speak – something which can be harder than 'going' to another people. He was to speak to people whom God described as 'a rebellious nation', and Ezekiel's message was that they had not merely rebelled against Assyria, Egypt and Babylon but against God and they were spiritually 'obstinate and stubborn' (2:3–4).

Ezekiel's mission was to be 'a watchman' for Israel (33:1–20; 36:16–27). This was a very important role: a watchman had to watch for the coming of an enemy and give a clear warning if any came. In this way the life of the people depended upon the readiness of the watchman and the clarity of his message (3:17–19). Ezekiel's warning message was that it was Israel's wickedness that had led to her difficulties (5:7–10) and that God's judgment was inevitable. 'This is what the Sovereign LORD says to the land of Israel: The end! The end has come upon the four corners of the land' (7:2). His message included some of the harshest words of judgment one could imagine (chapters 16 and 23), and in persuading the people of the need to repent he had to confront the popular belief that Israel would be saved from surrounding enemies and that Jerusalem was inviolable. This, said Ezekiel, was not so. Jerusalem was doomed! 'An unheard-of disaster is coming,' he prophesied as he spoke of the end. He spoke of doom, panic, the sword, plague, famine, bloodshed and terror. And this was from God! 'Then they will know that I am the LORD' (7:1–27). Would you want to be the bearer of news such as this? We can only imagine Ezekiel's feelings about being a watchman with this kind of news, especially among those who were utterly convinced that Jerusalem, the city of God, was a place which could never be destroyed. Jerusalem was the city which David established as the capital and which became the economic and political heart of the nation. But even more than that, it was the centre of divine kingship and the home of the ark of the covenant, the footstool symbolizing the presence of God with his people. Jerusalem, home to the temple, dominated the spiritual life of Israel and was a symbol of the whole nation.[4]

Despite this confidence in Jerusalem, just a few years later Ezekiel's undoubtedly unpopular prophetic ministry was tragically vindicated. King Zedekiah led yet another rebellion against Babylon which, in 587 BC, brought absolute disaster. His army was defeated and Jerusalem besieged by the Babylonians. Eventually the city, including the temple, was completely destroyed and the largest part of the population was sent to join the earlier exiles in Mesopotamia (2 Kgs 25:1–30). The arrival of the terrible news – 'The city has fallen!' – is recorded in Ezekiel 33:21–33. If they had done so before, now no-one could consider Ezekiel to be a false prophet. Those who assumed that Jerusalem would never be taken because it was God's city were wrong. The destruction of Jerusalem was both punishment for sin and the end of the illusion that the city of Jerusalem was Israel's only hope. There is a warning here for anyone who thinks that God must act in a particular way, especially if it involves an assumption that he will overlook 'our' sin while dealing with 'their' iniquity: God's sovereignty is absolute and his ways are completely just.

While this tragedy led to great despair, however, there was yet more to be revealed. Just as the people were wrong if they assumed that God would not allow Jerusalem to be destroyed, so they were wrong if they assumed that this was the end of God's action. Although Ezekiel's message still contained stern warnings it also included new hope. He promised that the Lord would look after his people and rescue them, cleanse them from their sins, remove their 'heart of stone' and give them a new heart and a new spirit. Moreover, the Lord promised, 'And I will put my Spirit in you and move you to follow my decrees and be careful to keep my laws. You

[4] 2 Sam. 5:6–10; Pss. 78:68; 132:13–18; 1 Chr. 28:2; 2 Sam. 6:17; 2 Chr. 3:1–17; 1 Kgs 6:1–38.

will live in the land I gave your forefathers; you will be my people, and I will be your God' (36:24–27). Through the presence and the power of the Spirit of God a transformation would take place. If it was hard to believe that God would not protect Jerusalem from destruction, it was even harder to accept this. Nothing less than a complete resurrection of Israel was needed. And that was exactly the point of the vision of the valley of dry bones in Ezekiel 37.

1. Preaching to the dead

a. The situation: death and destruction

Because of events such as those which took place in Auschwitz, Kosovo and Cambodia we are now all too well able to imagine the horrific scene which confronted Ezekiel in his vision. Our feelings when we see film of piles of skulls and bones from some human tragedy are probably little different from what he felt when he found himself *in the middle of a valley*[5] which was really a mass grave: *it was full of bones*. The cheerfulness of the spiritual song which sings about 'dem bones, dem bones, dem dry bones' does not really do justice to the starkness and the despair which Ezekiel faced: there were *a great many bones*. The bones *were very dry*, indicating that they had been there for some time since whatever disaster one might imagine brought this about. They probably looked like the aftermath of some great battle fought with much loss of life, for when they were raised to their feet there was *a vast army*. That these bones were unburied was a tremendous insult and a great misfortune. In the Ancient Near East only the cursed should remain that way. In Hebrew culture it was a tragedy not to be buried properly.[6] Even today in Israel where bombings regularly occur there are certain groups of Jews who volunteer for the awful task of clearing up as they are determined that literally every fragment of flesh and every drop of blood, no matter how far it has been spread, will be carefully retrieved for burial. This valley of bones represented a very great tragedy – a vast number of people who were never buried and who had died tragically and, quite possibly, apart from God.

b. The meaning: judgment on Israel

Ezekiel faced this valley of death because *the hand of the LORD* was upon him and took him there. Like the arm and the finger, *the*

---

[5] The word refers to a flat plain with hills around.
[6] 1 Kgs 13:22; Jer. 16:6.

hand of the LORD indicates the presence and the power of God.[7]
The fact that God was involved and that this was not just a terrible
nightmare brought on by a disturbed mind is emphasized by the
words *he brought me out by the Spirit of the* LORD. The Spirit
'came upon' Ezekiel and 'raised him to his feet' and 'lifted him up'
so that he could now see and understand things from God's point
of view.[8] The bones among which Ezekiel walked represented the
covenant people of God, *the whole house of Israel.* As they were
saying themselves, *Our bones are dried up and our hope is gone; we
are cut off.* These were the people who said, 'Our offences and sins
weigh us down, and we are wasting away because of them. How
then can we live?' They inhabited 'the desolate ruins and the
deserted towns that have been plundered and ridiculed by the rest
of the nations' and the people were 'scattered through the
countries' because the Lord 'judged them according to their
conduct and their actions'.[9] The picture in Ezekiel's vision
confirms their worst fears: they are effectively dead and, apparently, without hope.

c. The question: can these bones live?

The Lord then asks Ezekiel, *'Son of man, can these bones live?' I
said, 'O Sovereign* LORD, *you alone know.'* One can only speculate
on Ezekiel's feelings at this point. Some think he lacked sufficient
faith to respond positively to God, who had previously brought life
back to the dead.[10] And yet it has to be admitted that in Hebrew
thought there was no certainty concerning life after death. Daniel
was probably the first to declare belief in a general resurrection.[11]
New life for those recently deceased is one thing, but these were the
bones of the long since dead. And would God want to bring life
back to those who could well have died a cursed death? Whatever
thoughts went through Ezekiel's mind, he took a cautious route and
referred the matter back to God.

d. The call: preach to the dead!

If Ezekiel thought that by referring the matter back to the Lord he
had escaped any difficulty, he was mistaken. The Lord's response
was to put the onus back on him by saying, *Prophesy to these bones*

[7] Ps. 89:13; Jer. 32:17; Num. 11:23; Gen. 49:24; Exod. 6:1; 8:19; 31:18.
[8] Ezek. 2:2; 3:12, 14, 24; 8:3; 11:1, 5, 24.
[9] Ezek. 33:10; 36:4–21.
[10] 1 Kgs 17:17–24; 2 Kgs 4:18–37; 13:20–21.
[11] Compare Ps. 30:9 with Dan. 12:2.

and say to them, 'Dry bones, hear the word of the LORD*!'* It is no small thing to be asked to preach to those who have been dead for years. Imagine going down to the local cemetery and preaching to the graves! It is absurd. It is one thing to preach to resistant people – those who do not want to hear – and quite another to preach to those who cannot hear.

e. The result: resurrection to life

Ezekiel was to preach concerning new life: *This is what the Sovereign* LORD *says to these bones: I will make breath enter you, and you will come to life. I will attach tendons to you and make flesh come upon you and cover you with skin; I will put breath in you, and you will come to life. Then you will know that I am the* LORD. The message was a reaffirmation of the sovereignty and Lordship of God, just as he had earlier declared, 'I put to death and I bring to life' (Deut. 32:39). The one who had created Israel would now bring life back to the nation. The restoration of life to bones was to be a symbol of new life for the people of God. New life came to the dead in two stages paralleling the original gift of life in Genesis 2:7–8 where God first of all formed humanity (*'ādām*) from the dust of the ground and then brought life to the body by breathing into him the breath of life. In Ezekiel's vision the bones first of all gained flesh, muscle and skin, but were without life until Ezekiel was commanded to prophesy again, this time to enliven the bodies: *Come from the four winds, O breath, and breathe into these slain, that they may live ... and breath entered them; they came to life and stood up on their feet – a vast army.* Nothing is beyond the bounds of possibility for Yahweh. He is the Lord of life and death and by his Spirit can even revive the dead.

2. The Spirit of the Lord

Obviously the Spirit of the LORD is central to the account of Ezekiel's vision. It is the Spirit that comes upon Ezekiel and takes him to the valley of death, it is the Spirit that brings life to the bones and at the conclusion of the vision God's people are promised, *I will put my Spirit in you and you will live.* Before proceeding to examine further the implications of the revivification of the bones it will be helpful to consider the essential characteristics of the Spirit and the implications for the Christian doctrine of the Trinity. The vision demonstrates the following four characteristics of the Spirit.

a. The powerful Spirit

The Hebrew word for Spirit (*rûaḥ*) has a number of related meanings. It can refer to 'breath' or 'wind', as it does in *Come from the four winds, O breath, and breathe into these slain* (vv. 9–10), and then, by an extension of thought, because a person's breath can represent their life it can also be used to refer to the life or the spirit of a person.[12] When it does so, 'spirit' naturally takes on more personal associations, sometimes representing the whole person and at other times some aspect of their personality, as when it is used to refer to 'a spirit of stubbornness' or wisdom, lying or truthfulness.[13] Then, importantly for this passage, the same word is used for the Spirit of God. Just as the human spirit represents the human person, so the Spirit of God represents God. In doing so the Spirit's primary attribute is that of immense power. In common usage today 'spirit' has the sense of something which is immaterial, but in Hebrew thought it had a lot more to do with power and energy. If used of the movement of air *rûaḥ* could be a gentle breath or wind, but it was more likely to be a powerful wind, and when used of the Spirit of the LORD it was typically powerful and overwhelming. The Spirit could bring physical strength to fight a lion, military acumen and leadership to defeat the enemy or spiritual and moral strength to overcome evil.[14] In Ezekiel 37 the Spirit is able to take Ezekiel's mind to the terrible valley of bones and then it is the Spirit that has the power to bring life back to the dead. Finally it is the Spirit that will come upon all the people of Israel and enable them to live again and to know that it is God who has done this great thing. The point to be made is that the Spirit of God is powerful. The Spirit can not only win great battles but even bring life to the dead.

b. The prophetic Spirit

The Spirit of God is identified with God in such a way that the one overtaken by the Spirit is able to speak for God. The word of the Lord and the presence of the Spirit are closely associated in the Old Testament, especially with leaders such as kings and prophets. The Spirit was present with Ezekiel not only to take him to the valley but also to enable him to proclaim the astonishing message from God, *Dry bones, hear the word of the LORD!* Under the guidance of the Spirit Ezekiel preached a message which was, from a human perspective, not only impossible but also ridiculous. Yet through

---

[12] This connection is made in the account of creation in Gen. 2:7.
[13] Deut. 2:30; 34:9; 1 Kgs 22:22; Ps. 33:2.
[14] Judg. 3:10; 11:29; 14:6; Mic. 3:8; Zech. 4:6.

this apparently foolish preaching *there was a noise, a rattling sound, and the bones came together.* The lesson Ezekiel was to learn here was to be obedient to the leading of the Spirit of God. A willingness to listen to the Spirit is critically important for all believers and sometimes those who rely most heavily on what appears to be rational can find this hard to do. Rationality is a wonderful thing until it gets in the way and makes listening to the Spirit difficult. Faith involves one's intelligence, but it is not primarily a matter of the mind. It is more about the ability to trust in God's ways and God's wisdom.

c. The personal Spirit

The Spirit of God is 'personal' in the sense that the Spirit represents God as an extension of his life and activity. The psalmist asks the rhetorical questions, 'Where can I go from your Spirit? Where can I flee from your presence?'[15] in which the Spirit is obviously synonymous with the presence of God. And in Ezekiel's vision the Spirit's leading is the leading of the LORD. The intimacy of the relationship between God and the Spirit of God raises the question of whether there are any implications for the Christian doctrine of the Trinity. Do passages such as Ezekiel's vision, where the Spirit of God represents the presence of God, imply some form of divine plurality?

The term 'the Spirit of the Lord' implies that God *has* a Spirit in some sense. But this is not a 'possession' in the way one might speak of 'the car of Brian', that is, in the way that I possess a motor car which is a distinct and separable entity. The Spirit of the Lord is much more closely related to God than that. One comes closer to the sense of the term by paralleling it with a phrase such as 'the mind of Brian', in the sense that Brian possesses a mind not as something separate from himself but as an essential part of him. The Spirit is as close to God as one's mind is to oneself. But this analogy is by no means perfect. One of the complicating factors is that our modern way of viewing the person is different from the Hebrews' approach. Our perception of a person is more sharply defined and individual-istic. We tend to distinguish clearly between that which is internal to a person (his or her mind, will, emotions and so forth) and those things which are external to (or at least different from) the person (the attitudes of others, the life of the community, the prompting of God's Spirit and the influence of other spirits). In the Old Testa-ment there is a more corporate view of life in which the lives of

[15] Ps. 139:7; also see 51:11.

others (individuals, the community and various spirits) are more interactive with the life of the individual and less distinguishable. For example, Elisha can ask for a double portion of Elijah's spirit, an evil spirit creates depression in Saul and a lying spirit causes one to tell lies. The essential life of the person was, however, identified with his or her spirit,[16] and in a similar manner 'the Spirit of the Lord' represents God's essential being. It is a personification of God – that is, the Spirit of the Lord has personal attributes and is treated in every way as though a person but without any suggestion that the Spirit actually exists as a separable or distinct person or entity.

Understanding the Spirit in this way means avoiding two opposite errors. The first is that of assuming that more is intended by this description of the Spirit than simply a personification (in which the Spirit is treated *as if* the Spirit was a distinct person). Although it has been a minority opinion, both Jewish and Christian sources have suggested that the Spirit is intended to be taken as a separate entity with a different centre of thought and activity, related to but distinct from Yahweh. The Spirit would thus not be a personification but a separate (albeit related) person or hypostasis.[17] The problem with this is that it takes too literally the language of personhood as applied to the Spirit. The various personal descriptions of the Spirit as coming and going, speaking and acting and so forth are meant to represent the dynamic activity of Yahweh, especially those times when he acts in people's lives and transforms situations. The Spirit is God in action in much the same way as we might say when commending a person for helping someone, 'The counsellor in them really came out and they were able to help a lot.' There is no suggestion here that there actually was a separate person who was a counsellor, it is simply a way of describing those personal characteristics which were to the fore at that time. With regard to the Spirit it is important to note that the words and actions of the Spirit are 'one

[16] 2 Kgs 2:9; 1 Sam. 16:14; 1 Kgs 22:22; Ps. 31:5.

[17] Unfortunately in the relevant literature 'hypostatization' (which in English is a transliteration of the Greek *hypostasis*) is used with different meanings which often depend upon whether the context is Old Testament study, New Testament study or the theological debates of the third to sixth centuries AD. Some commentators on the Old Testament use 'hypostasis' (in its English sense) as a synonym for 'personification' while others, perhaps more accurately, distinguish personification from hypostatization. In New Testament studies *hypostasis* is used in very different ways to reflect its use in 2 Cor. 9:4; 11:17; Heb. 1:3; 3:14; 11:1, where it has non-technical meaning. In the theological debates of later centuries concerning the doctrine of the Trinity *hypostasis* was initially used almost synonymously with *ousia*, referring to the one substance or the essence of God, while later it came to be used as equivalent to the Latin *persona*, referring to the threeness of God. In the present discussion hypostatization is used to refer to the process beyond personification whereby the entity concerned should be considered as a distinct centre of activity.

way', that is, always from God to people through the Spirit, and the Spirit is not presented as responding to Yahweh or acting other than as Yahweh's voice or agent. The Spirit is the power of God acting through his people, not a separate entity.

On the other hand, while avoiding hypostatization it is also necessary to avoid the opposite error of viewing personification as nothing other than an anthropomorphic literary device with no significance for understanding the person of God. The Old Testament presentations of God as Spirit, Wisdom and Word play an important preparatory role in the overall development of the doctrine of the Trinity. The personification of the Spirit is not simply the same kind of literary device as found elsewhere, such as when mountains are described as jumping and trees as clapping their hands. These are anthropomorphisms, in which a non-personal entity is described in human terms for literary effect in order to make some point or other. The personification of the Spirit is different. Not only is it far more extensive, but it is intriguing in the way the personal characteristics attributed to the Spirit are so intimately connected with the personality of Yahweh. If the Spirit comes upon someone that person is filled with power from God, if the Spirit speaks it is the word of the Lord, if the Spirit is grieved it is because Yahweh is grieved, if the Spirit guides it is in the way of the Lord, and if the Spirit gives life it is life from God.[18] Whereas mountains and trees are personified in the sense that they take on a life of their own, that is, a life which would not have existed without the personification, the Spirit is specifically personified to take on the life of Yahweh – to the point where it is difficult to distinguish between them and one is equivalent to the other. There is no difference in will, thought, attitude or action. The personification of the Spirit creates an *alter ego* for God, but the full significance of this is not realized until the coming of Christ, who comes and lives in the power of the Spirit, breathes the Spirit on his disciples and promises that the Spirit, 'another' like him, will come in fullness after his own departure (John 14:16). The full significance for the doctrine of the Trinity of Ezekiel's personification of the Spirit can therefore only be fully understood in the light of the promise that one day the Spirit would be poured out on all people.

d. The promised Spirit

The personified Spirit of the Old Testament is the promised Spirit of the New. The theological implications are not spelled out in detail

[18] 1 Sam. 19:23; Isa. 63:16; Ps. 143:10; Neh. 9:20; Ezek. 2:2; 3:10; 11:4; 36:27; 37:14.

until later but God promised through Ezekiel and the prophets that what Moses longed for was to come about.[19] The promise of the Spirit's coming in fullness meant not only that the Spirit would come on more people but also that there would be a new and greater revelation of the nature of the Spirit. This is because it is in Christ that the Spirit is known. As Jesus said to his disciples, 'But when he, the Spirit of truth, comes, he will guide you into all the truth. He will not speak on his own; he will speak only what he hears, and he will tell you what is yet to come. He will glorify me because it is from me that he will receive what he will make known to you. All that belongs to the Father is mine. That is why I said the Spirit will receive from me what he will make known to you' (John 16:13–15). The significance of Ezekiel's experience of the Spirit has to be seen in connection with this later fulfilment, so that the work of the Spirit in breathing life into the dead in Ezekiel's vision is to be understood not only as a description of the new life which was to come to the nation of Israel, but also as an anticipation of what the Spirit was to do in the last days when the resurrected Lord Jesus, himself filled with new life, in an echo of Ezekiel's vision, breathed on his disciples and said, 'Receive the Holy Spirit.' This was in anticipation of both the outpouring of the Spirit at Pentecost and their own resurrection by the power of the Spirit and was the fulfilment of God's promise through Ezekiel, 'I will no longer hide my face from them, for I will pour out my Spirit on the house of Israel' (39:29). Another connection is made in John's revelation of the end when the army of those that the antichrist had killed is raised by the breath of God in the same way that the bones in Ezekiel's vision were brought to life.[20] In other words the New Testament is able to expand the teaching concerning the Spirit and when it does, it does so in a trinitarian direction.

The New Testament view of the Spirit is grounded in the Old, but it is not simply the same. The Spirit of Christ is no longer a personification but a person in his own right. Personhood is seen in the life, activity and character of the Spirit who knows the deepest thoughts of God, lives in the lives of believers, gives life, guides, desires and grieves.[21] These are descriptions of the life of a person, of God as Spirit. The New Testament also demonstrates how the Spirit brings new life to all. As Paul said, 'If the Spirit of him who raised Jesus from the dead is living in you, he who raised Christ from the dead will also give life to your mortal bodies because of his Spirit who

[19] Isa. 11:2; 32:15; 42:1; 61:1; Joel 2:28–29; Num. 11:29.
[20] Compare Ezek. 37:10; 2:9 – 3:3 and 40:3–4 with, respectively, Rev. 11:11–12; 10:8–11; 11:1–2.
[21] 1 Cor. 2:10; 3:16; 2 Cor. 3:6; Gal. 5:17–18; Eph. 4:30.

lives in you' (Rom. 8:11). The overall point of this is that the Spirit of God as known in the Old Testament is a personification of God which goes beyond being a mere literary phenomenon but which is, at that point, unresolved as to its true significance. The personal characteristics and divine activity of the Spirit are, however, subsequently shown in the New Testament to be a preparation for a fuller revelation of the nature of God, who lives as Father, Son and Spirit.

3. Resurrection through the Spirit

Having described the situation Israel faced and the vision Ezekiel received, and having examined the nature of the Spirit of the LORD, it is now necessary to turn to the implications of Ezekiel's vision for today. At its most fundamental level the message is that the Spirit of God has the power to bring new life to the dead. But to what does this refer? Does it constitute biblical evidence for personal life beyond death and, even more specifically, for a physical or bodily resurrection? Or is the revivification of the dry bones simply a metaphor promising that the nation of Israel as a corporate body will be revived?

a. New life for the covenant community

The primary interpretation of this miracle of new life is not left to chance. It is given to Ezekiel. The dry bones in the valley represented people who were spiritually dead and they are symbolic of *the whole house of Israel*. The people of Israel were the chosen ones, but they were disobedient and so were judged 'according to their conduct and their actions'. Consequently, God allowed them to fall into the hands of their enemies and they were 'ravaged and hounded from every side'. They became 'the object of people's malicious talk and slander' and were 'plundered and ridiculed' (36:19; 36:3). Their sin meant divine displeasure and exile from their own country. Israel in exile was spiritually and physically dead. Consequently, if the dry bones represent Israel in captivity then the revived bodies represent a renewed life for the covenant community and an end to their time of desolation. 'The towns will be inhabited and the ruins rebuilt. I will increase the number of men and animals upon you, and they will be fruitful and become numerous. I will settle people on you as in the past and will make you prosper more than before. Then you will know that I am the LORD' (36:10–11). The vision was a promise that the exile was not going to last for ever, that the nation would not disappear (as other nations have from time to time) and that there would be a renewed life for Israel.

Although Israel had spiritually departed from the Lord he would act to restore them. As Leslie Allen said, 'The vision exposes an organic relation between the two prophetic events, the wreaking of judgment and the bestowing of salvation. Salvation was to rise phoenix-like from the embers of judgment.'[22] It was God's intention to make Israel live again. Was this because they deserved it? No, the motive lay in God's commitment to love and redeem the world. In short, the primary meaning of the passage relates to God's intention to revive the corporate life of his chosen people and in so doing to preserve his promise to bring salvation to the world.

A secondary implication of the revivification of the dry bones, however, is that it serves as a powerful reminder of the fact that it is the same God who is Lord of the church today. The people of this new covenant community also fall into sin and sometimes the community life of the church is far less than perfect. There is evidence of this in various biblical descriptions of the life of the church. The Revelation of John speaks of churches where people have fallen away from their love of Christ, have allowed false teaching and have engaged in immorality (Rev. 2:4, 14, 23). No doubt one can also look to one's own church for further evidence of sin. There are always those who are, as the writer of the book of Hebrews says, 'ignorant and ... going astray' (Heb. 5:2). The church today is no more exempt from God's judgment than the nation of Israel in the time of Ezekiel. But neither is the church today any more separated from God's mercy, or from the possibility of forgiveness and the reviving power of the Holy Spirit. The church must always be alert to the possibility of spiritual stagnation and decay but must never be fooled into thinking that life and vitality cannot be restored. Those who fall away need to be brought back to repentance through the reviving power of the Spirit rather than cast aside as unworthy or unredeemable (Heb. 6:6; 3:7). Even those parts of the church which are morally or theologically in serious error can be restored. There is a tendency for Christians to assume that various people and churches are spiritually irretrievable long before the Spirit does. Thankfully, God specializes in bringing people and situations back from the dead.

b. New life for the individual

Although the primary meaning of the revivification of the dry bones is that God intends to restore the life of the nation of Israel, many people have wondered whether Ezekiel's vision of bones being

[22] Allen, *Ezekiel*, 188.

brought back to life constitutes biblical evidence for either Jewish or Christian belief in the resurrection of the body. Christian belief, of course, is primarily based upon the New Testament testimony to the resurrection of Christ and the general resurrection of believers, and any testimony from Ezekiel, Daniel or other Old Testament books is secondary. It has, however, appeared to many to be an anticipation of the Christian doctrine of resurrection. As regards the belief of Hebrew religion concerning the possibility of life after death the matter is less straightforward. What can be said with greater certainty about Hebrew religion and the afterlife is that Old Testament faith involved complete trust in Yahweh as the source of life, as the God of the living and as the eternal God whose power extended beyond human death. The faith of the covenant community meant trusting Yahweh in all circumstances and believing that, irrespective of the fate that befell human beings, God's life, his laws and his kingdom would endure for ever.[23] But there is relatively little about personal life after death. There are a few 'resurrections' where a deceased person returns to earthly life,[24] and Israel's leaders and kings are sometimes described as joining their ancestors in the afterlife,[25] while God 'took' Enoch and Elijah ascended to heaven in a chariot of fire and a whirlwind.[26] But these were not the standard experience of the righteous. The afterlife in the Old Testament is Sheol (or 'the grave', 'the pit' or 'destruction'), a shadowy form of existence in the depths of the earth.[27] Although there are references to Sheol being the place of all those who die it is not normally seen positively. It is a fate generally seen as more appropriate for the wicked than for the righteous.[28] A few passages do envisage some more general form of positive existence with God beyond death,[29] but the first, and possibly only, reference to resurrection is found in the promise of Daniel 12:2–3: 'Multitudes who sleep in the dust of the earth will awake: some to everlasting life, others to shame and everlasting contempt. Those who are wise will shine like the brightness of the heavens, and those who lead many to righteousness, like the stars for ever and ever.' However, this very positive affirmation of life beyond death did not serve to overcome completely either the frequent negative connotations or the uncertainty associated with dying in other passages such as Psalm 6:5,

[23] Gen. 21:33; Deut. 33:27; Ps. 119:89; Isa. 26:4.
[24] 1 Kgs 17:17–24; 2 Kgs 4:18–37; 13:20–21.
[25] Gen. 15:15; 47:30; Deut. 31:16; 2 Sam. 7:12.
[26] Gen. 5:24; 2 Kgs 2:11.
[27] E.g. Gen. 37:35; 42:38; Num. 16:30; Deut. 32:22; Pss. 6:5; 9:17; 89:48; Isa. 14:9–11.
[28] Pss. 49:14–15; 89:48; Eccl. 9:10.
[29] Pss. 16:10; 49:15; 73:24.

'No-one remembers you when he is dead. Who praises you from his grave?'[30] Consequently, in the first century AD there existed disagreement among the Jews about the afterlife. The Sadducees believed that the soul died at death and thus denied any form of afterlife, but there were others, such as the Pharisees and the Essenes, who believed in it.[31]

In this kind of context early Jewish scholars were divided on the significance of Ezekiel's vision. Some saw it as the revelation of a literal event and others saw it simply as a vision given to Ezekiel alone.[32] Because of their firm commitment to belief in the resurrection of all believers the early church was more disposed to see the vision as proof of the resurrection, but given the interpretation found within the passage[33] the basic meaning has to be taken to relate to the restoration of Israel rather than the resurrection of the body. The only safe interpretation leaves the matter there and treats the vision as a kind of parable which does not require a literal resurrection of the body, any more than Jesus' parable of the talents requires an actual king and particular servants who invested or buried the money they were given (Matt. 25:14–30). Nonetheless, the use of the resurrection of dry bones as a metaphor demonstrating that new life for Israel was possible would not be very effective unless the parallel was actually accepted as a genuine possibility itself. It would be counterproductive to make a comparison with something that could not happen. The vision is not a proof of the resurrection of the body, not least because it appears to involve a 'revivification' which returns the deceased to bodily life in this world, but there is perhaps a secondary message in it which affirms that God can indeed do anything, even that which is, humanly speaking, impossible. It is a message which is consistent with Yahweh who says, 'There is no god besides me. I put to death and I bring to life' (Deut. 32:39), and it finds its ultimate fulfilment in the Spirit's resurrection of Jesus Christ and, through that, the resurrection of all believers: 'And if the Spirit of him who raised Jesus from the dead is living in you, he who raised Christ from the dead

[30] Or Eccl. 3:19–22: 'Man's fate is like that of the animals; the same fate awaits them both: As one dies, so dies the other ... All go to the same place; all come from dust, and to dust all return. Who knows if the spirit of man rises upward and if the spirit of the animal goes down into the earth?'
[31] See the work of the Jewish historian Josephus in *Jewish Antiquities Books XVIII – XIX*, ed. G. P. Goold (Harvard University Press, 1965), VIII, 13–16; cf. Matt. 22:23–33. The issue of the afterlife does not appear to have been central, however, as people were able to change between parties.
[32] See Greenberg, *Ezekiel*, 749–751.
[33] Ezek. 37:11: 'these bones are the whole house of Israel'.

will also give life to your mortal bodies because of his Spirit who lives in you' (Rom. 8:11).

The apostle Paul described the spiritual state of those without Christ in terms as graphic as Ezekiel's vision of dead and decaying bones.

> You were dead in your transgressions and sins, in which you used to live when you followed the ways of this world and of the ruler of the kingdom of the air, the spirit who is now at work in those who are disobedient. All of us also lived among them at one time, gratifying the cravings of our sinful nature and following its desires and thoughts. Like the rest, we were by nature deserving of wrath.
>
> (Eph. 2:1–4)

Preaching new life for the dead is no easy message, yet it is at the heart of the Christian gospel. It is inevitable that preaching Christ crucified and Christ risen from the dead, and death to sin and resurrection to new life for believers will be misunderstood or thought impossible or foolish. When Paul preached about Jesus and resurrection in Athens some thought that he was preaching about two new gods – Jesus and Anastasia – because 'resurrection' (*anastasis*) was also a woman's name (Acts 17:18). And in the second letter to the Corinthians he emphasized the difficulty of preaching the Christian gospel yet affirmed that 'God was pleased through the foolishness of what was preached to save those who believe ... For the foolishness of God is wiser than human wisdom, and the weakness of God is stronger than human strength' (1 Cor. 1:21–25). But through obedience, and by preaching the word of the Lord, both Ezekiel and Paul discovered that God can bring new life. As Ezekiel watched, *the bones came together* and *flesh appeared*, then *breath entered them* and *they came to life*. New life came from the Spirit. And Paul was able to say that 'God, who is rich in mercy, made us alive with Christ ... God raised us up with Christ and seated us with him in the heavenly realms' (Eph. 2:4, 6). Can the spiritually dead live? Yes. As Paul said, 'When you were dead in your sins and in the uncircumcision of your sinful nature, God made you alive with Christ' (Col. 2:13). Should we reckon any to be 'too dead' to be raised? No. There is no person, group or nation beyond hope.

Part 3
The Trinity in the experience and teaching of Jesus

Luke 1:26–56
6. Incarnation: divine coming

The birth of Jesus was surrounded by miracles. From the time of the announcement of Elizabeth's pregnancy with Jesus' cousin, John the Baptist, through to the escape of the holy family into Egypt there were four angelic appearances, a number of special revelations, portents in the sky, inspired prophecies, several dreams with warning messages and other physical miracles including the conception of Jesus.[1] They witness to the fact that this was no ordinary birth. They point to the greatest miracle of them all – an incarnation: God coming in human form.

1. Gabriel the angelic messenger

The story of Jesus begins with the statement that *God sent the angel Gabriel* to the virgin Mary, who was engaged to a man named Joseph, a descendant of David. This angelic appearance is indicative of God's direct involvement in the birth of Jesus, but modern Western culture, dominated by a rational and scientific approach to life, has often viewed accounts of angels – especially those announcing miraculous conceptions – with scepticism. The effects remain with us today. In some mainline churches up to a third of clergy deny that any miracle was involved in the conception of Christ. This has an effect on faith. One newspaper writer observed that his theological reading had persuaded him that the birth story was a literary creation and that he needed to take a more 'mature' and less supernaturally orientated view. But while 'all this made me appreciate the literary skill of the evangelists, it was hard to see the Christmas story emptied out by modern biblical scholarship'.[2]

---

[1] Respectively, Luke 1:11, 26; 2:9; Matt. 2:12; Luke 1:41; 2:26, 38; Matt. 2:2; Luke 1:67; Matt. 2:13; Luke 1:20.
[2] Michael B. Kelly, *The Melbourne Age* (21 December 2002), Insight, 2.

When Billy Graham wrote his book on angels in 1975 it became a bestseller precisely because very little had been said or written about angels for decades. Its popularity indicated that there was an increasing sense that God acts in ways beyond human comprehension.[3] The situation changed even more rapidly in the latter part of the century as New Age spiritualities became popular, and eventually an article in *Time* magazine was able to place Western culture firmly on the side of the angels: 'If there is such a thing as a universal idea, common across cultures and through the centuries, the belief in angels comes close to it.'[4] Today angels and their messages are discussed in magazines and books, courses are offered to help people identify and communicate with angel-guides, and shops and fairs sell all sorts of paraphernalia related to angels. All in all, the present situation is complex: while popular culture has rediscovered angels and miracles with some enthusiasm, parts of the church continue to be sceptical.

a. Messenger of God's holiness

We have little information about what angels look like,[5] but their majestic and holy manner stands in marked contrast to that of the diminished angels of contemporary, commercialized New Age spirituality which are always kindly, non-judgmental, non-threatening entities who specialize in comforting messages of personal support. But an appearance by Gabriel or the other biblical angels inevitably causes great consternation. In this case *Mary was greatly troubled at his words*. Given that the most common initial reaction to an angelic appearance was fear, it is unlikely that the angels were 'angelic' in the sweet and saccharine manner in which the word is commonly used today. Meeting with God's messenger means meeting with a God who is awesome and holy. Holiness is always something to be feared, for God's holiness cannot stand sin. Yet God is also good and gracious. This tension is well expressed in C. S. Lewis's classic *The Lion, the Witch and the Wardrobe* when Lucy, Edmund, Susan and Peter are preparing to meet Christ, represented by the lion Aslan. Mr Beaver emphasizes Aslan's power and strength and the fear of those who enter his presence. ' "Then he isn't safe?" said Lucy. "Safe?' said Mr Beaver; "who said anything about safe? 'Course he isn't safe. But he's good." '[6]

---

[3] Billy Graham, *Angels: God's Secret Agents* (Hodder and Stoughton, 1975).
[4] Nancy Gibbs, 'Angels Among Us', *Time* magazine (27 December 1993), 58.
[5] Angels are, at times, described as being dressed in white, see Matt. 28:3; Rev. 15:6.
[6] C. S. Lewis, *The Lion, the Witch and the Wardrobe* (Penguin, 1959), 75.

b. Messenger of God's grace

God's intention is not to consume or destroy but to reveal and redeem, and so Gabriel says, *Do not be afraid.*[7] Like the other angels he comes with 'good news', revealing the purposes of God for the salvation of the world.[8] Gabriel announces that Mary *will conceive and give birth to a son.* It was perhaps inevitable that she would query this for, humanly speaking, it was impossible. She is described as *parthenos*, which refers to a young, unmarried girl and has strong connotations of virginity. This fits with the fact that she was engaged to Joseph. Betrothal could happen as early as twelve years of age, usually lasted a year, and while it was regarded as equally binding as marriage it was not normal for intercourse to take place during that time. Neither Mary nor Joseph had any claim to significance in human terms. Joseph was a descendant of Abraham, through King David, but this is noted in order to indicate that Jesus was the 'son of David' through Joseph his legal father,[9] rather than to claim any social significance in Jesus' immediate family. Marshall comments that Luke even has to note that their home town is in Galilee 'for the benefit of non-Palestinian readers who would probably never have heard of so insignificant a village as Nazareth'.[10] *The Most High* did not come with this announcement to a king and queen, or to anyone famous, wealthy or religiously prominent, but to an unknown girl barely into her teenage years who lived in an obscure town. This girl – not really yet a woman – is *highly favoured* by God. This, says Marshall, 'signifies the free gracious choice of God who favours particular men and women; the stress is on God's choice rather than human acceptability'.[11] God's choosing is reflected in the literal meaning of her name, 'exalted one', and is an example of the principle that 'he chose the lowly things of this world' to accomplish his purposes (1 Cor. 1:28). How often do we miss seeing divine action and godly wisdom simply because we overlook those who, humanly speaking, are the most unlikely of people to be bearers of divine grace? Children, teenagers, the obscure and unnoticed, the lowly, the uneducated and the poor are all loved, honoured and used by God.

[7] He does so to each of the recipients of divine visitations, Zechariah, Mary and the shepherds (Luke 1:12–13; 1:29; 2:9).
[8] Luke 2:10. 'Angel' translates *angelos* which literally means 'messenger', and this is related to *euangelion* which is translated as 'gospel' and literally means 'good news'.
[9] Matt. 1:1–16; Luke 3:23. It was normal to trace descent patrilineally.
[10] Luke 1:26; 2:4, 39; 4:31. Marshall, *Luke*, 64.
[11] Ibid., 66.

2. Mary the chosen mother

What was to make this conception unusual was the fact of direct, divine intervention: *the Holy Spirit will come upon you ... you will conceive and give birth to a son*. Here was God asking a young girl to bear his child! Asking for someone's womb is asking a great deal. But God knows who to ask.

a. Mary's faithfulness

Mary's gloriously faithful response is, *I am the Lord's servant ... May it be to me according to your word*. These are not words of resignation or obligation, they are words filled with deep faith, love and hope. They are perhaps the most profound words that can ever be said to God. In every situation the believer should offer his or her life and circumstances to God. Mary gave to God the most precious thing in her – her virgin womb, the deepest place where life is born, and through this came salvation for all.[12] In this relationship of call and obedience we have the gospel in a nutshell: God's grace works through faith (Eph. 2:8).

Mary's willing response was not undertaken unknowingly, foolishly or irresponsibly, for despite her youth she knew the one to whom she was committing herself. She clearly had a maturity of faith which is unusual but not unique for someone so young. Elizabeth Fry, the chief promoter of prison reform in Europe, also demonstrated an exceptional faith while young. It is said that 'as a girl she showed the benevolence of disposition, clearness and independence of judgment and strength of purpose for which she was afterwards distinguished'.[13] She achieved much for those in prison: the separation of the sexes, the classification of prisoners, female supervision for women, education and religious instruction. She said, 'Since my heart was touched at seventeen years old, I believe I have never awakened from sleep, in sickness or in health, by day or by night, without my first waking thought being, "how best might I serve my Lord?" '[14]

b. Mary's humility

When Mary says, *I am the Lord's servant* (v. 38) and then sings of *the humble state of his servant* (v. 48) she is not demeaning herself in any

[12] Valdir Steuernagal, 'Doing theology with an eye on Mary' (paper presented at the 2002 conference of the Federation of European Evangelical Theologians), 4.

[13] *Encyclopaedia Britannica*, Vol. 9 (William Benton, 1969), p. 974. Fry lived from 1780 to 1845.

[14] *Christian Quotations*, H. Ward (ed.), *The Lion Christian Quotation Collection* (Lion Publishing, 2002), Elizabeth Fry, 172.

way. In fact she is in the company of others who were known specifically as 'servants of God', including Abraham, Moses and David.[15] Humility means recognizing the lowliness of one's position before God. The focus should be on the presence and greatness of God rather than on one's own inadequacies. It is not something achieved in a moment or a month – any more than patience can be learnt quickly. It is an act of grace and the work of a lifetime. A cartoon in *Punch* magazine shows two monks walking the cloisters as one says, 'There's not a lot you can teach me about humility.' But humility is not a matter of formal learning. It is fruit that grows in our lives through the working of the Holy Spirit. The closer we come to God the more a natural humility emerges. It does not mean being perpetually fearful of God, disdainful of oneself or incapable of being a recipient of the grace of God. That would be to declare not only that God has created someone who is worthless but also that God is incapable of loving the lowly and unwilling to stoop and save.

Mary's humility and obedience have often been portrayed in paintings and sculpture. The most famous of these is Michelangelo's *Pieta*.[16] She is shown cradling the crucified Christ who has been taken down from the cross. But the Mary which Michelangelo sculpted was the young Mary, the teenage girl who bore a baby, rather than the woman of forty-five or fifty who would have cradled her crucified son in her arms. Moreover, if one imagines that Christ is not there, one sees Mary's cradling arms now held out in prayer, offering and commitment – just as one might imagine the young girl did some thirty or more years previously when she had said, *I am the Lord's servant ... May it be to me according to your word*. What is Michelangelo saying here? It is a potent reminder of the fact that young faith can lead to times of suffering and sadness. The joyous birth of Christ led to a horrific death. And yet Michelangelo does not allow the observer to despair; he accurately reflects in the face of Mary the biblical picture of one who has a firm and confident trust that God is in control.

3. Jesus the only Son

Gabriel accounts for Mary's pregnancy by announcing that *the Holy Spirit will come upon you*. The significance of Jesus' birth being by the Holy Spirit and without a human father can be examined both from a historical or physical perspective and from a theological or spiritual point of view.

[15] Ps. 105:42; Neh. 9:14; Ps. 89:3.
[16] It is on display in St Peter's Basilica in Rome.

a. Jesus' conception as a physical fact

Despite the obvious intention of the biblical text to describe this as a miraculous event, a modern, rational, scientific emphasis meant that it was 'obvious' to some that the so-called 'virgin birth' (actually a virginal conception) was not real history but rather a literary construction of the early church.[17] However, before eliminating the miraculous dimension it is necessary to consider the following points.

(1) Clearly the scripture intends the reader to understand the story as *historical* with the Holy Spirit as a direct, though spiritual, substitute for a human father, standing in contrast to the birth of Jesus' brothers born to Mary and Joseph (2:7; 8:19). Luke's account records Mary's declaration, *I am a virgin*, while Matthew describes it from Joseph's point of view as he knew there had been no sexual intercourse and had to be told by the Lord in a dream that 'what is conceived in her is from the Holy Spirit'. The nature of the material gives no clues that it is mythical; it has implied support in other parts of the New Testament and became a part of the Apostles' creed, one of the earliest and most foundational creeds of the church.[18]

(2) It is unlikely to be an *invented* story, as this would require the belief that it was first created many years after the event as a post-resurrection mythical explanation of the identity of Jesus which was applied retrospectively to the account of his birth. N. T. Wright exposes the improbability of this, arguing that it is difficult to see how a story deliberately invented as a way of making a theological statement could almost immediately be confused and pass, completely unchallenged, as an historical event.[19]

(3) It is unlikely to be a *borrowed* story, as some claim, modified from pagan religious stories of gods impregnating women. Marshall comments that the details are 'framed in so characteristically Jewish manner that the pagan parallels are extremely remote'.[20] Moreover,

[17] A. Richardson, *Introduction to the Theology of the New Testament* (SCM, 1958), 174; Küng, *On Being a Christian*, 451. In the 'modern' era it first came into dispute in 1892 when a German pastor named Schrempf refused to use the Apostles' creed because it affirmed this article (Donald Macleod, *The Person of Christ* [IVP, 1998], 27). Even some who strongly defend other miraculous events argue that this story is legendary and problematic; see Pannenberg, *Jesus – God and Man*, 143.

[18] Rom. 1:2–4; Gal. 4:4. The Apostles' creed affirms that Jesus was 'conceived by the Holy Spirit and born of the virgin Mary'. Although the creed did not achieve its final form until the sixth century it is derived from an early Roman creed of the second century.

[19] Wright, 'Born of a Virgin', 175–178.

[20] Marshall, *Luke*, 75.

what we have in Matthew and Luke is not the story of 'a divine being descending to earth, and in the guise of a man mating with a human woman, but rather the story of a miraculous conception without the aid of any man, divine or otherwise. As such, the story is without precedent in Jewish or pagan literature.'[21]

(4) Perhaps the most telling argument for the physical reality of this event is its *theological significance*. As Donald Macleod says, 'It stands on the threshold of the New Testament, blatantly super-natural, defying our rationalism, informing us that all that follows belongs to the same order as itself and that if we find it offensive there is no point in proceeding further.'[22] This miracle eliminates any possibility of understanding or grasping the nature of God in Christ in a purely intellectual fashion. It leaves only a spiritual understanding in which God's purposes are understood in God's own way.

b. Jesus' conception as a spiritual experience

The miraculous conception has its significance as a part of the whole question of the identity of Jesus Christ. R. E. Brown comments that the virginal conception is 'part of a Lukan scene which would make little christological sense without it'.[23] The significance of Christ's conception and birth is found in the following points.

(1) *The identity of Jesus*: although Jesus was fully human there is no doubt that the miraculous conception and the other events surrounding his birth clearly differentiate Jesus from the rest of humanity. As Karl Barth said, 'The virgin birth at the opening and the empty tomb at the close of Jesus' life bear witness that this life is a fact marked off from all the rest of human life.'[24] Jesus' life is different in origin for his sonship is related to the direct work of God through the Holy Spirit, and in purpose for he came to reveal the nature of God and bring salvation to the world.

(2) *A unique relationship with the Holy Spirit*: throughout the scriptural narrative the Holy Spirit inspires, empowers and guides many people. But now Gabriel tells Mary that *the Holy Spirit will come upon you*, and Mary conceives Jesus through the Holy Spirit. The primary theological point of the biblical account of the conception of Christ through the Spirit is that there is a real, essential connection of Jesus with God that is different from the

[21] Ben Witherington III, 'Birth of Jesus', in Joel B. Green, Scot McKnight and I. H. Marshall (eds.), *Dictionary of Jesus and the Gospels* (Inter-Varsity Press, 1992), 70.

[22] Donald Macleod, *The Person of Christ* (Inter-Varsity Press, 1998), 37.

[23] Brown, *The Birth of the Messiah*, 307.

[24] Barth, *Church Dogmatics*, I/2, 182.

relationship any other person has. A legendary approach to this narrative would undercut the very point that is being made.[25] The indispensable point concerning Christ's essential nature is only sustained by the conviction that the Holy Spirit was *really* involved in a unique manner.

(3) *An essential connection with the Father*: the way Jesus is conceived creates a connection of *essence* between Jesus and God. The absence of a human father points to God as the Father of Christ. Jürgen Moltmann says, 'These nativity stories are trying to say that God is bound up with Jesus of Nazareth not fortuitously but essentially. His Fatherhood does not merely extend to Christ's consciousness and his ministry. It embraces his whole person and his very existence.'[26] Jesus does not become God's Son at some point in his ministry; he is from the time of his conception the unique, messianic Son. His unique, essential relationship with the Father through the Spirit is the basis for the distinction noted when Jesus, speaking to the disciples, refers to 'my Father and your Father' (John 20:17). I would not normally say to any of my three brothers, 'I am going to see my father and your father.' Rather I would say, 'I am going to see *our* father.' But Jesus' sonship and the Father's fatherhood is of such a different nature that it has to be distinguished from the sonship we have with God our Father. We are children by adoption rather than by nature; Jesus is Son of God by nature and was so from conception.

(4) *The foundation of the Trinity*: the conception of Christ through the working of the Holy Spirit is the real beginning of the doctrine of the Trinity. In other religions and philosophies God is not defined according to his temporal nature or by reference to a specific historical event. By definition, God is usually considered to be radically different from, and even opposed to, the temporal and the physical. But God works precisely in this radical and astonishing manner and the incarnation reveals that the temporal and the physical have their part to play in understanding the nature of God. In the conception of Christ with the Father through the power of the Spirit there is a foundation for the Trinity. It includes a perfect union of heaven and earth, of spiritual and material: 'The Son is the image of the invisible God, the firstborn over all creation ... He is before all things, and in him all things hold together' (Col. 1:15–17).

[25] This is illustrated in Moltmann's discussion: the fine theological analysis quoted on this page (see n. 26) is sabotaged by his claim that it is permissible for us 'to assume that the nativity stories are secondary, retroactive projections of the experiences of the Easter witnesses' which they 'transfer to the pre-natal beginnings of Christ' (Moltmann, *The Way of Jesus Christ*, 82).

[26] Ibid., 84.

(5) *A sign of sinlessness*: although the New Testament does not use his spiritual conception as an explanation of the claim that Christ was 'holy, blameless, pure, set apart from sinners',[27] it nonetheless points towards his sinless nature. The announcement that he was to be given *the throne of his father David* and was to *reign over the house of Jacob forever* points to his messianic nature and later this was precisely the temptation which Jesus successfully resisted: to deny his messianic calling.[28]

(6) *A sign of salvation*: Jesus' conception by the Spirit has soteriological significance – that is, it points to the salvation which he was to bring to the world. It was not Mary or Joseph but God who said *you are to give him the name Jesus*. The name Jesus (a common Jewish name at the time), meaning 'Yahweh saves', was in this case deeply significant.[29] In Jesus God was beginning the work of salvation promised from the time that human sin had entered human history. The Gospel story of Mary the mother of Jesus stands in subtle contrast to the Genesis story of Eve the mother of humanity. Mary's conception of Christ is the fulfilment of the prophecy concerning the salvation of the world which is found in God's judgment on Eve after she and Adam sinned. God declared that a descendant of Eve would strike a fatal blow at the evil offspring of the deceiving serpent:

> I will put enmity
> > between you [the serpent] and the woman [Eve],
> > and between your offspring and hers;
> He will crush your head,
> > and you will strike his heel.
>
> > > > (Gen. 3:15)

Mary's humility clearly contrasts with Eve's pride. And just as Eve's disobedience was the start of the rebellion of the human race, now Mary's obedience is the beginning of its redemption. Although Eve's disobedience led to pain in childbirth this very event now becomes a source of blessing for the world.[30] Prophecy gives way to fulfilment with the birth of a child: the incarnation of the Son of God.

---

[27] Heb. 7:26ff. Also see John 8:46; Heb. 4:15.

[28] See the temptations in the desert at the beginning of his ministry (Luke 4:1–13) and in the garden of Gethsemane at the end (Luke 22:42).

[29] At this point in his Gospel Matthew records the further comment 'because he will save his people from their sins' to emphasize this point (1:21).

[30] Cf. Gen. 3:5–7; Luke 1:48. Also see Gen. 3:16.

> O holy child of Bethlehem! Descend to us we pray;
> Cast out our sin and enter in; be born in us today.

(7) *The value of human nature*: the circumstances of Jesus' conception and birth also say something about the value and significance of human nature. Every stage of human life – from conception to resurrection – is contained in the incarnation. Jesus was fully human, taking on even the weakest, the most difficult and the most vulnerable dimensions of personhood. The incarnation is an affirmation of them all, including embryonic life, and God's judgment is that they are all valued and important in his eyes. They are not to be discarded but assumed and redeemed. Can they be less for us?

(8) *The nature of true power*: the graciousness of God's decision to become incarnate, born as a vulnerable child, weak and helpless, is the foundation of the principle that 'God chose the weak things of the world to shame the strong' (1 Cor. 1:27). Jesus' vulnerability was real, but so too was God's providence. King Herod was outwitted by the Magi, who did not return to tell him where to find the Christ-child, and so he ordered the slaughter of all males under the age of two years. Jesus was certainly protected – until his own time of sacrifice should come – but it must be remembered that he was born in the midst of blood and savagery, weeping and great mourning. There is a sharp contrast between the vulnerability of the divine incarnation and Herod's aggressive actions. Real strength and divine blessing come through weakness and sacrifice rather than through aggression, selfishness or pride. Long before Jesus ever taught any disciple, God had, through his birth, given an important but surprising lesson on the source of true power. Henri Nouwen in *Gracias!* [31] wrote to his family after his sister-in-law gave birth to a child with Down's syndrome, 'Laura is going to be important for all of us in the family. We have never had a "weak" person among us. We are all working, ambitious and successful people who seldom have had to experience powerlessness. Now Laura enters and tells us a totally new dependency. Laura, who will always be a child, will teach us the way of Christ as no one will ever be able to do.'

4. God the wonderful Saviour

Mary's meeting with Elizabeth brings together two women involved in the one plan of God. Why did Mary go to see Elizabeth? It is unlikely that she went to hide her pregnancy as she left when it

[31] Henri Nouwen, *Gracias! A Latin American Journal* (Orbis, 1993), 65.

would have been unnoticeable and returned just as it would have begun to show. We should probably assume it was to see Elizabeth (who, the angel told her, was already six months pregnant) and to help with the birth (she stayed just long enough for that to happen) and almost certainly to tell her of the events surrounding her own conception.

Having prayed one of the most profound prayers that has ever been spoken, Mary is now recorded as singing a majestic song of praise rightly known as 'the Magnificat'.[32] Some suggest that Luke, or another Christian writer, is more likely to be the author as it is improbable that such a young and uneducated girl could have produced this beautiful hymn spontaneously. But it does not sound like the creation of a post-resurrection Christian believer as it is very Jewish both in style and concept.[33] It reflects the thinking of its day rather than a later period. There is no need to assume that it was produced instantaneously: Mary had plenty of time on her four-day journey to reflect on the song of Hannah,[34] which is clearly the basis for this hymn. It would have been natural for Mary to contemplate on this passage as both she and Hannah were chosen to be mothers of sons who would be saviours of Israel.

a. Jesu, joy of our desiring

Mary's hymn of praise emerges from a deep sense of joy:[35] *My soul glorifies the Lord and my spirit rejoices in God my Saviour.* The birth of any child is a joyful time for parents and family, but the birth of this particular child is marked with special joy 'that will be for *all the people* ... a Saviour has been born' (2:10–11). It is very appropriate that Christmas should be celebrated with great rejoicing, but one of the great difficulties faced in many countries that have been strongly influenced by the Christian tradition – but which now are sometimes described as 'post-Christian' – is that popular celebrations can easily focus on the actions marking the occasion rather than on the central event itself. Holidays, presents, parties and even Christian values dressed up in secular clothing (e.g. peace represented as being 'nice' to one another) can detract from the joy that should be felt at the fact that God has sent his Son

---

[32] So named after the first word of the Latin version.

[33] E.g. see Nolland, *Luke*, 63.

[34] Found in 1 Sam. 2:1–10.

[35] When Elizabeth met Mary, the baby in her womb (significantly John the Baptist, the one who was to announce the coming of the Messiah) leapt for joy at the presence of the Messiah. See also the prophecy about him in Luke 1:14: 'He will be a joy and delight to you.'

into the world to redeem it. How then should Christians celebrate this momentous event? This is a perennial question. In the middle of the seventeenth century the Puritan movement (generally a very positive and helpful holiness movement) perhaps went too far in trying to eliminate joy at Christmas. Winston Churchill commented,

> The feast days of the Church, regarded as superstitious indulgences, were replaced by a monthly fast day. Parliament was deeply concerned at the liberty which it gave to carnal and sensual delights. Soldiers were sent round London on Christmas Day before dinner-time to enter private houses without warrants and seize meat cooking in all kitchens and ovens. Everywhere was prying and spying.[36]

Fasting is an excellent spiritual discipline, but Christmas should be celebrated with great joy. The appropriateness of any specific form of celebration is determined by asking whether it helps to focus attention on the central, spiritual significance of the coming of Christ rather than only on the pleasure of those involved. Mary's song points clearly to the fact that Christ's birth is an expression of God's concern for the humble and the poor, so it is not only appropriate but actually essential that the joy of Christmas should be celebrated with practical demonstrations of love for the needy and justice for the oppressed rather than with purely self-indulgent obsessions. These sacrificial, celebratory acts should flow out of a sense of joy (rather than simply from duty) and a desire to find the deepest pleasure of God. As John Piper has pointed out, the likely problem 'is not that our desire for pleasure is too strong but too weak! We have settled for a home, a family, a few friends, a job, a television, a microwave oven, an occasional night out, a yearly vacation, and perhaps a personal computer. We have accustomed ourselves to such meager, short-lived pleasures that our capacity for joy has shriveled.'[37] The joy of Christmas is a deeply spiritual one which should exceed any material or physical pleasure.

b. God's character defined

Mary exclaims that *from now on* (a phrase often used to indicate a significant development in God's plan[38]) *all generations will call me*

---

[36] He was not only a British prime minister but also a historian of some note. See Winston S. Churchill, *A History of the English Speaking Peoples*, Vol. 2 (Cassell, 1956), 248.

[37] Piper, *Desiring God*, 78.

[38] Luke 5:10; 12:52; 22:18, 19; Acts 18:6.

blessed. Once touched by the grace of God, life can never be the same again. Mary's song nominates four of God's attributes for particular praise. Each of them reflects what is known of the character of God in the Old Testament, but Mary relates them directly to his creative work in bringing Christ to birth. Each attribute leads naturally on to the next.

(1) *God is my Saviour*: this is the Greek form of the Hebrew 'God of my salvation'.[39] God was previously known as Saviour for he saved Israel from their enemies. Now, in Christ, God has acted to do nothing less than save the whole world from the enemies of sin and death.

(2) *God is the Mighty One*: he is frequently described this way in the Old Testament.[40] The Saviour of the world has to be powerful and his ultimate power, the power of the Most High, 'overshadows' Mary in order to conceive Jesus.

(3) *God is holy*: something which is holy is unique, set apart in some distinctive way. God is known as holy by both his character and his actions and people become holy if they are specifically set apart to live for God. Mary praises God's holiness in that he set her apart for himself in a unique way: that he might be born in her.

(4) *God is merciful*: this holiness expresses itself in *mercy* which extends to all those who 'fear' him. In the Old Testament such people are variously described as those who seek God, those who acknowledge his position and authority and those who obey him and follow his ways.[41] Now mercy will be shown to all those who become followers of his Son, Jesus.

c. God's deeds outlined

Mary now turns from praise for what God has meant to her to thanksgiving for what he has done for all his people. These are not distinctly different. Verses 51 to 54 contain seven statements which have been interpreted variously, (a) as thanksgiving purely for God's past actions, (b) as statements with a present implication – they are expressions of what God always does, and (c) as statements indicating that what God has done in the past (as seen in the Old Testament) has now been continued in the birth of Jesus and they will inevitably be fulfilled perfectly in the future. Given the eternally consistent nature of God the last of these is preferable. In Christ

[39] This Greek form is often found in the LXX (the Greek translation of the Old Testament): e.g. Pss. 24:5; 25:5; Mic. 7:7; Hab. 3:18.

[40] E.g. Pss. 44:4–8; 89:8–10.

[41] See Ps. 103:17, 'The LORD's love is with those who fear him.' Also see Deut. 7:9; Isa. 55:3, 6; 57:15.

God has begun the final stage of salvation history and it can be considered as good as done. The central dilemma in Gilbert and Sullivan's *Mikado* is that any number of convicted criminals have not been beheaded despite decrees to the contrary. In order to achieve a happy and humane ending to the story it was suggested that because the emperor was an absolute monarch and all-powerful, if he decreed that something *should* be done then it was *as good as* done. For all practical intent it *was* done. And as he *had* decreed that these people should lose their heads then it *must have* happened! To the vain emperor this was a significant endorsement of the authority of his word and so he declares that 'nothing could possibly be more satisfactory'. Of course in the case of the *Mikado* it is very dubious logic, but in the case of God it is absolutely right: he has performed mighty deeds, brought down rulers and filled the hungry with good things in the past and they are not merely incidental to his purposes: these *are* general truths expressing the eternal nature and purpose of God, and in the birth of Jesus Christ *it is inevitable* that he will accomplish these things again, yet even more perfectly and fully. They are as good as done. This is a prophetic insight which does not demand of Mary any direct knowledge of the future; it is enough for her (and us) to know the constant, faithful character of God.

God is described as having *performed mighty deeds*. They can be summarized in three main actions. First, he reverses human notions of power. This is shown in the way he has *scattered those who are proud in their inmost thoughts* (which is something like the scathing dismissal of a boaster as 'a legend in his own mind'). He has *brought down rulers* while at the same time he has *lifted up the humble*.[42] This is part of what has been called 'the great reversal' of ethics and discipleship.[43] Communist leader Mao Tse Tung believed that 'power grows out of the barrel of a gun', but power does not come from any form of violence or coercion, or even from any position of strength. This is true in political, social, personal and even religious contexts. Power is not something to be possessed or owned, even by the faithful. Power belongs to Christ and the way to power is through him and his power comes through weakness. In Christ we see a profound contrast between the love of power and the power of love. The humble are the truly 'powerful' for they understand that power is not for domination but for self-control, self-denial and discipline. It is not for self-satisfaction but to build others up. The birth of Jesus speaks decisively of God's capacity to

[42] As he has done in the past: Isa. 2:12; Num. 10:35; Ps. 68:1; Job 5:11; 1 Sam. 2:7.
[43] E.g. see Alan Verhey, *The Great Reversal: Ethics and the New Testament* (Eerdmans, 1984).

134

achieve his purposes through that which, by human standards, has no ability or strength to achieve its ends.

Secondly, he brings justice to the world. This is seen in the way he has *filled the hungry with good things but has sent the rich away empty.*[44] This is another dimension of God's reversal of values. Christ was born at a time when rulers expected to govern, the rich were always well fed and it was the poor who were dominated and who had to expect to be hungry. But Jesus challenges those expectations. In understanding this we must avoid two opposite errors. One is to overspiritualize the material references in Mary's song to the point where responsibilities in terms of material good, social structures and political actions can be avoided. They cannot be: the birth of Christ is the means by which all aspects of life are to come into conformity with the will of God. Stanley Jones described this as 'the most revolutionary document in the world'. The other mistake is to interpret what is said in purely material, 'this-worldly' terms and so ignore the spiritual implications of this birth. It is of little eternal use, for example, to have peace in terms of the absence of war but not to have 'the peace of God which passes all understanding', which keeps our hearts and minds in Christ Jesus (Phil. 4:7). This may mean that at times we are to be disturbed out of a comfortable existence to press on to a higher goal. A Spanish prayer says, 'May God deny you peace and give you glory.' The rich are sent away empty for they do not understand the ways of God. Rudyard Kipling advised a group of university graduates not to care too much for money or power or fame, for 'someday you will meet someone who cares for none of these things, and then you will know how poor you are'.

The third of God's mighty deeds brings us, very appropriately, to the end of this chapter. God is praised for he has *helped his servant Israel, remembering to be merciful to Abraham and his descendants forever.* The nation of Israel had always been the focus of God's election. They were not chosen simply for their own sake, they had nothing to merit being chosen, and from the time of God's covenant with Abram they were elect in order to be a blessing to other nations (Gen. 12:2). Consequently, although Israel had suffered greatly and was at this time under Roman rule, God had not forgotten them and in the conception of Christ through the power of the Holy Spirit he was undertaking his greatest act of salvation. The descendants of Abraham are now to be all those who are filled with the Spirit and enter into a relationship with Jesus Christ. In his birth God was communicating with humanity in the only way that

[44] See 1 Sam. 2:5; Ps. 107:9; Job 15:29; Jer. 17:11.

135

everyone in the world could understand – through a person. Many are unable to comprehend sophisticated philosophies, but having a personal relationship is the most fundamental characteristic of being human. In the birth of Jesus Christ it is possible to see the divine Trinity at work bringing salvation to the world. The Father's intention is brought into being through the incarnation of the Son by the power of the Holy Spirit.

> Let earth and heaven combine,
> angels and men agree,
> to praise in songs divine
> the incarnate deity,
> our God contracted to a span,
> incomprehensibly made man.
>
> He deigns in flesh to appear,
> widest extremes to join;
> to bring our vileness near
> and make us all divine:
> and we the life of God shall know,
> for God is manifest below.[45]

[45] Charles Wesley (1707–88).

Mark 1:1–14
7. Baptism: heavenly empowering

There is a saying that 'a good beginning makes for a good ending'. In Mark's Gospel that is certainly the case, for the ending is found at the beginning. His opening sentence, *The beginning of the good news about Jesus the Messiah, the Son of God*, encapsulates everything that he wants to say and gives the answer to the question of Jesus' identity which will permeate the whole Gospel. Jesus is none other than the *Christ*, that is, the long-expected Jewish Messiah, and *the Son of God*. The end is known before the story has really begun. Anyone reading this Gospel now knows that they have to consider Jesus in the light of his relationship with God. It is likely that *the beginning* was meant to parallel the 'in the beginning' of the creation story in Genesis: as God once created all things so now in *the good news about Jesus* nothing less than the re-creation of the universe is under way (Gen. 1:1).

In a Jewish context the title 'Son of God' does not necessarily imply divinity – it could be used to refer to a human king and messiah[1] – but Mark would have known full well that such a beginning would make Gentile readers immediately think of divinity and it is hard to imagine that he would have begun this way if he had not intended them to consider that possibility. Moreover, Mark immediately proceeds to record those events which will raise questions about Jesus' identity and deity: his encounter with unclean spirits which recognize the divine power at work in him; various exorcisms and healings; his ability to control nature; his declaration of sins forgiven and even his power to raise the dead. Now, when Jesus forgives sins the readers know the answer to all that is implied in the question, 'Who can forgive sins

[1] As it was in the Old Testament. See 2 Sam. 7:14; Ps. 2:7. Not all manuscripts include 'Son of God'.

THE MESSAGE OF THE TRINITY

but God alone?' and when Jesus is called 'good' they will understand the significance of the statement, 'No-one is good – except God alone' (Mark 2:7; 10:18).

As he begins to explore the nature of Jesus' divinity Mark turns to the events associated with John the baptizer,[2] as they provide the reader with a fundamental insight into the nature of Jesus' deity. In the account of Jesus' baptism Father, Son and Spirit are brought together in a manner which is often taken as a classic representation of the Trinity. Only by understanding these relationships can one grasp the Christian understanding of God. The uniquely Christian trinitarian confession of faith is not something which is added to a prior, general conception of God; it is, in fact, the Christian way of speaking about God. It is, as Claude Welch says, 'a first principle of all Christian thought and life'.[3]

1. John the baptizer

Mystery surrounds John the baptizer. He came from virtually nowhere – out of the Judean desert region near the Jordan – with nothing but a message to proclaim. Yet he must have been a compelling figure for *the whole Judean countryside and all the people of Jerusalem went out to him.* Who was he?

a. A prophet calling for repentance

John came from the desert and *wore clothing made of camel's hair, with a leather belt around his waist.* This is indicative of the typically ascetic lifestyle of a prophet of God and, in particular, connects John with the prophet Elijah.[4] This is significant because Isaiah had prophesied that the final Day of the Lord would be preceded by *one calling in the desert, 'Prepare the way for the Lord',* and it was widely believed, on the basis of a prophecy of Malachi, that this would involve Elijah's return.[5] So John is, in a sense, the new Elijah, preparing the way for the king. What is the appropriate preparation for a monarch? Everything has to be ready and in first-class order. In Isaiah's time the appropriate preparation for an earthly king included road repairs, not least making *straight paths for him* – a king should not have to be troubled by going round a

---

[2] Mark refers to 'the baptizer', compared to the other Gospels which speak of 'the baptist'.
[3] Welch, *The Trinity*, 48.
[4] Elijah is described in just the same way. See 2 Kgs 1:8; Zech. 13:4.
[5] Mark refers to Isaiah's prophecy but he actually quotes Isa. 40:3 and Mal. 3:1. Also see Mal. 4:5–6; Mark 8:27–30.

138

bend! Such preparations still happen today: Prince Philip is recorded as saying that he was tired of the smell of fresh paint because everywhere he went had been recently recoated. But for the coming of the Lord what is required is nothing less than a radical change in life's direction, away from sin and towards God. By preaching *repentance* John was confronting Israel with a call which resonated with many, for it was the same message that Jeremiah had proclaimed: 'Turn from your evil ways, each one of you, and reform your ways and your actions' (Jer. 18:11). Indeed, the fifth of the Eighteen Benedictions which Jews prayed daily asked that Israel would return to God and praised him as a God 'who delights in repentance'.[6] And so *all the people of Jerusalem went out to him. Confessing their sins, they were baptized by him in the Jordan River.* His preaching produced results appropriate for those professing repentance.

Similarly today, the church must preach repentance, despite the cost. John was a forthright preacher who did not shirk his responsibilities to God or the people he was called to serve, and his preaching led to imprisonment and death at the hands of King Herod.[7] The significance of the fact that he emerged from the wilderness is that this was a place of prayer and preparation (Mark 1:12). John did not preach 'off the cuff' but thoughtfully and prayerfully. It is inevitable that if the church preaches repentance people will sometimes be offended. But the person whose words have never offended anyone has probably never done anything to change anyone either. As it has been said, the preacher's job is to comfort the afflicted and to afflict the comfortable. No-one is without sin – not even the preacher – and so hard words must be spoken with humility, as by a fellow traveller on the road, rather than as though they come from one who is without sin. I have a friend who makes this point with a joke: 'Too many people don't admit their faults. I would if I had any.'

John's preaching related the gospel to people's life and work. He gave instruction on the use of material possessions and how soldiers and others should fulfil their responsibilities. Recently I had an after-church conversation with someone on the ethical implications of his work. It was a complex matter which involved responsibilities to a number of different people with varied needs and requirements, but it was a common situation for him and probably was no more difficult than many issues faced by a range of people in the course of their work in trade, education, business or government. 'Let me

[6] Marcus, *Mark*, 150.
[7] Mark 6:14–29. More detailed accounts of his teaching can be found in other Gospels. See Matt. 3:7–10; Luke 3:7–19.

guess,' I said, 'the amount of help and guidance or even interest you have received from your church on this is probably about ... zero?' He ruefully agreed that this was a correct assessment and went on to describe how he had struggled alone for many years with these matters. In retrospect, one might think that this is a harsh assessment. No doubt the church provided general guidance on right and wrong and it would certainly provide motivation to do what is right. And perhaps those who face issues in their daily work could do more to raise the issues involved. But however it is done, the church still needs to do more to follow the example of John and address directly and clearly the ethical issues people deal with from Monday to Friday.

Repentance is important and must be preached, but not in such a way as to create a form of legalism. Repentance leads to *the forgiveness of sins*, but repentance is not the basis for this. Forgiveness is based in God's mercy and is offered freely. Repentance is the process whereby we turn to God to accept it gratefully. Repentance is not to be treated as though it is the basis of the forgiveness of sins, or as though it persuades God to be gracious. Repentance is the means by which one may receive the reconciliation which God freely offers. Repentance is *preparatory*, but it is not everything. As the preaching of John shows us, it prepares the way and inexorably leads to Christ. All preaching must do that and John illustrates that his message is Christ-focused: *After me comes the one more powerful than I.*

b. A baptizer preparing for a new covenant

As John preached, those who confessed their sins *were baptized by him in the Jordan River*. Why did he do this? It certainly was not Christian baptism.[8] What did it mean to a first-century Jew? At least three actions with water must be considered as part of the background to John's baptism.

The first is the presence of *Jewish purification rites*. Washing with water removes dirt so it was easy for this to become an appropriate metaphor for God's removal of both physical disease and spiritual sin (Lev. 14:1–9; 2 Kgs 5:1–27). The one who was sinful needed to use water as a sign of his or her repentance. Isaiah told sinful worshippers to 'wash and make yourselves clean', and the psalmist's answer to the question, 'Who may stand in his holy place?' was, 'He who has clean hands and a pure heart' (Isa. 1:16; Ps. 24:3–4).

---

[8] In Acts 19 some Ephesians who had been baptized by John were subsequently baptized as Christians.

Washing was to be a symbol of repentance, which was an actual change of heart and action.

Secondly, water was used in *proselyte baptism* – that is, a baptism for those who converted to Judaism. There is controversy, however, as to whether this was a pre-Christian practice or whether it only emerged later, in which case it could not really have influenced the thinking of John or those who were baptized by him.[9] Later on it achieved some importance as one of three required actions by converts along with offering sacrifice at the temple in Jerusalem and (for males) being circumcised. Although all three were expected, converts outside Judea found getting to Jerusalem difficult and that, combined with the obvious discomfort of circumcision for adult males, made baptism an attractive alternative. It would be unsafe to say more than that there could be a general parallel, rather than a direct dependence, between Jewish proselyte baptism and John's baptism.

The third possible antecedent of John's baptism is related to a ritual *washing of the new covenant* associated with the Qumran community (or the Essenes as they are also known), a Jewish sect which avoided every form of commerce, observed a strict Sabbath, avoided all oaths, maintained ritual purity and undertook washings in association with the establishment of the new covenant foretold in the Hebrew Scriptures. As Jeremiah said, ' "The time is coming," declares the LORD, "when I will make a new covenant with the house of Israel and with the house of Judah ... I will put my law in their minds and write it on their hearts. I will be their God, and they will be my people" ' (Jer. 31:31–33). Like the Essenes, John was a desert-based ascetic. Whether he was ever a member of this community is not certain, but his thinking seems to overlap with theirs and especially with their ritual washing of the new covenant which was the focus of their intense eschatological hope. It is not unlikely that people would have understood that John's baptism was related to the new covenant.

2. The baptism of Jesus

The baptism of Jesus is a wonderful and unique picture of God which establishes for us the New Testament foundation for what we may rightly call a doctrine of the Trinity. Jesus' baptism reveals the identity of God just as Christian baptism gives identity to the

---

[9] There is no clear evidence of Jewish proselyte baptism prior to AD 70. See, for example, McKnight, *A Light among the Gentiles*.

believer (Gal. 3:26–29; Rom. 6:3–11). This is a scene full of symbols and trinitarian significance.

- *Jesus* is present, indicating his solidarity with humanity through the symbol of *water*.
- The *Spirit* descends like a *dove*, uniting Jesus with God.
- A *voice* from heaven reveals *God as the Father* of Jesus the Messiah, his beloved son.

Jesus *saw heaven being torn open* and this is a mark of divine authority for what happens (Rev. 4:1). Later the chief priests, scribes and elders asked Jesus about his ministry, 'Who gave you authority to do this?' In reply Jesus asked them whether John's baptism was from heaven or a human source. To say 'from heaven' would be to concede that Jesus ministered in God's name, but to say it was not would anger the people, so they answered lamely, 'We don't know' (Mark 11:27–33). But the answer has already been given, for at his baptism the *voice came from heaven* and is from God.

God spoke from heaven on other significant occasions. 'The heavens were opened' to Ezekiel, he saw great visions, was filled with the Spirit and then sent on a difficult mission. Nathaniel declared to Jesus, 'Rabbi, you are the Son of God,' and so Jesus promised him that he would 'see heaven open' with the angels and the Son of Man. And Stephen, while being stoned, was filled with the Spirit; he looked up to heaven and saw the glory of God, and Jesus standing at his right hand.[10] These are wonderful things and we might idly wonder sometimes, 'Wouldn't it be nice if God opened the heavens and came down to earth a bit more often? Couldn't he appear in glory and majesty more frequently? If a voice came from heaven it might persuade a few more people to believe in him!' Or would it, so to speak, debase the currency too much? Any answer to this is bound to be a little complex, but probably should include at least the following four points.

The first is to note that *special revelations such as these are a privilege rather than a Christian's right*. God will reveal himself as and when he determines. Nonetheless, God's grace is such that while they may not be an everyday occurrence they are perhaps more common than we might at first imagine. This will depend on the culture and the church tradition to which one belongs. Some are far more expectant and ready to experience such things and some are more willing to be open and discuss them when they do occur. But even where people are reserved it is remarkable how many people

[10] Ezek. 1:1 – 2:4; Isa. 64:1; John 1:51; Acts 7:56.

will say that they have had special experiences of God which, from their perspective, are as real as the biblical messages from heaven.

Secondly, it is undoubtedly helpful for Christians to *encourage one another with them, but not to idolize them* as though they were a requirement for the spiritually minded. Even in biblical context they are the exception rather than the rule of the Christian life. God is known continually, not just occasionally, in quiet prayer, through worship, in the reading of Scripture and through the advice and guidance of other Christians. In particular, we should not expect the miraculous if we have studiously ignored the revelation he has already given in Scripture.

Thirdly, if we are tempted to think that God is remiss in appearing we must remember that *he has appeared fully and completely and in person* rather than just as a voice from heaven. He came to earth, God incarnate, and that is the revelation to which we need to pay attention. If all we want is a miraculous appearance or a disembodied voice, then we are implicitly downplaying the significance of the incomparable incarnation of God in Jesus. And besides, the spectacularly miraculous is not necessarily more persuasive. Jesus told a parable of a rich man who died and went to Hades. He begged for someone to be sent to warn his brothers, but the answer came back that this would not work: 'If they do not listen to Moses and the Prophets, they will not be convinced even if someone rises from the dead' (Luke 16:19–31). Faith does not come from seeing amazing things, it comes from the inner working of the Spirit of God in response to the Word of God concerning Jesus Christ.

Finally, while we must remember never to rule out the possibility of a special revelation of God, *we must be careful of what we seek*. Remember that Elijah expected God to speak in powerful wind, or an earthquake or a fire, but he spoke through a gentle whisper (1 Kgs 19:11–13). And be particularly careful, because special revelations are usually given to those about to face great adversity, or those who are being called to a seemingly impossible task. Special situations require special help.

As John said, the contrast between himself and Jesus was that *I baptize you with water, but he will baptize you with the Holy Spirit.* John's baptism is a sign of the new covenant which will actually be established through the ministry of Jesus. Why then does Jesus, the one who is to bring the new covenant, come himself for baptism by John? Others come to mark their repentance and be forgiven, but Jesus is without sin – he is the one who can forgive sins – and so his baptism is different. Its significance can be understood in three statements.

143

a. Jesus identifies with humanity

Mark simply says that *Jesus came from Nazareth in Galilee and was baptized by John in the Jordan*. He does not include, as Matthew does, John's reluctance to baptize Jesus or Jesus' insistence that it happen on the basis that 'it is proper for us to do this to fulfil all righteousness' (Matt. 3:13–15). But even without those additional words it is clear that Jesus' baptism marked a decision to identify himself with all sinful people. He was prepared to stand with them and be reckoned the same as all those who needed baptism – that is, with all those who are sinners; in other words, everyone. This act of solidarity points forwards towards his ultimate act of solidarity by which he dies for the sake of the world and, in so doing, fulfils all righteousness. This is made clear in the discussion which takes place when the disciples ask to be given the best seats in the forthcoming kingdom. 'You don't know what you are asking,' Jesus said. 'Can you drink the cup I drink or be baptized with the baptism I am baptized with?' The implication is clearly that they cannot do this, for Jesus' death is unique. Not in physical pain or suffering – there are many who have suffered far worse fates, but it is unique in that he bears the effect of the sin of the world and knows the full torment of separation from his heavenly Father (Mark 15:34). This is his unique ministry. But then he relents, saying, 'You will drink the cup I drink and be baptized with the baptism I am baptized with,' indicating that while only Jesus can identify with, and die for, the sins of the world they will be able to identify themselves with Jesus and share in death in the sense that they too may die for the sake of the gospel.

It is perhaps intimidating to be told that being a disciple of Jesus may lead to persecution, suffering or death (Mark 13:9–13), but it is something that every believer should consider carefully. For many Christians around the world today it is a reality or a genuine possibility. However, while Jesus never promised his followers that they would be able to avoid suffering because they were disciples, he did promise that they would be blessed, that he would always be with them and that they would one day share in heaven with him.[11] Moreover, in his baptism he indicates the extent to which he was prepared to go for others. He willingly identified himself with sinful people and was prepared to suffer for their sake. In so doing he set his followers an example to emulate. It has been said that a Christian is someone who shares the sufferings of God in the world. Belgian missionary priest Joseph de Veuster (known as 'Father Damien' in

[11] Matt. 5:1–14; 28:20; John 14:3.

the film of that name) was distressed when he heard about the lepers isolated on the small island of Molokai in the Hawaiian Islands. In 1873 he chose to give up the comforts of conventional ministry and join the lepers on their island, knowing that by doing so he would never be able to leave. He cared for the ill despite the most appalling circumstances, and gave hope to those in despair. Eventually de Veuster contracted leprosy himself. His response was, 'I thank God that now when I preach instead of "dear brethren" I shall be able to say "my fellow lepers".' After fifteen years of service to the people of Molokai he died. Joseph de Veuster followed his Lord Jesus in completely identifying with those in need of help. This was not help from a safe distance but 'up close and personal', just like Jesus.

b. Jesus is empowered for ministry

Jesus' baptism opened a new chapter in his life. As he came out of the water *he saw heaven being torn open and the Spirit descending on him like a dove*. The dove subsequently became a well known Christian symbol for the Holy Spirit, but what was it that made it suitable as a symbol for the Spirit in the first place? It is likely that there are two dimensions to this. The first is that the dove is *a sign of a new covenant*: it was a dove which returned to Noah with an olive leaf, indicating that the flood was coming to an end, and which therefore acted as a herald of God's forthcoming covenant never to send another flood to destroy the earth (Gen. 8:11; 9:8–12). In a similar way, at Jesus' baptism the dove acts symbolically as a herald of God's new, forthcoming covenant to be established through the Spirit.

The second dimension is that the dove is *a sign of God's power to create and give birth*. The phrase *descending on him like a dove* can be taken to mean that the Spirit *descended* like a dove – rather than just suggesting that the Spirit *looked* like a dove.[12] In this case the focus is on the fact that the Spirit descends in a gentle fluttering or shaking movement. What does this imply? It reinforces the fact that Jesus' power is *from above*, that is, from heaven, and therefore is none other than the power of God's Spirit. This is a necessary point to make as just a little later Mark records how certain scribes argued that Jesus' power to cast out demons actually came from demonic power,[13] but the manner of his baptism makes it clear that his power descends on him from God. The distinctive fluttering movement of

[12] The former way of reading the text takes it as an adjectival phrase, while the latter assumes it to be an adverbial phrase. Grammatically, either is possible.
[13] Jesus pointed out the absurdity of thinking that Satan would cast out Satan; Mark 3:20–27.

a dove coming down is also a reminder of the Spirit of God 'hovering over the waters' at creation (Gen. 1:2). The Babylonian Talmud makes this connection when it comments on this verse, 'And the Spirit of God was brooding on the face of the waters like a dove which broods over her young but does not touch them.'[14] The fluttering of a dove creates a slight movement of air, a gentle wind which is very appropriate for the creative Spirit as both the Hebrew and the Greek words for spirit have the literal meaning of 'wind' or 'breathe'. Seen this way, the fluttering, descending dove symbolizes the creative work of the Spirit both at the creation of the world and now, at the bringing into being of a new Son, a new kingdom and a re-created world.

The gentle wind and the soft touch of the dove are perhaps surprising images to use for the incomparable power of God which fills Jesus and which will soon be the means for overcoming evil spirits, stilling storms and bringing life to the dead. One might think that a clap of thunder and bolts of lightning would be more appropriate, but God's way is power with gentleness and mighty justice with infinite peace. God's power came to Jesus gently, quietly and probably unobserved by others.[15] The presence and the power of the Spirit in one's life is not known by flamboyant gestures or spectacular claims but rather by the actual, effective exercise of ministry – the work of the kingdom.

> Spirit of God, unseen as the wind, gentle as is the dove;
> Teach us the truth and help us believe, show us the saviour's love.
> Without your help we fail our Lord, we cannot live his way;
> We need your power, we need your strength, following Christ each day.[16]

The descent of the Spirit was the inauguration of Jesus' ministry, one characterized as a life lived with and through the Spirit of God. This is evident in three ways. First of all, Jesus *lived* by the Spirit. As soon as the Spirit came upon Jesus he was led by the Spirit out into the wilderness where he was tempted by Satan for forty days. The

---

[14] B. Hagiga 15a. This is a late Jewish writing which can only be used to lend support to the idea that in first-century Judaism the fluttering or brooding action of the dove was associated with the coming of the Spirit. See Barrett, *The Holy Spirit*, 38, and Keck, 'The Spirit and the Dove', 41–67.

[15] It is noted that as Jesus came out of the water *he* saw heaven being torn open and the Spirit descending; Mark 1:10.

[16] M. V. Old, 'Spirit of God, unseen as the wind', in *Sing to God* (Scripture Union, 1971).

wilderness was seen as the home of demons and a place of alienation, wandering and testing, just as it had been at the time of the exodus. Mark connects the wilderness with the exodus through the quotations from Malachi and Isaiah (vv. 2–3).[17] In the desert Jesus has to face and overcome Satan's temptations (v. 13) and the power of demons (Mark 5:1). But by entering the desert he redeems it and leads another exodus towards a new promised land. By the time he left the wilderness he was ready to preach the gospel and able to proclaim confidently that 'The kingdom of God has come near' (Mark 1:15). The Spirit knew that it was necessary for Jesus to undergo this testing. It was a time of strengthening for the trials that lay ahead and the difficulties of the temptations made Jesus better able to minister salvation to the world. As the writer to the Hebrews said, 'He had to be made like his brothers in every way, in order that he might make atonement for the sins of the people. Because he himself suffered when he was tempted, he is able to help those who are being tempted. Therefore, holy brothers, who share in the heavenly calling, fix your thoughts on Jesus, the apostle and high priest whom we confess.'[18] Life's difficulties are sometimes present as testing times to enable us to become stronger and more mature. As it has been said, 'If you can find a path with no obstacles, it probably doesn't lead anywhere.' Troubles are the tools by which God shapes us for better things. The aim of the Christian life is not to have an easy life, but to seek, find and do the Father's will in the Father's world with the fellowship of the Son by the guidance and strength of the Holy Spirit.

Secondly, Jesus now had the power to *minister* by the Spirit. Mark's Gospel presents a breathtaking array of evidences of the power of the Spirit in the life of Jesus. Following his baptism with the Spirit he was able to cast out evil spirits, heal the sick, preach the gospel, forgive sins, teach authoritatively, debate with opponents, still storms, raise the dead, form a community of disciples, walk on water, feed thousands, counsel the uncertain, cause a fig tree to die by a curse, prophesy concerning future events, suffer betrayal by friends, be crucified and, finally, be raised from the dead.[19] In these actions Jesus is revealed as the promised Messiah, the Son of God, which is precisely what Mark had asserted in the first sentence of the Gospel and is what Peter finally concluded in the light of what he and

[17] And later he makes the same connection through the feeding of the five thousand which takes place in the desert and is an echo of the manna which the children of Israel were given to eat (Mark 6:30–44; Exod. 16).
[18] Heb. 2:17 – 3:1, slightly abridged.
[19] Mark 1:30–32, 38; 2:5, 23–28; 3:20–27; 4:35–41; 5:21–43; 1:16–20, 6:7–14, 45–52; 8:1–10; 10:17–31, 35–45; 11:12–25; 13:1–27; 14:43–52; 15:16–39; 16:1–20.

the other disciples saw happening: 'You are the Messiah.'[20] It means, literally, 'anointed one' and is a term associated with those who, in the Old Testament, were anointed with oil for special office: kings, priests and prophets.[21] Jesus' baptism with the Spirit is his anointing, indicating his messiahship and pointing towards his subsequent ministry as the ultimate Prophet, the High Priest and the King of Kings.[22] As the Messiah he ministers in the power of the Spirit.

Finally, the descent of the Spirit on Jesus meant that he was now the one able to *bestow* the Spirit on others. As John said, *he will baptize you with the Holy Spirit*,[23] and this was just what God had promised much earlier through Ezekiel: 'I will give you a new heart and put a new spirit in you ... you will be my people, and I will be your God' (Ezek. 36:25–27). It is of the utmost significance that the Spirit comes to us through Christ. There are many spirits, pseudo-spirits and spiritualities to which people can give their lives. God's Spirit is identified as the One who comes as the gift of the Lord Jesus Christ. The Spirit of God has the character and the personality of Jesus and will do nothing other than point towards the way of Jesus Christ. The fruit of the Spirit (love, joy, peace patience, kindness, goodness, gentleness and self-control) is the character of Jesus (Gal. 5:22).

c. Jesus is revealed as God's Son

The declaration from heaven is usually interpreted in the light of two important passages of the Old Testament, Psalm 2 and Isaiah 42. (a) The first part of the phrase, *You are my Son*, is related to the declaration in Psalm 2, 'You are my Son; today I have begotten you.'[24] (b) The third part of the phrase, *with you I am well pleased*, appears to be a deliberate echo of Isaiah 42:1, 'Here is my servant, whom I uphold, my chosen one in whom I delight.' (c) The second part of the divine declaration, *whom I love*, can be translated as 'the beloved' and it is possible that it is intended to relate to Isaiah's 'my chosen one'. On the other hand, it is also an expression which was sometimes used with the implication that the beloved was an *only* child,[25] in which case it would then relate to the psalmist's 'today I

[20] Mark 8:29. The Hebrew 'messiah' is equivalent to the Greek 'Christ'.

[21] 1 Sam. 9:15–16; 16:3, 12–13; Exod. 28:41; 1 Chr. 29:22; Isa. 61:1–2.

[22] Heb. 1:1–3; 5:6–10; 6:20 – 10:18; Rev. 17:14.

[23] Mark 1:12, 25–26; 2:5–7; 3:22–27; 5:13, 41–42.

[24] It is actually the first of two such heavenly declarations in Mark's Gospel. See Mark 9:7.

[25] That is, a 'beloved' son or daughter is not beloved because he or she is more lovable than any brothers or sisters but because he or she is the *only* child.

have begotten you'. Or it could be that 'the beloved' provides a connection of thought between Psalm 2 and Isaiah 42 and relates to both of them. Irrespective of how the phrase *whom I love* is taken, there is a clear connection with both Psalm 2 and Isaiah 42 and the question now is, 'What is the significance of this for understanding the divine declaration of Sonship at Jesus' baptism?'

1. The divine Son is a saviour

The voice from heaven is clearly from God and declares, *You are my Son, whom I love*. This points towards a unique relationship with God the Father and therefore towards the fact of his own divinity: he is not merely an honorary son of God but the unique Son of God who shares in divine nature and love. This is the real meaning of the title *Son of God* attributed to Jesus in the very first verse of the Gospel. There are other descriptions of Jesus, including Son of Man, Messiah, Lord, Saviour, Servant and Prophet, but none have been as influential as this one for 'this title gave clearest expression to the subject of Jesus' relationship with God'.[26] That is, the Father-Son relationship is to be understood primarily as a relationship of love. The real basis of love is that it begins within the relationships of the Trinity. God is Father, Son and Spirit and therefore *is* love. Love is God's nature (1 John 4:16) and is revealed and defined in the Father's love for the Son. When we understand the depth of the love which the Father has for the Son, it becomes even harder to comprehend the extent of love that God has for humanity. The Father was prepared to offer his only Son, and the Son was willing to come in order to die for others. Although it was a terrible act, the death of the Son was no accident. It happened with 'God's set purpose and foreknowledge' (Acts 2:23). Such is the love of God.

Jesus' Sonship not only reveals the loving nature of God, it also points to the fully divine nature which Jesus has. As the Nicene creed says, he is 'the only Son of God, eternally begotten of the Father, God from God, Light from Light, true God from true God, begotten not made, of one being with the Father'. This is certainly creedal terminology rather than biblical language, but it is an accurate representation of biblical thought. While walking on the beach a child asked, 'Why did God send Jesus – why didn't he come himself?' A question came back in answer, 'Is there any difference between the water in the sea and the water in this bucket?' The child said, 'No, they are both the same water.' And so came the reply, 'There is as much water in there as you can fit. And there is as much of God in Jesus as can be fitted into one human life.' The

---

[26] Pannenberg, *Systematic Theology*, Vol. 2, 381.

implications are clear: his deity means that our worship of him is necessary. Our primary calling is to live our lives before God, to be available to him, to meet and know him. In so doing, in our worship and service of one who is Lord and King we receive the grace of the Lord Jesus Christ, we participate in the life and love of the Father, we experience the corporate fellowship of the Holy Spirit and we celebrate the Living God.

Anselm of Canterbury was right when he argued that only humanity *should* make reparation for sin (for it was human sin that separated the world from God) and that, given the seriousness of this problem, only God *could* make this reparation. While there are many illustrations of one person giving his or her life to save another, no-one can die for the sins of the world except Jesus. Any other person simply cannot avoid the twin facts of his or her finitude and sinfulness. Consequently, said Anselm, 'If none but God *can* make it and none but man *ought* to make it, it is necessary for the God-man to make it.'[27] In Jesus alone is there the possibility of salvation.

2. The royal Son is a servant
The declaration from heaven links Psalm 2 with Isaiah 42 and so connects *sonship* with *servanthood*. The royal, messianic Son of God is 'my servant, whom I uphold, my chosen one in whom I delight'. Moreover, the servant is revealed to be a suffering servant.[28] This is subsequently revealed in his ministry – 'the Son of Man did not come to be served, but to serve, and to give his life as a ransom for many', and in his teaching – 'Anyone who wants to be first must be the very last, and the servant of all' (Mark 10:45; 9:35). It is possible for Christians to get so accustomed to singing about 'the servant king' that we overlook the totally unexpected and radical, but fundamentally important connection of kingship and servant-hood. This servanthood gives content and character to the kind of kingship that Jesus was to exercise: 'My kingdom is not of this world' (John 18:36). At his baptism Jesus experienced the Father's blessing and the Spirit's filling, but the real test of his Sonship was to be found in his future ministry. Spiritual experiences are not the sum total of the Christian life. As Oswald Chambers said, 'The true measure of a spiritual life is not ecstasy but obedience.'

3. The Father's Son is a revelation
In Christ there is a great, mysterious synthesis of the human and the divine. The deity of Jesus Christ means that our understanding of

---

[27] *Cur Deus Homo*, Book 1, ch. 11 – Book 2, ch. 5. Anselm (*c.*1033–1109) was Archbishop of Canterbury.
[28] See Isa. 53. For Jesus, suffering and death are symbolized in baptism.

the nature of God can never be the same again. On the one hand, Jesus, the Son of God, is *completely and fully human*. At his baptism Jesus was declared to be the unique Son of God, but he had been so from birth and even from conception. This challenges our understanding of the nature and value of humanity and the whole created order. During nine months of pregnancy God was sharing our life, our world. He was vulnerable as a tiny one-cell embryo, sharing the complete process of growth and subjecting himself to life in his own creation. Subsequently, his baptism points to his desire to identify with humanity in every way. In Christ God lived among us, sharing our life. In so doing he makes clear the inestimable value he places on the physical, the ordinary, the material world. The Creator of the universe was present in a few cells, in a baby, then a child, and in every part of life through to death. In this way God shows his love for the world and his intention to redeem it (Col. 1:16–20).

On the other hand, Jesus of Nazareth, born of Mary, baptized with the Spirit, is *completely and fully divine*. Jesus did not 'become' Son of God at his baptism. He was not 'adopted' as God's Son at that point in time. He was 'declared' Son of God but he was intrinsically the Son of God, always, from birth. As Jesus is declared Son of God, so God is now known in a new way – as the Father of Jesus. This becomes *the* Christian definition of God: he is the one who is the Father of Jesus Christ. Clearly, our understanding of God has to take on a trinitarian form. God is intrinsically Father. Being Father defines the Christian view of God. God cannot be God without being the Father and the Father cannot be without the Son any more than light can be without shining. We must also note that Jesus is known as Son of the Father only through the ministry of the Holy Spirit. Only the creative Spirit of God can bring this about: that which is not of God cannot confer divine power or status. The Holy Spirit is in intimate relationship with both the Father and Jesus. The Spirit is the link, the unifier of the Trinity.[29]

In a spiritual age and at a time when there is a pervasive attitude that God can be whoever (or whatever) you define God to be, it is of the utmost importance to identify the nature and the character of the God Christians worship. The uniqueness of Christianity lies in

[29] This fits with the fact that both Ps. 2 and Isa. 42 operate in the context of the anointing of the Spirit. Ps. 2 implies this in the anointing of the new king and Isa. 42:1 explicitly refers to the fact that 'I have put my Spirit' on him. Also see Rom. 1:13 and 1 Tim. 3:16, which connect the Spirit with Jesus' Sonship. Although little more can be said in this regard until we have looked at other passages which focus more on the identity of the Spirit, we should note the implication here that these trinitarian relationships point towards an understanding of the Spirit as more than merely a power sent from God. The Spirit is the unique Spirit of God who shares divine nature with the Father and the Son.

the fact that God is to be defined as Father, Son and Spirit. All gods are not the same; all spiritual roads do not lead to heaven; the uniqueness of Christ and the message of the Trinity *are* at the heart of Christian faith. The Trinity is not an 'add-on', it is not an 'extra', it is the gospel.

> God has spoken by Christ Jesus,
> Christ the everlasting Son,
> brightness of the Father's glory,
> with the Father ever one;
> spoken by the word incarnate,
> God from God, ere time began,
> Light from Light, to earth descending,
> Man, revealing God to man.[30]

[30] George Wallace Briggs (1875–1959).

Matthew 12:15–32
8. Mission: spiritual encounter

What would you do if you were sent on a mission to change the world? In the film *Pay It Forward* eleven-year-old Trevor responds to his teacher's challenge to come up with a plan and devises the 'pay it forward' concept. This involves helping three people in some very significant way and, in so doing, encouraging them to 'pay it forward' (rather than 'pay it back') by doing something equally caring for three more people. They will then each do the same for three others, and so on, until the world is full of good deeds. The idealism of the concept perhaps does not deal fully with the difficulty people experience in consistently acting in this way and ultimately only the presence of God's Son, Jesus, the Lord of Life, can truly change the face of the world. Nonetheless, the 'pay it forward' principle of caring for others with no thought of reward for self is profoundly Christian.

Jesus' own mission was to change the world through love. It has been said that mission is 'the mother of theology' and indeed it is, for it is from our understanding of this divine mission that it is possible to understand the most fundamental nature of God. Jesus is sent on this mission by the Father in the power of the Spirit in order to redeem the world. Consequently, this passage from Matthew 12 gives us the opportunity to come to a deeper understanding of both the mission of Jesus and the dynamics of the life of Father, Son and Spirit.

1. The Messiah and his mission

a. The Messiah

Jesus' healings and exorcisms were bound to attract attention and inevitably he was besieged by crowds. He healed a man's withered hand and then sought to withdraw quietly to avoid further attention (Matt. 12:9–14), but *a large crowd followed him* and out of compassion for them *he healed all who were ill*. They also brought to him *a demon-possessed man who was blind and mute, and Jesus healed him, so that he could both talk and see*. It should be no surprise to read that as a result of this *all the people were astonished*, for this was a remarkable sign of nothing less than the presence of the kingdom of God. Yet Jesus was reluctant to have too much attention paid to what he was doing. Having already withdrawn from the people once, he again acted to minimize the attention he was getting, this time *he warned them not to tell others about him*. He insisted on this at other times as well (8:4; 9:30; 12:16; 16:20; 17:9) and this deliberate concealment is sometimes referred to as 'the messianic secret'. Various explanations for it have been proffered, but it is unlikely that he did this only to avoid antagonizing his opponents (something he could have achieved by being far less blunt towards them) or because he was simply not a publicity-seeking type of person (he was, after all, very concerned for people to know about the love of God, Mark 1:38–39). It is even less likely that the various statements about secrecy were literary creations written back into the Gospel events in order, it has been suggested, to explain the supposed belief of the later church that Jesus' messiahship was revealed only at the time of his resurrection.[1]

The explanation is to be found in theological rather than literary or pragmatic reasons. Jesus was ensuring that people did not develop a wrong and dangerous understanding of the nature of his messiahship. There was a risk that it would be interpreted in the light of popular expectations of a majestic, powerful, worldly figure who would come to dominate the political and social world of the first century. When the Roman-backed Idumean King Herod died in 4 BC the Jews sought social reforms from Archelaus, his son and heir. But the new king unwisely determined to assert his power and responded to this affront by massacring thousands of worshipping pilgrims at the Passover. Inevitably this produced revolt in every part of the kingdom in the form of messianic movements aimed at the complete overthrow of Herodian and Roman control of Palestine and the anointing of a new king.[2] Jesus' concern was that the crowds would interpret his ministry as the start of a violent or political movement and so he sought to restrain them while at the same time continuing to teach and minister in a manner appropriate

[1] This is tied to passages such as Acts 2:36 and the view is associated with the pioneering work of W. Wrede in *The Messianic Secret* (James Clarke, 1901).
[2] See Josephus, *Jewish Antiquities Books X – XVII*, ed. G. P. Goold (Harvard University Press, 1963), XVII, 195–207.

to his messiahship. It involved power of a different nature, which came though qualities such as peacefulness and quietness, service, gentleness, compassion and patience, grace and justice.

Having recorded the fact that Jesus warned them *not to tell others about him*, Matthew then comments that *this was to fulfil what was spoken through the prophet Isaiah*. He then provides his own translation of Isaiah 42:1–4 which is a prophecy of the forthcoming Messiah: *Here is my servant whom I have chosen, the one I love, in whom I delight*. As with many prophecies these words are fulfilled in more than one way. The ultimate fulfilment is in Jesus, but, surprisingly, the prophecy originally referred to Cyrus who founded the Persian Empire in 549 BC and soon controlled Assyria and Babylon. A politically astute leader, he decided that generosity would pay dividends and issued a decree by which those, including the Jews, who had been prisoners of the Babylonians were permitted to return to their homes and restore their deities in renovated temples.[3] The point is not that Cyrus was generous but that God can use whomsoever he chooses to fulfil his plans. Cyrus was, albeit unknowingly, Yahweh's servant and his 'shepherd' who would 'accomplish all that I please' (Isa. 44:28). Even an unbelieving king can be used by God and become a forerunner of the Messiah. God's ability to work in the world today is not restricted to those who consciously serve him. God can use the most unlikely people to achieve his purposes.

b. His mission

The initial reason for including this text from Isaiah is that it provides a biblical justification for Jesus' secrecy in that it says the Messiah *will not quarrel or cry out; no-one will hear his voice in the streets*. But Matthew quotes more of Isaiah than is necessary to make that particular point (and he is usually economical in his quotations) and the reason seems to be that he wants to be able to develop his interpretation of Jesus' ministry in the light of other aspects of Isaiah's prophecy. Of particular significance is the fact that in the quotation Yahweh identifies the Messiah as *my servant whom I have chosen, the one I love ... I will put my Spirit on him*. The point that Matthew is now making is that Jesus' healing of the sick and his refusal to act violently are valid parts of his messianic ministry and should not be seen as weakness but rather as the exercise of a different sort of power. His ministry is going according

[3] See Cyrus's Cylinder in Pritchard, *Ancient Near Eastern Texts* 316; Thomas, *Documents of Old Testament Times*, 92–94; Ezra 6:1ff.

to plan and the divine affirmation is that Jesus *is my servant whom I have chosen.*

To understand the mission of Jesus one has to comprehend the trinitarian nature of God, for the two are bound up together. The mission that Jesus has is to do the will of his Father and to love the world to death (his own death, that is). The power that he exhibits is not simply brute strength. His defeat of 'the strong man' itself requires great strength, but a paradox is involved in this. We see Jesus working in the power of the Spirit to fulfil the mission given to him by his Father and in it we see actions of great spiritual power associated with humility, patience and gentleness. On the one hand, he confronts the power of *the strong man* (v. 29) and *drives out Satan* (v. 26) as he heals a demon-possessed man (v. 22). But on the other hand, Matthew is concerned that his readers should understand that Jesus is one of whom it can be said, *A bruised reed he will not break, and a smouldering wick he will not snuff out.* These images from Isaiah are used to suggest a gentle, compassionate and patient approach to ministry in which even the weak and insignificant are cared for. A bruised reed was useless for any purpose (whether to make a flute, a measuring rod or a pen) and, in any case, was easily replaced by any of the many fine and unbruised reeds which grew in abundance by almost every piece of water. But it was not to be broken or rejected. A wick was meant to burn and give light, but one that smoked too much while it burnt not only gave little and irregular light, it was also a nuisance for it created a smoke-filled room. The solution was to extinguish it and replace it with another, but God's patience is such that he does not discard the most useless or the most insignificant or the one that is apparently the most worthless.

It is said that in the Middle Ages the elderly scholar Muretus became ill and, as no one recognized him, he was taken to a hospital for the poor. Two doctors discussed his case in Latin, never dreaming he could understand them. One suggested that they could use such an obviously worthless person for a medical experiment, whereupon Muretus looked up and surprised them by speaking in Latin: 'Call no man worthless for whom Christ died.' Today, while that kind of medical experimentation on adult human life is now carefully controlled, the value of life is degraded in many other situations. In a number of countries the protection and care traditionally afforded to the dying is being challenged. While there are situations where it is appropriate to refrain from providing distressful, ultimately futile and invasive medical treatment in the final stages of a person's death, there are now powerful moves towards euthanasia for an ever-increasing number of reasons, including psychiatric as well as physical suffering. In another context the most defenceless of human beings – the early embryo – is also increasingly vulnerable, as there is an increase in the medical uses that can be found for embryonic stem cells and other body parts. This is a difficult debate, but once again the mission of the kingdom is to protect the weak and the vulnerable. The mentally ill, the prisoner, the victims of abuse, the children of broken families and poverty are also those who are in need of protection and care. One cannot claim to be a disciple of Jesus and have no concern for others.

The benefits of this mission are to be for all. The Messiah's concerns will extend beyond Israel to 'the nations'. He will *proclaim justice to the nations* and *in his name the nations will put their hope*. The 'justice' that the nations are to receive is good news; they can confidently put their hope in him, knowing that through God's grace Gentiles are able to find salvation in Christ. This is not only a reminder that God's intentions were always broad, but there is also a marked contrast between the deliberate rejection of Christ by the Jewish religious leaders and the promise of salvation to the Gentile nations.

2. The Spirit and the kingdom

The tension continues to build. The crowds are continuing to search Jesus out and to bring him their sick for healing. The Pharisees, on the other hand, have become desperate in their attempts to minimize Jesus' influence and have determined to kill him (v. 14) while Matthew, in his own commentary, has increased the stakes by clearly connecting the ministry of Jesus with prophecies concerning the messianic servant. The situation is ready for an explosive confrontation and at this very point the crowds brought to Jesus *a demon-possessed man who was blind and mute, and Jesus healed him, so that he could both talk and see*. This was amazing and although the NIV translation says *all the people were astonished*, the language used is strong (as in Mark 3:21) and Hare suggests that a valid, if more colloquial, rendering would be, 'The crowds were going crazy over Jesus!'[4]

a. The crowd's question

On a previous occasion Jesus had healed a demon-possessed man and at that time, 'The crowd was amazed and said, "Nothing like this has ever been seen in Israel"' (9:33). Now the general mood has

---

[4] D. R. A. Hare, *Matthew: Interpretation, a Bible Commentary for Teaching and Preaching* (John Knox, 1993), 138.

shifted and the crowd has advanced in its thinking. The healing power involved in making a blind, mute, demon-possessed man well again recalled Old Testament prophecies and made the people wonder, *Could this be the Son of David?* Could he be the long-expected Servant of God, the promised 'son' of David who was to be king of Israel?[5] It is likely that some of the doubt they felt arose from the fact that Jesus' background and appearance – as a simple Galilean carpenter – did not seem to fit with the idea of a messianic king. But it is not appearances that matter, it is the power with which one works. And that is true not only for Christ: those who minister in Christ's name today, whether ordained or lay, do not need the trappings of title, status, position, power, wealth, numbers or any of those things which the world values and believes are essential. Whether those things are actually of use (which they may be) or are a diversion from what is really important (which can frequently happen), they are certainly of no value without the power to minister in the name of Jesus Christ.

b. The Pharisees' accusation

The Pharisees' response to the crowd's speculation was to claim that *it is only by Beelzebul, the prince of demons, that this fellow drives out demons*. It seems these miracles were so well attested that they could not be disputed and so they sought to undermine their significance by claiming they were done in the power of *Beelzebul, the prince of demons*. This was not the only time that people thought Jesus himself was demon-possessed (John 7:20; 8:48). The name Beelzebul may have derived from the Canaanite deity Baal, meaning 'head' or 'prince', and Zeboul, meaning 'height', 'dwelling' or 'abode'. Hence 'prince (or Lord) of the dwelling' where the implication is that it is the place of demons.[6] The tragedy of the Pharisees' response is that it constitutes a great blasphemy: the working of the Spirit of God in the ministry of Jesus to bring healing to the ill and oppressed is interpreted as a work of demons. It is this which will later lead Jesus to discuss the unforgivable *blasphemy against the Spirit*.

c. Jesus' explanation

Jesus responds to this criticism with three arguments demonstrating that the Pharisees' assertion is either ridiculous, a significant

---

[5] 2 Sam. 7:12–15; Ezek. 34:23; 37:34; Amos 9:11.
[6] Hill, *Matthew*, 191. Also found in 2 Kgs 1:2.

concession to the power of Jesus, or else a demonstration of the Pharisees' own complicity in evil. The first argument in response (vv. 25–26) points out that if Jesus casts out demons by using the power of the prince of demons then there is an obvious schism in the demonic kingdom. This would make no sense at all and clearly the Pharisees' conclusion is ridiculous. The second rebuttal (v. 29) is to argue that if he did cast out demons by demonic power then it at least proves that the Pharisees are conceding that Satan – the strong man – is now bound and powerless in the face of Jesus' ministry, because no-one can enter Satan's house *and carry off his possessions* (people like the possessed man who are under his control) unless he is first restrained. Thus the Pharisees' conclusion is a concession that Jesus has won a great victory. The third argument (vv. 27–28) is that if the Pharisees claim that Jesus casts out demons by Satan then the other Jews who practised exorcism and who were supported by the Pharisees must be doing the same thing. In that case *they will be your judges* and show that the Pharisees themselves are in league with Satan.

Jesus then presents a better alternative to the idea that he drove out demons by the power of Satan. Once again his explanation points us towards the Trinity, for Jesus works in the power of the Spirit to bring in the kingdom of God. As Jesus said, if *it is by the Spirit of God that I drive out demons, then the kingdom of God has come upon you*. The kingdom of God has come in the person of Jesus and this is demonstrated in the power he exercises to overcome evil. Others may have power and cast out demons, but the miracles of Jesus are fundamentally different precisely because they are the miracles *of Jesus*. They are not merely demonstrations of power, but the kingdom of God comes through them, for Jesus is the messianic Son of David, the one, as the psalmist says, whose father is none other than God (Ps. 2:7). 'What is decisive', says Allison, 'is not the exorcisms but the exorcist.'[7] It is the coming of Jesus that inaugurates the kingdom of God. The significance of this claim in the context of the development of Jesus' ministry is indicated by the fact that this is the only place that Matthew records a reference to the kingdom *of God* rather than to the kingdom *of heaven*. In every other place Matthew prefers the Jewish tradition of not referring directly to 'God', but here this is overridden by the importance of asserting very clearly and directly that God was present in Jesus through his Spirit and that the kingdom of God had come. One cannot be half-hearted about the presence of God.

[7] Davies and Allison, *Matthew*, 341.

In healing this demon-possessed man Jesus exercised extra-ordinary power. His own interpretation of this is that he drives out demons *by the Spirit of God* and that this is a sign of an even more significant truth, that *the kingdom of God has come*. This means that *the strong man* – Satan – has been defeated and that his 'house' is in the process of being plundered. This healing, therefore, is evidence of a far greater spiritual victory than one might first imagine. Others, like Peter and Paul, were able to exercise this kind of power for healing and exorcism as the Spirit was also operative in their lives (Acts 3:1–10; 5:12; 28:1–7), and yet at the same time there were significant differences. First, Paul and the other disciples attribute their ability to be bearers of the Spirit's power to the fact of their relationship with Jesus. Only those who are 'in Christ' receive the Spirit which enables such actions. Secondly, the miracles of Jesus, such as this exorcism, are associated with that deeper confrontation with evil which leads to the binding of Satan and the introduction of the kingdom of God. The uniqueness of his miracles, the extent of his power and the ability to overcome Satan are thus signs of the uniqueness of the ministry of Jesus.

One cannot remain neutral in the presence of Jesus. He follows the statement about the strong man with the saying, *Whoever is not with me is against me, and whoever does not gather with me scatters*. It is reported that John Wesley used to ask his probationer preachers two questions: 'Has anyone been converted?' and, 'Did anyone get mad?' If the answer to both was 'no' then he told them he did not think they had been called to preach. One cannot be neutral to the gospel. On this occasion Jesus said, *Whoever is not with me is against me*, but at another time he also said, 'Whoever is not against us is for us' (Mark 9:40). The former statement places those who do not actively support Jesus as enemies, while the latter says that they are friends. The two statements are not necessarily contradictory, given that they occur in different contexts. In the first case the ones not with Jesus are the Pharisees, who were clearly acting as enemies, while in the second case the ones not with Jesus are those who do good in the name of Jesus (even though they apparently do not really know him). They will be rewarded for the good that they do. No-one, however, can ultimately remain neutral. Everyone must decide on their relationship to Jesus. He continues, rather enigmatically, *and whoever does not gather with me scatters*. It is a reference to harvesting ('gathering') and it is applied to the harvest of believers at the end of time.[8] Harvesting has commenced, for in Jesus the kingdom of God is now present

---

[8] Matt. 9:37–38; 13:24–43; 21:41; 25:26.

and those who make the decision to be with him are those who are part of God's harvest. Those who are opposed to Jesus seek to *scatter* the harvest.

3. Jesus and the Trinity

Matthew describes how Jesus drove out demons, healed a blind and mute man, defeated 'the strong man' and inaugurated the kingdom of God. Elsewhere we read how he was able to still storms, walk on water, feed thousands of people, know people's minds, foretell unusual events and even raise the dead. Inevitably this led to declarations such as, 'Truly you are the Son of God' (14:33). On the other hand, the Gospel descriptions of Jesus also indicate that he did all the normal things of life: he ate, slept, bled, grew physically and intellectually, knew fear and temptation. He is presented as genuinely human. The only conclusion the faithful could draw was that Jesus was fully and completely divine and human. The church rejected the notions, (a) that Jesus was really divine and only appeared to be human; (b) that he was human and Spirit-filled but not really divine; (c) that he was divided in his life, being partly human and partly divine; (d) that he was a blend of humanity and divinity, somewhere between the two; and (e) that he was successively divine, then human, and then divine again after his resurrection. There was instead an insistence that he was truly God and truly man. This was later expressed in terms of two natures in one person. It is probably no surprise that thoughtful members of the church continue to wonder how Christ could simultaneously be God and man in body and, especially, mind and soul.

Was Jesus, as the Son of God, aware of all the needs of the universe? Did he know the thoughts of everyone he met? Was he aware of being God? The implications are significant. Sometimes there is a tendency among those who hold firmly to the belief that Jesus is both God and man actually to undermine the nature of his humanity. The very correct notion that Jesus is the perfect, sinless, Son of God is sometimes extrapolated so that Jesus is the one who never doubted or feared anything, who knew all things including the thoughts of all those around him, and who was sustaining all things by his power as God while appearing as a man with the divine plan of salvation in his mind. As God he was ready to die and be raised again knowing that this would bring salvation to the world. Some assume that Jesus always had complete divine knowledge at first hand, and if this is available by virtue of his divinity then it would seem to be logical to assume that this kind of

161

awareness was present to the infant Jesus. Some even attribute to him the full use of will and intellect and a full knowledge of God from the very first moment of his conception.[9] But it is hard to think of a Jesus like that being human in any recognizable sense and even harder to see in him an example of faith for us to follow. If Jesus, as the divine Son of God, lived permanently with an awareness of those things which are usually hidden from ordinary people, and if he had a spiritual strength beyond that of any other man, then one can ask whether he really shared our human life. In particular, if he was aware of being God, could he live a life of faith and trust as every other human is called to do? Would the incarnation not be somewhat more like the experience of the crew in the early days of the television series *Star Trek* who, when visiting an alien planet, could, in moments of danger, call out 'Beam me up, Scotty!' and be miraculously (or in their case very scientifically) transported back to the safety of the starship? This approach tends to blur the distinction between the Father and the Son. The incarnate Son is not the Father and the Father is not the Son. It is the Father who is aware, as God, of the divine plan of salvation and it is the Son who, while still being the divine Son, lives a human life with all its limitations and uncertainties and lives by faith in the Father, empowered by the Holy Spirit.

These issues have long been debated as theologians have struggled to preserve and explain how Christ can be truly human and truly divine while being one integrated person. Post-Reformation theology was agreed in affirming such a communion of natures in the one person, but differed on how these natures related. Lutherans argued that the various properties or attributes of each nature were communicated so that, for instance, it could be said that God shed his blood or was crucified and that Jesus was omnipotent (Acts 20:28; 1 Cor. 2:8). Calvinists argued that this communication of properties was verbal rather than real. The danger of the Lutheran approach of affirming the communication of properties is that of mixing or even blurring the two natures, while the danger of the Reformed approach is that of having a person divided and operating with two sets of actions. Any resolution has to affirm the reality of the two natures and the integrity of the person. There are two main types of explanation. One suggests that at the time of the incarnation Christ 'emptied' himself of some aspects of divine power and nature, while the second sees that as unnecessary and maintains that full humanity and full divinity coexist in an inexplicable paradox.

[9] Aquinas, *Summa Theologica*, Part 3, Question 34.

a. The 'self-emptying' God

The idea of 'self-emptying' is found in the early church and it was debated by seventeenth-century Lutheran theologians, but it has only been in the modern, scientific era[10] that people have seriously felt the need for a rational, logically defensible and non-paradoxical explanation of the relationship of Christ's two natures together in one person. The 'self-emptying' or 'kenotic' theory is named after the reference to the way Philippians 2:7–8 describes Christ who 'made himself nothing' (from the Greek *ekenōsen*), sometimes translated as 'emptied himself'. The self-emptying theory exists in various forms.

The modern debate began with the suggestion that at the incarnation Christ laid aside some attributes such as omnipotence and omniscience while retaining others, but soon went further and suggested a self-emptying so comprehensive that it meant Christ's divinity was called into question. At this point essential trinitarian relations were affected and biblically this approach did not fit with the fact that 'in Christ all the fullness of the Deity lives in bodily form' (Col. 2:9). Nowhere does Scripture suggest that Christ laid aside his divine *nature*.

An alternative form suggested that Christ retained all the attributes of God but voluntarily refused to use them, except in certain circumstances. This is consistent with the account of the temptations of Jesus, where he refused to give in to the suggestion that he use divine power to persuade people to believe in him. But it suffers from the difficulty that, if Jesus remains aware of all divine power and knowledge, this tends to remove him from the genuinely human dimension of uncertainty and fear and also from the need to live by faith and hope rather than by knowledge and certainty.

Finally, is it possible to say then that Christ laid aside *some* divine attributes, those which would detract from his life as a human? Charles Wesley's hymn 'And can it be?' contains a verse which says,

> He left his Father's throne above,
> (so free, so infinite his grace!)
> emptied himself of all but love,
> and bled for Adam's helpless race.
> 'Tis mercy all! Let earth adore,
> let angel minds inquire no more.

What can we conclude about the value of this way of thinking about Christ? We must first sound several cautionary notes. First, the

[10] Understood broadly, modern debate began in mid-nineteenth-century Germany.

notion of 'self-emptying' is easily developed in ways that are somewhat speculative and so care must be taken with it. Secondly, it should not be connected with the Philippians 2:7 passage as the 'emptied himself' translation is unlikely to be correct – it is almost certainly something more like the NIV's 'made himself nothing'. On the other hand, although the 'self-emptying' terminology and its connection with Philippians 2:7 has difficulties, and despite frequent criticism that kenotic theory is not biblical, it has to be accepted that many of the ideas associated with kenotic theology have become part and parcel of orthodox theology and it does in some way reflect the biblical picture of Jesus. The reality of Jesus' temptation, his suffering expressed in the cry of dereliction and the limitations on his knowledge are now much more a part of theological thinking. Mark 13:32 clearly indicates that Jesus did not know the time of the end of all things, something which an older orthodoxy found difficult to deal with, and Paul described the sacrifice of Christ by saying, 'Though he was rich, yet for your sake he became poor, so that you through his poverty might become rich (2 Cor. 8:9). 'Self-emptying' may not be the best word but in this discussion generally, as S. M. Smith puts it, 'The problem of who is Biblical cuts more than one way.'[11]

Nonetheless, any theory which empties Christ of divine nature is to be rejected, because in Christ 'God was pleased to have all his fullness dwell in him' (Col. 1:19). What is important is that Jesus is also clearly understood to be fully human in every respect. His divinity does not detract from his humanity. This is most important because it makes it possible to see Jesus as our example. It also reminds us that the incarnation is an act worthy of the highest worship and praise – rather than just intellectual analysis. Not even the angels can comprehend the nature of this act of love. This is certainly a theology which deserves to be sung!

b. The paradoxical God

An older and more traditional way of dealing with the two natures of Christ in one person begins by being far less concerned about actually finding a rational explanation for what is considered to be a divine mystery. This view means accepting that there is a paradox involved which cannot finally be resolved. The paradoxical view begins by rejecting the common perception that 'humanity' and 'divinity' are two entities in the same category which are inevitably

[11] S. M. Smith, 'Kenosis', in W. Elwell (ed.), *The Evangelical Dictionary of Theology* (Baker, 1996), 602.

opposed to one another. That is, it is often assumed that something which is human is not divine, and vice versa, in just the same way that some elements can be either solid or gas, the animal at my feet can be a cat or a dog, and the object outside my window can be a carved stone birdbath or a tree – but not both, for one excludes the other. But this, says the paradoxical view, is not helpful. While we tend to think of humanity and divinity as opposed, God does not. We find them together, both fully present in Christ. The two natures differ more in the way that water and music differ.[12] They both exist but they do not exist in exactly the same way. They can interact, just as sound can travel through water, but they do not exclude each other. More music does not mean less water. In this way divinity is not some distinct or separable part or aspect of the life of Jesus. It is something known as a result of knowing and fully understanding his whole life, which is itself the outworking of God's trinitarian nature. Jesus, the incarnate Son of the Father, is the second person of the Trinity who lives in relation to Father and Spirit, and he comes into relationship with humanity to draw people into communion with the life of God.

Jesus is not just a Spirit-filled person, Jesus is God and one should not divide Jesus' life into divine and human parts or assume that a divine attribute eliminates a corresponding human one.[13] For example, divine omniscience in Jesus is not a super-enhanced human psychological capacity. He is omniscient in as much as he is divine, and of normal, limited human knowledge in as much as he is human. His omnipotence is not an abstract power that is human strength magnified many times; his omnipotence is such that he can assume weakness and triumph through it. His eternity is such that he can enter time without ceasing to be eternal. These divine and human attributes are different, they can be related and may be considered to exist paradoxically, but they are not contradictory or opposed. For some, that is more than enough to say about the mystery of God.

4. Sin and the Spirit

Jesus' words about 'the unforgivable sin' are somewhat shocking given all that he has said about the importance of forgiveness. Elsewhere he has taught quite clearly that if a brother sins he should be forgiven and that forgiveness of others is the way to be forgiven by the Father. Forgiveness, according to Jesus, should not be

---

[12] This is a poor and imperfect analogy and should not be taken too literally.
[13] See, for example, Barth, *Church Dogmatics*, IV–1, 187–188; and Turner, *Jesus, Humanity and the Trinity*, 12–13.

exercised reluctantly or with a mean spirit.[14] Now though, he pronounces a word of judgment, that *blasphemy against the Spirit will not be forgiven*. His teaching on this comes in the form of two couplets found in verses 31 and 32. They are not precisely the same but there is clearly a parallelism. In verse 31 the first statement is that *people will be forgiven every sin and blasphemy*, and its parallel in verse 32 is that *anyone who speaks a word against the Son of Man will be forgiven*. Some think that they are meant to be interpreted as exact parallels, so that a word against 'the Son of Man' is to be understood as a word against 'a human being'. This is thought to match the first statement which, it is assumed, refers to sin and blasphemy against people. While it is possible to translate 'Son of Man' in this way (as in Mark 3:28 where blasphemies 'of men' is, literally, 'of sons of men'), given that Matthew has consistently used the term in the titular sense (as indeed he does later in verse 40 of this chapter[15]), it is much more likely that it is a reference to 'a word against Jesus, the Son of Man'. This immediately makes the overall saying more difficult to understand, however, for it is now not merely a general statement that every sin and blasphemy will be forgiven (except that against the Holy Spirit), but an assertion that even blasphemy against Jesus can be forgiven while blasphemy against the Holy Spirit cannot. Yet this is the teaching that we need to reckon with.

What is it that makes blasphemy against the Spirit so different and unforgivable? As we reflect on this we must bear in mind three important facts. The first is technical, that the text does not explicitly interpret the meaning for us. Consequently, Dale Allison claims, 'As it stands Mt. 12.32 has no obvious meaning.'[16] One therefore has to be careful in determining the meaning of this verse. The second point is a pastoral concern: many people have suffered the fear of having inadvertently committed the unforgivable sin. They need some clear help in this matter. The third is that to understand the unforgivable sin one needs to treat it as a matter of trinitarian relations, given that sin against the Son of Man, the second person of the Trinity, is specifically said not to be unforgivable, while sin against the Hoy Spirit, the third person of the Trinity, is unforgivable. A number of solutions have been proposed.

(1) It has been suggested that the claim that a sin is unforgivable is simply hyperbole. Elsewhere Jesus uses this technique to make a point: one must 'hate' father and mother to be a disciple; the disciples should 'cut off their hand' if it sins. But there is no indication in the text that this is purely an exaggeration. The

[14] Luke 17:3–4; Matt. 6:14; 18:21, 31–35.
[15] Also see Matt. 8:20; 9:6; 10:23.
[16] Davies and Allison, *Matthew*, 348.

language is devoid of the imagery that is sometimes used with hyperbole, it is measured and careful language and repeated to give clarity. It does not seem to be hyperbole.

(2) Another suggestion is that this does nothing more than restate the Old Testament position that there are some who are not forgiven and who are lost to God.[17] However, any explanation has to deal with the fact that this is Jesus' teaching and it has to be interpreted in the light of his new teaching on the radical importance of forgiveness. It also seems that there is an additional element involved here: not only is this sin not forgiven, it seems that this sin *cannot* be forgiven *in this age or in the age to come.*

(3) A third possibility is to say that those who rejected Jesus in the time of his earthly ministry can be forgiven because he was, at that time, not fully revealed as the divine Son of Man. On the other hand, those who spoke against the Holy Spirit after Pentecost cannot be forgiven as they have a fuller knowledge of what they are doing in rejecting God. But this is not convincing, as this sense is not reflected in the tenses used in these sayings.

(4) A related possibility is that the rejection (at any time) of the 'human Jesus' can be done in ignorance of his true significance because the identity of the incarnate Son of Man is veiled. The Spirit, however, has to be recognized as the Spirit of God before any rejection is possible and so it is a deliberate, wilful sin which cannot be forgiven. This interpretation means, of course, that wilful sin cannot be forgiven and this will leave some people who have resisted God in the past with great uncertainty concerning their salvation. This is a very real pastoral problem for some and it does not seem to fit with the grace of God as expounded elsewhere in the New Testament. It also seems inconsistent to suggest that the apostle Peter can be forgiven for his wilful and knowledgable denial of Jesus,[18] while one who at some point in his or her Christian walk deliberately denies the presence or the work of the Holy Spirit can never be forgiven.

(5) Consequently, at least since the time of Augustine, it has been argued that 'the unforgivable sin' does not refer to any single act, whether done in ignorance or wilfully, but has to do with a long-lasting, even permanent attitude of impenitence. This requires a state of moral insensitivity which is caused by the refusal to respond to the guiding work of the Spirit. This was the Pharisees' condition when they declared what was good to be evil. It is only by the Spirit that one can recognize goodness and truth (John 16:8). If one rejects

---

[17] Num. 16:30, 31; 1 Sam. 3:14; Isa. 22:14.
[18] Matt. 26:75; John 21:15–20.

THE MESSAGE OF THE TRINITY

the guidance of the Spirit then it eventually becomes impossible to be forgiven simply because one no longer cares whether one is forgiven or not. One's own deliberate insensitivity is the means by which one cuts oneself off from forgiveness. Understanding the 'unforgivable sin' as being a state of complete resistance to the Spirit therefore has trinitarian implications. Resistance to the Spirit means that there can be no union with Jesus Christ and therefore access to the Father is impossible.

More positively, those who respond to the Spirit will be led towards Christ and will come to know the Father. Our lives and our characters are gradually transformed as we listen to, or reject, the guidance of the Spirit.[19] It has been observed that 'every little action of the common day makes or unmakes character'. The truth is that we grow in virtue as we practise it. As character informs action so action informs character. This does not mean the elimination of all sin. Indeed, as one moves on in the Christian life one should become more and more attuned to sin, because as the Holy Spirit works on our lives we will recognize that what was not sin yesterday may be seen as sin today. This is not because the sin has changed, but because we have. All the great saints are agreed that growth in holiness involves an increased sense of sinfulness. This should keep us from the delusion that we can, in this life, completely rid ourselves of sin. This should make us ever more ready to rely upon the indwelling and guidance of the Spirit, the grace and forgiveness of Christ and the love of the Father.

[19] Rom. 9:1; 1 Cor. 8:7; 2 Cor. 1:12; 1 Tim. 4:2.

John 14:15–31
9. Teaching: knowledge of God

1. The God of life

Although he does not use the word 'Trinity' there are few descriptions of the inner, trinitarian life of God as profound and as important as the words of Jesus recorded in John 14. The trinitarian character of his teaching is seen both in the overall structure of the passage and in particular verses. In terms of structure Jesus' teaching is presented in three sections (15–17; 18–21; 22–24) which parallel one another in content as they discuss the coming of the Holy Spirit (the Advocate), then the resurrected presence of Jesus and finally the indwelling of the Father. Each of the three sections contains parallel propositions concerning (a) the relationship of love and obedience, (b) the presence of God (either Father, Son or Spirit), and (c) the world's rejection of God (either Father, Son or Spirit). Before we consider the implications of this let us look in a little more detail at the parallel statements which produce this trinitarian structure.

(a) *The love of God*: each of the three sections has as its premise statements which connect loving Jesus with obeying him.

- *If you love me, keep my commands* (v. 15).
- *Whoever has my commands and keeps them is the one who loves me* (v. 21).
- *Anyone who loves me will obey my teaching* (v. 23).

The first statement makes the connection of love and obedience, the second presents it in reverse, while the third section generalizes it to refer to anyone. They all make essentially the same point, emphasizing that genuine love entails obedience.

(b) *The presence of God*: each of the love-obey statements is followed by a promise of divine presence.

169

- The Holy Spirit is *another advocate to ... be with you forever* (v. 16).
- Jesus promises that *I too will love them and show myself to them* (v. 21).
- Jesus comes with the Father: *we will come to them and make our home with them* (v. 23).

The call for love and obedience is explicitly and carefully associated with the presence of each member of the Trinity. Clearly there is a message in this.

(c) *The rejection of God*: the parallelism then continues in that each section contrasts the presence of God in the life of the believer with the world's rejection of Father, Son and Spirit.

- The Spirit: *the world cannot accept him, because it neither sees him nor knows him* (v. 17).
- Jesus: *the world will not see me anymore* (v. 19).
- The Father is rejected because the rejected words of Jesus *belong to the Father who sent me* (v. 24).

The overall message of this section is clear, and is repeated in different ways for each of the members of the Trinity: to love God is to obey him, but this is only possible when God is present, and if God is absent it is because he has been rejected. This is then followed up with a brief but explicitly trinitarian conclusion (vv. 25–26) in which Jesus speaks of *the Advocate, the Holy Spirit, whom the Father will send in my name*. With this in mind we can now turn to the practical implications involved in this teaching, beginning with the love-obey statements.

a. Security in obedience

Jesus' conditional statement, *If you love me, keep my commands*, and the two related love-obey statements establish as a basic principle the connectedness of love for God with obedience to his commands. The connection approaches the level of the definition found in 1 John 5:3, *This is love for God: to keep his commands*. The asymmetrical form of this relationship – that God commands and people obey – is an important and enhancing aspect of the relationship between God and his people. It is a mistake to imagine (as some do) that God's requirement for obedience turns the relationship into an austerely authoritarian, distant or domineering form of relationship. Love of another often requires such an asymmetrical relationship in which one party takes the initiative. While the love between a parent and a young child is equal in many senses (including, for example, emotional commitment and intensity), the parent has to exercise a greater level of care and responsibility for guiding the child and ensuring that the relationship is able to continue in a healthy way. The parent needs to be thinking and acting on behalf of the child and this includes seeing things from the child's side and actively helping him to develop the strength of character which will enable him to be obedient to the guidance which is given. For the sake of the relationship the parent sometimes needs to command and for his own sake the child needs to learn to be obedient. In a similar way God has taken the responsibility for establishing a love relationship with his people and one aspect of this being a healthy relationship is that people need to obey his commands. Love and obedience go hand in hand.

What are these commands that are to be obeyed? Primarily Jesus is referring to the things he has just been teaching them, concerning *servanthood* ('I have set you an example, that you should do as I have done for you', 13:15), *love* ('As I have loved you, so you must love one another', 13:34) and *faith* ('believe me when I say that I am in the Father and the Father is in me', 14:12). Ultimately though, the commands which are to be obeyed include the whole word of God found in the Scriptures, for Jesus himself affirms the validity of 'all the Law and the Prophets'.[1] These commands concern every dimension of human life and relationships and they are given for one reason only: because they are good for us. God does not command in order to demonstrate his power, or in order to boost his ego, or to assert control over the less powerful. These are human motives for control. God loves us and so his commands are always and only given for our good. Sometimes it is patently obvious that these commands are for our own good, such as when God commands us not to murder, simply because it is damaging, in different ways, to all sorts of people. At other times it is not so obvious to everyone that what God commands is always good. Scriptural injunctions against premarital intercourse, for example, are sometimes assumed to derive from a God who is somewhat austere and joyless. But social research indicates that the widespread practice of living together prior to marriage seems to contribute to higher levels of relationship difficulties and a higher breakdown rate within marriage, because the critical, initial phase of the relationship which sets the pattern for the later stages has been based on something less than full commitment. This illustrates the fact that whether it is immediately apparent or not, God's commands are for our good.

[1] Matt. 7:21; 22:40; Rom. 3:21.

Some commands of God, particularly those Jesus was teaching about in this passage, concerning servanthood, love and faith, are very open-ended. They require the children of God to act with initiative and love in treating others with all possible care. Obviously this produces results which are good for the other, but for many Christians the desire to serve others is countered by the feeling that it involves an indefinite, possibly very great, cost to oneself in time, effort, money, emotion or energy. What is needed is a commitment to love and obedience which is grounded in the security of knowing that God always acts for our good. It releases our hold on 'self' and deals with those concerns that our obedience will diminish our own life in some way. In fact, obedience produces character, develops the life of the individual and helps us move towards a maturity in love.

b. Maturity in love

To love God is to obey him, and to be obedient is to love him. Indeed, the Christian life could be defined as a life of obedient love. It is interesting that Christians are often known simply as 'believers' without any need to say anything further, as in the book of Acts where we read that 'Peter stood up among the believers (a group numbering about a hundred and twenty)'.[2] However, Christians could just as easily have become known simply as 'the lovers' – in which case it might have been said, for example, 'All the lovers were together and had everything in common' (Acts 2:44). That would have been at least as appropriate as a reference to 'believers'. Obedient love is central to the Christian life. Obedience is, of course, the dimension of love that people are likely to find the hardest to accept. Even a secular culture can accept the simple message that 'all you need is love' and is likely to agree with Augustine's oft quoted saying, 'Love God and do as you like.' But Augustine's epigram is often misunderstood. It certainly does *not* mean that if you have the right motive – love – you can do whatever you like. In no way does it invalidate the use of moral rules or the need to be obedient to God's commands. In the original context it was said with respect to the use of arms against a schismatic group known as the Donatists and the saying is more like, 'Do in love what needs to be done, whether it *looks* loving or not.'[3] To suggest that it implies love without rules is to ignore the

---

[2] Acts 1:15; and subsequently in 2:44; 4:32; 5:12, etc.

[3] See J. Fletcher who, in *Situation Ethics* (SCM, 1966), 79, recognizes that this is not an encouragement to antinomianism, and Fairweather and McDonald, *The Quest for Christian Ethics*, 85–86.

view of ethics which Augustine was putting forward in which the individual is transformed and redirected by God and is guided entirely by his grace. If we follow the way the world understands love it is necessary to say that love is *not* all you need. The real basis of love is that it begins within the relationships of the Trinity. The love of God is revealed and defined in the self-sacrifice of God in his Son. And our response to him is to be one of obedient love, involving discipleship and commitment. Perhaps the way the church has taught about 'love' has been influenced by the way the world understands love, so that a call to obedience to a set of moral standards runs counter to the self-indulgent freedom that the instruction to 'just love' *appears* to offer. But God is a God of holy love. There is such a thing as sin and life is not just a playground for self-gratification or an arena in which the form of love can constantly be remoulded to fit human desires.

Dietrich Bonhoeffer is well known for his discussion of the way that belief is connected with obedience. Love is connected with obedience in the same way. Bonhoeffer argued, first (in line with the thinking of his day), that only believers will obey the commands of God and, secondly (in opposition to the trends of his day), that only the obedient actually believe. There is, he said, no such thing as a disobedient believer. It is no use claiming to be a believer while failing to obey the call of the gospel. The failure to obey is evidence of a lack of belief. In this way he challenged a complacent church satisfied with what he called 'cheap grace' – grace without commit-ment.[4] This applies to love and obedience: only lovers of God obey his commands, and only the obedient are actually lovers of God, irrespective of what they may say. In any relationship, when people *say* they love but do not obey the necessary obligations of that relationship it causes pain and grief. Love is not emotion without commitment or an attitude devoid of action; love is a commitment to action and a failure to be obedient is a sign of immaturity in love.

As time goes by greater responsibility is to be expected in any relationship. Parents would be desperately disappointed if their young children did not gradually move beyond being told to get dressed or how to speak politely. Parents want their children to grow and mature in every way and this occurs when the child is able to internalize appropriate behaviours, rather than having to continue to rely on an external authority. Obedience to God is internalized through the presence of the Holy Spirit and the Christian life is a continuous, lifelong exploration of this relation-ship. It is important to note that each of the three love-obey

---

[4] D. Bonhoeffer, *The Cost of Discipleship*, 69.

173

statements is immediately followed by a promise that God would come to those seeking to love and obey. After the first one there is the promise of *another advocate to ... be with you forever*, after the second Jesus promises, *I am in you*, and says, *I will show myself* to you, and finally the Father and Jesus together promise that they will *make our home with* the one seeking to love God (14:15, 21, 23). The point is made that the command to obey is not something that we are able to do in our own strength: it can only be done with God. There is a stress on the continued presence of God in the life of the lover of God. How important is this fact? It is absolutely critical. Fortunately, the fundamental Christian message concerns not what we ought to do, but what God has done and is willing to do. In fellowship with him we can be lifted above what is humanly possible.

c. Community in God

Jesus teaches the disciples that he, the Spirit and the Father will enter into a new and close relationship with those who love him. The nature of this liaison is expressed in a number of ways, each with increasing intimacy. First, there is the language of *association*: Jesus promised, *I will not leave you as orphans*, and he will 'come to' believers. Likewise the Spirit will be 'with' them (vv. 15, 18). Secondly, there is the language of *revelation*: Jesus promises that he will 'show' himself to them and they will be able to 'see' and 'know' the Spirit and he will 'teach' them (14:21, 17, 26). This is significant, for the Spirit is the *Spirit of truth* who teaches *all things*. Finally, there is the language of *habitation*: the Spirit actually comes to 'live with', and the Father and the Son 'make their home with', the believer. The word used for the *home* that God makes with the one who loves him is the same word that is used of the Father's heavenly house where believers will meet with him (14:2). Here, though, it is used for the indwelling of the Father and the Son with the believer. God does not just live 'with' his people, for the Spirit and Jesus live 'in' the believer while the believer is said to be 'in' Jesus (14:17, 23, 17, 20). Humanly speaking, while it is possible to live closely with another we cannot live 'in' them. This is obviously a most intimate and unique form of relationship for which there is no parallel. This life 'in' God is closely related to the intimate, inner life of the Trinity. As the persons of the Trinity are 'in' each other, so the persons of the Trinity are (in a related, though not identical, sense) 'in' the believer.

The early Fathers of the church used to describe the inner relational dynamic of the persons of the Trinity in one another as *perichoresis.* This concept denotes a unity of three persons in one. It is defined in many ways, as 'an intimate indwelling', 'complete interpenetration', 'mutual life' and 'coexistence'. All these are attempts to explain the biblical terminology of 'living together' and being 'in' one another. Jesus makes the perichoretic relationship of the three persons of the Trinity the foundation for the union of God with the believer when he puts them together, saying, *I am in my Father, and you are in me, and I am in you.* It is often said that *perichoresis* originates from a reference to dancing ('to dance about'), but this is an unlikely origin for the word – although that is perhaps a pity as it is a helpful image. It can also be a wonderfully dynamic picture of the life of God as it suggests that Father, Son and Spirit are engaged in a close, joyful, loving dance, weaving together in perfect harmony. The Shakers, an eighteenth-century faith community, used dance as the main basis of their worship.[5] They danced before God and the intricate patterns of their dance reflected his divine nature. Sydney Carter adapted a Shaker tune and used dance as a metaphor for the divine life in his song 'The Lord of the Dance'. The analogy suggests that when Jesus seeks union with believers (*I am in my Father, and you are in me*) he is inviting us to join in the divine dance.

> Dance, then, wherever you may be,
> I am the Lord of the Dance, said he,
> And I'll lead you all, wherever you may be,
> And I'll lead you all in the Dance, said he.

Of course, there are other analogies for the way Christ lives in us and we live in Christ. Picture a bottle which is tossed into the sea: the sea is in the bottle and the bottle is in the sea. A more personal analogy for the relationship the believer has with God (or which the Beloved has with his lovers) is marriage. It is a relationship in which 'two become one' and it is described in Ephesians as a relationship which reflects something of the mystery of God's relationship with his people (Eph. 5:32). Marriage is probably the closest one can come to experiencing life 'in' another, but even there the analogy is not perfect. God is in the believer and the believer is in God in a unique manner.

The presence of the three members of the Trinity in the life of the believer (or 'lover') is undivided: the presence of Jesus means the presence of the Spirit and the Father as well. Jesus says, *I will come*

[5] They were a North American group related to the Quakers (The Society of Friends).

175

to you and the Father *will give you another advocate*, and finally Jesus brings the Father: *we will come to them and make our home with them*. The crucial factor in this is the individual's relationship with Jesus and his command to love and obey. The Spirit does not come unless Jesus asks the Father and the Father does not come apart from Jesus. Conversely, the rejection of Jesus is a rejection of all. Tragically, people do this. Jesus contrasts those who love God with *the world* which cannot or will not accept him because it refuses to hear the words of Jesus and does not love Jesus (14:17, 19, 24). In the end, as Augustine said, 'love separates the saints from the world'.[6] Clark Pinnock says, 'It would be nice to be able to say that all will be saved, but the question arises, "Does everyone want to be saved?" What would love for God be like if it were coerced? There is a hell because God respects our freedom and takes our decisions seriously – more seriously, perhaps, than we would sometimes wish. God wants to see hell completely empty; but if it is not, He cannot be blamed. The door is locked only on the inside.'[7]

2. The life of God

a. The love life of the Trinity

It is through love and obedience that each person finds his or her way into union with God. But love and obedience are not only important for human life, they are also at the heart of the inner relationships of the Trinity: *Jesus loves the Father and does what the Father commands* (14:30). The apostle John, who, alone of the Gospel writers, recorded the teaching of Jesus found in chapters 14 to 17, obviously understood the divinely internal and eternal significance of love. For him love was not just a good way to behave, an apt personal philosophy, an attitude which gave a good return or even an obligation required of disciples. It was the essence of God which provided the form of the relationships of the members of the Trinity and a foundation for understanding all things. His focus on love is seen in the fact that John was almost certainly 'the beloved disciple' (21:20), he was the author of the epistles of love[8] and, according to a legend recorded by Eusebius, the fourth-century 'Father of church history', he was known in his old age for having no other theme than love. There are not too many difficulties in imagining that the author of a Gospel in which love is such a central subject would never stop talking about it. From his

---

[6] Brown, *John*, 648.
[7] Pinnock, *Reason Enough*, 116–117.
[8] 1, 2 and 3 John.

records of Jesus' teaching concerning love it is possible to begin to comprehend the various trinitarian relationships which emphasize the distinctions of Father, Son and Spirit, for they are rooted in a dynamic love relationship. These three are persons-in-love with distinctive relationships and functions. Father, Son and Spirit are not just three equivalent, interchangeable names. They are persons who can be distinguished and they relate to each other. Jesus can refer to himself and the Father as 'we' and the Spirit as 'another', and they are all able to love. The Spirit is the member of the Trinity most frequently misunderstood as either an impersonal force or simply a way of talking about the presence of Jesus, but this is to diminish the Spirit's nature. Michael Ramsey put it this way:

> To say only that the Spirit is the impact of God or the impact of Jesus is to do less than justice to the Christian experience, for the Holy Spirit was felt to be one who from within Christians' own lives makes a response to Jesus and to the Father ... It is here that the doctrine of the triune God begins to emerge, not only as a mode of divine activity but as a relationship within the life of deity ... Christians were encountering not only their own response to God but the relation of God to God ... The fourth Gospel takes the further step of suggesting that the divine relationship, known in the historic mission of Jesus and its sequel, reflects the being of God in eternity.'[9]

By revealing the Father in the Spirit, Christ has disclosed for us 'the secret nature of the living God'[10] and has shown us the depths of love in the Trinity. Only the Father knows the Son and the Son the Father, and the Holy Spirit knows the Father and the Son. There is a unity in the Godhead for one is never without the other. God is the perfect unity of persons, an eternal relationship of love, and in each person there is a unique way of giving and receiving love. It is this nature which overflows in love for the world and which seeks to draw people, and the whole created cosmos, into this divine, dynamic relationship.

b. The social relationships of the Trinity

While love is the essence of the trinitarian life of God, the various persons and their relationships (Father-Son, Father-Spirit and Spirit-Son) are all different. The Spirit, for example, is not simply

[9] Ramsey, *Holy Spirit*, 119–120.
[10] Diodochus of Photike Catechesis, cited in Oliver Clement, *The Roots of Christian Mysticism*, 59.

another 'son' for it is the Son who becomes incarnate; it is the Spirit who witnesses to the Son rather than the Father; and it is the Father who is the origin of life for the Son and the Spirit rather than the other way around. To blur these distinctions or confuse the relationships would be to lose sight of the complete work of God and the proper ordering of the trinitarian relationships. In the early church, for example, the 'patripassianists' said that the Father suffered as the Son, but the church rightly regarded that as a mistaken view. The Father may suffer as one who loses a child but only Jesus dies upon the cross. A right understanding of the persons and the relationships of the Trinity enriches the worship, the spiritual life and the discipleship of the church.

A widespread recognition of this has led to a resurgence of interest in the social relationships of the Trinity, to counter what many see as the Western tendency towards stressing the unity of God at the expense of the sociality and relationality of the persons. These explorations have taken a number of approaches.

(a) Some, like John D. Zizioulas, have argued that the philo-sophical trinitarianism of the ancient Fathers is the best approach.[11] In fact he argues that the critically important concept of 'person' owes its form to the trinitarian reflections of patristic theology. Zizioulas emphasizes the fact that relationality is of the very essence of personhood – whether human or divine. Divine and human 'being' only exists in communion and there is no person without relationships. He links together the communion of divine and human persons and the doctrine of the Trinity with the doctrine of the church, the community of God.

(b) Jürgen Moltmann also stresses a 'social' doctrine of the Trinity but does more to base it in the events of salvation, centred in the cross, though his trinitarian reflection on it is not primarily focused on the cross as the salvation of the world but as an event in the life of God.[12] It reveals the inner relationship – and the alienation – between the Father and the Son exemplified in the cry of dereliction, 'My God, my God, why have you forsaken me?' (Matt. 27:45): God is defined and known by this death. Amongst other things, Moltmann was trying to deal constructively with the problem of suffering, a universal human concern which, he argued, also lay at the centre of God's being. God knows suffering and can deal with it. Moltmann was also trying to strengthen the idea of trinitarian thinking as a category of thought in its own right rather than (as it is usually understood) as a subset of monotheism. He argued that to

[11] Zizioulas, *Being as Communion*.
[12] Moltmann, *Trinity*.

subsume the Trinity under the heading 'monotheism' is to lose the most distinctive Christian doctrine of all. Evaluations of Moltmann's work have varied. He has been criticized for his view of the way God suffers (the Father as well as the Son), and his repudiation of monotheism as a primary description of Christian thought has led some to think he veers too close to tritheism. But he is right to say that the Father shares in the suffering of the Son as a result of the break in their relationship and, although it is probably confusing to talk of rejecting the term 'monotheism' (as trinitarianism needs to be closely related to the teaching of the Old Testament which is consistently and correctly described as monotheistic), he is right that any description of Christianity which operates only in terms of monotheism is inappropriate.

(c) One aspect of the social approach to the Trinity is the view that the relations of the triune persons are not just modes of existence but are themselves just as substantial as the persons. This has been taken up in different ways by a number of writers, including Paul Fiddes who has written 'a pastoral doctrine of the Trinity' in which he rightly argues that the understanding of the Trinity affects the way Christians practise and experience pastoral care.[13] He connects the notion of the Trinity existing as 'subsistent relations' with aspects of life such as prayer, suffering, forgiveness and death. He argues that because persons only exist in relation to each other, it is the relations which constitute the divine nature. The perennial problem of having three persons understood as individual subjects without slipping into tritheism is overcome by refusing to be bound by the 'misleading' analogy between human and divine 'persons'.[14] A trinitarian theology, says Fiddes, cannot be built on the idea that a divine person is a subject in a way analogous to that of a human person. Therefore, the persons of Father, Son and Spirit are to be understood *as* relationships rather than as persons *in* relationships. '[T]he triune God must not, as I have been suggesting, be visualised as three individual subjects who *have* relationships.'[15] It is more correct to say that the Triune God is an event of relationships; not three persons with relationships but three relationships. Fiddes connects this dynamic view of God with the possibility of human participation in the life and work of God. Prayer, for instance, is not an action undertaken towards the person of the Father but is participation in the dynamic divine movements which take place between Father, Son and Spirit, and human suffering is interpreted in the light of the internal pain of the

[13] Fiddes, *Participating in God*.
[14] Ibid., 49.
[15] Ibid., 36–37 (his emphasis).

Trinity at the death of Christ. The undoubted positives involved in this approach are mitigated, however, by what is effectively a dismissal of the persons. While one may, for instance, be able to pray *within* a relationship ('in the Spirit'), one cannot pray *to* a relationship. The logical problem with a Trinity of pure subsistent relations is that they cannot act. And biblically, in order to do justice to the account of the Father's salvation of the world through the incarnation of the Son and the life of the Spirit, one must understand the trinitarian persons *as subjects able to act and relate*. It is certainly true that there are no persons without relations, but it is equally true that there are no relations without persons. Father, Son and Spirit are not merely descriptions of God as fatherly, filial and spiritual: Scripture bears witness to active relationships between them. The three mutually indwell each other without ceasing to be distinct persons (John 17:21). They are distinct though related centres of consciousness and action.

While there is now a wealth of trinitarian theology to draw upon, calling something 'trinitarian' does not automatically make it so and does not guarantee that it is right or useful. It is important to avoid the tendency, inherent in any theology which stresses the 'essential' nature of trinitarian thought, to neglect the importance of the external work of salvation. The danger is of creating the doctrine of the Trinity out of purely formal concepts such as revelation, community or even love. This does not mean that Barth's concept of the Trinity as three dimensions of revelation, or Zizioulas's development of the idea of three persons out of community or Augustine's Trinity of love are to be ruled out altogether. But they have their validity and creative power only to the extent to which they accurately reflect the actual historical action of God in Christ. The doctrine of the Trinity must begin with the way Father, Son and Spirit are revealed in bringing salvation to the world and there can be no prior understanding of God other than the way God is revealed as the God of Israel. With that in mind, it is now necessary to see what this passage says in this regard.

The relationship between Jesus and the Spirit begins with Jesus indicating that he has asked the Father to send *another advocate to be with you forever* who will *teach you all things* (14:16, 26). The Spirit is *another* counsellor or teacher and in this way is like Jesus, who has previously been described as the disciples' 'teacher'. They teach in harmony and the inspiration of the Spirit can never contradict what Jesus says. The connection is emphasized by the fact that the Spirit is sent *in the name of Jesus*. This means that the Spirit is Jesus' *representative* (literally, he 're-presents' Jesus to people) and not just 'another' in the sense of a *replacement* (Gal. 4:4–6). The role of the Spirit is primarily to bear witness to Christ rather than to draw attention to himself. It is only through Jesus that we can come to know God. Jesus leads us to the Father and sends us the Spirit.

There is also a close, but different link between the Father and the Spirit. The Father sends the Spirit, who is 'the Spirit of God'. This connects the life and character of the Spirit with the life and character of the Father. This is important as there are, potentially, many 'spirits' to which one can give oneself, but the true Spirit only comes from the Father and only does as the Father says. The Paraclete lives with the believer and exhibits personal characteristics such as teaching, reminding and guiding.[16] The self-effacing nature of the ministry of the Spirit has sometimes been interpreted in terms of a subordination of the Spirit to both the Father and the Son, and in much Western theology since the time of Augustine the Spirit has been seen in a rather impersonal way as simply the mutual relationship, or the love, between the Father and the Son. In John's Gospel, though, the advocate (*paraklētos*) is fully personal and is described as 'he' even though *paraklētos* is grammatically neuter. The Spirit has a distinctive role but is fully personal and divine, equal with the Father.

In this passage from John 14 the relationship between the Father and the Son is the most problematic because Jesus describes the Father as *greater than I*. What is the meaning of this within the context of a Trinity of persons all considered to be divine? Various answers have been offered.

(1) *Eternal subordination according to nature*: some have interpreted this to mean that Jesus had a different nature from the Father, was therefore less than divine and not eternal but created at some point in time. The early church repudiated this interpretation and Origen was the first to speak of the 'eternal generation' of the Son in order to make clear the full divinity of the Son.[17] 'Eternal generation' simply means that, while the incarnation takes place at a specific point in time, the Son pre-existed and lived eternally with the Father who was the one giving ('generating') the life of the Son. This way both the Son and the Father are eternal and fully divine and the statement that *the Father is greater* than the Son cannot be taken to refer to a difference in essential nature. The point has been made in other places that if I say, 'The Queen is greater than I,' no-one would assume that it was intended to be a statement that

---

[16] John 14:16, 26; 16:13, 18.
[17] Origen (c. AD 185–254) was an Alexandrian theologian.

Her Majesty was more human than I am or different in basic human nature. Nor should it apply here: Jesus is not lesser than God in nature. This interpretation must be ruled out.

(2) *Temporal subordination according to function*: others suggest that the Son is only lesser than the Father while incarnate and living 'in the form of a servant' (Phil. 2:7). Colin Kruse suggests that the phrase *the Father is greater than I* should be interpreted in the light of both the earlier statement that no messenger is greater than the one who sent him (13:16) and the later statement that in returning to the Father he would once again receive the glory he had before the world began (17:5).[18] These indicate that the Father is 'greater' simply because he sent the Son into the world and that on returning to the Father from the world he would again receive his glory. That is, the subordination is said to be related to Christ's temporal function or work rather than to his essential nature. This is perhaps what Paul meant in 1 Corinthians when he said that 'the Son himself will be made subject' to the Father (1 Cor. 15:28). Humility and obedience were necessary characteristics of Jesus' life and they became salvation for the world. According to the writer of the book of Hebrews, 'During the days of Jesus' life on earth ... he learned obedience from what he suffered and, once made perfect, he became the source of eternal salvation for all who obey him' (Heb. 5:7–9). Salvific obedience like this is not possible without some form of subordination, and yet in it the Son remains coequal with the Father. Love and obedience do not diminish the divine relationship between Father and Son; in fact, servanthood, humility and obedience do not diminish *any* person or relationship but only serve to enhance their quality and value. If the inner relationships of God involve love and obedience, should they not be part of the life of those made in the image of God?

(3) *Differentiation according to relationship*: although contrasting the temporal with the eternal is part of the answer to the question of the nature of divine subordination, it is not the full story. When Jesus says in John's Gospel that *the Father is greater than I* it can be argued that the context is that of the *eternal* Father-Son relationship rather than a description of the temporally different functions they perform. Nonetheless, understanding this as an eternal relationship does not imply 'subordination' as much as 'differentiation'. An eternal subordination threatens the fundamental equality of the divine persons. The claim that the Father is greater should be taken, according to this view, as a statement

[18] Kruse, *John*, 312.

concerning the unique origin or source of the Son's life. He is
'subordinate' only in the sense in which a son is subordinate to his
father as the one who gave him life, or as a river is subordinate to
its source as that which gives life and controls the initial direction
in which the river flows. But, while they are the essential beginning, a biological father and the source of a river do not control the
child or the river in the rest of their life or journey. The father is
not a 'managing director' who controls everything. As Rudolf
Schnackenberg says, 'The Father is "greater" because everything
that happens originates with him and is taken to its end by him.'[19]
A relational understanding of this kind also makes sense of the
preceding phrase, *if you loved me, you would be glad that I am
going to the Father*. This means that if the disciples really knew
what it was to love Jesus fully (which at that time they could not,
for the Spirit had not yet been given to them), then rather than
operating according to their own desires (to have Jesus stay with
them) they would instead rejoice because he is returning to the one
who *is greater than I* – that is, he is returning to the place he came
from, which is where he lives in love with the Father. 'Subordination' in this sense is primarily related to a proper 'subordering' of
relationships. Each person has his relationship with the others in
complete unity and eternal harmony.

At this point it becomes clear that there are difficulties in
resolving this debate, not least because of the terminological
problems involved. 'Subordination' is used variously (and often
qualified as functional, relational, derivative, ontological, numerical
or naïve) for everything from heretical Arianism to what I have
referred to as relational differentiation (which others refer to as
'relational subordination'). This is less than helpful. At the very
least 'functional' should be distinguished from 'relational' and
'subordination' from 'differentiation' or 'ordering'. And even
though John's Gospel has been greatly used in philosophical
discussions of the inner nature of the Trinity, a text such as this
should not necessarily be expected to provide answers to debates
which did not exist when it was written. What can be affirmed is, on
the one hand, the essential equality of the persons of the Trinity
without any eternal subordination[20] and, on the other hand, the
differentiation of the three persons – whether by temporal subordination and/or relational differentiation, both of which are
orthodox formulations of the trinitarian life of God who is Father,
Son and Spirit.

[19] Schnackenberg, *John*, Vol. 3, 86.
[20] As expressed by Millard Erickson in *God in Three Persons* (Baker, 1995), 226.

3. Truth, peace and love

The three-part trinitarian structure of verses 17 to 25 (outlined at the beginning of this chapter) is followed by further reflections on the specific persons of the Trinity. Truth, peace and love are associated with, respectively, the Spirit, the Son and the Father.

a. The Spirit of truth

Jesus said that he would ask the Father to send another advocate (*paraklētos*) to be with the disciples. Commentators and translators have used many different words to translate *paraklētos*, including counsellor, advocate, convincer, friend, teacher, comforter, protector and helper, as well as the transliteration 'paraclete'. It is probably impossible to find one English word which satisfactorily equates to the original. It is primarily used of one who comes to give assistance in a law court as a friend of the accused (hence 'advocate'). The Spirit is described as *another* paraclete – like Jesus – and in 1 John 2:1 (which refers to Jesus) 'advocate' is clearly appropriate. The TNIV puts it this way: 'If anybody does sin, we have an advocate with the Father – Jesus Christ, the Righteous One.' One alternative to 'advocate' in certain contexts is 'counsellor', as long as a legal counsellor is assumed rather than a therapist. The Greek word could also be used in a more active sense than is usual for a legal advocate in a modern, Western context. As well as defending, a paraclete could teach and guide the one being helped. This is the sense found in 14:26 where it is said that the paraclete *will teach you all things and will remind you of everything I have said to you*. Indeed, context is very important for getting the right nuance. The meaning shifts between two broad senses. The first includes advocate (15:26; 16:17), teacher (14:26) and even encourager (he is *to be with you forever*, 14:16), while the second sense refers to a paraclete as one who *indwells* or *lives with* (14:17) the believer and strengthens him or her to obey. Hence comforter, convincer, friend and encourager can be appropriate translations. R. E. Brown prefers this general sense: 'This *paraklētos* does not function so much to advocate the disciples' cause before God as to mediate the presence of Jesus to the disciples.'[21] John Wycliffe used 'comforter' to translate paraclete and while today this would be taken to relate primarily to a form of sympathy, at that time it had more to do with producing courage (*con* – together, *fortis* – brave). The paraclete removes inadequacies and makes one strong. God calls us to obey and provides the strength to do it. The two senses of the word

[21] Brown, *John*, 274.

represent, on the one hand, the *acquisition* of truth and, on the other, the *ability* to live it. Of course, knowing the truth should never be separated from living it, although that separation probably occurs more in English thought and terminology than in Hebrew. Hebrew thought assumes that truth is not only to be *known* but *lived*. God now provides the means to know and live the truth, first through Jesus who is *the truth*, and then through the paraclete who is *another* like him. The Spirit *will teach you all things and will remind you of everything I have said to you*. Rudolf Schnackenberg comments, 'A Christian who lets himself be "taught" and "reminded" of Jesus' words by the Spirit is led by that Spirit into a closer relationship with Jesus ... he can more easily understand the present and the future and find an answer to the questions raised by the contemporary world and his existence.'[22] The connection of the Spirit and the words of Jesus is important for the Christian. It is important today to reflect deeply on the words of Jesus found in Scripture, and as we do so the Spirit will work to enable a deeper understanding not only of God but also of our own age. The Spirit will interpret the words of Jesus to us. The connection of word and Spirit has also been put this way: 'If you want to be filled with the Spirit then fill yourself with Scripture.'

b. The Lord of peace

Jesus told his disciples that in a little while he was going away (13:33). By this he was referring to his imminent death. He promised them, however, *I will not leave you as orphans; I will come to you*. In the Hebrew context it was not uncommon for disciples to be described as 'orphans' at the death of their rabbi,[23] and in the Greek context Plato described the disciples of Socrates as orphaned after his death.[24] The statement *I will come to you* has variously been taken to refer to the return of Jesus at the parousia, the gift of the Holy Spirit, and the presence of the resurrected Jesus. The associated promise, *Because I live, you also will live*, clearly points to the last of these options. It will be *on that day* of resurrection that the unity of life and purpose of the Father and the Son will be known, for the resurrection of the Son takes place through the Father. Then the believers will know that *I am in my Father, and you are in me, and I am in you*. As well as his continued presence as the resurrected Lord he also promises them another gift:

[22] Schnackenberg, *John*, 154.
[23] Brown, *John*, 640.
[24] Plato, *Phaedo*, 116a, in F. J. Church (ed.), *Phaedo: Library of Liberal Arts* (Pearson, 1951).

Peace I leave with you; my peace I give you. The peace which Jesus gives is virtually synonymous with salvation. It is one of the most distinctive marks of the messianic kingdom promised through the prophets. For Ezekiel the new covenant is to be 'a covenant of peace ... an everlasting covenant', and for Isaiah to 'proclaim peace' is the same as to 'proclaim salvation'.[25] It is a peace which is sharply differentiated from other forms of 'peace'.

There are two dimensions to the peace which Jesus leaves with his disciples.

(a) *Personal peace – more than a greeting*: the most common Jewish greeting is *Shalom*, which means 'peace'. It is also a blessing. Paul often combined it with 'grace' in his greetings,[26] and the church adopted 'May the peace of the Lord Jesus Christ be with you' as a formal, liturgical greeting. Any set of words can become a formality, nonetheless this greeting is vastly preferable to some alternatives. It is interesting to observe the things that people say when they meet. Where I live it has been traditionally very common to say, 'Hello, how are you?' or, 'How are you going?' or (very colloquially), ''Ow ya goin'?'. The appropriate response is, 'Well, thank you. And you?' or (more colloquially), 'No worries, mate.' Recently, however, there has been a significant and very common shift of terminology. The greeting is more likely to be, 'How are you? Keeping busy?' and the appropriate response is, 'Yes, pretty busy.' Or if the greeting is just 'How are you?' then the response is 'Keeping busy.' It is as though one has a responsibility to 'keep busy'. There is everything to commend in hard work and all sorts of activities. But the pressure to make sure that everyone is 'keeping busy' (with work or recreation) seems to reflect the worst of our culture's obsession with avoiding inactivity, as though rest or (even worse) silence or meditation or peace were inappropriate or lazy. It is possible to deny genuine 'peace' by doing too much of the wrong kind of work. This is not to suggest that the 'peace' of God is simply equivalent to doing nothing! The peace that Jesus gives can exist in the midst of activity and in quiet. While some miss the peace of Christ by inactivity (failing to engage in the work of Christ), others miss it by being preoccupied with all sorts of activities which become a substitute for seeking and trusting in God. It is his peace rather than our busyness which saves us. Is it our prayer for our brothers and sisters that they should be 'keeping busy' or 'keeping at peace'?

We can be at peace because of the promise *you are in me, and I am in you.* In Christ there is a perfect peace which is greater than

[25] Ezek. 37:26; Isa. 52:7.
[26] E.g. Rom. 1:7; 1 Cor. 1:7.

any problem we can have. His peace should permeate our lives: *Do not let your hearts be troubled and do not be afraid.* Jesus encourages us to face all our difficulties with him. Just as some people deny Christ's peace by their work, others deny this peace by their worry. There is nothing wrong with giving attention to the practicalities of life, but Jesus told his disciples not to worry about food, drink, their body, their life or how long it is, tomorrow or what to say about their faith.[27] Anxiety is a denial of the peace that God gives to his children. God cannot give us joy or peace apart from himself, because there is no such thing. The peace which Jesus gives is nothing less than his own presence in our lives.

(b) *Political peace – more than the absence of war*: the statement that Jesus brings 'political' peace does not mean that Jesus brings an end to party politics. It is a reference to peace *between* people in the broadest sense, as distinct from peace *in* people. It is social, corporate, intercommunal and international peace. It is not just a reference to the absence of war, hatred, mistrust and envy, but is meant to be a positive statement about harmony, love, community and sharing. This is an important dimension and the church must not narrow down the message of the gospel of peace to purely inner, personal, private peace. Without doubt the peace that Jesus gives is personal. But Christ's peace has many effects and the corporate life of a community, a nation and the world are important and are a focus of God's concern. On the one hand, peace is nominated as one of the fruit of the Spirit and these fruit operate in a very personal dimension as part of the transformation of one's sinful nature (Gal. 5:22–23). But, on the other hand, 'peace' is also listed with 'justice' and 'joy' as manifestations of God's kingdom (Rom. 14:17) in a context relating very much to the corporate life of the community. Peace between people is part of the gospel as well as peace in people. The political is as spiritual as the private. Just as the peace of Christ can be found in the life of the believer and yet will not be fully realized until the end of all things, so his peace can be found in the present corporate, political context and yet will not be completed until the kingdom comes in its fullness.

Jesus told the disciples that the world cannot see or know the Spirit, the Father or himself (14:17, 19, 24) and this became a matter of some confusion for Judas,[28] who wanted the world to know Jesus now. He asked, *Lord, why do you intend to show yourself to us and not to the world?* Judas wanted an immediate socio-political change. But this is not what Jesus brought. Judas's problem was probably

[27] Matt. 6:25, 34; Luke 12:23.
[28] Not Iscariot, probably Judas son of James, Luke 6:16.

that he was too influenced by contemporary messianic expectation which led him to expect the promised messiah to be publicly revealed and the reign of God to be politically all-powerful.[29] In his typical manner Jesus does not directly answer the question (3:5; 4:13) but uses it to explain further what it really means for anyone to *see* him. In this way he explains why the world cannot see him. The answer lies in the fact that *anyone who loves me will obey my teaching*. Because obedience is the key to seeing Jesus, the world cannot see him for (it is implied) the world as a whole *does not love me [and] will not obey my teaching*. But the fact that the world does not love Jesus does not mean that the kingdom of God cannot be found. The kingdom is present in Jesus and is like a tiny mustard seed which grows to become a great tree.[30]

The kingdom is real and present but not to be found in fullness and it must not be confused with either *stability* or *complacency*. At the time of Christ there was a peace of sorts. It was known as the *pax romana* – the Roman peace – and was a 'peace' established and maintained by force. But this is not peace. To believe that peace can be established by force is an illusion, a scandal. Stability is not peace, nor is complacency, and it is a mistake for anyone to claim that peace exists where there is injustice. To do so is reminiscent of the Lord's condemnation in Jeremiah of the greedy and the unjust who proclaimed 'peace, peace' while injustice, greed and dissension abounded. ' "Peace, peace," they say, when there is no peace' (Jer. 6:14). True peace requires justice and so no Christian can live complacently with injustice. There is a significant truth in the statement, 'If you want peace then work for justice.' Jesus' gospel of peace is a peace that the world cannot give and it is wrong to see peace where it does not exist. True peace is salvation, the presence of the kingdom, and it is something achieved by the life, death and resurrection of Jesus. But this is no excuse for not seeking to bring peace to the political world. Peace is a sign of the kingdom and a part of the gospel message and the teaching of Jesus.

c. The source of love

The truth of the Spirit and the peace of the Son are grounded in the reciprocal love of the Father, the Son and the Spirit. *Anyone who loves me will be loved by my Father, and I too will love them and show myself to them.* If we ask, 'What kind of being is God?' we might answer by reference to this verse or perhaps the related verse in 1 John

[29] This is also seen in John 7:4.
[30] Matt. 13:31; Mark 4:31; Luke 13:19.

4:7–8, 'Dear friends, let us love one another, for love comes from God … Whoever does not love does not know God, because God is love.' God is the ultimate reality in the universe and God is fundamentally 'being-in-love'. To believe in the Trinity is to affirm this truth and it involves being drawn into love: 'To be a human person is to be drawn progressively into the Love-life that is God's Being.'[31] What does John record Jesus as saying about love in these verses?

The triunity of love: there is no conflict between the Father and Son, they are united in love: the one who loves Jesus *will be loved by my Father* and so, says Jesus, *I too will love them*. It is in love that the Father sends the Son and it is in love that the Son willingly lays down his life. This is trinitarian unity. Unfortunately, sometimes people have misunderstood the relationship of the Father to the Son. Some have thought the Father to be cruel, even monstrous, in sending his Son to die for the sake of the world. One such misunderstanding was put in a church newsletter. It included strong criticism of any view of the doctrine of the Trinity which held that the Father sent the Son to die. Such a view, it argued, held that:

> the death of Jesus was the only way of appeasing a God who was so angry and so outraged over our sinfulness that his sense of justice could only be satisfied by the death of one without sin … If God has to be appeased and the only way of doing it is with a murder which is totally outrageous and unjust by almost any standards, just what has that got to say to our hurting community? Is that really a creative way of loving? … That is *not* what love is about! Certainly you do not love your own children or look for them to love you on such a basis. A God who operates like that amounts to nothing but a bully.

This is a tragic misunderstanding of the nature of the Trinity. Not only does the Son willingly lay down his life, but the Son shares in the life of the Father and the Spirit: they are united in a single will, purpose and nature. God does not seek another to die in his place. The essence of the gospel of salvation is that God in Christ comes to die in our place. The sacrifice of the Son is the sacrifice of God.

Love as giving: God's love is defined by its gracious, giving character. It has been said that 'you can give without loving but you cannot love without giving', and anyone wanting to imitate God's love will need to become a giving, gracious person. This is not hard; it simply depends where our heart lies, for it is a principle of love that we tend to become like that which we love. This is why God

---

[31] Kelly, *Trinity of Love*, 170.

became man – his love for humanity led him to become like us. It also explains how we can become like Christ. We inevitably become like that which we love, for in love we give ourselves over to it. It does not matter so much what we do, what counts is the love with which things are done. Paul said, 'Let us not become weary in doing good' (Gal. 6:9), not even weary of doing little things for the love of God, 'who regards not the greatness of the work, but the love with which it is performed'.[32]

Unconditional love: God's giving in love is *unconditional*. It would be wrong to think that Jesus' statement that *anyone who loves me will be loved by my Father* makes the Father's love dependent upon ours, as though he waits for us to love before he will do anything in return. No, God is not like that because before we could ever love God he acted in love for the world by sending the Son. Because God's love is expressed in the Son, those who turn away from the Son inevitably turn away from God's love. So God's love is conditional only in the sense that those who do not love the Son *cannot* receive God's love.

Love is known in Jesus: love expresses God's grace and is at the heart of Christian life and discipleship. After all other things disappear love remains. It is important to note, though, that theology and the Christian way of life are not based upon the general notion of 'love'. They are more precisely based upon the fact that 'God is love' (1 John 4:8) and even more precisely upon the love of God which is expressed in Jesus Christ. John says in his first epistle, 'This is love: not that we loved God, but that he loved us and sent his Son as an atoning sacrifice for our sins' (1 John 4:10). It is through Jesus' willing obedience to the Father that salvation comes: *I love the Father and do exactly what my Father has commanded me.*

Sometimes, however, the authentic trinitarian concept that 'God is love' is changed into 'love is God'. Deliberately or unconsciously people try to re-create divine purposes into a form which they believe 'love' would involve, rather than defining love in terms of the nature and purposes of God. It becomes a problem when people believe that it is appropriate for them to be arbiters of what 'the loving thing to do' is and disregard biblical principles. Such an approach is simply not focused enough on Jesus. Christian discipleship is not just a life of love, it is a life of love and obedience to Jesus Christ. The basis of the Christian life is not an abstract concept or philosophy but a person: Jesus Christ, who, through the Spirit, is the way into the life of God.

---

[32] Brother Lawrence, *The Practice of the Presence of God* (Whitaker House, 1982), 60.

Matthew 28:16–20
10. Resurrection: commissioned to discipleship

Matthew's account of the life of Jesus is the only one with a decisive ending. The Gospel of John may have finished originally at the end of chapter 20,[1] the ending of Mark is uncertain,[2] and Luke's Gospel finishes in such a way that it can move on to the sequel in the book of Acts. Matthew, however, chose to finish clearly and decisively and to leave his readers with the final words of the risen Lord Jesus ringing in their ears.

> All authority in heaven and on earth has been given to me. Therefore go and make disciples of all nations, baptizing them in the name of the Father and of the Son and of the Holy Spirit, and teaching them to obey everything I have commanded you. And surely I am with you always, to the very end of the age.

The words of the Great Commission found in Matthew 28:16–20 have continued to resound down through the centuries as a constant and challenging call for Christians to mission. Those who have come to know the life of God through the missionary activity of the Son are themselves given the privilege of becoming 'co-missionaries' with God. The universal and timeless nature of this commission is made clear by the way Matthew strips the context bare of all detail in order to focus entirely upon the words of Jesus. He says almost nothing about the setting (the mountain where it takes place is

---

[1] Chapter 20 finishes well but then chapter 21 seems to contain some additional thoughts.
[2] Some ancient manuscripts do not have Mark 16:9–20.

'unnamed and mysterious'[3]) and, unlike the other Gospels, there is no description of Jesus' appearance, nor is there any attempt to prove the reality of it. He does not record anything of what the resurrected Jesus did, there is no reference to his final ascension, and these few words are all that Matthew selects out of Jesus' extensive post-resurrection teaching.[4] Clearly Matthew wanted them to stand out as being of the utmost importance and he certainly achieved his aim, for they have served to form Christian life and discipleship for two thousand years.

1. Commissioned to make disciples of Jesus

The mission which is given to all Jesus' disciples – *therefore go and make disciples of all nations* – is based on the fact that God the Father redeemed the world through the life, death and resurrection of the very first missionary, his own Son, Jesus Christ. Now in these few words Jesus in turn commits his followers to a disciple-making mission. In many situations brief segments of long speeches have captured people's imaginations. Patrick Henry's speech considering the forthcoming American war for independence from the British late in the eighteenth century powerfully concluded, 'Is life so dear, or peace so sweet, as to be purchased at the price of chains and slavery? Forbid it, Almighty God! I know not what course others may take; but as for me, give me liberty or give me death!'[5] Winston Churchill's wartime speeches also contained many memorable and inspiring passages, such as when he both warned and challenged the British people, 'I have nothing to offer but blood, toil, tears and sweat.'[6] In a struggle of a different kind, civil rights campaigner Martin Luther King Jr famously preached, 'I have a dream that my four children will one day live in a nation where they will not be judged by the colour of their skin but by the content of their character.'[7] Then there is Nelson Mandela's 'there is no easy road to freedom' speech,[8] and John F. Kennedy's famous words, 'Ask not what your country can do for you ... ask what you can do for your country.'[9] These are all memorable words which sum up a powerful message. They can define a movement, inspire a nation and even

[3] Smith, *Matthew*, 336. Although it is possibly the mountain where the 'Sermon on the Mount' was given. Cf. Matt. 5:1.
[4] Luke 24:13–53; Mark 16:9–20; John 20:19 – 21:25.
[5] Patrick Henry (23 March 1775).
[6] Winston Churchill (13 May 1940).
[7] Martin Luther King (28 August 1963).
[8] Nelson Mandela at his inauguration as President of the Republic of South Africa (10 May 1994).
[9] John F. Kennedy (20 January 1961).

change the course of human history. This is what Jesus has done. Matthew records a mere fifty of all the words of teaching given by the resurrected Jesus, 'yet nothing more and nothing greater could be expressed with a thousand words.'[10] With these words the followers of Jesus are commissioned to become disciple-makers and world-changers. It is 'the unifying climax of the entire Gospel's teaching on mission that is anticipated in many ways throughout Matthew's narrative'.[11] It is a brief statement which encapsulates a whole theology.

Although these words are the culmination of Jesus' ministry they do not constitute an ending, for they also speak of the *continuation* of this ministry in the life of the disciples. The disciple-making ministry of Jesus is a privilege in which Christians may share. The Great Commission is not just an obligation which must be dutifully shouldered (though it is that), it is also a privilege which may be entered into joyfully. God allows ordinary people the opportunity to become participants in his life and mission. It is a high calling and a great privilege that Christians are able to share with the Lord Jesus, one that Christians should undertake with great commitment. The fact that disciples are called to share in his mission is not the result of necessity or desperation, it is not an act of last resort, nor is it done out of frustration. It is God's choosing and he delights in the ministry of his people. God wants to work through his people so that we can share in his creative endeavour and in his missionary love. To be a missionary is to share in an act of love with God and to be involved in mission is to discover grace. The Great Commission is not a problem to be faced, nor an obligation to be fulfilled. It is not a duty to perform, but a possibility to be explored. In mission we discover what God can do. Often Christians operate out of a sense of duty, but there are much better motives than that. Our question to ourselves should not be, 'What do I have to do?' but, 'What are the possibilities that are open to me?' By sharing in the mission of Jesus we not only benefit others, we also bless ourselves. God is revealed to us as we reach out to others.

2. Baptized in the name of the Trinity

The Great Commission calls people into discipleship and fellowship through baptism *in the name of the Father and of the Son and of the Holy Spirit*. The distinctive nature of this formula has led to the idea that it is not original, but a later insertion reflecting the theology and

[10] Smith, *Matthew*, 336.
[11] Köstenberger and O'Brien, *Salvation*, 87.

the baptismal practices of a later age when, it is suggested, baptism in the threefold name supplanted the earlier practice of baptism in the name of Jesus.[12] But it is a mistake to read this phrase from the standpoint of later theology or to treat it as the liturgical formula which it later became, and the absence of any actual textual evidence for the view that it is not original certainly counts against it. Theologically this statement need not be considered out of place at all as Matthew has already recorded Jesus' own words in which he variously describes God as Father, himself as the Son and the Spirit as the source of his power.[13] This trinitarian statement is simply a summation of the teaching Jesus has already given and is only new in the form he has used to bring these themes together. Baptism, then, is not primarily defined in terms of an action which takes place with water (although it does of course involve that) and the greatest issue is not the age at which it takes place (although that is not a matter of no consequence); it is primarily part of the disciple-making mission of the church which is defined theologically by the fact that it takes place *in the name of the Father and of the Son and of the Holy Spirit*. Baptism is a trinitarian action – it is the gracious gift of God the Father through which believers are incorporated by faith into the life, death and resurrection of Jesus Christ,[14] and become part of the forgiven, gifted and sanctified community of the Holy Spirit,[15] which is a sign of the forthcoming kingdom of God.[16] Baptism is a missionary, disciple-making activity. Too often baptism is domesticated, it becomes an in-house rite, something with little connection to the wider world, a private act of faith undertaken by individuals, rather than a missionary activity, a public act which challenges the broader community about God's grace and people's response of faith. Baptism is part of the trinitarian mission of the church.

While it is quite clear that baptism links mission with both Trinity and church, the precise nature of that relationship needs to be carefully defined. There have been a number of interpretations of it and some have been less helpful than others. A brief review of how mission has been related to Trinity and church will help ensure that the church's mission is undertaken in healthy and helpful ways.

(a) *Mission as the trinitarian activity of God*: for more than a thousand years 'mission' was understood as an activity of the

---

[12] Acts 8:12, 16; 10:48.
[13] Matt. 11:27; 12:28; 16:27; 24:36.
[14] Rom. 6:3–11; Col. 2:13; 3:1; Eph. 2:5–6.
[15] Acts 2:38; 1 Cor. 12:1; 6:11.
[16] 2 Cor. 1:21–22; Eph. 1:13–14.

trinitarian God alone. *Missio Dei*, the mission of God, referred to the Father's sending of the Son and to the sending of the Holy Spirit by the Father and the Son (John 14:26). Mission was *an action of God* rather than an activity of the church in spreading the gospel.[17] As Christianity became established in Europe as the dominant religion it was also isolated from the rest of the world by the presence of Islamic nations. These factors, when combined with the conceptual separation of mission from the life of the church, meant that the church lost most of its missionary impetus. A theological understanding of mission as the trinitarian activity of God with no reference to the mission of the church inevitably meant that the ongoing divine mission of disciple-making was unfulfilled.

(b) *Mission as an activity of the church*: eventually, the role of the church in mission re-emerged in both seventeenth-century Catholic[18] and post-Reformation Protestant traditions. Indeed, the concept of mission was turned around so that it was primarily thought of as *an activity of the church* rather than of the Trinity. The Protestant version of this can be traced through the early Lutheran missions, the German Pietist movement, the Great Awakening in North America, the Wesleyan revival in Britain and the founding of numerous mission societies devoted to the communication of the gospel around the world. The transition from the idea of mission as purely the activity of God to the conviction that the church has a responsibility for it is illustrated in the controversy surrounding John Wesley's innovation – evangelism outside church buildings![19] The belief that disciple-making was an activity the church should practise in fields, marketplaces and at work was an idea resisted by many churchgoers at that time. The same kind of shift in thinking is illustrated in the well known account of William Carey's call to mission.[20] As a young man Carey developed a vision for world mission at a time when this was not generally considered to be the church's responsibility. Some supported the idea but there was also considerable resistance to it. At a meeting of Baptist pastors Carey suggested that they discuss the Great Commission but was told by a more senior minister, 'Sit down, young man. If God wants to convert the heathen, he will do it without consulting with you, or

---

[17] Other words and phrases such as 'propagation of the gospel', 'preaching of the gospel' and 'apostolic proclamation' were used for that. See Bosch, *Transforming Mission*, 228.

[18] When they started to use the word 'mission' to describe the work of some monastic settlements (Ibid., 229).

[19] Wesley (1703–91) was the founder of Methodism.

[20] Carey (1761–1834) was a Baptist pastor who became a pioneer of the modern missionary movement.

195

me!'[21] Here was a conflict between those who understood mission as purely an activity of God and those who saw the necessary role that the church plays in it.

(c) *The church as the basis of mission*: the shift to recognize the church's responsibility in mission was, in many ways, positive but there was a tendency to focus on ecclesiology at the expense of the fundamentally theological and trinitarian dimensions of mission. This produced at least two problems. The first was that the stress on ecclesiology led to a tendency to view the purpose of mission as being to reproduce clones of the sending church. Presbyterians, Anglicans, Baptists and so forth saw their responsibility, at least in part, as being to establish their own denomination in other countries. The second problem was that the neglect of the theological, trinitarian foundation led many to operate on the basis that missiological issues were primarily methodological when, in fact, they are theological. A number of popular mission strategies have focused on purely pragmatic issues aimed only at increasing numbers attending church while neglecting other important aspects of church life. Disciple-making is not just about numbers, and it is not complete when someone is baptized. It involves an ongoing process of applying the gospel to all dimensions of life, including matters of justice, equality, oppression and politics. The Micah Declaration expresses this in terms of 'integral mission', saying,

> God by his grace has given local churches the task of integral mission ... the church is not merely an institution or organization, but communities of Jesus that embody the values of the kingdom ... Integral mission or holistic transformation is the proclamation and demonstration of the gospel. It is not simply that evangelism and social involvement are to be done alongside each other. Rather, in integral mission our proclamation has social consequences as we call people to love and repentance in all areas of life. And our social involvement has evangelistic consequences as we bear witness to the transforming grace of Jesus Christ ... Justice and justification by faith, worship and political action, the spiritual and the material, personal change and structural change belong together. As in the life of Jesus, being, doing and saying are at the heart of our integral task.[22]

[21] S. Wellman, *William Carey: Father of Modern Mission* (Barbour, 1997), 48.

[22] The Micah Network is a coalition of over 200 evangelical churches and agencies from around the world committed to integral mission. It is named after the prophet Micah whose book contains the words, 'He has showed you, O man, what is good. And what does the LORD require of you? To act justly and to love mercy and to walk humbly with your God' (Mic. 6:8). The Declaration was formulated in 2001.

(d) *Mission as the basis of the church*: this enhanced recognition of the role of mission since the time of Wesley, Carey and others led to further developments. The creation of numerous mission societies was indicative of the growing importance of mission in the minds of many people. Mission societies generally understood themselves to be fulfilling the most essential activity of the church, but the broader church was consequently able to feel exonerated from any further mission activity as long as they supported the mission societies prayerfully and financially. To some extent those who understood mission the most – the mission societies – were complicit in this alienation of mission from most church people by the focus on the 'call' (which only some people would hear and respond to) and the general need to engender support for their mission from those they identified as 'sending churches'. This reinforced the notion that mission was, on the one hand, an important activity but, on the other hand, something engaged in only by certain groups and individuals from churches. Gradually, however, the significance of mission as an activity of the church grew and developed. It came to be understood that not only is the church not the final object of mission, it is not the sending agency either. It is the church itself that is sent. This means that mission becomes an activity of the *whole* church rather than of some societies or individuals who are sent out on behalf of the church. Consequently, a failure to engage in mission is not just a failure of the church in one of its activities, it is a failure to be the church. If a church exists for its own sake it is no church. As it has been said, 'The church exists by mission as a fire exists by burning.' No burning, no fire. No mission, no church.

(e) *The Trinity as the basis of mission with the church as the means*: at this point church and mission were becoming more firmly integrated and they can be seen in their proper order, with mission as fundamental to church. It is now also possible to relate theology and Scripture to mission and church in a more helpful way. And just as it was helpful to reverse the mission–church relationship (so that mission becomes the basis of the church, rather than the reverse), so it is helpful to reverse the relationship of Scripture and mission. The significance of mission is often defended in sermons, Bible studies and courses at theological colleges by exploring 'the biblical basis of mission'. But to talk about the biblical basis of mission is to imply that missiology needs to be justified or approved by biblical theology. Of course that is, in one sense, completely legitimate, but it is also possible, and perhaps more helpful, to reverse this relationship and argue for 'the missiological basis of the Bible'. Not every good and spiritual writing is included in the canon of Scripture. The various writings of the Old and New Testaments are considered to be Scripture because they speak about God who reached out to the world in Jesus Christ his Son in order to redeem humanity. Scripture is specifically the story of God's mission to the world. Mission thinking is the foundation and the beginning of Christian theology.

The missiological basis of theology can easily be seen by reflecting on what would happen to theology generally if there was no theology of mission. (a) Without mission the doctrine of God and Trinity are lost. The mission of God reflects the inner nature of God as love. (b) Without mission Christology is a story of Jesus, a good and wise teacher, but it is not an account of the first missionary, the Son of the Father, the Saviour of the world. (c) If mission is not theologically foundational, then the church is not a community of the redeemed living in the fellowship of the Spirit – it becomes more like a social club or a private school (or even a ghetto). (d) Without a mission focus preaching will not be the message of salvation found in Christ, but will become moral advice for those who want to improve themselves. (e) Even one's theology of creation suffers if mission is not foundational. Instead of a world in the process of being redeemed, a creation that will one day be completely transformed, one would have to conclude that this – what there is now – is all there is and all there will be. By the time one has evacuated the doctrines of God, Christ, church and creation of all missionary – and therefore of all trinitarian – meaning there is not much left of Christian faith. Where a part of the church neglects the theology of mission and its relationship to the Trinity, it is in danger of ending up with a diluted and irrelevant theology.

Of course, this is not the way it is with Scripture, which is the story of God's mission to the world. A triple mission is involved. First the Father sends the Son to proclaim and embody the kingdom and to reconcile all things to God. Then the Father and the Son send the Spirit to empower, to create community, to conform people to the image of the Son and to give gifts to the church. These gifts, including the presence of the Spirit, enable the church to engage in the third act of the divine mission in which the church is sent to make disciples of all nations. Whereas previously the doctrine of the Trinity was seen as a *barrier* to mission, there is now a greater recognition that it is actually the *basis* of the mission in which the church participates. Karl Barth, often considered the premier theologian of the twentieth century, developed his entire theology in terms of the mission of the trinitarian God and related this to his theology of the church. And the International Missionary Council at Willingen, Germany, in 1952 affirmed the following statement:

198

Mission is not only obedience to a word of the Lord, it is not only a commitment to the gathering of the congregation; it is participation in the sending of the Son, in the *missio Dei*, with the inclusive aim of establishing the Lordship of Christ over the whole redeemed creation. *The missionary movement of which we are a part has its source in the Triune God Himself.*[23]

Missiological reflection continued to develop the idea of the trinitarian foundation of mission,[24] and this has helped the church move towards a new understanding of mission as primarily a divine activity. While it is important not to dismiss mission as something disciples are involved in, the emphasis should be upon the paradigmatic missionary activity of God. This is the heart of missionary activity and it should be at the centre of the teaching ministry of the church which is so important for making disciples. Theologically, mission is not primarily a human activity, it is God's mission in which we have been included. Or, as Lesslie Newbigin said, 'The beginning of mission is not an action of ours, but the presence of a new reality, the presence of the Spirit of God in power.'[25]

The most immediate implication of this is that *mission therefore starts with the trinitarian love of God which overflows in love for the world*. While it is important to understand that this love deals with human sin, mission is, first and foremost, an expression of divine love. The most important message of the church is not that the world is sinful (though this is an essential aspect of the gospel) but that Christ is beautiful, lovely and loving. If we first of all proclaim Christ Jesus and teach people to obey everything he has taught, then people will soon enough understand the seriousness of their sin. The trinitarian foundation also reminds us that the church is not the source of mission. It is God who sends and it is the church itself which is sent. The whole church is therefore called to mission for the church. The church is God's agent for mission in the world. Mission cannot be left to mission societies – unless, of course, the church as a whole sees itself as a mission society. The Great Commission has commissioned all disciples of Jesus to be partici-pants in the divine mission and baptism is not the end-point or the culmination of those disciples' commitment, rather it is the begin-ning of a life of discipleship in which they are to share in God's own mission by making disciples of others.

---

[23] N. Goodall, *Missions Under the Cross* (Edinburgh House Press, 1953), 189.

[24] E.g. Newbigin, *The Open Secret*, and Bosch, *Transforming Mission*.

[25] Newbigin, *Open Secret*, 119.

3. Sent with the Father's authority

The Great Commission is grounded in the fact that Jesus is able to say that *all authority in heaven and on earth has been given to me*. It is, in fact, nothing less than a royal decree issued by the King of Kings. It is a divine command for the church based on the royal authority given to Jesus by God the Father. This commission appears as the final verses of Matthew (28:16–20) and it needs to be understood in the light of the close parallel it has with another royal commission found in the very last verses of 2 Chronicles (36:22–23). In the sixth century BC, in the first year of the reign of Cyrus, the Persian king who took control of Babylon and Assyria, the LORD moved the heart of Cyrus to make a proclamation throughout his realm. Cyrus was demonstrating his political acumen by issuing a decree by which those Jews who had been prisoners of the Babylonians were permitted to return to their homes in Israel and rebuild the temple. Cyrus proclaimed,

> The LORD, the God of heaven, has given me all the kingdoms of the earth and he has appointed me to build a temple for him at Jerusalem in Judah. Anyone of his people among you – may the LORD his God be with him, and let him go up.

Cyrus's commission appears as the very last words of 2 Chronicles 36:22–23, in the same position that Matthew places Jesus' commission in his Gospel, indicating that Cyrus's commission to build a temple to the Lord in Jerusalem was a prophetic foreshadowing of the Messiah's commission to establish a universal kingdom throughout the world. The similarity of these commissions is seen in three ways.

(a) Each has a statement of *authority* which is given by God. Cyrus's authority is that 'The LORD, the God of heaven, has given me all the kingdoms of the earth'. Jesus' authority also comes from God but is even more extensive, for he has been given 'all authority in heaven' as well as 'on earth'. Jesus' authority has far greater dimensions.

(b) Both commissions involve a *task*. In Cyrus's case he has the earthly authority 'to build a temple for him [Yahweh] at Jerusalem in Judah'. The temple, of course, held a central place in Jewish theology. It was the centre of worship, the place where God was (Pss. 42:2; 63:2). The destruction of the temple had created an enormous sense of loss and Cyrus's commission to restore it was of critical importance. The temple even went beyond being the focus of Jewish faith and hope as it was to be 'a house of prayer for all nations' (Isa. 56:7). Jesus' commission picks up the universal and eschatological dimensions of Cyrus's commission as he called the disciples to 'go and make disciples of all nations'. The physical building of the temple is replaced by a process of spiritual building. The stones of the new house of God are faithful disciples from all nations (Eph. 2:19-22).

(c) Both commissions have the promise of *divine presence*. Cyrus allows any Jew who wishes to do so to return to Jerusalem and expresses the hope, 'may the LORD his God be with him.' In other words, as they 'go' (or, more precisely, as they 'go up' as it was usually said when one went to Jerusalem, which was on Mount Zion) God would go with them. Matthew carefully records Jesus' commission as promising that 'surely I will be with you always, to the very end of the age', maintaining the parallelism by noting that this takes place precisely when the disciples 'go and make disciples'.

Earlier, in 12:15-21, Matthew had already quoted from Isaiah to show how the pagan Persian king Cyrus was a servant of Yahweh and a forerunner of the Messiah. It is certainly an amazing thing that a pagan king is interpreted in this way, but neither Isaiah nor Matthew are disturbed by the comparison. Matthew allows the words of Jesus' commission to the disciples to stand in the same prominent place in his Gospel as Cyrus's commission stands in 2 Chronicles and, in so doing, suggests that Jesus' commission to the disciples is to be obeyed as an imperial decree given by a royal Son. Cyrus's commission concludes 2 Chronicles with the expectation that Cyrus's royal command will, in fact, be obeyed and the temple will be rebuilt, and Matthew's Gospel finishes with the same expectation that the royal command of Jesus, the Son of the almighty God, will be obeyed and that his ministry will continue through the disciple-making mission of the disciples. The point is clear: this commission is not an optional extra, not a mere suggestion, not just a good idea – it is a royal command of the King of Kings.

4. Discipled in the Spirit's power

The trinitarian character of the Great Commission continues as the disciples are made in the power of the Holy Spirit.

(a) *Disciples*: Jesus' disciples were those who responded to his call (4:18-22) and they were not chosen because of any particular virtue of their own (9:15). Although there was a group of 'the twelve' who were particularly close to him, discipleship was not restricted to them (10:2-4). Having called them to be disciples (4:18-22) Jesus immediately began what is of the essence of discipleship: 'he began

201

to teach them' (5:2). No-one can be a disciple who is not willing to be taught. Jesus' initial teaching (commonly known as 'the Sermon on the Mount', 5:1 – 7:28) provided a definitive outline of the life of a disciple of Christ. This teaching was given to the disciples in the context of large crowds (5:1) and so it is simultaneously instruction for those who are his followers and a challenge for others to become disciples as well.

(b) *Make disciples*: although followers of Jesus are often described as disciples,[26] the verb 'making disciples' is comparatively rare[27] and only Matthew 28:19 explicitly describes the disciples' responsibility in this way. Yet it encapsulates the fundamental and universal responsibility of the disciples of Jesus until the end of the age. It is a commission possible only through the unlimited power and the universal presence of the Holy Spirit, and for this to occur Jesus had to leave (John 16:5–18). The Great Commission is given by Jesus, but its fulfilment in the life of the church is only possible through the presence of the Spirit. It is the Spirit who brings Jesus to the disciples and who provides the power for the church's mission.

(c) *Go and make disciples*: it is sometimes assumed that there are two different main activities involved in the Great Commission: to 'go' and to 'make disciples', with two subsidiary, explanatory actions, 'baptizing' and 'teaching'. But the Great Commission has only one main verb, one primary action, and that is the instruction to 'make disciples'. In technical terms 'go' is a participle (literally, 'going') which is linked to the imperative ('make disciples') and so, although it shares in the force of the imperative verb, the emphasis falls on the main action, which is to 'make disciples'. It could be translated 'make disciples as you go, baptizing them ... teaching them'.

This stress upon disciple-making, or, conversely, the de-emphasis of the 'going', may be disappointing to those accustomed to using this verse as a stimulus for encouraging people to become missionaries involved in 'going' into cross-cultural mission. But, without diminishing in any sense the important place such mission has, it is ultimately unhelpful either to diminish the singular importance of 'disciple-making' by making 'going' of equal importance with it, or to identify 'mission' as an activity which only takes place when one 'goes', especially as the problems associated with equating the Great Commission with some sort of physical, cross-cultural 'going' are often compounded by the assumption that mission is therefore an action undertaken only by full-time (probably career) Christian

---

[26] Seventy-three times in Matthew.
[27] It is only found elsewhere at Matt. 13:52; 27:57; Acts 14:21.

missionaries. To think in that way is to downplay the universal importance of the Great Commission as an activity which can and ought to be fulfilled in every place, by those who have 'stayed' as well as those who have 'gone' and by every Christian disciple, not only those who are 'full-time' Christian workers. It is vital to the health of the church to understand that those who stay at home and those who work in so-called 'secular' occupations can fulfil this royal disciple-making decree just as much as those who are full-time missionaries in another culture. Indeed, sometimes those who are most deeply involved in the life of the church are the least well equipped to be missionaries on the fringes of the church or in places where the people are least aware of church or gospel.

(d) *Of all nations*: it has to be said, though, that although the stress is upon 'making disciples' rather than upon 'going', disciple-making is not an activity that can be undertaken passively, as though one can produce disciples of Christ without effort or intention, or without thought or time. The 'going' expresses the dynamic sense of the discipling mission. It is a positive activity and not something which happens accidentally or inevitably. Disciple-making involves a call to be guided and led by the Spirit into new contexts and situations. It always involves 'going' in some sense and it should be no surprise that it may mean 'going' in a geographic sense. Jesus emphasized the active, geographic nature of the Great Commission by specifying that they were to make disciples *of all nations*. The commission to make disciples of all nations deliberately removes any restriction on the gospel. Previously Jesus had spoken in more restrictive terms (15:24; 10:5-6), but now he shows clearly the full extent of the disciples' responsibility. From the very beginning of this most Jewish of Gospels, Matthew (knowing, one suspects, the words of Jesus he was going to use to conclude the Gospel) made sure that the Gentiles were well portrayed.[28] The Great Commission confirms the universal nature of God's love for the whole world. Consequently, whereas God has previously been defined in terms of relationship to Israel – as 'the God of Abraham, Isaac and Jacob' – the Great Commission now emphasizes his relationship to *all nations* and identifies God in terms of divine relationships, and once again the trinitarian implications are revealed. Rather than being the God of the Jews, the trinitarian God is revealed as the universal Lord of the whole

---

[28] Four non-Israelite women are included in the initial genealogy; the first to worship Jesus (the Magi) come from the east; Isaiah's prophecy extends to 'Galilee of the Gentiles'; Jesus ministers to people from outside Israel; and the Gentile centurion and the Canaanite woman are particularly commended for their faith (Matt. 1:1–16; 2:1–12; 4:15, 23–25; 8:5–13; 15:21–28).

world. God is now known as 'the Father of the Lord Jesus Christ' rather than as 'the Father of Israel' and so mission now takes place *in the name of the Father and of the Son and of the Holy Spirit*.

There is a fivefold use of 'all' in the Great Commission: all authority, to all nations, teaching all things, all the days, with Jesus always present. There is a stress on the universality of mission. It is worthy of note that the commission is not just to make disciples of 'all individuals' or even 'all people' but specifically all *nations*. Of course, individuals are in view – one cannot baptize nations, only individuals. Nonetheless, the use of 'nations' emphasizes the global nature of the mission: disciple-making needs to take place within each and every culture and nation. It thus affirms the value of the many cultures and people groups which exist in the world and points to the way the gospel needs to go to such people, rather than have them leave their culture in order to come to the gospel.

5. Taught to obey all things

The instruction to make disciples involves baptizing believers and also *teaching them to obey everything I have commanded you*. The ongoing spiritual development of disciples depends upon this fundamental Christian ministry.

(a) *Teaching them*: Matthew describes Jesus as 'teaching' believers, while among unbelievers he 'preaches'.[29] Given Jesus' own practice of teaching disciples in the context of crowds, however, these two activities should not be too sharply distinguished (4:23; 11:1). They are both part of the disciple-making mission. Teaching is an important aspect of evangelism, because those who are to become disciples must understand the nature of their calling and the lifestyle of the kingdom. The Sermon on the Mount is an example of this. Jesus taught about God's grace, the law, personal attitudes and responsibilities, love, prayer, wealth and true wisdom and not only the disciples but also 'the crowds were amazed at his teaching' (5:1 – 7:28). Although it may begin with a specific response to the grace of God offered in Jesus, being his disciple is not a matter of only a moment. It involves an ongoing commitment to being taught. Jesus emphasized this in saying, 'Not everyone who says to me, "Lord, Lord," will enter the kingdom of heaven, but only those who do the will of my Father who is in heaven'

---

[29] He 'teaches' his disciples (Matt. 5:2; 7:28) and those in synagogues and the temple (4:23; 9:35; 13:54; 21:23). He 'preaches' throughout towns and villages – usually the good news of the kingdom (4:23; 9:35; 10:7).

(Matt. 7:21). The making of a disciple is an activity of a lifetime. It is not a matter of absorbing a certain amount of information, it is learning for living.

(b) *Teaching them to obey*: teaching for Jesus is not just teaching for teaching's sake but something undertaken so that the disciples will *obey everything* that he has taught. The focus in this falls upon obeying *Jesus* rather than adhering to some system of teaching. 'For Matthew, then, being a disciple means living out the teachings of Jesus, which the evangelist has recorded in great detail in his Gospel. It is unthinkable to divorce the Christian life of love and justice from being a disciple.'[30] Christianity is not primarily about following some theological or theoretical system, it is not a set of ethical principles or a form of ritual, nor is it just a social system or an ecclesiastical structure. Being a disciple is about following a person. It's about Jesus, and being a Christian means knowing him and obeying him in everything. The Trinity is known through Jesus.

(c) *Teaching them to obey everything I have taught you*: it is very important to note that Jesus calls his disciples to obey everything he had taught them. Disciples are not at liberty to select what they want from the teaching of Jesus. His teaching was aimed at making a difference. Christians are to be salt and light in the world, lamps are not to be hidden away, and 'if the salt loses its saltiness, how can it be made salty again? It is no longer good for anything' (Matt. 5:13–14). If we do not obey everything that Jesus commanded then we may become stumbling blocks to others. It is said that when Mahatma Gandhi[31] was asked by some missionaries, 'What is the greatest hindrance to Christianity in India?' his reply was, 'Christians.' Before we look anywhere else for hindrances to Christian mission, let us look at ourselves. Those who listen to football commentaries may well be aware of the rather hackneyed comment about a footballer who is consistently failing to play at his expected standard: 'He needs to take a good, long, hard look at himself.' It seems to be the sportsman's equivalent of Plato's well known philosophical observation, 'The unexamined life is not worth living.' If we are not obeying everything that Jesus has commanded us, are we real disciples? True disciples of Jesus are committed to obeying all that he commanded, and Jesus describes these disciples as wise, righteous and blessed (7:24; 5:20; 5:1–12).

---

[30] Bosch, *Transforming Mission*, 81.
[31] Gandhi (1869–1948) was the architect of Indian independence.

6. Guaranteed the presence of Jesus

Although Jesus departs, he does not leave his disciples. The words of the Great Commission are followed by the promise of Jesus' continued presence, *and surely I am with you always, to the very end of the age*. These final words of Matthew's Gospel echo some of its first words, where Jesus' birth is interpreted in the light of Isaiah's prophecy, ' "They will call him Immanuel" – which means, God with us.'[32] Jesus is God who lives with his people. Although the mode of his presence may change, Jesus is always with his disciples.

While this promise of Jesus' presence is given to all disciples in every era until *the very end of the age*, in the immediate context it comes as a direct response to the doubt which some of the disciples expressed when they saw the resurrected Jesus. The eleven disciples met with Jesus on a mountainside in Galilee and Matthew says that *when they saw him, they worshipped him; but some doubted*. Morris suggests that it should be 'hesitated', as if they were not sure it was Jesus, while Köstenberger and O'Brien say 'they lacked resolve'.[33] Whichever word is used, it indicates significant uncertainty and it should not be ignored. It does not seem to be the case that *some* worshipped Jesus while *some* doubted. Apparently *all* of them worshipped him, but *some* of them also doubted. What did they doubt? Did they doubt themselves? Did they doubt that they actually saw anything? Did they doubt that the person they saw was really Jesus? Or did they doubt that he should be worshipped as Lord?

It is difficult to know which of these doubts was foremost in the disciples' minds, but whichever it was, this kind of hesitation is consistent with other descriptions of the interactions between the disciples and the resurrected Jesus.[34] Interestingly, references to the weaknesses of the disciples are apparently important to Matthew,[35] and his recording of them ought to be greatly encouraging to those today who are hesitant in faith or who doubt some aspect of their experience of God. Being a disciple of Jesus does not mean that one is immune to doubt. There are always some who have 'little faith' and it is important to recognize that doubt is not the alternative to faith or worship. Matthew is clear that they can be connected. Interestingly, there are only three occasions in his Gospel where the

---

[32] Matt. 1:23; Isa. 7:14.
[33] Morris, *Matthew*, 744–745; Köstenberger and O'Brien, *Salvation*, 103.
[34] Luke 24:16, 22, 36; John 20:8, 11, 24; 21:4.
[35] Matt. 8:26; 14:31; 16:6; Luke 8:25; 12:26.

disciples are said to worship Jesus and in all three cases doubt or fear is also present.[36]

Sometimes we have exaggerated pictures of the heroes of the faith and it is possible to think that stressing their utter faithfulness and their total commitment will be encouraging to other disciples. While that is indeed often the case, sometimes followers of Jesus can become only too aware of their fallibility, their lack of faith and their less than complete obedience. In those situations this passage helps in two ways. First, it is good to be reminded of the example of the very human disciples of Jesus. Followers of Jesus today can be assured that hesitation or doubt does not exclude one from the kingdom now, any more than it excluded the disciples of Jesus' day. Their example is an encouragement to disciples today. Bosch comments that 'mission never takes place in self-confidence but in the knowledge of our own weakness'.[37] Secondly, and far more importantly, this passage shows us what Jesus does. He meets the disciples' doubt and hesitation with a gracious promise that they will not be left alone: *surely I am with you always, to the very end of the age.* The disciples doubted what they had seen, but now it is what they hear that counts. The words they hear are Jesus' own promise and it is a reassuring conclusion to the Gospel.

The disciple-making mission which has been given to the church takes place not only in the tension between faith and fear but, more importantly, in the presence of Jesus himself. What makes mission possible is not self-confidence but confidence in Jesus. Early in Martin Luther King's struggle against racial discrimination a threat was made to kill him and his family. Later he recalled in a sermon how, sitting at his kitchen table full of fear for his wife and children, he prayed, 'Lord, I'm down here trying to do what is right ... I think the cause that we represent is right. But Lord, I must confess that I'm weak now. I'm faltering. I'm losing my courage.' Then he described what happened next. 'And it seemed to me at that moment that I could hear an inner voice saying to me, "Martin Luther, stand up for righteousness. Stand up for justice. Stand up for truth. And lo, I will be with you, even to the end of the world" ... I heard the voice of Jesus saying to fight on. He promised never to leave me, never to leave me alone.' The promise of the presence of Jesus made it possible for King to continue in the face of tremendous opposition. Although it eventually cost him his life (he was killed by an assassin's bullet) he was able to achieve much, and even though his own life was a mixture of fear and doubt as well

---

[36] Matt. 14:31–32; 28:9–10, 17–20. Also see Mark 9:24.
[37] Bosch, *Transforming Mission*, 76.

as faith, the most important truth was that Jesus was present.[38] He is always present as his people engage in the mission to which they have been called. God's promises are like the stars: the darker the night the brighter they shine.

The promise of Jesus' presence is part of the Great Commission to make disciples of all nations. It is therefore sometimes suggested that it only applies to certain people or at certain times – that is, to those who are actively engaged in disciple-making (such as missionaries and pastors), or only to people when they are actually engaged in mission (as defined in a fairly restricted manner) and, perhaps by implication, not at other times. On the one hand, it is right to connect the promise of the presence of Jesus with his command to engage in mission, as it is quite clear that Jesus will not desert or let down those who serve him. But, on the other hand, it is not necessary to see the promise as being narrow, restricted or limited in some way. The presence of Jesus in the life of his disciples does not depend primarily upon their faithfulness to Jesus but on Jesus' faithfulness to them. Moreover, the disciple-making commission itself is not restricted. It is not given to some people, some societies, for some periods of time. It is given to *all* disciples for *all* time until Jesus returns. Perhaps, rather than suggesting that if disciples go out in mission then Jesus is with them, it would be better to say that because Jesus continues to be present with his disciples they go out in mission. Looked at in that way, it helps us see again that mission is something which begins with and belongs to God. By grace he allows his disciples to join in it. Because disciple-making is primarily the mission of God, and only secondarily the mission of the disciples, those who engage in it are not only working for God but also living and working with God and participating in the divine life and the mission of God. Mission thus becomes less of a human responsibility, less of a burden and more of a joy and a privilege. While it has become commonplace to speak of mission as a mandate or a responsibility, this is not so helpful if it locates the motive for mission in something like duty or obligation rather than simple joy or thankfulness.[39]

Finally, as mission is intimately connected to the inner life of God, it is not really possible to be involved in mission without being involved in the life of God. God does not call us to mission because of some inability to achieve his purposes without us, as though he just needed workers; God calls us to mission because as we engage in it we have fellowship with him and share in the trinitarian life of

[38] From a sermon tape cited in Philip Yancey, *Soul Survivor* (Hodder and Stoughton, 2001), 20.
[39] Newbigin, *Open Secret*, 116.

God. This will support and bless the disciples of Christ whatever their circumstances. David Livingstone, the famous missionary to Africa (also known as an explorer), spent over sixteen years struggling with discomfort and physical danger (including being mauled by a lion) and repeated bouts of tropical fever as he sought to make disciples for Christ. He wrote in his journal about the impact this promise had upon him and he was well known for speaking about it later. 'Would you like me to tell you what supported me through all those years of exile among a people whose language I could not understand, and whose attitude towards me was always uncertain and often hostile? It was this, "Lo, I am with you always, even unto the end of the world." On these words I staked everything and they never failed.'[40]

[40] Cited in the sermon by F. W. Boreham in *The Protestant Pulpit: An Anthology of Master Sermons from the Reformation to Our Own Day*, compiled by Andrew W. Blackwood (Abingdon-Cokesbury Press, 1947), 164–169.

Part 4
The Trinity in the experience and teaching of the early church

Acts 2:1–47
11. The day of Pentecost

It is often said that Luke's account of the life of the early church known as the Acts of the Apostles would be better known as *the Acts of the Holy Spirit*, for it is the Spirit who is constantly empowering, inspiring and guiding the early church.[1] The second chapter of Acts is critically important, for it describes in detail the day of Pentecost which many refer to as the real birthday of the church. God had always had his chosen people and Jesus had lived for years with his disciples, but now there was a fundamental difference: the believers became Spirit-filled disciples, transformed members of the church of Jesus Christ, guided and empowered by the Holy Spirit. Luke's account of this event describes the work of the Spirit in three dimensions:

- *Spirit-filled disciples*: in verses 1–4 he describes the dramatic coming of the Holy Spirit on the followers of Jesus and in verses 5–13 the response of the crowd.
- *Spirit-filled Christ*: the second section, including verses 14–41, consists of the apostle Peter's explanation of these events in which he connects the coming of the Spirit with the life and ministry of Jesus Christ.
- *Spirit-filled church*: the final part, verses 42–47, provides an outline of the lifestyle of this infant church.

The Spirit appears throughout as the connecting theme, filling the disciples, empowering Jesus and being poured out on the young church as its source of life and strength. While much of this material deals with the relationship of the Spirit to the church, it is also possible to gain a greater understanding of the Trinity, initially

[1] See, e.g., 1:8; 4:8; 8:39; 9:31; 11:12; 13:2, 9; 15:28; 16:7; 20:23; 21:4.

because the Spirit is the gift of God and particularly through appreciation of the relationship of the Spirit with Jesus.

1. Spirit-filled disciples

When the day of Pentecost came, they were all together in one place. Who were *they*? They would certainly have included the eleven disciples and Matthias who had just been chosen to replace Judas, but the group could also have included some or all of the 120 who believed in Jesus at that time (1:23–26). They were all *in one place*, which would have been difficult for 120 if it was in someone's house, but where they gathered is not described with any more precision than that it was somewhere in Jerusalem. While neither the precise number of disciples nor the place has any great significance, the timing is important. The coming of the Spirit occurred on *the day of Pentecost*, a Greek name derived from the word for fifty and used to refer to the Jewish Feast of Weeks which took place on the fiftieth day (i.e. seven weeks) after the Passover. The theological meaning of the coming of the Spirit has to be seen in relation to Pentecost and the symbols associated with the event.

a. A new harvest

Pentecost was a harvest festival and, specifically, the time for celebration of the gathering of the firstfruits of the harvest. On that day Jews would give to God an offering of new grain and would give thanks to him.[2] Previously Jesus had used the image of a harvest to describe those ready to come into the kingdom of God,[3] and it is possible that a parallel is intended between the Old Testament harvest of the firstfruits and the beginning of the new 'harvest' of believers which began on the day of Pentecost when three thousand trusted in the Lord Jesus (2:41). These were the 'firstfruits' of what was to be a great harvest and Peter and the other disciples were the first workers in this field, sent out by the Lord of the harvest.[4] The coming of the Spirit means that this harvest, which will last until the return of the Lord Jesus, can now begin, and the Holy Spirit is clearly seen to be both the Spirit of mission and evangelism and the Spirit of the last days. Pentecost thus marks the beginning of the end and the time of the growth of the church.

[2] Deut. 16:9–12; Num. 28:26.
[3] Matt. 9:37; Luke 10:2; John 4:35.
[4] Matt. 9:38; Rom. 1:13; Rev. 14:15.

b. An inner power

Pentecost was celebrated fifty days after the Passover feast which commemorated God's rescue of the children of Israel from captivity in Egypt, when the Lord's angel 'passed over' and kept safe all those in houses marked with the blood of a lamb. This rescue was understood by Christians to be an Old Testament foreshadowing of God's release of people from their captivity to sin which was fulfilled through the sacrifice of Christ. It is likely that Luke saw, in a similar way, the gift of the Spirit as the ultimate fulfilment of the feast of Pentecost. While the Jewish celebration of Pentecost originally focused on it as a harvest festival, it eventually included a commemoration of the giving of the law at Mount Sinai. Exodus 19:1 describes this as taking place 'in the third month' after the Passover, and therefore at a time close to the harvesting of the firstfruits, allowing the two events to be assimilated. Some scholars, however, suggest that this parallel is not possible because the connection of the giving of the law at Sinai with the harvest thanksgiving at Pentecost had either not been made or was not very common in the first century AD.[5] Others suggest that is 'possible, but not certain'[6] that the festival was associated with the giving of the law at that time. It is certainly true that this emphasis was more prominent after the destruction of the temple in AD 70. But even if the law-Pentecost connection was not widely noted in Jewish teaching prior to this, it does not mean that it did not exist at all and it certainly does not preclude Christians such as Luke from seeing a parallel between the giving of the law and the giving of the Spirit.[7] Just as the law was a gracious provision of God as a means by which they were able to remain faithful to the covenant he had entered into with them, then so the giving of the Spirit can easily be seen as an even more gracious act of God by which he not only guides but also empowers his people to live out the new covenant he has established through the sacrifice of

[5] 'Some commentators have suggested that Luke intends a parallel between Moses' giving the law and Jesus' giving the Spirit, but the law-Pentecost connection may be later than Luke, and little in Acts 2 suggests that Luke makes the connection, even if some Jewish Christians before him might have' (Keener, *Bible Background Commentary*, 326–327).

[6] B. Witherington III, *The Acts of the Apostles* (Eerdmans, 1998), 131.

[7] This connection is hinted at in the way Luke describes these events as happening *when the day of Pentecost came*. Literally this reads as 'when the day of Pentecost was being fulfilled', which perhaps encourages readers to consider the true fulfilment of Pentecost. It is also interesting that fire and loud noises are associated with the giving of both the law and the Spirit (Exod. 19:16–19; Acts 2:1–3).

Christ.[8] The Holy Spirit is the Spirit of God poured out on God's people.

c. A global community

Although the significance of Pentecost is illuminated by the parallel with the giving of the law at Sinai, C. K. Barrett argues that when interpreting Acts 2 'a more important OT passage is the account of the building of the Tower of Babel'.[9] The story of this tower, found in Genesis 11, begins with the declaration that 'the whole world had one language and a common speech'. The building of a tower 'that reaches to the heavens' was the idea of those who said they wanted to 'make a name for ourselves and not be scattered over the face of the earth'. But the LORD saw what was happening and confused their language, 'so they will not understand each other', and consequently all the peoples of the earth were divided and scattered. This was the catastrophic end result of the accumulation of the effects of the sin which had come into the world with Adam and Eve, and which led to the murder of Abel by his brother Cain and then to the all-pervading wickedness which persuaded the LORD to decide to 'wipe mankind from the face of the earth' through a great flood.[10] The story of the tower was the final act in this tragedy. It highlighted both the pride of those who sought to usurp God's position and God's determination that this would not happen, and so he 'confused the languages of the whole world' and scattered the people. The coming of the Spirit at Pentecost was marked by a miracle of tongues which reversed this division. All those who spoke different languages were able to hear the one message: *we hear them declaring the wonders of God in our own tongues.* The scattering is symbolically ended and the divisions between the nations are overcome by the presence of the Holy Spirit.[11] The various nations are listed (2:9–11) to make the point that unity

[8] This parallelism is foreshadowed in Jeremiah, who contrasted the written law of Moses with the new law which would be 'in their minds' and 'on their hearts'. In the new covenant God's Word is not external, in writing, but internal, through the presence of the Spirit. See Jer. 31:31; John 14:26; 15:26; 16:13.

[9] Barrett, *Acts*, 112.

[10] Gen. 3:1–21; 4:1–26; 6:7; 7:1 – 10:32.

[11] Another interesting connection is seen in the fact that it is specifically noted that there was 'bewilderment' at Pentecost, just as there had been at the Tower of Babel. The same word is used in Acts 2:6 as is used in Gen. 11:7 in the Greek translation of the Hebrew Scriptures which was in common use at that time. It appears deliberately to suggest an allusion to Babel, but whereas previously it came from the introduction of different languages it now comes about as a reaction to the miracle of languages. See Barrett, *Acts*, 119.

comes through the gift of the Spirit and it is noted that the community grows rapidly.[12] The Holy Spirit is the one who overcomes divisions, creates the community and brings about growth.

Some, however, have questioned this interpretation. It has been noted that Luke does not make much use of the parallel, and it has been suggested that a more obvious and precise reversal of the scattering into different language groups would have involved the elimination of all the various languages and a return to unity through the speaking of a single language. Nonetheless, the miracle of hearing which is described has exactly the same practical effect and also the advantage of affirming the validity of each and every one of those languages and cultures that was represented. It is a clear declaration that one does not have to cease being a Mede or Elamite (or American, British, Chinese, Dutch or Egyptian) in order to be filled with the Spirit and become a Christian. This is an important point, especially in the light of the fact that it was not long before some Christians were arguing that people ought to become Jews first before they became Christians.[13] Christians who today take the gospel to other people and cultures or subcultures must likewise avoid suggesting directly or implicitly by word or by action that 'to be a Christian you must become like us and take on our customs and habits and way of life'.

Luke lists the nations which were present at Pentecost by moving, generally, from east to west. It starts with the *Parthians, Medes and Elamites* who came from beyond the Roman empire, though not beyond the reach of the widely spread Jewish dispersion, moves through Mesopotamia, Asia Minor and North Africa and finishes with references to *visitors from Rome*, which was, of course, the heart of the empire, and *Cretans and Arabs*. The symbolism of this is clear: they are representatives of the whole world and are forerunners of a global community of Christians. This points to God's intention to build his church in every place and is an affirmation of the value God attributes to people of all nations, races, cultures and language groups.

The filling of the disciples with the Holy Spirit was associated with spectacular phenomena. These were symbolic events. This is not to say that they did not occur, but they were not natural events, they were symbols of the nature of the Spirit. There was, for instance, no actual wind, but simply a *sound* which was *like the blowing* of a strong wind. There was no actual fire, rather it was an

---

[12] At the end of the chapter three thousand people believed (Acts 2:41).
[13] Hence the debate of Acts 15.

event that *seemed to be tongues of fire*. Moreover, when the crowd is amazed because *each one heard their own language being spoken*, the emphasis falls on the hearers' perception rather than the nature of the speakers' words. It is clear that some phenomenal things occurred, but Luke is cautious in defining their precise physical nature, because the focus should fall upon their significance so that they are understood as pointers towards the indisputably real event which is taking place: the coming of the Holy Spirit into the lives of the disciples. It would be a diversion to think that the nature of the associated phenomena is of greater importance than the event to which they point. So, then, what do wind and fire teach us about the filling of the Holy Spirit?

(1) *A creative wind*: the disciples were gathered together and a sound like the blowing of a violent wind came from heaven. In Scripture 'wind' (*pneuma*) has a double meaning and is frequently a symbol for God's creative Spirit.[14] God is described as moving on the wind, and he used it as his messenger to fulfil his purposes and sometimes to execute his judgment.[15] The fact that this wind is said to come from heaven is a further indication that it was a spiritual rather than an ordinary event, and the fact that it was the sound of a strong, even violent, wind points to the power and strength of the Spirit who comes to bring life to the church and enable it to fulfil God's purposes. Just as God breathed into Adam and brought life (Gen. 2:7), and just as a wind from God gave life to the bones in Ezekiel's vision (Ezek. 37:9), so now the Spirit comes to bring life, energy and power to the disciples.

(2) *A burning fire*: the disciples also saw what seemed to be tongues of fire. Fire had long been a potent Hebrew symbol of the presence of God,[16] with particular connotations of God descending from heaven with power to overcome sin and evil. Fire was a symbol of divine warfare and a mark of the defeat of the enemies of God.[17] It was a sign of justice and the punishment of wrongdoers[18] and of sacrifices and the destruction of sin.[19] This also made it a powerful symbol of the end-times when the final judgment would take place.[20] All this made fire a very appropriate symbol for the Holy Spirit, the Spirit of the end-times, who came in power to reveal and deal with sin (John 16:8). John the Baptist had already

[14] Exod. 19:6; 1 Kgs 19:11; Ezek. 37:9, 14; John 3:8.
[15] 2 Sam. 22:11; Pss. 11:6; 18:10; 104:4; 135:7; Jer. 4:11–12; 18:17.
[16] Gen. 15:17; Exod. 3:2; 19:18; Deut. 4:12.
[17] Num. 21:28; Isa. 10:16; Zech. 12:6.
[18] Gen. 38:24; Lev. 20:14; Josh. 7:15.
[19] Isa. 6:6–7; Heb. 12:29.
[20] Zeph. 3:8; 2 Thess. 1:7; Heb. 10:27.

associated fire and the Spirit, prophesying that Jesus would baptize his people 'with the Holy Spirit and fire' (Matt. 3:11). The Pentecostal descent of the Spirit in the form of fire is reminiscent of the confrontation which occurred between Elijah and the prophets of Baal, when Elijah declared, 'The god who answers by fire – he is God' (1 Kgs 18:24). Just as God spoke then through all-consuming fire rained down from heaven, now, at Pentecost, he was again acting in decisive fashion to pour out the Spirit of holiness on the world, through the life and ministry of his disciples.

(3) *A Holy Spirit*: wind and fire were symbols of the real event – the filling of the disciples with the Holy Spirit. The initial experience of being filled with the Spirit is what makes someone a Christian. Without the Spirit it is not possible to be a believer,[21] for it is the Spirit alone who brings new life in Christ.[22] Luke says the disciples were 'filled' with the Spirit, while elsewhere this initial experience is described as being 'baptized' in the Spirit.[23] While 'baptism' is used exclusively for the initial experience, 'filling' is also used of the ongoing, repeated experience of the Spirit.[24] These subsequent fillings do not mean that believers are repeatedly emptied of the Spirit. Some illustrations suggest that the believer is like a glass of water that needs to be filled when it is empty. But one cannot be a believer without the Spirit, and Christians should be assured that the Spirit will not leave them. Yet believers who have the Spirit can, without being emptied of the Spirit, be filled again. This is no more contradictory than many other aspects of life. Someone who is cheerfully engaged in what is a long and difficult task does not have to become completely discouraged in order to benefit from an encouraging word from a friend or colleague. The Spirit is always with the believer but that presence is, at times, more obvious than at other times, and sometimes the Spirit strengthens, guides and empowers believers in their life and ministry in very particular and special ways.

The ongoing nature of the Holy Spirit in the lives of all believers was what made Pentecost something completely new. The Spirit was poured out on the church in a way that had not occurred previously. This does not mean that the Spirit had not been present previously, for the Spirit of God had already played an important role in the life of the Old Testament,[25] but now there was a fundamental

[21] Acts 19:1–6; 1 Cor. 12:3.
[22] John 6:63; Rom. 8:2, 11; Gal. 6:8.
[23] Mark 1:8; Acts 1:5; 2:4; 9:17; 11:16; 1 Cor. 12:13.
[24] As in Acts 13:52; Eph. 5:18.
[25] Gen. 1:2; Exod. 31:3; Num. 11:26; Judg. 6:34; 1 Sam. 10:10; Ps. 51:10; Isa. 61:1; Ezek. 3:12; Zech. 4:6.

difference in the mode and extent of God's presence with his people. Prior to Pentecost the work of the Spirit was (a) to create and bring life,[26] (b) to inspire minds and hearts,[27] (c) to empower Israel's leaders,[28] (d) to make the Lord's people holy,[29] and (e) to be a sign of hope concerning the future of God's plans for the world.[30] Note that this was almost exclusively achieved through the leaders of Israel, the judges, kings and prophets. The Spirit is not usually associated with the ordinary person. The action of the Spirit on these leaders could involve spectacular physical power and spiritual ecstasy, but it was also unpredictable and impermanent. The Spirit usually came for a specific task and a particular time. From Pentecost onwards, however, the Spirit came to stay permanently with God's people. This was no temporary empowering but an ongoing presence. Moreover, the Spirit fell on all God's people. Every believer was blessed with the gift of the Holy Spirit and was inspired in a way that had previously been the preserve of just a few. Through the Spirit God was transforming all people and enabling them to participate in the life and mission of God. There were none who lacked the gifts and graces for Christian life and ministry.

This multifaceted work of the Spirit was continuous with the ministry exercised prior to Pentecost, as noted in the five points above, but now it had a different orientation: (a) the creative work of the Spirit was now focused on bringing new life to believers,[31] (b) the inspiring work of the Spirit was now directed towards guiding the church in the fulfilment of its gospel mission to the whole world,[32] (c) the strength which the Spirit brought now enabled the disciples to preach boldly and resist persecution,[33] (d) the sanctifying work of the Spirit was orientated to enabling people to follow the example of Jesus,[34] and (e) altogether the presence of the Spirit leading the church in this way was a sign of hope that God was in control, and the spread of the gospel to the Gentiles was, in particular, a sign of the approach of the last days.[35]

[26] Gen. 1:2; 2:7; Ps. 104:30.
[27] 1 Sam. 16:13; 2 Chr. 15:1.
[28] Judg. 14:6, 19; 1 Sam. 10: 6, 10.
[29] Pss. 51:10–11; 139:7; Isa. 32:15.
[30] Isa. 11:2–19; 42:1–4; Ezek. 36:26; Joel 2:28.
[31] Acts 2:38; 8:15; 10:44; 11:24; 19:2, 6.
[32] Acts 2:17; 5:32; 6:3; 8:29; 11:12; 13:2; 15:28; 16:6; 20:22.
[33] Acts 4:8, 31; 6:10; 7:55–59.
[34] Acts 5:3; 10:38; Rom. 1:4; 8:9, 10.
[35] Acts 2:17; 10:45–47; 28:25–28. Altogether Pentecost was the fulfilment of God's promises calling on people to wait 'till the Spirit is poured upon us from on high' (Isa. 32:15).

This change in the mode of presence of the Holy Spirit has to be understood in trinitarian terms. It could not occur previously, and the difference that made it possible was the ministry of Jesus. In Old Testament terms the Spirit existed in close relationship to the very being of God and was the active presence of the transcendent God among his people. But through the incarnation much more was revealed. Jesus' life, death and resurrection decisively defined the character of God, and the Spirit was then revealed as the Spirit of Jesus and thus was irrevocably connected with his character and purpose. Consequently, in the New Testament there is a shift away from seeing the Spirit just in terms of power and force and even beyond the idea of the Spirit as the action of God in the world, towards an understanding of the Spirit as God who enters personally into a relationship with his people, guiding, revealing and inspiring them. The connection of the Spirit with Jesus tends to personalize the Spirit and provides a foundation for a doctrine of the Trinity. In his explanation of the Pentecostal events Peter explained it in this way: God has raised this Jesus to life, and we are all witnesses of the fact. Exalted to the right hand of God, he has received from the Father the promised Holy Spirit and has poured out what you now see and hear (2:33). The Spirit now brings to the believer remembrance of all that Jesus did, produces faith in him or her and develops the character and the gifts of Jesus in the believer's life.[36]

2. Spirit-filled Christ

The crowds which gathered in Jerusalem for the Jewish feast known as Pentecost were, according to Luke, *in bewilderment* and *utterly amazed* at this turn of events. Some of the crowd were amused by the apparently enthusiastic behaviour of the disciples and *made fun of them and said, 'They have had too much wine.'* This was, in fact, a great moment in the life of the church. It involved the coming of God into the lives of his disciples and the confirmation of the life, ministry, death and resurrection of Jesus, the Son of God. And what did the crowd think of it? They were making fun of it, mocking the disciples and treating them like a bunch of party-going drunks! This kind of reaction is not discouraging, however, and there are two reasons for this.

The first is that it tells us that what was happening was so exciting and that the disciples were filled with so much passion that it

---

[36] This is also found in John's Gospel, where Jesus is recorded as telling the disciples that it was for their own good that he was going to leave them, for then the Spirit would come, sent by the Father in the name of the Son (John 16:7; 14:26).

appeared to the ordinary bystander that there had to be some unusual explanation for this explosion of enthusiasm. We might ask whether people would say the same about the church today. Is the church's corporate life, worship and attitude so outgoing, enthusiastic and spontaneous that people will get confused when they see it and wonder what on earth has got into these people? Of course, it will not be like that all the time – even the early church did not exist perpetually in that state. But if this account of the first filling of the Spirit is anything to go by, then there ought to be times of joy, excitement and enthusiasm in the life of the church. A church that is always boring, always under complete control and unable to explode at times with joy and spontaneity is not a church which reflects the dynamic presence of the Holy Spirit as illustrated at Pentecost.

At various times throughout the history of the church there have been Christians who have been derided for being zealous in the expression of their faith. In eighteenth-century England, for example, some Christians were known disparagingly as 'enthusiasts'.[37] At a time when there was a lot of nominalism and apathy in the church it was not considered socially acceptable to be too enthusiastic about faith. Whenever the church lacks any experience of the dynamic work of God in the life of believers, it is difficult to discern rightly the difference between the genuine work of God in renewal and the fanciful imagination of some of his followers. How are visions, healings, miracles and dramatic conversions to be interpreted – especially when they are associated with breaches of church order, social disruption and claims of personal perfection?

The early Methodists faced this problem when some, like George Bell, attempted (unsuccessfully) to give sight to the blind and to raise the dead. Yet the leader, John Wesley, was concerned that he should not find himself fighting the work of God or stopping the dramatic conversions and it did appear that Bell had healed a woman with painful lumps in her breast by prayer. Wesley found himself in opposition to the majority of churchmen of the day who condemned all such enthusiasm because they believed that such charismatic phenomena – including instant conversion – were confined to the apostolic age. Wesley was censured for believing in 'an imaginary new birth, an imaginary new faith and an imaginary

---

[37] The English word 'enthusiast' actually comes from two Greek words, *en* meaning 'in' and *theos* meaning 'God', so that, although the contemporary meaning is much broader today, it is derived from the behaviour of one who is excited by the presence of God. This is a great thing to be excited about. It should be no surprise if observers sometimes get confused about what is happening.

assurance'.[38] Wesley, of course, could never believe that these things were contrary to the will of God and he was not opposed to seeing the miraculous in other ways. Amongst other things he believed in direct providential intervention to stop it raining when he preached. His actions provide a model for discernment. He observed the controversial meetings for himself, he carefully evaluated their claims and was not reluctant to apply principles of reason and sound judgment. He repudiated those things which were contrary to Scripture, including the notion of special, unique revelations (though he was not opposed to the idea that God revealed himself to people). He dissociated the movement from the claim that the world would end in 1750. The kind of situation Wesley faced is by no means unknown today. There are always enthusiasts who expect more evident results from the grace of God than others and it can be difficult to find a way between the excesses of well-meaning but overzealous faith and a failure to appreciate the extent of God's grace. The application of scriptural precedent and rational evaluation is not out of place and an assessment of the personal conduct of those involved is important. Church meetings should not, said Wesley, be as rowdy as a bear garden, and he opposed the self-focused nature of some ministries. This self-centredness was also found in the claims of certain people that they did not sin, something Wesley opposed (it was not what he meant by 'perfection'), and he described people who claimed special, unique revelations as those who think they are God but are not. While care is needed, it is of the greatest importance to be open to the radical working of God in the lives of his people.

When Jesus made claims that seemed outlandish and performed inexplicable miracles, many people misunderstood and thought that he was demon-possessed. His family were kinder and assumed he had just gone mad,[39] showing that even those closest to the believer may misunderstand the nature of spiritual influences. But it is more important to be in tune with the will of God than with what others want of us. If we spend our time trying to be normal and aiming not to stand out then we may miss something of what it means to be Christian. In a piece of somewhat satirical, but nonetheless thoughtful, self-analysis the head of one denomination asked what might have happened if the young church had responded to the confusion, the enthusiasm, the strange phenomena and the apparently negative public perceptions associated with the Pentecostal outpouring of the Spirit in the same way that the contemporary church usually

[38] F. Baker (ed.), *Letters of John Wesley*, Vol. II (Epworth, 1931), 263.
[39] See Mark 3:13–27, specifically v. 21: 'He is beside himself' (RSV); 'He's gone mad' (TEV).

deals with unpredictability, outlandish enthusiasm and uncontrolled growth. In that situation the disciples would, he thought, appoint a review committee to perform an analysis of how it could be better controlled and structured in future, probably recommending a new administrative structure, a revised public relations programme (to overcome the negative public perceptions of the church) and a new building programme (to avoid the continued and unexpected use of public places and to cope with the three thousand new converts as well).[40] Of course, it is possible to argue that many of these suggestions are actually good, helpful and necessary, but the challenge is that they ought not to come at the expense of the vitality and unpredictability which can occur when the Spirit leads the church.

The second positive thing to note about the crowd's reaction to the disciples' enthusiasm is that people were not indifferent to it. Even though the initial reaction was dismissive, it did not stay that way. Their negative response was, in fact, preliminary to a radical change and soon three thousand people converted to faith in Jesus Christ. An indifferent response is far worse. It means that they do not see anything worth reacting to. This is not an invitation deliberately to provoke negative reactions in those who are not believers. The church must be gracious and loving in its proclamation, but the gospel itself speaks in such a way that it calls for a response of some kind. S. J. Kistemaker points to a rather ominous progression in attitude towards Christians by those who did *not* believe. The initial bewilderment soon turned to ridicule and this was followed by a negative, questioning, even inquisitorial, approach. Then came threats, imprisonment, beatings and finally murder.[41] In short, repentance and conversion on the one hand, and mockery and persecution on the other, were the responses to the preaching of the church. Both should probably be considered normal.

The dramatic events which created such a disturbance needed to be explained, and so *Peter stood up with the Eleven ... and addressed the crowd*. Peter interprets these events against both the backdrop of Old Testament belief[42] and the more recent events surrounding the life, ministry, death, resurrection and ascension of Jesus. It is not too speculative to suggest that his ability to speak in this way was not only inspired by the Spirit but also related to the forty days he and the other disciples had spent with Jesus during

---

[40] Alan Marr, *The Witness: The Voice of Victorian Baptists* (July 2003), 2.

[41] Acts 2:13; 4:7; 5:18, 40; 7:58.

[42] Referring in particular to the words of the LORD through the prophet Joel 2:28–32 and the writer of Psalms 16:8–11 and 110:1.

which they had discussed the kingdom of God (1:1–3). It would be surprising if, during this time, they had not considered many of the very things which Peter spoke about. His interpretation required an explanation of the work of the Trinity, although, of course, he did not use that word.

- First there is an explanation of the outpouring of the Holy Spirit based on Joel's prophecy (vv. 14–21).
- This is then connected with the person of Jesus and the ministry he received from the Father (vv. 22–36).
- It then culminates in a discussion of the relationship between Jesus, the Spirit and the Father (v. 33). After this Peter makes an appeal to the crowds to repent and be baptized.

Peter's preaching was very theological. His explanation of the nature of the divine relationships – Father, Son and Spirit – is what constitutes most of the sermon. The actual appeal is short and to the point and is only made after the character, the relationships and the work of the trinitarian God have been clearly explained.

(1) *The Spirit is the Spirit of God*: Peter uses the prophecy from Joel to show that the Spirit which came upon the disciples was actually God's Spirit, even though the Spirit had never fallen on a group of people in this way previously (vv. 17–21). But Peter's point is that this is exactly what had been promised through Joel many years before – that one day God would pour out his Spirit upon *all people*. In this way Peter shows that the amazing events which have just taken place can be interpreted as the work of the Spirit of God.

(2) *The Spirit is the Spirit of Jesus*: Peter then moves on to link the Spirit with Jesus (vv. 21–24). Peter is quite sure that the promise found in Joel – *I will pour out my Spirit in those days ... And everyone who calls on the name of the* LORD *will be saved* – has been fulfilled through two events: the coming of the Spirit at Pentecost and the life of Jesus of Nazareth, *a man accredited by God to you*. In other words, the Spirit is poured out now because Jesus has come and the Spirit brings new life to all those who trust in Jesus.

(3) *Father, Son and Spirit*: having related the Spirit of Pentecost with both God and Jesus, and having related Jesus with God, it now simply remains to link all three together and at this point the trinitarian theology which is implicit in the events of Pentecost becomes most explicit (v. 33). Peter says of Jesus, *Exalted to the right hand of God, he has received from the Father the promised Holy Spirit and has poured out what you now see and hear*. Jesus is described as *the Holy One* and as *both Lord and Messiah*, and he

225

is also *raised* to life and *exalted to the right hand of God*, with God the Father and the Holy Spirit. The language is so powerful as to compel one to conclude that Jesus has the position and the honour of God. Father, Son and Spirit are together in the heavenly realms, together but distinct, sharing the divine life, nature and honour of God. The Father is God and the originator of all, he sends the Son to the world and also gives the Spirit to the Son, and the Son pours the Spirit out on all his people. The Spirit, then, is from God and is God, but only comes through the Son. There is no other way of being the recipient of God's Spirit other than by knowing the Son. Clearly, the early preaching of the church was trinitarian in form. This was a theology which formed the life of the church, united the Christian community and inspired its worship.

At the heart of this trinitarian action of God is the determination of the Father to work through the Son and the Spirit in order to save the world. These three are not at odds with each other in this, they share a common purpose, and so Peter says that it is *by God's deliberate plan and foreknowledge* (v. 23) that the Son was handed over to be crucified. This election of the Son by the Father coexists with the next statement, which places the responsibility for the death of Christ squarely on human shoulders rather than describing it as a result of divine purposes. The death of Jesus was done, says Peter, by *you, with the help of wicked men*. Here is a mystery of divine will and human freedom. Humanity's guilt and God's plans go together. There can be no attempt to exonerate humanity's culpability in the worst of sins, nor can there be any suggestion that God was not in ultimate control of these events. Through crucifixion God works out his purposes. There is a piece of ancient graffiti which dates back to sometime around the second century. It shows a rather scrawled picture of a man on a cross – certainly a reference to Christ – but the man has been drawn with the head of a donkey. This was presumably done to make the man shown kneeling before the cross in worship appear even more foolish. The inscription below reads, 'Alexamenos worships his God.' We do not know who Alexamenos was, but presumably he was known as a Christian and someone was mocking his beliefs. It is no surprise that this should have happened and it is no less amazing today that God should determine to redeem the world in this way.

3. Spirit-filled church

When the crowd heard Peter's explanation of what had happened *they were cut to the heart* and asked, *what shall we do?* Peter's response is to issue a call expressed in trinitarian terms. Repentance marked by baptism is to take place *in the name of Jesus,* and the disciples will receive the forgiveness of sins and *the gift of the Holy Spirit.* This is for all those *whom the Lord our God will call.* Thus the faithful share in the whole life of God, embraced and surrounded by his love. Repentance means turning away from evil to God. It is something which John the Baptist and Jesus called people to do (Mark 1:4, 15), but it is also a gift of God (5:31; 11:18) associated with faith. Faith produces repentance and repentance leads to faith; one cannot do either without the other. Repentance means *the forgiveness of your sins* and this act of faithfulness means receiving *the gift of the Holy Spirit* marked by baptism, the sign of God's grace, *in the name of Jesus Christ.* Every society and every person has to deal with the concept of sin in some way. Although that word may not be used, there is no-one who does not believe at some time or another that they have been unjustly dealt with or sinned against. And there is no-one whose conscience does not at some point condemn them and tell them that they themselves have done what is wrong. One approach to dealing with this which is common in contemporary Western society is to deny that there really is a problem, or at least to minimize it. If there is no sin there is no problem, no guilt, no regret, no condemnation, no need for forgiveness. Consequently, a number of trends have combined to suggest that everything is all right. There is a tendency to limit the concept of wrong to ever more limited areas of life, mainly social acts such as violence, abuse of children and outright crime, while defining many other immoral acts, including most personal acts, as not only legal but also as valid moral options. Pluralism and tolerance certainly have their rightful place, for without them fascism and fanaticism are likely to rule, but they can also suggest that many wrong and unhelpful things should be tolerated. N. T. Wright says,

> Instead of genuine forgiveness, our generation has been taught the vague notion of 'tolerance'. This is, at best, a low-grade parody of forgiveness. At worst, it's a way of sweeping the real issues in human life under the carpet ... Jesus' message [of forgiveness of sins] offers the genuine article and insists that we should accept no man-made substitute.[43]

All those who respond to Peter's invitation to repent and be baptized will receive *the gift of the Holy Spirit* just as the disciples did. There is no distinction, the Spirit is poured out on all those who

---

[43] Wright, *The Lord and his Prayer*, 50–51.

believe[44] and empowers them to live Christian lives. The final verses of Acts 2 provide an insight into the effect of the presence of the Holy Spirit. There are ten characteristics of a healthy church of Spirit-filled people.

- Four of them are primary or *essential characteristics* of a church. The disciples *devoted themselves* to these things.
- Then there are five further, *specific illustrations* of the life of the church at this time. These should be taken as typical illustrations of church life.
- Finally, there is described *one result* which specifically relates to what God (rather than the believers) does for the church.

a. Four essential characteristics

These are found in Luke's description of the spiritual life of the first Christians: *They devoted themselves to the apostles' teaching and to fellowship, to the breaking of bread and to prayer*. The teaching of the apostles became foundational for the life of the church,[45] for they had been with Jesus from the very beginning and had heard his teaching (1:24). But even more importantly they had been witnesses of his resurrection and the heart of their message was that Jesus was not just a teacher but, as Peter proclaimed, both Lord and Christ. The priests and the Sadducees were 'greatly disturbed' that the disciples were 'teaching the people, proclaiming in Jesus the resurrection of the dead' and tried to stop it, but despite persecution the disciples 'never stopped teaching and proclaiming the good news that Jesus is the Messiah'.[46] In short, the lesson is that the authenticity of Christian teaching and preaching is determined by whether Jesus is proclaimed as the resurrected Lord.

The second primary characteristic of the early church was its fellowship (*koinōnia*). Although the idea permeates all the descriptions of the early church this is the only place the word itself is found in the book of Acts. It means to participate or share in something together, or to have something in common. It was a word that could be used in a secular sense, such as when it is used to refer to the fishing 'partnership' of Simon Peter, James and John. They shared in a partnership and were, presumably, co-owners of one or more boats and equipment. They shared in that business together (Luke 5:9–11). In a Christian sense the believers share together in God. This is variously described as sharing 'in the Holy Spirit', 'in

[44] Acts 8:15–17; 9:17; 10:44; 15:8; 19:6.
[45] Also see Paul on this, 1 Cor. 12:28; Eph. 4:11.
[46] Acts 2:36; 4:2; 5:42. Also see Acts 13:1, 12; 18:11.

Christ' and 'in the divine nature'.[47] It is through the gift of the Spirit that they are able to share together in God's life and thus they are able to have fellowship with one another. Christian fellowship is not primarily about sharing with those who are the same as us. Christian fellowship exists between people who are very different because fellowship is with all those who are *in Christ*.

The reference to *koinōnia* is followed by two further fundamental characteristics of the life of the church: *breaking bread* together and *prayer*. These are expressions of fellowship, but are not to be equated with it as there are other expressions of it as well. Paul described the monetary gift which the church at Rome made to the poor church at Jerusalem as being their *koinōnia* and he used the same word to describe the bread and the cup at the Lord's Supper as their 'participation' in the body and blood of Christ (1 Cor. 10:16). Christian fellowship is a spiritual reality exhibited in a number of very specific, visible and tangible ways which reflect the grace shown by God in coming into relationship with humanity. What is meant by *breaking bread* beyond the fact that it involves eating together? Is it a reference to normal meals which the disciples shared in, or is it a term intended to describe a special, perhaps symbolic, meal associated with Sunday worship which was the beginning of that celebration known variously today as the Lord's Supper, Holy Communion and the Mass? Later in Acts Luke describes the church meeting on the first day of the week 'to break bread', and in 1 Corinthians Paul appears to discuss and even promote the use of a symbolic meal.[48] However, verse 46 refers to the disciples meeting at the temple *every day* and goes on to refer again to the fact that they *broke bread* in their homes. This makes it sound as though the reference is to normal meals, and yet it is specifically noted that they ate *with glad and sincere hearts, praising God*, which perhaps points to a significance beyond that of a purely routine meal. It is very possible that the kind of distinction which later developed, between symbolic and full meals, may not have existed at this time. Every meal was an opportunity for the believers who were gathered together to give thanks to God for what he had done. They also devoted themselves to prayer. Literally, this is to 'the prayers', referring to specific prayers said in worship. This would certainly have included the regular Jewish prayers (which would be consistent with the fact that they were also continuing to meet in the temple), but it may also be a reference to specifically Christian prayers and perhaps an allusion to the Lord's Prayer in particular.

[47] Rom. 8:9; 12:5; 1 Cor. 1:30; 2 Pet. 1:4.
[48] 1 Cor. 10:16; 11:17–33.

b. Five typical illustrations

These first four characteristics are set out as the basic elements of the life of the early church to which the disciples *devoted themselves*, and they remain today as indispensable parts of church life. Together, teaching, fellowship, breaking bread and prayer constitute the essential worship life of the church. The next five characteristics which Luke describes were part and parcel of the life of the early church and yet they are not in the same category as the first four. The early believers did not, for instance, 'devote themselves' to 'wonders and miraculous signs' or to selling their 'property and possessions' in order to be able to give the proceeds away. Indeed, the actions of Ananias and Sapphira soon made it clear that the sale of property was voluntary rather than a requirement (5:1–4). Nor was it mandatory then, any more than it is today, for believers to meet daily in the temple courts for worship. Nonetheless, miracles occurred, great generosity was shown and they worshipped daily in the temple. These things are more illustrative of the effect the grace of God had on the first disciples than prescriptive for the life of the church in every time and situation. Nonetheless, they do provide us with an outline of the life of a healthy church.

Everyone was filled with awe and many *wonders and miraculous signs* were done by the apostles. These are the same words Peter used to describe the works of Jesus which were evidence of his being accredited by God. They indicated that he was the fulfilment of Joel's prophecy (2:16–22). These miracles perform the same function – that is, they demonstrated the veracity of the message of salvation in Jesus alone. The community life of the believers meant that they *were together and had everything in common*. S. J. Kistemaker comments that 'the aim of the early Christians was to abolish poverty so that needy persons, as a class, were no longer among them'.[49] For a short while at least the Christian community became economically classless and 'there were no needy persons among them' (4:34). This was an expression of the conviction that God owned everything. Corporate ownership meant that they sold their possessions and gave *to anyone who had need*. Charity was an important part of their life together and became the occasion for a new step in the visible organization of the church as disputes arose over the distribution of money (6:1–7). This radical form of sharing did not continue to be typical of the life of the church, although there have always been those who have lived in this way and have done the church a great service by holding out radical equality and

---

[49] Kistemaker, *Acts*, 112.

even voluntary poverty as viable options for Spirit-filled believers. It appears to be a truth of the spiritual life that the richer we become materially, the poorer we become spiritually. Another of the effects of the Spirit on the lives of believers is the presence of a new attitude which involves *praising God* and having *glad and sincere hearts*. These are described repeatedly throughout Acts as the result of the work of the Spirit, and in Ephesians Paul likewise describes praise as one of the primary effects of being filled with the Spirit.[50]

c. One final result

The final result of the presence of these characteristics is the fact that the church grew. *The Lord added to their number daily those who were being saved.* It is specifically noted that this final characteristic of the early church is something that is attributed to the work of *the Lord* rather than to the effort or achievements of the disciples. They could devote themselves to teaching, fellowship, prayer, praise, breaking bread, charity and so forth, but not to growth. In his letter to the Corinthians, when discussing the rivalry which existed in that church, Paul was unwilling to claim credit for what others had done and observed, 'I planted the seed, Apollos watered it, but God has been making it grow. So neither the one who plants nor the one who waters is anything, but only God, who makes things grow' (1 Cor. 3:6). It is the Lord who gives the growth and no-one should take credit for what they do not control. One cannot in any way guarantee individual conversions or overall growth. The responsibility of the church is to be faithful in those things to which it is called, including teaching, prayer, fellowship, worship, charity and so forth. It is God's responsibility to grow churches as he sees fit. This does not mean that we should become uninterested in the growth of the church. Indeed, we should perhaps be concerned about making churches full of people, but we should certainly be very concerned with helping to create a community of disciples, prayerful, praising and well taught in all the ways of the Lord. Before Christ sent the church into the world he sent the Spirit into the church and the same order of things must be followed today.

---

[50] Acts 8:8, 39; 13:48; 15:3; 16:34. Eph. 5:18–20.

Romans 8:1–17
12. Christian experience

One of the most famous photographs of the twentieth century shows a burnt, naked and traumatized nine-year-old Vietnamese girl running with outstretched arms away from a napalm attack on the village of Trang Bang in 1972 during the Vietnam War. One of the helicopter pilots involved in that raid was John Plummer. He was subsequently haunted by the image and by guilt for twenty-four years, until a Veterans' Day Memorial in Washington at which Kim Phuc spoke of her suffering, saying that she had reached the point where she no longer held any bitterness towards those who had committed this act and forgave them for it. Plummer was moved to tears, for in those words he found the forgiveness he sought. He was no longer condemned for what he had done.[1] Similarly, *there is now no condemnation for those who are in Christ Jesus* (8:1), for whoever they are, they too have been forgiven. The difference is that this particular message of liberation is offered to all people, for all sin, for all time. The negative construction translated as *no condemnation* is emphatic in form,[2] just as we might say 'there is no condemnation *at all*'. It is completely removed, not because Christians are sinless but simply and only because they are *in Christ Jesus*. This is the only way to deal with the effects of sin so powerfully described in earlier chapters of Romans. It is an illusion to think that time cancels out either the effect or the guilt of sin, foolish to assume that sin is trivial, unfortunate or simply inevitable, and arrogant to believe that sin can be dealt with by human means. Sin is defiance, it

---

[1] The photograph, by Nick Ut, won a Pulitzer Prize. Kim Phuc's story is told in Denise Chong's *The Girl in the Picture* (Penguin USA, 2001).

[2] The negative 'no' is emphasized by its placement at the beginning of the sentence.

is rebellion against God, a statement of independence which, unless resolved, inevitably leads to a final alienation from the ultimate and only source of life.[3] It can only be dealt with by God through the death of Christ and the life of the Spirit. No-one can forgive themselves for their sin any more than John Plummer could forgive himself for what happened in Vietnam. We need God to forgive our sins, and the message of Romans is that this is just what has happened. God loves people as they are, but he refuses to leave them that way. He is a transforming and redeeming God.

The removal of the believers' condemnation for sin means that not only has their *status* been changed but their actual *situation* has been transformed. *Katakrima* ('condemnation') is only found in the New Testament here and at 5:16 and 18 and it refers to more than a simple conviction (i.e. a change of status), F. F. Bruce describes it as a reference to the actual process of condemnation or 'penal servitude' which a convicted criminal suffers.[4] The removal of this 'condemnation' means that for the Christian there is now no continuing penalty, no further punishment. In other words, there is no reason to go on living as though not really liberated. Life is actually, experientially different, it is to be lived in the Spirit. This emphasis on life in the Spirit is seen in the simple fact that *pneuma* ('Spirit' or 'spirit') is used of the Holy Spirit five times in the first seven chapters of Romans and eight times in the final eight chapters, but *nineteen* times in the single intervening chapter 8,[5] including fifteen times in the first seventeen verses, which are discussed here. There is no doubt that authentic Christianity is not merely theoretical, not only cerebral, nor solely moral, but also definitely and clearly experiential. Of course, it can be difficult to get the right balance. Some are scared of experience for they do not want to get carried away into an ecstatic, subjective, mystical faith, while others have majored on personal experience to the exclusion of other important aspects of Christian faith such as practical, caring service and various ministries to others. However, the best form of balance is not necessarily achieved simply by being moderate in everything. Sometimes it is achieved by the enthusiastic acceptance of very different aspects of faith. A healthy recognition of the personal experience of the Spirit is best balanced, for example, by an equally wholehearted commitment to the study of the Scriptures on the one hand, and an active life of service to the needy on the other. The experience of

[3] See, e.g., Rom. 1:19–32; 2:12–16; 3:9–10, 23; 5:12; Eph. 2:1–5, 11–12.
[4] Bruce, *Romans*, 159.
[5] And twice more *pneuma* is used to refer to the human spirit (15a, 16b).

233

God is critical.[6] From a biblical point of view it is the role of the Spirit to work in the believer's life to enable him or her to know God through the experience of salvation as well as through the written word of Scripture.[7]

When God comes to a person he comes completely. It is impossible to have 'one third of God'. To be *in Christ* means *the Spirit of God lives in you*. In verse 9 'Spirit of God' is used synonymously with 'Spirit of Christ': *You, however, are not controlled by the sinful nature but are in the Spirit, if indeed the Spirit of God lives in you. And if anyone does not have the Spirit of Christ, they do not belong to Christ*. This does not confuse the persons of the Trinity, but it emphasizes that although distinct they share divine nature and will. Robert Jenson refers to these words of Paul as 'the most remarkable trinitarian passage in the NT ... amounting to an entire theological system' in which the attempt is 'not merely to speak in a trinitarian fashion but to speak about the trinity in explicit respect of his triuneness'.[8] That is, the Trinity is primarily known in the experience of being saved. The doctrine of the Trinity is not mere theory, not just academic knowledge. It is a truth revealed by God in the gifts of Son and Spirit and known in the experience of believers. There are four aspects of trinitarian salvation in this passage, which may be briefly outlined as follows.

- *Liberation* (vv. 1–4): in which God sent *his own Son* so that *through Christ Jesus the law of the Spirit who gives life* could set believers free.
- *Transformation* (vv. 5–9): in which *the Spirit of God* who is *the Spirit of Christ* lives in the believer.
- *Resurrection* (vv. 10–13): in which *the Spirit of him who raised Jesus from the dead is living in you*.
- *Adoption* (vv. 14–17): *those who are led by the Spirit of God are the children of God ... and co-heirs with Christ*.

[6] Immanuel Kant began his *Critique of Pure Reason* (1781) with the words, 'There is no doubt that all our knowledge begins with experience.' and proceeded from there to critique the idea that reason alone can ever bring knowledge. This was a critical work for the modern era. If ever it was appropriate to ignore or downplay the importance of spiritual experience, it can certainly be so no longer.

[7] Leonard Sweet emphasizes this point in his *Post-modern Pilgrims* (Tennessee, 2000), in which he describes what he calls EPIC churches – that is, churches which are Experiential, Participatory, Image-driven and Connected. This may be a very postmodern expression of certain aspects of church life that are important for today, but all four of them reflect very biblical themes related to the work of the Spirit in the corporate life of believers.

[8] Jenson, *Triune Identity*, 44.

Each of them develops a different dimension of the Christian life in a trinitarian fashion.

1. Liberation: freedom through Christ

There is no condemnation for sin, says Paul, because *through Christ Jesus the law of the Spirit who gives life has set you free from the law of sin and death* (vv. 1–2). The ministry of the Son in setting the believer free from sin was achieved in harmony with both the Spirit (who lives with the believer) and the will of the Father (who sent the Son). Yet liberation is primarily the work of the Son, *For what the law was powerless to do because it was weakened by the sinful nature, God did by sending his own Son in the likeness of sinful humanity to be a sin offering. And so he condemned sin in human flesh* (v. 3). No longer is the believer condemned; instead it is sin itself which is condemned as being powerless and with no hold over the believer. The *law of sin and death* which is now powerless is primarily the Torah,[9] but it also includes the conscience which every person has (Rom. 2:14). In the previous chapters Paul has just shown that this law has a double function. On the one hand, it is holy, righteous, good and spiritual (Rom. 7:12, 14; cf. 7:22), but, on the other hand, it leads to sin and death because through it three things happen: (a) people understand that they have not obeyed God's will, (b) they learn new ways of rebelling, and (c) they become liable to the dire consequences which exist for those who disobey it (Rom. 3:20; 4:15; 5:13; 7:7–12, 21–23).[10] Of course, Paul has gone to great lengths to show that this applies to all people, and not just some. Whether Jew or Gentile, 'no-one will be declared righteous in his sight by observing the law' (Rom. 3:20). It makes no difference whether one has a great understanding of the Jewish Torah or simply the law of one's own conscience – the point is that no-one can ever claim to have lived up to the standard of whatever law they know.

[9] A Hebrew term for 'law' referring to the covenant established by God with the children of Israel as found in the Pentateuch, the first five books of the Hebrew Scriptures, which formed the foundation of life and religion for Jews.

[10] In the English-speaking world, E. P. Sanders has been the one most responsible for what is now known as 'the new perspective on Paul'. Greater attention has been paid to the specific circumstances of Paul's mission and the nature of Jewish religion so that, for example, Romans is interpreted less abstractly and with a more positive assessment of Jewish religion. The problem of the law is interpreted less in terms of it being something simply associated with sin and death and more as a problem for evangelism among Gentiles, when it is seen as an expression of Jewish privilege. The solution lies in affirming faith as the means of salvation. See Sanders, *Paul and Palestinian Judaism*; Dunn, *Romans*; Wright, *Climax of the Covenant*. The 'new perspective' continues to be debated.

Paul says that this is the result of living according to the *sarx* (vv. 4, 5, 8). Literally, this is the 'flesh' (as in the NRSV), but this translation may be deceptive as Paul does not mean to refer to the physical nature of the person (as in the expression 'flesh and blood') or the specifically sexual dimension (as in a reference to 'the desires of the flesh'), but to a much more spiritual dimension of the person which includes the non-physical (that is, the emotional, the volitional and the mental) as well. It is more like 'human nature' but with an emphasis on its sheer weakness, its inability to do what is right. Because of this the TNIV prefers to use *sinful nature* to denote this spiritual life which is lived apart from Christ and the Spirit.[11]

Martin Luther, whose commentary on Romans was so influential at the time of the Reformation, noted that it was commonly said that human nature generally knows and does what is right in most circumstances, but sometimes errs and thinks and does what is wrong. He insisted, though, that it was necessary to say that human nature sometimes knows and does what is right, but generally does not. Human nature 'knows only what *it* regards as good, honourable, useful and not what is good in the sight of God and neighbour. Therefore it knows and wills the good only as it is connected with our own interests.'[12] Luther's blunt assessment of human sinfulness is needed in a society in which certain trends want to minimize or deny the reality of sin. This is part of the prevailing relativism which denies that there is anything which is either fundamentally 'true' or 'false'. What is needed is the kind of refreshing honesty exhibited by the writer G. K. Chesterton when *The Times* newspaper was conducting an ongoing discussion on the topic 'What's wrong with the world?' Chesterton wrote a letter to the editor which simply said, 'Dear Sirs, I am. Sincerely yours, G. K. Chesterton.' The problem is sinful human nature and God's answer is found in Jesus Christ.

a. God sent his Son

The answer to the problem of sin lies in God *sending his own Son in the likeness of sinful humanity to be a sin offering* (v. 3). This is the greatest miracle possible, one that lies beyond human invention. It is not only a theological statement to be analysed and dissected, it is

---

[11] It is variously explained by commentators as 'our fallen, ego-centric human nature' (Cranfield, *Romans*, 372), 'the sin-dominated self' (Ziesler, *Romans*, 195), 'the unregenerate person' who cannot please God (Bruce, *Romans*, 44), and a 'this-worldly orientation' (Moo, *Romans*, 478). The works of the flesh are outlined in Gal. 5:19.

[12] Luther, *Romans*, 118, translated as 'man's own interests'.

the basis of Christian life and faith and it is important to stop in awe and worship before the God who makes this possible. We should kneel – perhaps metaphorically but perhaps literally – in prayer, for in Christ and his death we see God at work. This is a divine action which reveals the inner nature of the love of God. Yet, astounding as this is, it is hidden to some (1 Cor. 1:18). It is said that the early church leader Augustine was once accosted by a heathen who showed him his idol and said, 'Here is my god; where is yours?' Augustine replied, 'I cannot show you my God; not because there is no God to show, but because you have no eyes to see him.' Some things have to be seen to be believed, but other things have to be believed in order to be seen. And it is the Spirit of life who opens our eyes to the amazing work of God in Christ.

b. In the likeness of sinful humanity

God's grace and love involved sending his own Son in the likeness of sinful flesh (*harmartias sarkos*), which the TNIV translates as *in the likeness of sinful humanity*. As we shall see, this is a very careful description of the nature of the incarnation which avoids a number of misconceptions. First, reference to Christ's coming in 'the flesh' (or as a 'man') shows that Christ truly shared in our human nature. This assumption of human nature is essential in order to bring about the transformation of the believer's human nature into a new and eternal form of life. Secondly, reference to the specifically 'sinful flesh' of Christ is important in order to make the point that it is *fallen* (or 'sinful') human nature that needs redeeming. Christ came to save real people whose human nature leads them into sin, subjection to law and death. He did not come to redeem an unreal, idealized form of human nature which was without weakness. While most Christians today are formally orthodox in accepting the true humanity of Christ, in practice many devout believers allow their belief in Christ's divinity to overwhelm his humanity so that he appears to them as a kind of Superman. Christ shared our weaknesses, our limitations and even our temptations. He shared in all things except sin itself. Finally, the qualifying expression *in the likeness of* is important, as without it the reference to Christ coming as *sinful humanity* could have been taken as inferring either that he was *sinful* in the sense of actually sinning (rather than just being subject to the effects of sin) or that he came and 'changed into' human form and was then human instead of divine.[13] This was an

---

[13] Elsewhere Paul was not afraid to emphasize the human nature of Christ (e.g. Phil. 2:7), though this always needed balancing with references to his divinity (e.g. Phil. 2:6).

237

issue with which the early church had to struggle and Tertullian (c. AD 160–c. 225) was the first to directly address whether Christ metamorphosed (or 'transfigured') into human form or 'clothed' himself with it. He quickly opted for the latter and, although a lot more had to be said about the nature of the incarnation, he was right to assert that a transformation into human nature is wrong if it implies in any way that Christ's nature *was* divine and *then* became human. Christ was fully human *and* divine. Paul wants to emphasize a genuine humanity which does not detract from divinity.[14] Altogether, Christ's coming *in the likeness of sinful humanity* is a carefully nuanced phrase which balances Christ's sinless divinity with his fully authentic humanity.

c. To condemn sin

The dramatic nature of Paul's theology of Christ continues as he declares that the Christ, the Son of God, was made to be nothing less than *a sin offering* by which he *condemned sin in human flesh* (v. 4). Although sin offering (*peri hamartias*) is the common expression for an Old Testament sacrificial offering,[15] the context does not seem to relate it specifically to the sacrificial system and it is probably better to take it in a general sense as a statement of Christ's mission of offering his life for sin.[16] In so doing he has *condemned sin* in sinful humanity, which means that the atoning sacrifice of Christ on the cross has effectively removed the power sin previously had over sinful people. Christ, who is our substitute, was made sin for us (2 Cor. 5:21). Through having, on the one hand, a profound awareness of the seriousness of sin and, on the other hand, a knowledge of the power of forgiveness, the Christian is able to understand the deepest needs of the human heart. Dietrich Bonhoeffer wrote about the way Christians can open their lives up to one another because of the cross:

[14] It is sometimes argued, though, that the expression 'in the likeness of' was included to qualify the fact that Jesus specifically came in '*sinful* flesh' and that its absence would imply that Jesus sinned. This is not a problem for Paul elsewhere, however. He is able to say that Christ came to 'be sin' for humanity without implying that he actually sinned himself (2 Cor. 5:21), although this would be a little more difficult in the present context. Overall, it is more likely that 'in the likeness of' qualifies 'sinful *flesh*' to indicate that Christ assumed human nature while retaining his divinity. Paul certainly needed to include reference to the qualifying expression 'in the likeness of' in order to indicate that Christ shared our human nature without sinning himself.

[15] As found in the LXX, e.g. Lev. 4:24; 5:11; Ps. 40:6.

[16] As in Cranfield, *Romans*, 382, and Morris, *Romans*, 303. Although, obviously, the underlying idea is not too different anyway.

The most experienced psychologist or observer of human nature knows infinitely less of the human heart than the simplest Christian who lives beneath the Cross of Jesus. The greatest psychological insight, ability, and experience cannot grasp this one thing: what sin is. Worldly wisdom knows what distress and weakness and failure are, but it does not know the godlessness of men. And so it also does not know that man is destroyed only by his sin and can be healed only by forgiveness. Only the Christian knows this. In the presence of a psychiatrist I can only be a sick man; in the presence of a Christian brother, I can dare to be a sinner.[17]

Dare to be a sinner? Dare to recognize our real situation? Yes, because the Christian also knows that in Christ there is no more condemnation. To try to ignore, hide or deny the reality of one's sin is not only to risk future salvation, but also psychologically unhealthy in the present. The work of Christ in condemning sin allows each person's sin to be named, known and, of course, treated as something which has been dealt with by Christ. The believer is liberated, for now there is no condemnation for sin.

d. To fulfil the law

By sending his Son, God condemned sin *in order that the righteous requirements of the law* might be fulfilled. Note, first, that the statement is actually singular in form, referring to 'the righteous requirement of the new law'. While the old law demands many things (see Rom. 2:26), the requirements of the new covenant are summed up in only one thing: life *according to the Spirit* (v. 4). The singular nature of life under the new covenant is expressed in a similar way a few chapters later (Rom. 13:9), where the various commandments of the new 'law' are summed up in one rule: 'Love your neighbour as yourself.' This requirement to live a life of love is no different from the 'law' of living by the Spirit. They are closely connected, for one leads to the other, 'because God's love has been poured out into our hearts through the Holy Spirit' (Rom. 5:5).

Secondly, note that not only is *the righteous requirement of the law* singular, it is also passive in form: the righteous requirement of the law is *fully met in us*. That is, it is something done in us and for us by God, rather than simply by us.[18] This in no way excuses

---

[17] Dietrich Bonhoeffer, *Life Together* (SCM, 1954), 93.
[18] Moo, *Romans*, 483.

believers from their own part in the transformation of their life. Believers are not to *live according to the sinful nature but according to the Spirit*, and this requires them to be open to the work of the Spirit in them. By the Spirit the believer is enabled to live *now* according to the will of God (i.e. *what the Spirit desires* [v. 5]) and so the Christian will seek to turn away from those things which *are according to the sinful nature*. In this regard, although times change, people stay very much the same and the words of Richard Rolle on 'The Amending of Life' are as appropriate a commentary on human nature today as they have ever been. 'People who live in affluent circumstances are prone to be deceived by five things which they love: riches, dignity, independence, power and honour. They are thus enslaved to sin.' Rolle agrees that the believer will be set free from these things at death, but rather poignantly adds, 'To be set free from these at last, when only remorse is left, is to be set free too late.'[19] Through the Spirit life can be changed *now*.

2. Transformation: led by the Spirit

The first aspect of salvation is the *liberation* of the believer from the power of sin, which takes place as God sends his Son so that believers could be set free through the work of the Spirit. The second continues this trinitarian theology, for it involves the ongoing *transformation* of the life of the believer with the life of the Spirit of God who is the Spirit of Christ. A contrast is drawn between life lived according to the sinful nature and life lived according to the desires of the Spirit.

a. Life according to human nature

Those who *live according to the sinful nature*, says Paul, are distinguished in three ways. The first is that they *have their minds set on what that nature desires* (v. 5). That is, they have a 'this-worldly' emphasis and so cannot please God (vv. 7–8). Ironically, in seeking to please itself, the sinful mind actually loses all possibility of joy and pleasure, for those things which it seeks for itself can never produce happiness. This does not necessarily mean that each and every human desire is intrinsically evil. Anger can be good or evil depending on whether it is anger at sin or simply the result of impatience. Money and material things can be used for great good, but if they become the focus of one's mind then they are only what the sinful nature desires. On one occasion the Lord Jesus said to

[19] Rolle, 'The Amending of Life', 66–67.

Simon Peter, 'You do not have in mind the concerns of God, but merely human concerns' (Matt. 16:22–23). Peter's fault was in rebuking Jesus for predicting his own death. In doing this Peter's intention was undoubtedly honourable – he wanted to protect the Messiah – but it was in conflict with the plan of God. Even that which is good in itself can become evil if it is not part of life in the Spirit.

The second distinguishing mark is the stark truth that *the mind controlled by the sinful nature is death* (v. 6).[20] This is the result for all those who are not in Christ and Paul needs to put this bluntly, for while the ones who live by the Spirit recognize both their failings and their need for God's grace, those who serve human nature are liable to deceive themselves and believe that they are being righteous. It has been observed[21] that there are only two kinds of people: the righteous who believe themselves sinners, and sinners who believe themselves righteous.

The third distinguishing mark of the mind set on what human nature desires is that it *does not submit to God's law* (v. 7). In so doing it is *hostile to God*.[22] Morris observes, 'It is not simply being slightly un-cooperative; it is downright hostility.'[23] The tragedy of this is that God's laws are given for human good. God is not a divine killjoy who makes up rules just to spoil people's fun. No law is given without a reason. The law is given for our good and obedience to it benefits us (Ps. 19:7–11).

b. Life in the Spirit

Those who *live in accordance with the Spirit* (v. 5) have their mind *set on what the Spirit desires* or are *controlled by the Spirit* (vv. 5–6) because, says Paul, *the Spirit of God lives in you* (v. 9). The differences between these expressions are not great, and they all stress a life completely given over to God. Paul also describes this as *the law of the Spirit who gives life* (v. 2), which is more unusual as 'law' and 'Spirit' are usually in sharp contrast in his theology. Here Paul is using *law* in a somewhat different and more general sense as a 'law' or 'principle' of life in the Spirit which releases the believer from that 'law' which inexorably leads to sin and death. One law liberates us from another. The new 'law' or 'principle' of the Spirit

---

[20] Death is the inevitable conclusion. Paul puts it very bluntly in v. 6: there is no verb, literally it is 'for the mind of flesh death'. RSV says 'is death', while Barrett and TEV have 'results in death'.

[21] It is attributed to Blaise Pascal (1623–62) among others.

[22] See also Rom. 5:10; Jas 4:4.

[23] Morris, *Romans*, 306.

means that God is at work in the believer to produce new attitudes and actions which are described elsewhere as the 'fruit of the Spirit': love, joy, peace, patience, kindness, goodness, faithfulness, gentleness and self-control (Gal. 5:22–23). 'Law' in the old sense does not produce this kind of fruit any more than a vine produces grapes by a law of parliament.

Life in the Spirit stands in contrast to life according to the sinful nature (the flesh) and it is through the Spirit that one is able to overcome the habits of sin which are a result of the weakness of human nature. Each time we sin, we reinforce a pattern that becomes harder and harder to break. It has been said that 'the chains of sin are too light to be felt until they are too heavy to be broken'. Through the Spirit, however, there is the power to overcome sin. F. F. Bruce notes of Romans 8 that 'this is the first place in the epistle where the Spirit of God enters the argument. It is no accident that with his entry there is no further talk of defeat.'[24] The Spirit overcomes sin, but the main thrust of Paul's theology of life in the Spirit is not upon a gradual victory but upon the overwhelming comprehensiveness of the presence of the Spirit. Those who live in accordance with the Spirit *have their minds set on what the Spirit desires*. This could be interpreted to mean that believers 'set their mind towards' what the Spirit wants or that 'their minds are set' on those things which the Spirit desires them to be set on. The former stresses the role of the individual and the latter the work of the Spirit. Although the two dimensions can never be completely separated, the overall context suggests that Paul wants to place most emphasis on the role of the Spirit in the life of the believer. Christians often say they are 'led by the Spirit', but here Paul is probably referring to a basic orientation of life, rather than to special, specific instances where people are guided in a very particular way. Although such special situations occur, life in the Spirit is not sporadic or occasional. It should be habitual, a normal state of affairs, for the believer lives by the 'law' (or the 'principle') of the Spirit. Evangelist D. L. Moody illustrated this point by holding up a glass and asking how he could get the air out of it. 'Suck it out with a pump!' was one suggestion. But Moody replied that this would create a vacuum that would shatter the glass. After other suggestions Moody simply picked up a pitcher of water and filled the glass. 'There,' he said, 'all the air is now removed.' He then went on to explain that victory in the Christian life is not accomplished by 'sucking out a sin here and there', but by being filled with the Holy Spirit.[25]

[24] Bruce, *Romans*, 160.
[25] Moody Bible Institute, *Today in the Word*, September 1991, p. 4.

3. Resurrection: new life – present and future

The first dimension of salvation was adoption through the work of the Son, the second was life in the Spirit and the third is the resurrection of the believer through the ministry of both Son and Spirit. First of all the passage shows that *if Christ is in you*, then although the body may be dead (or dying) because of sin, the spirit is nonetheless alive. This presence of Christ in the life of the believer is then paralleled with the statement that *if the Spirit ... is living in you*, the Father will give you life. These two statements lead to the claim that *we have an obligation* to live according to the Spirit.

a. Life in the Spirit

Those who are in Christ receive the Spirit and those with the Spirit will receive resurrection life from the Father: *if the Spirit of him who raised Jesus from the dead is living in you, he who raised Christ from the dead will also give life to your mortal bodies because of his Spirit* (v. 11). The intratrinitarian relationships are such that the Holy Spirit is both 'the Spirit of the Father' and 'the Spirit of Jesus', just as Jesus is both 'the Son of the Father' and 'the character of the Spirit', and the Father is both 'the Father of the Son' and 'the source of the Spirit'. This connectedness means that it is not possible to experience the presence of the Spirit or the resurrecting power of the Father without the presence of Christ. All authentic spiritual experiences are to be tested by their relationship to him. While there may be many spiritual experiences and many 'spirits', the test of genuine Christian experience is the person and the character of Jesus. That which is consistent with the life of Jesus and that which is based upon his presence in the life of the believer may be counted as Christian. Any other spiritual experience is to be rejected as contrary to Christ. If Christ and the Spirit live in a person, then the promise is that God *who raised Christ from the dead will also give life to your mortal bodies*. The resurrection of believers is connected to the life and work of the trinitarian God. The power is from God the Father, but is exercised through the Spirit for those in whom Christ lives.

There are two implications of this. The first is that at some future time he *will also give life to your mortal bodies* (v. 11). This is the work of God in which the whole person will be transformed. Death has been overcome and resurrection has been guaranteed. Of course, the fact that believers are free from death does not mean that they are free from dying. Our mortal nature will still pass away

243

and the death of the body remains a reality, but the significance of death has been completely transformed. Its power of destruction has been removed. As Paul says in his letter to the Corinthians, 'Death has been swallowed up in victory' (1 Cor. 15:51–57). The Rule of St Benedict exhorts people, 'Day by day remind yourself that you are going to die.' This is not such a popular theme today, although at other times Christians have paid great attention to this inescapable fact of life. There is a pretty tough-looking motorcycle club whose members wear the name 'Coffin Cheaters' on their leather jackets. Macabre though it might be, it would be a suitable name for Christians!

b. The obligation of life

The second implication of the power of God is the idea that the resurrection not only brings eternal life in the future, but also transforms the way the present is lived now. Paul notes this when he says that *we have an obligation* in the way that we live (v. 12). At this point he shifts from 'we' to 'you', so it is an instruction that *you* put to death the misdeeds of the body through the working of the Spirit. Those who do that will live. This means putting an end to sinful practices and living according to the ways of the Spirit. At this point the tense is present, it is an ongoing activity. It requires our commitment: *you put to death the misdeeds of the body*. But this cannot be done by the believer alone: it is *by the Spirit* we are to put to death the misdeeds of the body. It is an illusion to believe that anyone can overcome sin by themselves; the only power for this comes from the Spirit. The TNIV refers to *misdeeds* of the body, even though it is literally just *deeds*, because of the implication that things which have to be *put to death* must be wrong (v. 13). But there are also things, although not wrong in themselves, which nonetheless need to be put away or left behind for the sake of a life lived under the guidance of the Spirit. All Christians have to examine their life to see if there are aspects of what they do and think and watch which, although not intrinsically wrong, are simply indulgences which hold them back or divert them from that which they are called to do.

4. Adoption: part of the family

The fourth and final trinitarian dimension of salvation is the adoption of believers by God the Father. This image of salvation is derived from God's election of Israel as his 'son' and of the people of Israel as his 'children',[26] and it carries with it the notions of choice (God alone is the one who calls people to belong to his family), commitment (when he does he is fully committed to them) and closeness (his children are close to him and can know him intimately). The full implications of this work are expressed in trinitarian terms, as follows.[27]

a. Children: a new relationship

Believers are described both as *sons* and as *children* of God.[28] There is no real difference in meaning between 'sons' and 'children' and speaking of 'daughters' as well as 'sons' of God is, at least in this context, quite appropriate. Hence TNIV uses *children* in all of these verses. Being a child of God means being a brother or sister of Jesus Christ. Indeed, becoming a child of God is only possible because of the relationship believers have with Jesus Christ who is, by nature, *the* Son of God. Believers who are 'in Christ' are 'conformed to the likeness of his Son' (Rom. 8:29) and become sons and daughters of God through adoption. As such they are not like Jesus, who is a Son *by nature*, but they do share in a special relationship with Jesus, as his brothers and sisters and as his co-heirs in the family of God. Adopted sons and daughters may not share the same nature as God, yet they have the privilege of knowing God as *Abba, Father*. This intimate terminology expresses the experience that Christians have of being close to God. Feelings do not bring about salvation, but salvation affects the feelings. It is a sign of the authenticity of our relationship with God that through the Spirit we are able to know God as closely and as intimately as a child knows a loving father.

b. Heirs: a new status

Salvation means not only that believers enter into a new relationship with God as Father, but also that they take on a new status as heirs of God: *if we are children, then we are heirs – heirs of God and co-heirs with Christ* (v. 17). Heirs inherit from their Father's estate and as *co-heirs* with Christ believers share in what Christ has already received from the Father. It is normal for someone anticipating an inheritance from a wealthy relative to consider the

[26] Exod. 4:22 refers to Israel as his 'firstborn son'; also see Hos. 11:1, and for 'sons' see Deut. 14:1 and Isa. 43:6. Also see Hos. 2:1 for a reference to the children as 'brothers and sisters'.

[27] Material related to the implications of adoption is also found in chapter 14.

[28] 'Sons' in vv. 14, 19 and 23 and 'children' in vv. 16 and 17. Also see Rom. 9:26; 2 Cor. 6:18; Gal. 3:26.

245

possibility of inheriting wealth, houses or land. But Paul thinks of inheriting the suffering that Christ endured. In fact, believers are co-heirs with Christ *if indeed we share in his sufferings*. The Father gave to Christ a mission which involved suffering and those who are co-heirs with Christ will suffer with him (Phil. 3:10; Col. 1:24–29). This is the suffering which the church has endured and does endure today for the sake of Jesus Christ. This suffering is not evenly distributed, but nor is it pointless or uncontrolled. It is endured *in order that we may also share in his glory* (v. 17). Suffering is the route to glory for the church just as it was for Christ (John 17:1–4). Without denying the tragedy, the pain or the personal cost involved in suffering, it is also necessary to point out the positive dimension of it.

First, suffering can *reveal the nature of the gospel*, including (a) the character of God (2 Cor. 4:7–18), (b) the faith of believers (1 Pet. 1:6–12), (c) the reality of sin (2 Thess. 1:3–10), and (d) the spiritual unity and corporate responsibility of Christians (Jas 5:13–17; Matt. 9:1–8; Luke 13:1–5).

Secondly, suffering can *strengthen the believer*, by (a) leading them to repentance (2 Cor. 7:5–13), (b) being a discipline (Heb. 12:3–10), (c) developing maturity and perseverance (Jas 1:3), (d) bringing blessing (Matt. 5:10–12; 10:16–23), (e) being a means of encouraging others (2 Cor. 1:3–11), and (f) enhancing the believer's ability to empathize with others (2 Cor. 11:16–28).

Finally, suffering can *benefit others*, (a) when it enables witness to non-Christians (2 Cor. 6:1–10), and (b) when it helps spread the gospel (Phil. 1:12–18; 2 Tim. 2:1–13). As Christ's co-heirs we can therefore, through the privilege of suffering, share in his glory.

c. Spirit-filled: a new life

Being led by the Spirit is a definitive sign of being a son or daughter of God. Paul emphasizes this point by saying, first, that *those who are led by the Spirit of God are the children of God* (v. 14) and then that *the Spirit himself testifies with our spirit that we are God's children* (v. 16). Käsemann suggests that being *led by* the Spirit should really be 'driven by' the Spirit. Paul, he notes, 'was not so timid as his expositors'.[29] While this may be to overstress the role of the Spirit,[30] his leading is by no means purely passive. It is a dynamic leading, guiding and strengthening. The Holy Spirit brings to believers an internal testimony, an assurance of salvation. This is

---

[29] Also in Gal. 5:18 and 1 Cor. 12:2. Käsemann, *Romans*, 226.

[30] L. Morris, for instance, disagrees with this, arguing that it is not linguistically supported in this situation (Morris, *Romans*, 313).

known as believers share in the desires of the Spirit. Christians may be disturbed by the way that sin persists in their life, they may be shaken in their faith by events that test them, or they may have doubts about some aspect of belief, but the mark of genuine faith and discipleship is not found in human strength or intelligence but in the presence of the Spirit. Those who are concerned about spiritual matters, who rejoice in the conversion of others, who delight in seeking God, who love to know more of Jesus – these are the ones who know the testimony of the Spirit, who share in his desires and who are marked as children of God.

d. Fearless: a new character

Paul goes on to describe the relationship that believers have with God in this way: *The Spirit you received does not make you slaves, so that you live in fear again; rather, the Spirit you received brought about your adoption to sonship* (v. 15). The opposite of the love, security and confidence involved in being a child of God is *fear*. The apostle John makes the same point: *We know and rely on the love God has for us. God is love. Those who live in love live in God, and God in them. This is how love is made complete among us ... There is no fear in love. But perfect love drives out fear, because fear has to do with punishment. The one who fears is not made perfect in love* (1 John 4:16–18).

The Spirit of sonship stands in sharp contrast to the spirit of fear. Unfortunately there are too many Christians who live with unhealthy and unbiblical images of God and who have, in one way or another, become precisely what Paul warns against here – 'slaves again to fear'. Unhealthy images of God often emerge from negative feelings which remain entrenched in a person's life as a result of destructive relationships and damaging situations. Those, for example, who have known abuse as children may well experience inappropriate feelings of guilt, having been led to believe that the problems were their fault. Defensiveness, distrust and fearfulness in life's experiences can mean that God is seen as a judge and not a saviour, as angry rather than loving, as demanding rather than forgiving, as a law-maker rather than as a source of strength. Sometimes these negative and fearful perceptions of God are actually reinforced by churches. Paul, however, does not want any believer to fall back into anything which makes him or her *live in fear again*. Instead, he encourages his readers to understand that they have received *the Spirit* which brought about *adoption to sonship* by which they cry *Abba, Father*. Christians should have an image of God which reflects this reality and should see themselves as God sees them – as his beloved sons and daughters. Where fear reigns instead of love Paul's famous hymn to love in 1 Corinthians 13 might, in part, read this way:

> Fearful people are not patient, and have difficulty being kind. Fear makes people envious of what others have, and boastful and proud in response. Fear leads to rudeness; it is self-protecting and it often covers itself up with anger. Fear makes people look for weaknesses in others and has a pathetic joy when others suffer in the vain hope that this will advance their own cause. Despite what it tries to do, it is unable to protect anyone, it makes them devoid of hope and liable to give up on life.
>
> (1 Cor. 13:4–7)

If it is the case that love sets us free while fear is crippling, why does Scripture tell us to 'fear God' as well as to 'love God'?[31] If 'perfect love drives out fear' (1 John 4:18), then clearly the 'fear' that is driven out cannot be the same thing as the 'fear' Christians are encouraged to have of God. This proper, appropriate 'fear' of God is closely related to 'obedience', to 'walking in his way' and to having 'trust' in him.[32] It is a proper response to God's majesty, power and salvation and should be associated with giving God worship, honour and reverence.[33] The one who 'fears the LORD has a secure fortress, and for his children it will be a refuge' (Prov. 14:26) – which hardly speaks of the kind of terror usually associated with the English word 'fear'. In other words, Christians can fear God and yet not be afraid of him. Those who 'fear' God in this way – that is, they trust, obey and offer him reverence, worship and praise – need not 'fear' anything else. Any sort of fear concerning family, famine, finances, failures, sickness or death can be overcome if we trust God. This is the proper sort of fear that supplants all other fears.

Postscript: the people who most need to hear this message of love conquering fear are the ones who are most likely to misunderstand it – precisely because they have a tendency to operate out of the constraints of fear rather than the freedom of love. For such people every word of the gospel of salvation becomes another burden laid upon them. Those who hear this message as, 'I ought to be less fearful, I really ought to be more loving,' and those who preach it as, 'You ought to be more loving and less fearful,' have transformed the

[31] On 'fearing God' see Exod. 2:20; Deut. 6:2; Ps. 66:16; Prov. 2:5; 1 Pet. 2:17; Rev. 14:7; 19:5. On 'loving God' see Deut. 6:5; Josh. 22:5; Matt. 22:37; Mark 12:30; 1 Cor. 2:9; 1 John 4:7–9; 5:3.
[32] See, e.g., Deut. 5:29; 6:2; 10:12.
[33] See Rev. 14:7; 1 Pet. 2:17; 1:17.

'good news' into the 'guilt news' and fear will reign once more. The gospel is the good news of the grace of God, union with Christ and the power of the Holy Spirit, and change takes place as people immerse themselves in God and his love and as their image of him becomes more and more aligned with his perception of us as his beloved children. *Those who are led by the Spirit of God are the children of God. The Spirit you received does not make you slaves, so that you live in fear again; rather, the Spirit you received brought about your adoption to sonship. And by him we cry, 'Abba, Father.'* The emphasis must fall on the invitation to be changed, on the possibility of transformation, on the trinitarian relationship believers have with Christ, on the leading role of the Holy Spirit and on intimacy with the Father.

1 Corinthians 12:1–11
13. Christian community

Some time ago a publisher produced a catalogue for use by retailers showing three virtually identical versions of the one book. The cover of one had information on nineteen spiritual gifts, another version referred to twenty-one gifts, as it included speaking and interpreting tongues, while the third (with a slightly more creative-looking cover) had twenty-four or so, as it added music and other creative arts ministries.[1] Presumably bookshops could make a judgment as to which version was most likely to be acceptable to their market. It seems, however, to diminish the divine sovereignty to suggest that one can choose (or reject) the gifts of God at will. As Paul said, *all these are the work of one and the same Spirit, and he distributes them to each one, just as he determines* (v. 11). Paul's primary concern, however, is not with establishing a definitive list of gifts. Each of his lists of gifts is different from every other one,[2] because the gifts relate to the specific situation being addressed and he devotes very little time to actually defining them (none in the present passage). Much effort has been expended in recent times on establishing a comprehensive list of gifts and determining the right form of categorization for them,[3] but it is likely that Paul would not have recognized many of them. He was more concerned about the theological principles which governed their use: (a) understanding

[1] See, e.g., Exod. 28:3–4 (creative ability), 1 Cor. 14:26 (music), Exod. 31:3; 35:31; 28:3 (art and architecture). Some would also include military and political leadership as gifts (Num. 27:18; Deut. 34:9; Judg. 3:10; 1 Sam. 11:6; Isa. 11:2) and at least one well used survey tests for an aptitude for martyrdom.

[2] See, e.g., the lists in Rom. 12:4–8; 1 Cor. 12:8–10, 27–31; Eph. 4:7–11; 1 Pet. 4:10–11.

[3] For instance, it has been suggested of the gifts in 1 Cor. 12:8–10 that (a) they are listed in order of importance, and (b) they deal with gifts of instruction, followed by gifts of supernatural power and finally by inspired utterances. Also see Kistemaker, *1 Corinthians*, 420–421.

their true nature, (b) discerning their authenticity, (c) ensuring that they are used correctly, and especially (d) making sure that they are not the cause of division.[4]

1. There are different kinds of gifts, but the same Spirit

a. The spirituality of gifts

Whenever Paul uses the expression 'now about ...' (*peri de*, as in 7:1, 25; 8:1; 16:1; 12:1) it indicates that he is responding to one or other of the disputed matters which the Corinthians have raised with him: marriage, celibacy, food offered to idols, financial responsibility and, in the present case, 'spiritual things' (*pneumatikōn*). It is usually translated as *spiritual gifts* and sometimes 'spiritual persons' (2:15; 3:1; 14:37). Both are grammatically possible and one has to rely on the context for clues as to the precise meaning. As the present discussion focuses specifically on gifts (see v. 4), that expression is usually preferred, but it is possible that it could be taken in the more general sense as 'now, about spirituality ...' That would be appropriate, as it seems that Paul was concerned about the way the spirituality of the Corinthians was tied to the exercise of spectacular spiritual gifts and he was determined to show them a more excellent way (12:31). In doing so he addresses the Corinthians as *brothers* (TNIV is not theologically out of place in adding *and sisters*) – a term he tends to use when he wants to speak firmly[5] – and continues, *I do not want you to be uninformed*, indicating that they have yet to learn something about the proper use of gifts which they ought to know,[6] on which Paul was about to set them straight. He begins by pointing them beyond their one-dimensional and sensationalist view of God's gifts as *pneumatikōn* (a term they used, which he does not reject), with its connotations of power and the spectacular, towards a new understanding of God's gifts as undeserved gifts of grace (*charismatōn*), practical services (*diakoniōn*), the working (*energōn*) of God and diverse manifestations (*phanerōsis*) of the Spirit, not given for personal benefit but for the common good.

The basic Corinthian problem seems to be that they had an overspiritualized theology which led them to deny the physical or material dimension of Christian life. They denied the value of

[4] See, respectively, (a) 12:1, 4–6, 8–11; (b) 12:33; 14:29–33; (c) 12:7, 13; (d) 12:12–26.

[5] See 1 Cor. 1:11; 2:1; 3:1; 7:29; 8:12; 11:33; 14:20.

[6] As at Rom. 11:25; 1 Cor. 10:1; 15:34.

251

sex and marriage, the physical aspect of the resurrection, and considered the ecstatic and miraculous gifts, especially speaking in tongues, as of greater value than the others.[7] Paul, however, implies that their spirituality was derived from what they learnt when they were pagans. They had been *influenced and led astray* by Greek religious practices, which included ecstatic prophecies at pagan shrines, fortune-telling and various forms of divination, and although they were now Christians they were still convinced that spectacular experiences were proof of a genuine experience of God and of spiritual maturity. But, as Paul indicates, whatever ecstatic utterances emerged in the pagan context and irrespective of what the fortune-tellers said, these were really *mute idols* with no genuine word from God, and any view of the nature of the spiritual life derived from that source was inevitably faulty. Consequently, in chapters 12 to 14 Paul addresses the general question as to whether spiritual gifts *necessarily* make for a spiritual person.[8] He argues that there is a lot more to a mature spiritual Christian life than the exercise of gifts – any gifts, let alone simply the more miraculous ones. Christianity today still has to resist absorbing its understanding of spirituality from outside sources, and the temptation to think that the spectacular is an indication of spiritual maturity remains. It is just as much a mistake today as it was then.

b. Gifts, diversity and the Trinity

In order to ground a genuinely Christian, rather than pagan, understanding of spiritual gifts theologically, one has to turn away from idols to the one, true God. In verses 3–6 Paul relates the diversity of gifts at one and the same time to the unity and the triunity of God. Observe the structure of verses 4–6:

> There are different kinds of gifts, but the same Spirit.
> There are different kinds of service, but the same Lord.
> There are different kinds of working, but the same God.

This should not be interpreted as though 'gifts', 'service' and 'working' refer to three different categories. They all refer to the same entity but without being synonymous, for the gifts which God gives are multidimensional and each word points to a different aspect of them. Similarly, 'Spirit', 'Lord' and 'God' refer to the same

---

[7] See, respectively, 1 Cor. 7:1; 15:12, 35; 12:10; 13:1; 14:1–25.
[8] See Prior, *1 Corinthians*, 193; Carson, *Showing the Spirit*, 22–23.

being but to different dimensions of the divine nature. Is this an example of trinitarian thought or is it simply three ways of describing the one God, just as one might describe God as Lord, Friend and Master? When seen in relation to the rest of Paul's theology and his way of thinking, it becomes apparent that he uses Spirit, Lord and God as terms for persons in relationship rather than just as varied descriptions of one person. Both the Lord Jesus and the Holy Spirit are sent from God, but the sending of the Spirit differs from God's Fatherhood of Jesus. The Spirit cannot simply be equated with Jesus, nor Jesus with the Father. This threefold description of God's relationship to spiritual gifts is another example of Paul's way of thinking. Gordon Fee says that the trinitarian implications of this particular passage are 'striking' and C. K. Barrett describes it as 'impressive', not least because 'it seems to be artless and unconscious. Paul found it natural to think and write in this way.'[9]

Repetition of the fact that *there are different kinds* of gifts makes the point that diversity is needed for a healthy church – but not any and every kind of diversity. There is 'diversity' which is really just duplication (that is, too many churches or Christian groups doing the same thing separately when they ought to be working together), and there is 'diversity' of doctrine (which sometimes is simply a way of overlooking erroneous beliefs) and 'diversity' of ethics (which can be a way of avoiding the need to challenge certain behaviours). The diversity which Paul affirms is, very specifically, the diversity of the gifts of God. This applies not only to spiritual gifts, but also to the gifts of character and personality, race and culture, the natural world, calling and ministry. The church can never have too much of the diversity which God gives, but it must be wary of creating inappropriate forms of diversity.

The different gifts are from *the same* source, the one who is *Spirit, Lord* and *God*. Paul associates different names for the gifts with each of the members of the Trinity: *gifts* with the Spirit, *service* with the Lord, and *working* with God. The unity of God means that all these words could be related to each member of the Trinity, but in the present context it is very appropriate to recognize the *grace-full* nature of the Spirit in sending gifts, the *servant* nature of Christ and the powerful *working* of God the Father. Yet God is not divided, the whole character of God flows through all the gifts, and every individual gift is a specific manifestation of God who is at work in the lives and ministries of his people.

[9] Fee, *God's Empowering Presence*, 162–163; Barrett, *1 Corinthians*, 284.

c. The Giver, the Gift and the gifts

Having made it very clear that the gifts are only properly understood as the work of the whole Trinity, Paul can now agree (six
times, in fact) with the superspiritually minded Corinthians that
gifts are *the manifestation of the Spirit*.[10] It is possible to discern two
different, yet related, meanings for the term 'gift'. On the one hand
there is 'the gift of the Holy Spirit', which is really the same as
talking about the gift of salvation.[11] This gift is given to all believers
and as a result of it every Christian receives his or her own specific
spiritual gift as a personal involvement in the ongoing work of the
Spirit. That is, 'the Gift' of the Spirit brings 'the gifts' of the Spirit.
This participation in the life and ministry of the Spirit is both a
present witness to believers that God is with them and a future
guarantee that he will one day be with them in fullness.[12] When
people give gifts they usually select something appropriate for the
situation and the person. The value of the gift will vary greatly
depending on the relationship and the purpose, but gifts are nearly
always 'things' designed to please the recipient. In this case God has
given a much more personal gift – nothing other than the gift of
himself. He could not possibly give *any* greater gift. It is the gift
of God. This is his guarantee of redemption. He has come to live
with us himself.

d. Ministry and the priesthood of all believers

Many congregations have pew sheets which, amongst other things,
list the names of the pastor, the youth pastor, the church secretary
and so forth. Some churches have added to the list, 'Ministers: all the
people of the congregation,' in order to emphasize the corporate
nature of ministry. Indeed, any thought that there is one 'minister'
in a church has to be repudiated in the light of Paul's teaching about
spiritual gifts: *to each one* the manifestation of the Spirit is given for
the common good. No one person can undertake all ministry, the
gifts are given *to each one ... to one there is given ... to another ... to
another ... to another* (vv. 7–11). No-one is excluded from receiving
gifts from the Spirit. Yet, despite this, some Christians are discouraged because they cannot find their spiritual gift. Either their

[10] As well as being *manifestations of the Spirit* the gifts come *through the Spirit ...
by means of the same Spirit ... by the same Spirit ... by that one Spirit ...* and are *the
work of one and the same Spirit* (12:7–11).
[11] The gift of the Holy Spirit (Acts 2:38; 10:45) is the gift of eternal life (Rom. 6:23)
and the gift of righteousness (Rom. 5:17).
[12] Cf. Eph. 1:14; also see 2 Cor. 1:22.

spiritual gift self-assessment test knows nothing of the 'gift' which they had always thought they had, or they cannot see themselves in any of the gifts which are described in a book (or even in the Bible). Often, however, the problem does not lie with the person but with the way the tests are framed and the way the interpretation of the gifts is undertaken. When Paul says that each person receives *the manifestation of the Spirit . . . just as he [the Spirit] determines* (vv. 7, 11), it seems to imply that the gifts actually manifest themselves in different ways in different believers. It is a common but unnecessary assumption that the gifts consist of a specified number of different and discrete gifts with a fixed content. There is perhaps a greater degree of fluidity in their nature than is usually noted. The Spirit not only determines how gifts are distributed but also how they are expressed in each person's life. Michael Griffiths speaks of them as existing on a spectrum rather than being distinctly different gifts. He suggests that they should not be thought of as (for example) apostle, prophet, teacher and shepherd but more as apostleprophet-teachershepherd.[13] Flexibility is seen in the way Paul speaks of the *message of wisdom* and the *message of knowledge* (v. 8). Comment-ators are quite undecided about how to differentiate these two gifts clearly. Does *knowledge* refer to factual information or data? Or is it a form of insight which makes clear the meaning or significance of Scripture or the character of God? Or is this word intended to refer to any sort of understanding which is derived in some special or even miraculous manner? And how does it relate to *wisdom*? Don Carson comments, 'It is not entirely clear how or even whether these two gifts differ from one another.'[14] Paul does not stop to explain the difference and perhaps precise definition was not the main point of what he was saying. Given the main thrust of the passage as a whole, it seems safe to say that Paul was more interested in arguing for a greater recognition of diversity and flexibility than in devising a rigid categorization of the various gifts. Just as wisdom and knowledge are overlapping concepts, so too there is potential for all of the gifts to emerge in different ways in different people.

We can call the teaching that every believer is gifted and able to serve the community 'the ministry of all believers'. Unfortunately, this principle is often confused with another doctrine known as 'the priesthood of all believers'. They are not the same thing. Priesthood is a particular form of ministry and under the covenant God made with the children of Israel a priest was one who was able to help others to come into the presence of God by offering sacrifices and

---

[13] M. Griffiths, *Cinderella's Betrothal Gifts* (OMF, 1978), 20.
[14] Carson, *Showing the Spirit*, 38; also see Barrett, *1 Corinthians*, 285.

prayers on their behalf (Heb. 5:1–4). Then the death of Christ established a new covenant in which he became the great and perfect High Priest and the old covenant was swept away (Heb. 7:17–22). As the new High Priest Christ calls all believers to share in his ministry and become priests with him: 'you also, like living stones, are being built into a spiritual house to be a holy priesthood, offering spiritual sacrifices acceptable to God through Jesus Christ ... you are a chosen people, a royal priesthood, a holy nation ... the people of God' (1 Pet. 2:4–12). As a nation of priests *all* Christians have the direct access to God that priests have. This takes place through union with Jesus Christ, the High Priest. No other means are needed, no other way is possible (Heb. 4:14–16). Every Christian, from the newest to the oldest, from the most immature to the spiritual giant, has the same opportunity to relate to God in Jesus Christ. There is no hierarchy, no waiting, no barriers, all are welcome in the presence of God. This is the doctrine of the priesthood of all believers and it is a fundamental and wonderful doctrine.

The priesthood of all believers, however, does not mean that everyone has a 'gift' in the sense of the spiritual gifts referred to in 1 Corinthians 12. It is true that according to the doctrine of the *ministry* of all believers everyone does in fact have a gift in that sense, but the priesthood of all believers concerns the universal Christian privilege of access to God. This is not the same as the spiritual gifts, which are distributed very differently. When Christian priesthood is seen as one of the 'spiritual gifts' then it is assumed that only some people have the gift of being a 'priest' by which people can come into the presence of God. An equally erroneous reaction to that is to deny that anyone ought to be set apart to be a 'priest' or 'pastor' or 'minister' in any special sense. Both are wrong. The former view denies the priesthood of all believers which ensures that everyone can come directly to God themselves, while the latter denies the ministry of all believers which includes the possibility of some people being recognized by the church community as having gifts which build up through leadership in worship, teaching, preaching and pastoral care. The church needs to defend carefully both the doctrine of the priesthood of all believers and the doctrine of the ministry of all believers.

2. There are different kinds of service, but the same Lord

a. Service not status

The second of the three parallel phrases indicates that *there are different kinds of service, but the same Lord* (v. 5). The connection of 'service' with the Lord Jesus is neither exclusive (as though it could not be said of the Father or the Spirit) nor arbitrary (as though these different words were used purely for rhetorical effect) but entirely appropriate. It was the Lord Jesus who said to his disciples, 'You know that the rulers of the Gentiles lord it over them, and their high officials exercise authority over them. Not so with you. Instead, whoever wants to become great among you must be your servant, and whoever wants to be first must be your slave – just as the Son of Man did not come to be served, but to serve, and to give his life as a ransom for many' (Matt. 20:25–28). His example of service is foundational for the Christian life and it permeates everything. In Romans 12:7 service (*diakonia*) is one of the specific gifts listed, something which can be defined according to intent but not in terms of specific action. It could involve virtually any action. In the present situation service (*diakoniōn*) is one of the four general words used to describe the nature of *all* the gifts. Service is an attitude which ought to permeate the use of all the gifts. They are all 'services' which are given *for the common good* (v. 7). Believers should imitate Jesus, who declared, 'I am among you as one who serves' (Luke 22:27). Ministry is about function rather than status. If Jesus became a servant his followers cannot do anything less themselves. According to tradition, St Laurence lived in Rome during the persecution of Emperor Valerian (AD 253–60) and was a remarkable example of service. During a period of persecution Christians were ordered to hand over their treasure to the state. Laurence, who was deacon in charge of welfare, immediately sold everything and gave the money to the poor. When required to appear before the authorities to hand over the church's wealth he gathered together the poor, the sick and the homeless and presented them, saying that they were the treasure of the church. The emperor had no sense of humour and no understanding of the servant nature of the church and ordered that Laurence be executed. But that attitude of service is not easily extinguished and his example has encouraged many others in their own life of service. The church as a whole is called to a ministry of service and spiritual gifts contribute to that. God does not call those who are equipped for this ministry, he equips those he calls to it.

b. Jesus is Lord

The test of authentic Christian spirituality is conformity to Christ. Consequently, *no-one who is speaking by the Spirit of God says, 'Jesus be cursed.'* The idea of someone cursing Jesus could relate to the Jewish saying, 'Cursed be everyone who hangs on a tree'

(Gal. 3:13), but it is more likely to relate to the way Christians were persecuted. Pliny, the Roman governor of Bithynia (part of present-day Turkey), described early in the second century how he established the guilt or innocence of those charged with the crime of being Christian: those who prayed to the pagan gods 'and moreover cursed Christ – things which (so it is said) those who are really Christians cannot be made to do' he would release. Some who had been Christians but claimed to have ceased being so some years before were also released when they worshipped the emperor 'and cursed Christ'.[15] Some time later Polycarp, the leader of the church in Smyrna, was also arrested and the authorities 'addressed him persuasively', 'Come now,' they said, 'where is the harm in just saying "Caesar is Lord", and offering incense, and so forth, when it will save your life?' Polycarp refused to do so and was pressed by the governor to 'revile your Christ'. Polycarp's famous reply was, 'Eighty and six years have I served Him, and He has done me no wrong. How then can I blaspheme my King and my Saviour?'[16] Paul, of course, had personal experience as a persecutor of Christians. At his own trial before Agrippa Paul reflected on his former life and how he arrested Christians and 'tried to make them blaspheme' (Acts 26:11). His attempts to make Christians curse Jesus would certainly have been in his mind as he wrote.

Rather than cursing Christ, the Spirit of God honours Jesus as Lord and this declaration separated Christian faith from every other belief. The brief statement, *no-one can say, 'Jesus is Lord,' except by the Holy Spirit* (v. 3), is implicitly trinitarian in form because the title 'Lord' was full of divine significance in Roman, Jewish and Christian contexts. It was used both as a polite form of address (Acts 9:5) and in a religious sense to refer to the gods including, by the first century BC, the Roman emperor who was considered to be more than a mere human. Consequently, it was an act of rebellion worthy of death to refuse to affirm 'Caesar is Lord' and to worship him as a god. In the Jewish context Jews used this word to indicate divinity, using 'LORD' in the Greek translation of the Old Testament in place of the proper name of God, Yahweh, in order to avoiding saying the sacred name. The Jewish historian Josephus notes that Jews refused to call the emperor 'Lord' because they reserved that name for God.[17] In other words, in both Roman and Jewish contexts 'Lord' was associated with divinity and so the meaning was clear when early Jewish Christians worshipped Jesus

[15] Pliny, *Epp. X.96*, in J. Stevenson, *A New Eusebius* (SPCK, 1957), 13.
[16] 'The Martyrdom of Polycarp', in E. Radice (ed.), *Early Christian Writings* (Penguin, 1968), 158–159.
[17] Josephus, *Jewish Wars* (Harvard University Press, 1928), 418–419.

as 'Lord'. They could not say 'Caesar is Lord' or deny that Jesus was Lord without undercutting their belief in the divinity of Christ. But this was not a statement one could arrive at by human understanding, this was knowledge that was not known *except by the Holy Spirit*, for only the Spirit of God knows God. Only God the Spirit can reveal that the man Jesus is the incarnate Son of God, equal to, and of the same nature as, God the Father.

c. Gifts and natural ability

A natural ability (which simply emerges in a person's life) is distinguished from an acquired skill (which comes about as the result of training and discipline) by the way it is obtained and it is sometimes assumed that a spiritual gift is distinguished from both of these because it is obtained in yet another way – via a supernatural impartation from God. But the method of acquisition is not the issue for Paul. Spiritual gifts come from God, but so too do natural abilities and acquired skills. God is able to provide his children with all they need in numerous ways and that which is spiritual may come through inheritance, hard work or miracles. What distinguishes a spiritual gift from the other 'gifts' of God is the way it is used in building up the church. As Paul says, *the manifestation of the Spirit is given for the common good* (v. 7), and this is why they ought to 'try to excel' in gifts 'that build up the church' (1 Cor. 14:12). The Spirit may choose to use a natural ability to become the basis of a spiritual gift. A person who has demonstrated a natural ability in teaching may be inspired by the Spirit to utilize that talent in the service of the church as one who teaches the faith. In other situations, however, that kind of natural ability may not become a spiritual gift precisely because it has, in the past, been a person's strength and to develop this would encourage the person involved to continue to be self-reliant in the exercise of it, rather than completely dependent upon God who is the true source of the ability. It is not unknown, though, to find that after a person has learnt the lesson of reliance upon God and has matured in faith, the natural ability is allowed to develop as a spiritual gift. God is, after all, the God of all talents and abilities (Jas 1:17).

d. Gifts and occupation

If the gifts referred to in the various New Testament lists are not intended as completely comprehensive, then what else can be included? In his commentary on this passage, William Barclay writes, 'The mason, the carpenter, the electrician, the painter, the engineer, the plumber all have their special gifts, which are from God and can be used for him.'[18] This approach certainly recognizes the essential value of those occupations, but undertaking these things is not the same as exercising a spiritual gift. The gifts listed – *wisdom, knowledge, faith, healing, miraculous powers, prophecy, discernment, tongues* and *interpretation* (vv. 8–10) – are clearly of a different order. Paul does not include fisherman, tentmaker, soldier, farmer or shopkeeper in any of his lists. Elsewhere Scripture assumes and affirms involvement in trade and business and so forth, but when it talks about the Christian life, and when it makes mention of discipleship, those who are fishermen, tax collectors, tradesmen and homemakers are said to be gifted by the Holy Spirit to be apostles, teachers, pastors, prophets, healers, carers, servers, evangelists, elders and so forth. The assumption is that the gifted ministers of the church will be ordinary folk. The New Testament knows nothing about a professional ministry of the kind we have today if it implies in any way that others are not equally ministers in the church. That is not to say that training, recognition, remuneration and professionalization are necessarily wrong, but these things should not be allowed to overshadow the fact that ordinary people are called to engage in ministry in the midst of their occupations. God is concerned about ministry in every area of life.

The idea of *working* has intrinsic value in that it allows people to share in the stewardship of the world to which all people are called (Gen. 1:28), it enables us to be like God the worker who created and who constantly sustains the universe, and it provides the means for us to live as children of God. *Gifting*, for its part, enables Christians to be ministers of Christ, serving on his behalf and through his strength in whatever situation they are found. Ministry and vocation are not in opposition, but they are different aspects of God's call on our lives. They can be closely related, for a trade or a profession can open up many opportunities for ministry, and what could otherwise be done for selfish motives can be done as a ministry to others. The manual work Paul engaged in to support his ministry was not unimportant, but nor was it his gifting, which was to be an apostle. It may be that he was able to use the time of work to share the gospel (Acts 20:34; 1 Cor. 4:12; 1 Thess. 2:9; 2 Thess. 3:8), but work has its own integrity and value even where this is not possible. Likewise the gifts of the Spirit have their own place and Christians need to be aware of their calling to work and of their gifting for ministry. The situation of the financially supported Christian worker or missionary who is, in a sense, a 'professional

---

[18] Barclay, *Corinthians*, 109.

Christian' for whom 'work' and 'ministry' come together in one is not the standard against which all others are measured, but is the more unusual (though not the less valuable) situation. It is possible for Christians to focus on their work to the exclusion of their gifting and it is possible for those who focus on the gifting of the Spirit to look down on work. Neither is appropriate.

e. Gift and leadership

So much is expected of leaders today, and not only in the church. Society generally is very interested in finding dynamic, charismatic, visionary leaders. There is a whole industry which revolves around writing about, searching for and training leaders. There are numerous philosophies about leadership, many techniques for developing it and different ways of assessing its effectiveness. Much of what has been developed is helpful, but not all of it is appropriate for the church. The first problem is that there has not been enough theological assessment of approaches to leadership originally developed outside the church. The second problem is that so much is expected of so few leaders. The push to find and develop ever better leaders is well meaning and helpful in many respects, but it also generates higher expectations and greater responsibilities. Many do not feel up to this task and so more is expected of fewer people. This leads to the third problem, that of stress and burnout among church leaders. Craig Blomberg comments, 'Ours is an age that delights to exalt Christian celebrities, to demand that our pastors entertain, have charismatic personalities, and display more spiritual gifts than any one Bible character ever had! Little wonder that burn-out from full-time ministry seems to be at an all time high and that moral failure often results from stress.'[19] There is a clear need to go beyond the secular stress on individual leadership and to recognize that Christian leadership is a corporate activity shared by the whole community through the exercise of spiritual gifts.

Paul does not focus directly on 'leadership' but rather upon the exercise of gifts such as apostleship, prophecy, teaching and pastoring (12:29–30; Eph. 4:11–12) which can, of course, be exercised in such a way that they become recognized 'offices' or positions in the life of the church.[20] They certainly have in them significant dimensions of leadership, but categorizing them as 'leadership gifts' means that, inevitably, their nature will be defined primarily in terms of leadership rather than the exercise of the gospel, teaching and

[19] Blomberg, *1 Corinthians*, 257.
[20] Acts 6:1–7; 15:1–41; 1 Tim. 3:1–16.

prophecy. Indeed, 1 Corinthians 12:8–10 does not list either apostles or teachers and the impression is not given that *prophecy* deserves a position of eminence or leadership beyond that exercised by the other gifts in the list. It is potentially available to all, rather than just to certain 'prophets' (14:1, 3–4, 24), indicating that even this ministry, nominated later as being of importance (12:28), is one that is shared by the community. The gift itself has little to do with ecstatic or miraculous utterances. The prophets understood their words and were able to control their speech (14:32). Nor is prophecy defined by the ability to predict the future. Paul says that its essence lies in 'strengthening, encouragement and comfort' in order to 'edify the church'. Prophecy involves 'intelligible words to instruct others' and is related to the word of God (14:1, 3–5, 19, 36). It may well be a prepared message akin to teaching and preaching, or it may be a spontaneous revelation (14:29–30). The means the Spirit uses to inspire the prophet is not the primary issue.

Generally, Paul's theology of spiritual gifts suggests that leadership is a corporate function shared by the community. Leadership does not mean having some individual with a specific gift of leadership which stands apart from those gifts which Paul actually lists. Leadership is not a separate, all-embracing function but an attribute of the gifting each person receives from the Spirit. Every Christian is a leader – albeit in different senses – because every Christian is gifted. This does not exclude the possibility of individuals being recognized by the community as having a particular role, as some gifts require public recognition by the community in order for them to be exercised properly. One cannot, for example, be a pastor without knowing one's people and without the people knowing and accepting the ministry of the pastor as their shepherd. When Paul instructs and exhorts he generally addresses the whole congregation (1:10, 26; 2:1; 3:1; 4:14–20), and 'this can only mean that responsibility for responding to such exhortations lay with the congregation as such and not merely with one or two individuals within it'.[21] Paul expects each spiritual person to make judgments (2:15) and test everything: *distinguishing between spirits* (v. 10) was important.

Paul is very careful to limit his own leadership, even though he has had the most important role in the birth and growth of the Corinthian church. On the one hand he wants to establish his credentials very clearly, but on the other he carefully limits his authority and refuses to become a leader who usurps the rightful responsibilities of the community. Note that with regard to his own

[21] Dunn, *Theology of Paul*, 593.

gifting, (a) Paul's calling to be an apostle was based on a personal communication from the Lord,[22] (b) the authority inherent in his ministry was grounded in the gospel – there was no personal authority in being an apostle other than what was found in the gospel which was exhibited in his ministry (Gal. 1:11–12), and (c) the evidence of the presence of a gift is found in its exercise – Paul's success in founding churches meant that he was, indeed, an apostle (4:15; 9:2). These principles apply to all ministries – they are given by God, are grounded in the gospel and are evidenced by their successful exercise. This means, amongst other things, that their authority is limited to the area in which they operate and Paul acts consistently with these principles in his dealing with the Corinthians. He restricts his apostolic authority to the area of his own ministry – the churches he has founded (9:2), and even then he limits his authority to those things that are part of his commission – the preaching of the gospel. He is not concerned about his own position but, as an apostle, with the truth of the gospel. He refuses to assume that he has all power or authority and clearly differentiates between 'the Lord's command' (14:37) and his own advice (7:1, 8, 12, 25, 32, 40).

The implications of this are that while authority and leadership are necessary no-one has complete control. Each person has leadership in the area of his or her own gifting and not outside it – in that situation even an apostle will advise rather than command. Authority and leadership are found in the gospel rather than the person and mutual submission is the key principle (Eph. 5:21). Those who are 'leaders' – and groups will inevitably have some individuals who will play more decisive roles in a community's overall thinking and direction than others – must listen, and even submit, to those who exercise gifts in the area of their ministry. This is why those people who have New Testament roles which may be described as 'leadership roles' are those who have the maturity to do this, rather than those who have some other 'need to lead'. Paul recognized that there were certain ongoing positions like this, including the ministries of deacons, elders/bishops and pastors/teachers, and these offices are primarily defined in terms of spiritual maturity rather than gifting (1 Tim. 3:2–12; Titus 3:1–3). So while some gifts are appropriate for certain offices (e.g., service for deacons, teaching for elders), the possession of a gift does not itself necessarily constitute the right to hold a particular, ongoing position within the church if maturity is lacking.

[22] See 9:1. This was something the Twelve previously considered essential for this particular ministry, see Acts 1:18–26.

3. There are different kinds of working, but the same God

a. Through us or despite us?

Spiritual gifts are described as 'workings' (*energōn*) which come from God: *there are different kinds of working, but in all of them and in everyone it is the same God at work* (v. 6). Here the emphasis is on the way the power of God is shown in the exercise of spiritual gifts, and two complementary truths emerge from this. The first is the recognition that people are the means through which God achieves his purposes. Spiritual gifts exist wherever the Spirit of God dwells, they are part of each person's participation in eternal life and represent the privilege of sharing in ministry with God. God's plan includes using humanity to display divine life and power. That, of course, is the basis of the incarnation, that in Christ humanity becomes the ultimate revelation of God to the world. One can also see a reflection of the divine nature in all those who are 'in Christ' and 'in the Spirit' (2 Pet. 1:3–4; Rom. 8:29). Thus God's great power is seen both in Christ and in his people.

The second truth to consider is that God works not because of us, but despite us. There is a real sense in which we must admit that God does not need us. He can achieve his purposes in other ways if he so desires. Yet he has *chosen* to work in this way and to give us the privilege of sharing with him in his work. When she was much younger my daughter wanted to be able to use our motor-mower to cut grass around the house. She was small, some of the grass is on rough ground and the mower is large and heavy, so, for safety reasons, I would not let her. But she begged to be given a chance and eventually I relented and allowed her to stand between me and the mower, holding the handle and pushing while I, rather awkwardly, leant around and over her to hold on and push the mower and control its direction and speed. It was far more difficult to do it this way than by myself. Yet out of a desire to let her experience something that she would appreciate I was prepared to put up with the difficulty and the fact that the grass was not cut as well as it would have been otherwise. I have to concede, though, that after some time of working against each other a system developed and when the mower was travelling in a straight line on flat ground I could feel that she was actually making a contribution to the mowing. This is how God works with us. It is for our sake rather than out of his own need that he grants us the privilege of participating in his ministry of serving others, and while our contribution can sometimes be counterproductive this does not negate the fact that we can actually share in this ministry.

God's work is seen, on the one hand, in the power exhibited in gifts such as *gifts of healing* and the working of *miraculous powers* (vv. 9–10) and, on the other hand, in the fact that he works through weak and fallible people. It has been suggested that Paul refers to *gifts of* healing to indicate that no-one has the power to heal all people at any time but that healing is something which occurs from time to time. In that sense God's power is not under any human control. The New Testament records times of healing by various people but also occasions when healing was not granted – at least not in the more apparent manner.[23] Miraculous healing is aimed more at strengthening faith rather than relieving suffering. God's power can be evidenced through weakness and suffering as well as through the exercise of miracles. This ought to be a great encouragement to every believer and a reminder of the privilege we have when God works his ministry through us.

b. Discerning gifts

The gifts of God must be used with discernment. This principle can be applied in several ways.

(a) *Distinguishing spirits*: Paul includes *distinguishing between spirits* (v. 10) in his list of gifts. It means distinguishing between that which is from the Spirit of God and that which is from a human or evil spirit. The apostle John wrote about the need to 'test the spirits to see whether they are from God, because many false prophets have gone out into the world' (1 John 4:1). This is a critical issue and the principal criterion revolves around Jesus Christ and whether the spirit 'acknowledges that Jesus Christ has come in the flesh' (1 John 4:2). Although phrased in view of the particular circumstances John faced, this is essentially the same as Paul's test concerning the proclamation that Jesus is Lord (12:3) and it is the same test that must be applied today. All those claiming spiritual giftedness must acknowledge Jesus as Lord.

(b) *Exercising control*: as well as distinguishing between spirits discernment can also mean weighing up the particular value and the appropriateness of specific contributions made by those who exercise spiritual gifts. The fact that an individual has evidenced giftedness in a particular area does not mean that he or she will always act perfectly correctly and most helpfully in every situation. Gifts can be used in more and less helpful ways, they can sometimes conflict and they can be exercised inappropriately. We should not be surprised at this, and it was perhaps the main point which Paul

[23] Acts 5:16; 6:8; 8:6–7; 14:8–10; cf. 2 Cor. 12:9; 1 Tim. 5:23; 2 Tim. 4:20.

was making to the Corinthians. Paul insisted on the need to weigh carefully what prophets said (14:29) and to control the exercise of speaking in tongues (14:1–25), but there is a need to discern the proper use of *all* the gifts. The Spirit who gives the gifts works with believers to guide them. Individuals are not free to do as they please, there must be mutual accountability in all things. It is, unfortunately, possible for words of *knowledge* to be used manipulatively, for *teaching* to be exercised in a self-aggrandizing manner, for *service* to be done neurotically out of a sense of deprivation rather than love. In many ways, that which enables a gift to be most effective in a person's life can be distorted so that it becomes a hindrance rather than a help to the community. Gifts do not operate automatically, like machines, gifted people need to exercise their gifts in relationship with the Spirit, and all gifts can only exist and grow in a community where Christians can help one another.

(c) *Distinguishing genuine from false*: while those who work for the community at the expense of their own income are deserving of support (1 Tim. 5:17) the gifts of the Spirit are not given for profit, prestige or self-promotion. They are for the community good. The problem of the misuse of gifts in this way, however, is not new. One of the earliest non-New Testament Christian documents, 'The Didache' ('The Teaching'), gives advice on how to distinguish genuine from false prophets. There are observations on how long itinerant prophets should accept hospitality in one house before being expected to work and there are comments on their general behaviour, but most of it boils down to two blunt warnings: 'If he asks for money he is not a genuine prophet,' and, 'If his deeds do not correspond with his words he is an impostor.' Those who are living in idleness are 'only trying to exploit Christ'.[24]

(d) *Discerning change*: the expression *gifts of healing* (vv. 28, 30) perhaps indicates that this gift is not given as a permanent ability but that each occasion of healing is separate. Every Christian manifests the gifts of the Spirit in a different way (12:7) and there is no assumption that the gifts are automatic, permanent or unchanging.[25] The variations in the gift lists and the contextualized approach Paul takes in the various places he discusses gifts should probably lead us to conclude that God will provide whatever is needed and that this may well mean there will be changes. The Spirit gives as he chooses and it is possible that a gift may be rescinded, perhaps because other gifts come to the fore or perhaps through disuse, but believers will never be left without a gift any more than they will be left without

[24] 'The Didache', in Radice, *Early Christian Writings*, 233.
[25] Rom. 11:29 occurs in a different context and has a somewhat different meaning.

the Spirit. Experience also seems to indicate that growth and maturity on the one hand and a change in context on the other can lead to the emergence of new gifts in a person's life. Churches should avoid institutionalizing gifts and ignoring issues about the changing context of ministry and should encourage growth and development in the ministries of all the people.

c. Corporate and individual

It is of the essence of gifts that they exist in relation to each other. Paul uses the image of the body to illustrate their complementary nature (12:12–31). A full recognition of the way the body works together means that the various members of the body will no longer focus on their own gift as being superior or most important. Indeed, the gifts should be seen as gifts of the body rather than of the individual. Even though they may be exercised through an individual, they belong to the whole body. What does this mean?

First, no-one should think simply of 'my gift'. As David Prior says, 'Any tendency nowadays to talk of "my church ... my gifts ... my ministry" can have Corinthian overtones.'[26] Independent, itinerant ministries operating apart from any responsibility to the wider church are in danger of being insufficiently integrated into the body as a whole. Complete independence is the beginning of separatism and the division of the body.

Secondly, in seeking gifts, the focus should be upon the whole body rather than the individual. C. Keener comments on Paul's instruction to 'eagerly desire the greater gifts' (12:31): 'The fact that God is sovereign over the distribution of the gifts (1 Cor. 12:7) is no reason not to seek the gifts. God is sovereign over our food too, but though he desires to provide it for his children (see Matt. 6:25–34) and wants us to seek his kingdom first (Matt. 6:9–10, 33), he expects us to pray for him to provide our food (Matt. 6:11; 7:7–11).'[27] This desire for the good of the body should be distinguished from the attitude which wants forthrightly to 'claim' particular gifts for oneself as if the individual had that authority which rightly belongs to God. However, the instruction eagerly to desire the greater gifts is usually taken out of context and interpreted individualistically, with the only corporate aspect being that it is taken to apply to every individual. But it comes at the end of a passage (12:1–31) in which independent and individualistic attitudes towards gifts have just been soundly rejected. The whole purpose of Paul's discussion

[26] Prior, *1 Corinthians*, 201.
[27] Keener, *Bible Background Commentary*, 34.

of the body is to point out just how much each part needs the other. The instruction to 'eagerly desire' gifts should be taken to refer to the whole body. That is, a community (and each member of it) should eagerly desire those gifts which are going to build up the church, not as something which they seek for themselves but as gifts which the community needs and which should be exercised by the one the Spirit chooses (12:7).

Thirdly, the corporate nature of the gifts does not mean that they cannot be of great benefit to individuals, for as individuals are strengthened so too is the body. It is important, however, that this should occur in the appropriate context. A public gathering of the whole body of Christ is not the place for individuals to exhibit gifts for their own benefit. This is seen in Paul's instructions concerning speaking in tongues. The principles involved in this actually apply to all the gifts, it is just that at Corinth it was tongues which were the primary problem. Speaking in different kinds of tongues (v. 10) is a Spirit-inspired utterance which is unintelligible without special revelation (14:2). It is not beyond the control of the speaker, though, and the one exercising this gift in a service of worship must speak in turn and not speak if there is no interpretation (14:6–28). The principle is that in corporate worship the gifts must contribute to building up the whole body. Thus, as an example, uninterpreted speaking in tongues must be avoided in public and should be exercised as Paul presumably used the gift – in private (14:18–19, 28). As the individual is built up in that way, then so is the body.

d. Character is fundamental

The final point is one which was at the heart of Paul's message to the Corinthians. It is that if a choice has to be made (and without Paul's words in 13:1–13 it would probably be foolish to attempt to do so), one has to say that character is more important than gifting. The fruit of the Spirit, especially love, constitutes the indispensable core of the Christian character. This reflects the being of God, for the closest thing to a definition of God is the statement, 'God is love' (1 John 4:8). It is character, more than our abilities, which determines who we really are. A right character is more important than intellect, training, position, status and even gifting or ability. In the various lists of qualifications for ministry as bishop, deacon and elder the first and most prominent characteristics relate to character, holiness and maturity.[28] Let us not be seduced by the kind of conspicuous, dynamic, 'effective' and popular leadership that is

[28] 1 Tim. 3:1–16; Titus 1:5–9; 1 Pet. 5:1–5.

sought after today by businesses, political parties and many churches. Spiritual gifts are needed by the church, but forget about 'charisma' in the populist sense and go for character every time. The final words go to the apostle Paul: 'If I have the gift of prophecy and can fathom all mysteries and all knowledge, and if I have a faith that can move mountains, but do not have love, I am nothing' (1 Cor. 13:2).

Galatians 3:26 – 4:7
14. Christian security

At the start of this millennium the largest gathering of people in the history of the world took place when no less than 70 million people gathered in one place, in Allahabad, India, at the confluence of the Ganges, Jamuna and Saraswati Rivers on the first day of the Kumbh Mela religious festival. They came to bathe and wash away their sins, reducing the number of incarnations before achieving nirvana in the afterlife. This ritual bathing is but one example of the myriad human attempts to gain salvation. But it is only one example, and there are others of a more secular nature. A newspaper featured a photograph of a group of people undergoing ritual washing at Kumbh Mela and then a day or so later a cartoon appeared which was strangely reminiscent of it, although in this case it featured a group of Western people sitting in their lounge, totally absorbed in their television, with the caption, 'We call our television Ganges because we immerse ourselves in it, and are saved.' It was an ironic commentary on the fact that people seek salvation in many different ways and it is just as possible to seek it through entertainment and consumption as through any religious practices. In secular society many people seek meaning in the religion of self-entertainment and the ritual of the shopping centre. In his letter to the Galatians the apostle Paul spoke of the need for people to be released from all principles, rituals and desires which keep them in slavery. This occurs when people live their lives in conformity to either externally enforced or internally gener-ated beliefs in the hope that they will bring salvation, give meaning to life or provide that deep-seated satisfaction with life which is essential for well-being. Without Christ, said Paul, everyone was *in slavery under the elemental spiritual forces of the world* (Gal. 4:3).

The term 'elemental spiritual forces' (*ta stoicheia*) is a relatively general one which could, in other contexts, be used to refer to the basic elements of which the world is constructed (earth, water, air and fire as it was assumed at that time), or the letters of the alphabet (the elements used to construct all words and phrases), or even the 'elementary truths of God's word' (Heb. 5:12). In this situation, though, Paul uses it to refer to the basic principles of religion which enslave people but which cannot bring salvation. This is a universal situation that extends to *all* the laws and principles governing the social operation of the world in every nation. No human law or action, not even the Mosaic law, can make people righteous or bring salvation to anyone at all, and slavery to the basic principles of the world only comes to an end when the trinitarian God acts. In this passage Paul describes how God the Father sends two gifts from the divine, inner nature to be the means by which people can be saved. First of all, the Father *sent his Son* into the world in order to redeem those under the law (4:4–5), and secondly, the Father *sent the Spirit* of his Son into our hearts to enable us to know God as '*Abba*, Father' (4:6). In this way we can know experientially and certainly that God has come to us. This distinctly trinitarian teaching is expounded from the point of view of believers and their relationship with God as Father, Son and Spirit. The three dimensions of this experience are as follows.

- *Adoption by the Father*: the rights and the obligations of being made *sons of God* (3:26, NIV).
- *Union with the Son*: the soteriological and social results of being *all one in Christ* (3:28).
- *Confirmation through the Spirit*: the personal effects of the experience of *the Spirit in our hearts* (4:6).

1. Adoption: sons of the Father

Paul's declaration to the Galatians that *you are all sons of God*[1] through faith in Christ Jesus was a claim which was at once both unremarkable and shocking. It was unremarkable in that it involved describing people as *sons of God*, something that would have been familiar in both Greek and Hebrew contexts. The heroes of Greek mythology, for example, were often called *sons of God*. Dionysius and Heracles were sons of Zeus by mortal mothers. Egyptian rulers were also called sons of God – the Ptolemies were 'son of Helios', and by the time of Jesus Romans were referring to Caesar Augustus as a 'son of god'. This influence is seen in Paul's own quotation from Stoic philosophy in his preaching at Athens concerning 'the

---

[1] TNIV is right to translate this as 'children of God' rather than 'sons of God' as the intention is not to exclude women. However, the NIV 'sons of God' is used in this section in order to relate the significance of the term to its original cultural setting.

unknown God' when he observed, 'As some of your own poets have said, "We are his offspring"' (Acts 17:28). Of even greater significance for many of Paul's readers, however, was the Jewish notion of Israel, or individual Israelites,[2] being God's son. Consequently, readers from both Greek and Hebrew backgrounds would have been familiar with the term and the difference in their understanding should not be exaggerated. James Dunn notes, 'The degree of similarity between the use of "son of God" within Jewish writings and its use in the wider Hellenistic world is noticeable ... both inside and outside Judaism human beings could be called "sons of God" either as somehow sharing the divine mind or as being specially favoured by God or pleasing to God.'[3] So, the idea of *sons of God* was a familiar one but Paul's declaration, *you are all sons of God through faith in Christ Jesus*, would still have appeared as a most surprising, even radical claim to many, especially his Jewish-Christian readers, because he asserted:

(a) that Gentiles were entitled to a position of sonship which Judaism had long identified as being specifically for the children of Israel;
(b) that sonship came about through faith rather than according to the Mosaic law;
(c) that because Gentile Christians were children of God by faith they did not need to become Jews as well; and finally, and most importantly for his present purposes,
(d) that this concept of sonship could be developed in such a way as to involve an intimate and unparalleled relationship between the believer and God. This relationship connects the believer with the trinitarian life of God.

The primary difference between the Christian concept of believers being 'sons of God' and all other concepts lies in the trinitarian nature of God who redeems, adopts and empowers. This relationship involves the following five aspects. Note that, although all primarily expound the believer's relationship with the Father, the process of adoption is thoroughly trinitarian in that it can occur through the ministry of Son and Spirit.

(1) *A different status*: adoption means that a change of status takes place, the believer is *no longer a slave, but a son*.[4] Being a son and part of a family means having a new, permanent relationship

---

[2] Such as the king (2 Sam. 7:14; Pss. 2:7; 89:26f.), the righteous man (Wisdom 2:13 16, 18; 5:5; Sirach 4:10; 51:10), or the Maccabean martyrs (2 Maccabees 7:34).

[3] Dunn, *Christology*, 16.

[4] Cf. John 15:15.

Family relationships are, or should be, for ever. One can have a 'former servant' but not a 'former son' or 'former father'. Moreover, being part of a family is not something determined by one's ability, efficiency, character, intelligence or any other personal quality. One is simply born, or adopted, into the family. We do not even cease to be children because we are disobedient children. Of course, this can never be an excuse for deliberate sin or rebellion, but the sign of our participation in the trinitarian family of God is not some arbitrary standard of goodness but the presence of the Spirit, who creates within us a desire for God and a love for Christ and who calls out with us, 'Abba, Father.'

(2) *A greater intimacy*: it is appropriate to refer to believers being 'sons', 'daughters' and 'children' of God, because sonship in this situation does not denote gender (as in Rom. 8:14–17, where 'sons' and 'children' are interchangeable) but rather the new level of intimacy that one can have with God. This new relationship is brought about because *God sent the Spirit of his Son into our hearts* (4:6). It is only by the Spirit that we are made sons and daughters of God. In Paul's thought sonship and receiving the Spirit are so connected that one cannot speak of one without the other.

(3) *A new motivation*: in some situations a servant and a son may act in the same way towards their master or father, but the motivation and the feelings are completely different. A servant acts out of obligation and duty, while a son acts out of affection and love. Obligation is the motive when one is under law, but love motivates one's family relationships and especially obedience to God the Father.

(4) *A better knowledge*: a slave does as he or she is told, and can only do that and no more, because (as Jesus said) 'a servant does not know his master's business'. But the situation is different with friends (and family), for the 'master's business' is the 'family business' and so Jesus says, 'everything that I learned from my Father I have made known to you' (John 15:15). Having this knowledge is not like understanding a philosophy or knowing as much as an encyclopaedia. It is not a theorem or final equation. It is knowing Jesus who is the end and the goal of all things, the centre around which everything revolves. Whoever knows Jesus knows the reason, the goal and the nature of the whole of God's creation.

(5) *A future inheritance*: in 4:7 Paul shifts from the plural ('sons', 'our hearts') to the even more personal and emphatic singular: *so you are no longer a slave, but a son, and since you are a son, God has made you also an heir*. This brings it home to each and every reader that he or she is a son or daughter of God, and because of that he or

she is also his heir. While being a son has implications for *present* status, being an heir is a way of speaking of *future* blessings.[5]

Altogether the adoption language which Paul uses here links the believer with the Father and the Father's family – the Son and the Spirit. It demonstrates the new privilege which believers have and holds out the promise of even greater blessing in the future. Paul then moves on to the second dimension of the believer's experience of the Trinity, which explains how this new status is achieved. He utilizes the second of the three images found in this passage: union with Christ Jesus.

2. Union: all one in Christ Jesus

Those who are sons and daughters of God are united together in one family. They are *all one in Christ Jesus* (3:28). This union with Christ is not restricted to some especially fortunate believers; it is characteristic of the life of every Christian. As we just saw above concerning 4:7, Paul moves between 'we' and 'you' very deliberately and at this point he emphasizes the universality of union life by shifting from the 'we [Jewish Christians]' of 3:25 to 'you [Galatians: Jews and Gentiles]' and by placing 'all' (*pantes*) at the start of the sentence, which in Greek is a position of emphasis. The main point is that because we are all *in Christ* then we are *all one* together. He demonstrates that believers are in fact all *in Christ* by reminding them that:

- they have all been *baptized* into Christ,
- and have *clothed* themselves with Christ,
- and so *belong* to Christ.[6]

Although they have their distinctive elements, these three claims are virtually synonymous. In the early church being baptized was connected with repentance and faith in Christ and with 'clothing oneself' with Christ (Rom. 13:14; Eph. 4:24), which means to take on Christ's characteristics.[7] Some time later the church took on the symbolic act of changing clothing at baptism as a sign of a change in life and character. To be clothed with Christ means to take on the character of Christ. Whatever we see in him should be seen in us.

Those who are baptized are *in Christ*. The term is used eight times

[5] Cf. Gal. 3:29; Heb. 11:9–19; 1 Pet. 1:4.

[6] Gal. 3:27–29.

[7] Similarly, it could be said that one was clothed with righteousness, salvation, strength, glory, virtue or immortality, or, less positively, shame – e.g. 2 Chr. 6:41; Job 29:14; Ps. 131:9, 16, 18; Prov. 31:25; Isa. 51:9; 52:1; 61:10; Zech. 3:3–5; Col. 3:12; 1 Thess. 5:8; 1 Cor. 15:53–54; Job 8:22; Ps. 131:18.

in Galatians. On some occasions it has the *instrumental* sense of, for example, being justified 'by' or 'through' Christ (2:17; 3:14; 5:10). At other times it has a *locative* sense: the life of the believer is actually, in some way, found or located 'in' Christ (1:22; 2:4; 3:26, 28; 5:6). Here it is used in the locative sense. It is impossible to understand the passage as a whole without comprehending something of the significance of this term. Indeed, Longenecker says, 'Without treating the "in-Christ" motif we miss the heart of the Christian message.'[8] Without it Christian faith is likely to fall back into the kind of law-based religiosity which Paul was trying to leave behind. But what does it actually mean to say that one person can be 'in' another? In a famous treatise A. Deissman argued that in Greek it made no sense to put 'in' with a personal name, as 'in Christ', because one person cannot be inside another.[9] It has also been observed that it is problematic that the writers of the New Testament 'take for granted the possibility of certain sorts of relationships which are not, on the face of it, compatible with common sense'.[10] Some writers have used the term 'corporate person' to describe Christ's relationship with believers so that the form of his life is distinguished from the more commonly understood 'individual person' with which we are more familiar. The fundamental problem is that we are dealing with a relationship that is unique and there is simply no analogy or parallel which can describe accurately what our relationship with Jesus Christ means. We can, in a limited sense, share in the life of someone else by sharing experiences, thoughts and feelings, especially if we are as close as being married, but even then we are not able to live someone else's life from the inside. The 'in Christ' concept requires a new and different understanding of personality that allows for a unique and 'mystical union'.

The various writers of the New Testament have different emphases regarding union with God:

- John stresses union with the *life* of Christ.
- Paul focuses on union with the *death and resurrection* of Jesus.
- Peter emphasizes *participation in the divine nature*.[11]

Yet there is strong agreement on the basic concept of union with God through Christ and the Spirit. The life of the believer and

[8] Longenecker, *Galatians*, 159.
[9] In 1892, cited in C. F. D. Moule, *The Origin of Christology* (Cambridge University press, 1977), 60.
[10] H. Oppenheim, *Incarnation and Immanence* (Hodder and Stoughton, 1973), 17–18; also referred to in Moule, *Christology*, 60.
[11] See, e.g., John 6:41–51; 14:6; 15:6; Rom. 6; 2 Pet. 1:4.

God 'in' one another is a mutual indwelling. Paul speaks freely of *Christians in Christ* but less often of Christ in believers, although he does so on occasions (4:19; Eph. 3:17). Christ is the God in whom 'we live and move and have our being' (Acts 17:28). It is more characteristic of Paul to speak of *the Spirit in the believer*, as he does here. One of the best-loved prayers of the English-speaking church is the Prayer of Humble Access, which concludes with reference to the hope 'that we may evermore ever dwell in him, and he in us'.[12] It is a reference to an experience that is virtually inexplicable and yet readily verifiable by those who have experienced it. Paul is speaking about the experience of intimacy with Christ, the deepest religious experience of God that anyone can have.

3. Confirmation: the Spirit who cries '*Abba*'

a. The procession of the Spirit

This is the only place in Scripture where the expression *Spirit of his Son* occurs.[13] There are many 'spirits' and 'spiritualities' but the true Spirit only replicates the character of Jesus. Both Son and Spirit are, of course, one with the Father. These biblical relationships of Father, Son and Spirit were expressed by the early church in the form of two statements in the Nicene creed – first, that the Son is born (or eternally 'generated') of the Father, and secondly, that the Spirit 'proceeds from the Father'. Unfortunately, the Western part of the church unilaterally[14] added a single Latin word to the agreed form of the creed so that it said that the Spirit proceeds from the Father 'and the Son' (*filioque*). This seemingly innocuous addition created a division between Eastern and Western churches, not only because it varied from the mutually agreed version but also because it represented a difference in theology. This cannot be ignored just because it does not seem to be of primary importance for Western Christians. The *filioque* remains a serious problem for Christian brothers and sisters in Eastern Orthodox churches and is a major cause of the division which exists today.

What is at issue? Some say that the failure of the East to include the Son in the procession of the Spirit distances the life of the Spirit from that of the Son. This means that the Spirit does not sufficiently take on the character of the Son and so there is a tendency, for example, to

---

[12] From *The Book of Common Prayer*.

[13] Although in John's Gospel Jesus makes the same connection when he refers to the Holy Spirit whom the Father will send 'in my name' (John 14:26), and Luke refers to 'the Spirit of Jesus' (Acts 16:7).

[14] Starting at a council in Toledo in AD 589.

see the Spirit operating more outside the church. One effect, it is said, is that the authority and power of the state can be used legitimately by the church to implement its policies.[15] On the other hand, critics in the East think that the Western understanding of the Spirit deriving from the Father and the Son not only diminishes the Father's role as the originator of all, but also creates a hierarchy of Father, then Son, and finally Spirit which inevitably leads to the creation of hierarchical structures in church, ministry and society. The Eastern view, it is said, is that of a more communal and socially dynamic structure. These are not easy matters, especially when it comes to connecting fundamental theological principles to large-scale social outcomes. Many factors can intervene. Biblically, the Spirit must be connected with the Son and the Father or else the identity of the Spirit can become blurred. Perhaps it can be best expressed as the Spirit proceeding from the Father through the Son.

b. The assurance of the Spirit

What evidence do believers have that they are actually saved? What proof is there that God's promise of salvation is actually true *for them*? Many Christians have asked the question, 'How can I know that I am saved?' The answer is found in the double 'sending' of God the Father: the sending of the Son (4:4) and the sending of the Spirit (4:6).

First of all the believer can be assured that there is an *objective* basis for salvation which is grounded in the Father's sending of Jesus. As Paul says, *when the set time had fully come, God sent his Son, born of a woman, born under the law, to redeem those under the law, that we might receive adoption to sonship* (4:4–5). The believer's salvation is based on the life, death and resurrection of Christ as found in the testimony of the Scriptures and the witness of other believers. Although this provides the believer with a sure foundation for faith, it is always possible for doubts to arise. It is possible for Christians to be uncertain about the testimony of Scripture, the historicity of the resurrection and even the evidence of their own relationship with God. It may be fuelled by the sceptic who argues that, while there is no doubt that people have special experiences, there is no guarantee that they are actually experiences of God. They may be purely psychological. Consequently, believers can become uncertain about their ability truly to serve God, discouraged at their lack of obedience and unsure that their

---

[15] Thielicke, *Evangelical Faith*, Vol. 2, 183, believes that the rejection of the *filioque* leads the Orthodox Church to see church and state as a unity (Caesaro-papalism).

communication with God is real. They should first be reassured that, while doubt can ultimately be destructive, it is not immediately evidence that a person is no longer under God's grace. Doubt can be faith in two minds – a struggle between a genuine knowledge of God and an uncertainty derived from the awareness that anyone can be mistaken, even about the apparently obvious when the evidence is strong and deserves acceptance. Christians can find themselves in a spiritual parallel to the scientists who not only refused to believe the first reports about the Australian platypus but continued to deny its existence despite being shown the carefully preserved remains of one. Perhaps this is not surprising as it is a mammal which lays eggs, lives for much of its time in water, and has webbed feet, a broad, flat tail, and a bill similar to a duck! They argued that the pelt they were shown was a hoax put together from various parts of other animals. Perhaps it was inevitable that some would doubt the evidence they should have trusted – just as Christians sometimes doubt their faith when there is an abundance of evidence for the life and work of Christ in the world and their own lives.

Fortunately, the Father not only sent the Son into the world to redeem it, he also sent the Holy Spirit into the lives of believers as the *subjective* basis of salvation, making them aware that they are a son or daughter of God and able to experience God as their loving, heavenly Father. *Because you are his sons, God sent the Spirit of his Son into our hearts, the Spirit who calls out, 'Abba, Father'* (4:6). The presence of the Spirit means that we do not only know God 'from the outside' in the way that we know all other persons, but we know God 'from the inside' and can know of our salvation with certainty. It is part of human nature for people to doubt their ability to serve God, to question their holiness and to have misgivings about their virtue or strength, but it would be wrong to assume that the honest recognition of one's own weaknesses meant that one was alienated from God. The truth is precisely the reverse of this: God does not come to those who are already strong, but to the weak. Christians should not look to their own strength or achievements for final certainty, but to the Spirit at work in their heart. As Paul said in his letter to the Romans, 'God's love has been poured out into our hearts through the Holy Spirit' (Rom. 5:5). If we feel in ourselves a love for Christ, a desire for God, if we delight in the Word or celebrate the salvation of others, then we can be sure that we are held fast in the loving arms of God, for these feelings do not come from any human source but only by the working of the Spirit in our lives. It is the Spirit who speaks for us, *who calls out, 'Abba, Father'*, and who nurtures in us a love for God and a desire for Jesus. There is an invitation to the Lord's Table which says, 'Come, not because you are strong, but because you are weak; come not because of any goodness of your own, but because you need mercy and help; come, because you love the Lord a little and would like to love him more; come because he loves you and gave himself for you.' All those who recognize that they love the Lord a little and who would like to love him more are children of God.

Romans 8:15 is a close parallel to Galatians 4:6, but in that passage it is *the believer* who cries '*Abba*, Father', whereas in Galatians it is *the Spirit*. God the Spirit comes so close to the believer that what they do cannot always be distinguished and there is one cry simultaneously from two sources. Just as no-one can say 'Jesus is Lord' except by the Spirit (1 Cor. 12:23), no-one can call God '*Abba*, Father' other than by the Spirit. In this way there is an experiential confirmation of the believer's sonship. This intimacy with God and the assurance it gives is not reserved for the especially righteous, the mature in faith, the ordained minister or the missionary, but is a reality for the newest and youngest child of God. For even a young child knows to call out, 'Father!' when they are in need. Nor should our failings as sinful believers, which sometimes figure so prominently in our own assessment of our spiritual state, be allowed to blind us to the intimacy we share with the Father and the Son through the presence of the Spirit and the desires which this generates within us. A sense of failure associated with any desire to love God more is actually evidence of the presence of the Spirit. Only the one who desires God is concerned about a failure to do so completely. Believers can be secure in the knowledge that it is not a matter of our own strength, for the Spirit is present to unite us to the Father and to testify to Jesus at the most difficult times of life. When internal fears and doubts plague us and when disasters that are outside our control fall upon us, then 'the Spirit helps us in our weakness. We do not know what we ought to pray for, but the Spirit himself intercedes for us through wordless groans' (Rom. 8:26).

A desire for assurance was one of the main factors that led to that world-shaking revolution which was the Reformation of the church in the sixteenth century. Martin Luther, the man who sparked the fire which changed the world, had suffered great personal doubt and torment because he had been taught that there could be no assurance of salvation. After his own transformation he wanted everyone to know that they could be fully assured that they were under grace, with sins forgiven, adopted as sons and daughters of God and recipients of the gift of the Holy Spirit. If we are assured in this way, said Luther, then we will not be so dependent upon other resources. 'We should not be so addicted to worldly things, trusting unto them when we have them, lamenting and despairing when we lose them;

but we should do all things with great love, humility and patience.'[16] Assurance liberates us from our concerns about the present world and lifts our minds to be with Christ. 'Since, then, you have been raised with Christ, set your hearts on things above, where Christ is seated at the right hand of God. Set your minds on things above, not on earthly things' (Col. 3:1–2).

4. The doctrine of the Trinity transforms culture

Paul, however, is not only concerned with the personal, experiential implications of being in Christ. In fact, his reason for raising it is to point out to the Galatians that there is a practical, social dimension to life together in Christ that will affect the way they live and relate to one another and the wider community. What begins with the mystical ends with the political. All Christians are in union with the same Christ, there is one God, one Lord, one Spirit and one faith, baptism, hope, body and church, and so in Christ *there is neither Jew nor Greek, neither slave nor free, neither male nor female*. These specific relationships reflect the three blessings which appear at the beginning of Jewish morning prayer: 'Blessed be He that did not make me a Gentile; blessed be He that did not make me a brutish (i.e. an ignorant peasant or slave); blessed be He that did not make me a woman.'[17] There is no evidence that this particular prayer was recited as early as the first century, but the thought it expresses certainly extends back to that period. In fact, it is similar in concept to a sixth-century BC saying attributed to the Greek philosopher Thales, who said he was glad that he had been born a human and not a beast, a man and not a woman, and a Greek and not a barbarian. Similar ideas are found in other places. In 1 Corinthians 7 Paul puts together the same three issues and discusses them in the light of the gospel. F. F. Bruce comments, 'It is not unlikely that Paul himself had been brought up to thank God that he was born a Jew and not a Gentile, a freeman and not a slave, a man and not a woman. If so, he takes up each of these distinctions which had considerable importance in Judaism and affirms that in Christ they are all irrelevant.'[18] Paul's teaching perhaps reflects his own transformation with regard to attitudes towards slaves, women and Gentiles.

Galatians 3:28 has been called the Magna Carta of Humanity,[19] a fundamental statement of equality before God. There is no doubt

---

[16] Luther, *Galatians*, 378.
[17] Longenecker, *Galatians*, 157.
[18] Bruce, *Galatians*, 187.
[19] Witherington III, *Grace in Galatia*, 280.

that Paul's primary focus is soteriological – that is, to assert that the salvation which Christ brings is equally applicable to all people. As Martin Luther said, 'Here might be added many more names of persons and offices which are ordained of God, as these: there is neither magistrate nor subject, neither teacher nor hearer, neither schoolmistress nor scholar, neither master nor servant, neither mistress nor maid, etc. For in Christ all states, yes, even those ordained of God, are nothing … in Christ, that is, in the matter of salvation they are nothing.'[20] Some argue that Paul's teaching at this point is purely about salvation and has no social implications, that it is a statement that all believers have the same position in Christ and his teaching does not change the social relationships and distinctions to which he refers. Others say that, while Paul is speaking about salvation, this passage also has social implications which must be addressed. Unfortunately, both positions implicitly assume that salvation is something personal and that the only question to be debated is whether it has broader, social implications for slavery, ethnic relationships and male-female roles, etc. But the distinction between 'personal' and 'social' is arbitrary; salvation is not something personal with social implications, it *is* both personal and social in nature. Christ came to redeem the whole world, not merely individuals from within it. He came to inaugurate a new kingdom and to transform relationships as well as to enter into union with each believer. Paul's teaching at this point is that salvation is about human relationships – ethnic, social and sexual – and this is derived directly from the trinitarian, relational and interpersonal nature of God. Salvation is not to be understood as something 'personal' in the inadequate sense of 'individual', for no individual life can be understood purely in terms of itself. Human life can only be understood in terms of relationships with God and, through union with God, with others. The failure to incorporate a social dimension to salvation is usually the result of an inadequately formed trinitarian theology. If God is treated, as Western theology has often done, *de facto* as 'one' without a proper integration of the relational diversity of the 'three', then salvation will inevitably be individualistic and people will have a deep suspicion of what should be an equally essential social dimension to God's salvation of the world.

It is distasteful to recount the shameful parts of Christian history, but honesty requires the admission that there have been many times when racial and social groups have been considered to be beyond the range of God's grace. In every age and on every continent there have been situations where racism, sexism and imperialism have

[20] Luther, *Galatians*, 341.

impugned the God-given value of certain people. Slaves, poor, black, indigenous, Asian, Arab, female and others have, at times, been treated as subhuman and, rather than loving, caring and praying for them, opposition to them has been justified by vilifying them and painting them as 'the enemy' and undeserving of God's love and salvation. There is an underlying assumption that *some* people (including 'us') deserve God's grace while others do not. It is of little use pointing to the sins of others, though: it is always necessary to ask *ourselves* whether we as individuals, or our church or our society as a whole, are treating any social, racial or political group as less than those whom God loves.

The doctrine of the Trinity teaches that individual persons cannot be separated, understood or treated apart from their relationships. The three couplets imply a radically reshaped social world which Paul bases on a very relational doctrine of the Trinity in which God demonstrates his desire for intimacy with all people. A society's perception of God has implications for the way people live and society is constructed, and the doctrine of the Trinity has had profound historical implications for the way various societies have acted. In the fourth century Augustine used the doctrine of the Trinity to provide a new paradigm for thought in the Western church, while in the East the Cappadocian Fathers[21] made their contribution to the growth of trinitarian thought and the structure of society. The doctrine of the Trinity did nothing less than transform the way people thought about the world. Since the time of Aristotle everything had been described in terms of either their inner, essential nature ('substances') or their more external, observable and very changeable characteristics ('accidents'). But this did not allow for an adequate description of God as Trinity, because the differences between Father, Son and Spirit could not be expressed as being a difference of 'substance' (as that would have meant that only the Father was really God) or a difference of 'accidents' (as God's characteristics cannot change). So Augustine used the concept of 'relationship' to distinguish the Father from the Son and the Spirit and spoke of God having one substance or essence and three 'persons'. This description of God in terms of persons also had profound implications for understanding human nature as people are made in the image of God. Philosophically, this was revolutionary and C. N. Cochrane described it as 'the discovery of personality'.[22] Of course, people had understood about 'personality'

[21] Gregory of Nazianzus (329–90), Basil the Great (330–70) and Gregory of Nyssa (335–94).
[22] Cochrane, *Christianity and Classical Culture*, chapter 11, referring especially to chapters 9, 10 and 15 of Augustine's *Trinity*.

in its common sense before that time, but at this point it became a new conceptual tool. It stressed the reality and the value of the individual person against the common idea of the time that the real person was an inner 'spark' which was actually a part of a very impersonal divine substance. It also stressed the fact that the person cannot be properly understood independently but only in terms of relationships, and especially in relationship to the Creator. Ultimately this transformed society's attitude to the value of people. Everyone was important, everyone had value and everyone existed in relationship with others and with God. The idea of the sanctity of human life developed and it led to the establishment of a vastly higher standard of care for *all* people, whether slaves, gladiators, infants, the ill and dying or foreigners.[23] This new understanding of God and the world was influential for nearly a thousand years and 'shaped the barbarian tribes of the western extension of Asia into a cultural entity that we call "Europe" – it was this way of thinking that shaped public discourse'.[24]

The foundation for all these changes is to be found in the doctrine of the Trinity and, in particular, Paul's exposition of its implications in this passage. Richard Longenecker comments,

> Certainly the proclamation of the elimination of divisions in these three areas should be seen first of all in terms of spiritual relations: that before God, whatever their differing situations, all people are accepted on the same basis of faith and together make up the one body of Christ. But these three couplets also cover in embryonic fashion all the essential relationships of humanity, and so need to be seen as having racial, cultural and sexual implications.[25]

(1) *Cultural and ethnic unity*: in terms of the particular argument that Paul was making to the Galatians the Jew–Greek distinction was the most important of the three. It was a deep-seated division of the first century that Paul dealt with on a number of occasions.[26] Earlier in Galatians Paul had made the point that no-one is justified by observing the law, but only by faith in Jesus Christ (2:15–16), and now he draws the implication that Jew and Gentile are united in Christ and any distinction is irrelevant in matters relating to salvation. One immediate effect of

---

[23] See W. E. H. Lecky, *History of European Morals from Augustine to Charlemagne*, 11th edn (Longmans, Green and Co., 1894), Vol. II.
[24] Lesslie Newbigin, 'The Trinity as Public Truth', in Vanhoozer, *Trinity*, 3.
[25] Longenecker, *Galatians*, 157.
[26] Acts 10:1–18; 1 Cor. 12:13; Eph. 2:15; Col. 3:11.

this was that any actual separation of Jew and Gentile in the church had to end. Christian Jews could not regard themselves as superior in any way or require Gentiles to embrace Jewish law even if they continued to adhere to it themselves. Jewish and Gentile believers could, and should, worship together (1 Cor. 3:4), and because they shared equally in the gift of salvation there could be no distinction in ministry which would suggest that one was more competent, or that one was more restricted in what he or she could do, or that one was in any way superior to the other. Previously the priesthood had been for Jews alone, but now, in a transformed state, it was open to all believers and leadership within the church was based on gifting and not race (1 Cor. 12:1–31; 1 Pet. 2:1–12). To believe that all are *one in Christ Jesus* meant that for Paul it was impossible to try to restrict the grace of God to one ethnic group or to disadvantage any particular group. But the effects of Paul's proclamation are a long way from permeating our world. Our carefully drawn national boundaries have become barriers that encourage us to feel and behave less responsibly towards people in other countries than we do towards those in our own. Those attitudes and actions which serve to overcome these barriers are often both difficult and controversial: overseas aid, missionary work, multiculturalism, interracial marriage, intercountry adoption and any action that promotes foreign relations on the basis of need rather than national priorities. Yet they are essential forerunners of a world in which racism and the more evil dimensions of nationalism are condemned like slavery. The unity and the community of the church should reflect trinitarian unity (John 17:21) and this should become a model for the whole of society.

(2) *Social and economic equality*: in the Roman empire of the first century slavery was not thought of as necessarily immoral and it is reckoned that a majority of people were actually slaves. Paul's claim that in Christ there is *neither slave nor free* was, therefore, in one sense a radical statement which challenged prevailing moral attitudes, although it would, no doubt, have been a popular notion among slaves. As indicated above, Paul's primary intention was to make a statement about the fact that salvation was available to all. Consequently, in his letter to the Corinthians he was able to say, 'Each of you should remain in the situation you were in when God called you. Were you a slave when you were called? Don't let it trouble you – although if you can gain your freedom, do so. For those who were slaves when called to faith in the Lord are the Lord's freed people' (1 Cor. 7:21–22). The main point was that being enslaved could not deprive a person of his or her relationship with God. Nonetheless, it was a revolutionary step to suggest that

the lowest of the low in social terms could become a son or daughter of God. But Paul's encouragement to remain in the situation they were in when God called them (*not* 'to which God called them') has led some to suggest that he was not very concerned about the morality of, or perhaps was even a supporter of, slavery. There is another side to this, however. First he encouraged those who could to get out of it (1 Cor. 7:21). Then he insisted on changes within the church: economic and social issues were not to define participation in, the ministry of, or the relationships within the Christian community. Elsewhere Paul required that if there was a slave and his master in the church then Christian status should take precedence over social status (Phlm. 15–16; Eph. 5:21).

It is significant that the contrast Paul draws is between *slave and free*, while in Ephesians 6 there is a related contrast between *slave and master*. In Ephesians he is speaking about the immediate Christian responsibilities of those two groups and although he does not demand an immediate end to it he quite pointedly indicates the fundamental theological position, that there is no such favouritism with God (Eph. 6:9). When it comes to his discussion in Galatians he does not, *could not*, say that in Christ there is neither *slave nor master*, because he could not suggest that it was a matter of indifference for those *in Christ* as to whether one was a slave-owner or not. We do not know whether, as a man of his own day, he could envisage an immediate end to slavery given the way it was firmly entrenched in the society of his time, but he certainly could *not* envisage a kingdom of God *with* such injustice. Paul created the atmosphere for change. 'While Paul did not set up a social agenda, he created an atmosphere that would eventually lead to the abolition of slavery throughout the whole world.'[27]

What does this mean for us? As with Paul, there may be times when we are powerless to prevent injustice, but there must never be a time when we fail either to protest against it or to proclaim God's justice. Dante Alighieri (1265–1321), the renowned Italian poet, suggested in his typically graphic and literary manner that the darkest places in hell are reserved for those who maintain their neutrality in times of moral crisis. Today, despite universal condemnation, slavery and related abuses still exist in many places. In addition to traditional slavery the United Nations reports that the sale of children, child prostitution, child pornography, the exploitation of child labour, the forced use of children in armed conflicts, bonded labour, the sale of human organs and the exploitation of prostitutes all exist today and constitute a form of slavery. One

[27] McKnight, *Galatians*, 204.

hundred million children are exploited for their labour,[28] and in India another form of slavery exists as the Dalits ('broken people', formerly known as 'untouchables' and 'harijan') suffer from the officially outlawed but still operative caste discrimination. Relegated to the worst jobs, they are often openly oppressed and may be assaulted if they do what is forbidden by the caste system. Many teach that they are cursed of God, they are often barred from temples and they are made to live in separate areas, use separate wells for water, and are separated in shops and schools. The Christian's responsibility is clear: it is to act in accordance with the basic principles of the gospel. We cannot be like the mythical character who thoughtfully commented to a friend, 'You know sometimes I'd like to ask God why he doesn't do something about famine and injustice, when he *could* do something about it.' His friend replied, 'Well, what's stopping you asking him?' and the rather sheepish but revealing answer is, 'I'm afraid he might ask me the same question!' As Catherine Booth (1829–90), co-founder of the Salvation Army, observed, 'There is no improving the future without disturbing the present.' What is essential in this is the recognition that these matters of social structure are not incidental to the gospel, nor even merely long-range implications, but they are directly related to the way that God is understood and specifically to the form of the doctrine of the Trinity.

(3) *Gender and sexual complementarity*: in both the Jewish and the Graeco-Roman worlds of the first century women were considered to be lesser than men. The Roman philosopher Seneca (4 BC–65 AD) classified women as innately inferior to men,[29] while the Jewish historian Flavius Josephus (AD 37–c. 101) summed up the scriptural situation as, 'A woman is inferior to her husband in all things.'[30] While this is a distortion of Mosaic law, it nonetheless summed up the common perception of the times. But once again, Paul was convinced that the Christian gospel required a somewhat different view. He begins by affirming that women are spiritual co-heirs along with men in the salvation which is found in union with Christ. Gender does not affect salvation. In practice, what did this mean for the life and ministry of the church? F. F. Bruce observed that, while Paul's ban on discrimination on racial or social grounds has been widely accepted by the church, 'there has been a tendency to restrict the degree to which there is no "male and female"'. But he continues:

[28] The website of the United Nations High Commissioner for Human Rights provides current information.

[29] Cited in Longenecker, *Social Ethics*, 72.

[30] Flavius Josephus, *Against Apion*, Book 2, chapter 25 (Kregel Publications, 1981), 632.

No more restriction is implied in Paul's equalizing of the status of male and female in Christ than in his equalizing of the status of Jew and Gentile, or of slave and free person ... if a Gentile may exercise spiritual leadership in Church as freely as a Jew, or a slave as freely as a citizen, why not a woman as freely as a man? ... [S]uperiority and inferiority of status or esteem could have no place in the society whose Founder laid it down that among his followers 'whoever would be first ... must be slave of all.[31]

Ministry and spiritual leadership within the church should not be determined by race, nor by social status, nor by gender. Other texts must be taken into account in determining Paul's complete position on the matter and there is dispute about them. It is possible to see, though, that women worked along with Paul (Phil. 4:3), even, arguably, as apostles,[32] and they certainly prayed and prophesied in public worship (1 Cor. 11:5). Whether one accepts that the restrictions that are placed on the ministry of women (1 Cor. 14:33; 1 Tim. 2:12) relate to specific, cultural situations rather than being general principles will depend on arguments that go beyond what can be included here.

It can certainly be affirmed, however, that this particular text suggests that there should be no restriction on anyone's ministry simply by virtue of their being a woman, and it is a recognition of the part women play among the redeemed who are *all one in Christ Jesus*.

Conclusion: transformation today

It is most important for Christians today to remember that theological influences do not stop at the doors of the church. As we have seen, it is possible for the doctrine of the Trinity to become a powerful force for positive change. Colin Gunton argues that, because what people think about God is eventually reflected in their understanding of the world, as post-Enlightenment, modern Western society lost its understanding of the importance of the doctrine of the Trinity it experienced a lack of relatedness between people and especially between people and God. The more extreme forms of modernism eventually abandoned God completely, while those that retained some understanding of the one God lost the sense of the divine threeness and God ultimately became a 'transcendent and apparently oppressive single deity'. The pathos of modernity, says

[31] Bruce, *Galatians*, 189–190.
[32] See Rom. 16:7, and see, e.g., Dunn, *Romans*, 894, and Fitzmyer, *Romans*, 737, for discussions of the gender of Junias.

Gunton, is the fact that the loss of the Trinity means that 'in both the failed experiments of modern totalitarian régimes and the insidious homogeneity of consumer culture there is a tendency to submerge the many in the one'.[33] In searching for a more communal and personally related church and society, the great need for our world today is for Christian theology to present a gospel of God as Trinity which not only converts individuals but also provides a new foundation for public dialogue and ultimately leads to the transformation of our society. The Christian understanding of God as Trinity is just as important as ever in demonstrating that the world does not operate by impersonal processes, showing that the human person is not just a sophisticated machine or a biological organism, proving that relationships are real, important and achievable and persuading people that through Christ and the Spirit there is meaning and purpose in life.

[33] Gunton, *The One, the Three and the Many*, 38, 210–211.

Ephesians 4:1–16
15. Christian unity

Some people have a remarkable ability to understand things as they really are and not as they might seem to the rest of us. If you were held in prison for more than four years without your case even being heard, while suffering severe hardship and being expected to offer a bribe to secure your release, would you view this very positively? This happened to the apostle Paul, who was arrested under Governor Felix and languished in jail for two years while Felix waited for a bribe. Under his successor, Festus, Paul was able to exercise his right as a Roman citizen to be tried in Rome and so was sent there under guard, where he again waited for more than two years for his case to be heard by Caesar (Acts 21:33 – 28:31). Yet when he writes to the Ephesians he is not in despair, he does not even describe himself as a prisoner of Caesar – as anyone who saw him in his cell would have done – but as 'a prisoner of Christ Jesus' (3:1) and *a prisoner for the Lord* (4:1). His view of life was controlled by an absolute confidence in God as the one who was to be found in each and every situation. While aware of the actions of friend and foe, the presence and power of God were the greater reality for Paul. In every situation he had learnt to be content with his circumstances and confident in the goodness of God (Phil. 4:11–12; Rom. 8:28–39). And so he was able to say to the Ephesians, *I urge you to live a life worthy of the calling you have received*, because if he remained a faithful *prisoner for the Lord* despite his own lengthy captivity and many other hardships (2 Cor. 11:23–33), then the Ephesians ought to follow his example and not allow anything to prevent them from living in a manner appropriate to their own calling as Christian believers.

Paul's reminder that they had been called by God reinforces what he has already emphasized about the action of God on their lives: that they have been chosen, predestined, adopted, included in Christ

289

and marked with the seal of the Spirit (1:4, 5, 11, 13). But this divine initiative does not exempt believers from the responsibility to respond to God, and so he urges them to live up to their calling. In so doing he emphasizes the fact that being a Christian is not a solitary endeavour but a life which can only be lived in community. There are many things that individuals can do on their own, but being a Christian is not one of them. The central theme of this passage, therefore, is the unity of faith which is derived from the unity and the community of God as Trinity: a unity which permits diversity, a community which produces love and a oneness in which believers *grow up into him who is the Head, that is, Christ* (4:15). In verses 4–6 there are seven[1] 'ones': one body, one Spirit, one hope, one Lord, one faith, one baptism, and one God and Father of all. This unity is grounded specifically in the triple unity of Spirit (v. 4), then Lord (v. 5), and finally the Father (v. 6). With each step there is a development, an expanding circle of significance which links life in the Spirit with a community of faith in the Lord Jesus and then with a truly universal union of all things through the Father. Theologically the move is from anthropology to ecclesiology and then to cosmology.

Even though the order was subsequently reversed (from Spirit, Lord and Father to Father, Lord and Spirit), the trinitarian structure found here and the association of Spirit with body and hope, of Lord with faith and baptism, and the description of Father as over, through and in all things, profoundly influenced the development of the ancient creeds of the church, including the Apostles' and the Nicene creeds. Ephesians 4 has been a significant influence on the Christian understanding of both the nature of the church and Christian unity.

The Trinity as a model of unity

The Trinity, especially the relationships of the three persons, provides a model for the structure, the unity and the mission of the church. Biblically, this connection is found in various places[2] and the most obvious point of connection is baptism in the name of the Trinity, which places believers in communion both with God the Trinity and with other believers, that is, the church. The connection of Trinity and church is such that 'where two or three come together in my name, there am I with them' and believers are 'one' just as Christ and the Father are 'one' (Matt. 18:20; John

[1] Possibly symbolic of perfection.
[2] Not only in Eph. 4, but also Matt. 28:18–20; John 17:20–23; 1 Cor. 12:4–6; 2 Cor. 13:13.

17:21). The unity and diversity of God the Trinity is, therefore, a model for the unity and diversity of the church. These are concepts which, traditionally, have been expressed in the idea of the catholicity of the church. For true catholicity, unity and diversity have to be held together, for without unity one has fragmentation and even contradiction or disintegration, while without diversity one has uniformity and neither creativity nor any real community of persons. As with the Trinity, the diversity of the community of the church is held together in unity by the love of God.

More detailed expressions of the way in which the Trinity provides a model for the nature of the church have to be undertaken carefully, as many different church traditions have found their own very particular understanding of church in their interpretation of the relationships of the Trinity. There is a danger of reading back into the doctrine of the Trinity characteristics which justify one's own position. All connections between the Trinity and ecclesiology must be justified biblically.

(a) John Zizioulas operates from an *Orthodox* perspective, for example, when he argues that the relationship between the universal church and local churches reflects trinitarian relationships. The universal church exists precisely as local churches and there is no universal church other than that which is given reality through local expression, just as, analogously, there is no God existing independently 'behind' the Father, the Son and the Spirit. The church exists only in local expression just as God only exists in Father, Son and Spirit.[3] The universality of the church, therefore, is found in its existence as a communion of churches – a view which is amenable to the Orthodox view of the relationship of churches.

(b) It is, however, at variance with the *Roman Catholic* view, in which the oneness of the Trinity requires a more concrete form of communion. The oneness of God, the unity of divine nature and the concept of there being one centre of action in God, tends towards a hierarchical understanding of church in which one Lord, one Christ and one church imply one universal pope, one bishop for each area and one priesthood to represent Christ.

(c) *Protestant* churches, by contrast, claim that an understanding of catholicity determined by visible communion in geographic, institutional and episcopal form is too narrow when compared with an understanding of catholicity and unity expressed primarily in spiritual terms and then – despite the diversity of denominations and churches – in and through local churches because of the presence of Christ in the power of the Spirit.

[3] Zizioulas, *Being as Communion*, 257–260.

THE MESSAGE OF THE TRINITY

In any dialogue on these matters it is important not to rely too much on logical and philosophical arguments concerning the Trinity without continual reference to the biblical narrative, through which is revealed the triune nature and the connection with the church. For instance, it can be argued on biblical grounds that God as Trinity is not presented as a single subject but as a communion of interdependent subjects who perceive and relate to the others as 'other' (or 'another' – another counsellor). The Father relates to the Son and the Spirit, and the Son to the Spirit, as others. They are not merely modes of one being but each is a centre of consciousness.[4] This plurality of trinitarian persons and their community is then reflected in the life of the church: in the way in which the presence of the Spirit is found in every person; in the fact that gifts of ministry are universal; through worship which is the privilege and responsibility of all; in the recognition of the priest-hood of all believers; and in the fact that there is a mission which belongs to the church as a whole.[5] Thus there is a multiplicity and diversity with unity in the church through Christ and the Spirit which reflects the life of the Trinity.

The problem of multiplicity

The multiplicity of the church in its many local expressions brings with it various strengths, but it is also necessary to be aware of the problems. While the diversity of the church can be likened to a garden of many coloured flowers, it can also be likened to a broken glass or vase. One does not usually speak admiringly of the pluriformity and beautiful diversity of a vase which lies shattered in pieces! In this situation multiplicity is problematic and ought not to exist. This is a truth which cannot be denied, but even though it has to be admitted that many of the divisions and multitudinous forms of church and para-church are the result of unedifying dissension, failure to communicate and unnecessary duplication, *in principle* the unity and catholicity of the church is not destroyed by diversity. The true unity of the church is grounded in the triunity of God, which is expounded in trinitarian fashion in Ephesians 4.

- This unity is seen, first, from a very personal perspective through *the unity of the Spirit*, which endows God's people with three qualities (humility, gentleness and patience) that are essential for the church to be *one body*, with *one hope* (vv. 2–4).

[4] Although, it must immediately and strongly be emphasized, they are not *independent* centres of consciousness as human persons are.
[5] See 1 Cor. 12:3, 7; 14:26; 1 Pet. 2:9; Matt. 28:18–20.

- Then it is seen from a communal point of view through the unity of the *one Lord* Jesus, which is the foundation of *one faith* and *one baptism* (v. 5).
- Finally, unity is seen from a universal perspective through the *one God and Father of all, who is over all and through all and in all* (v. 6).

Expositions of these three dimensions of divine unity will be followed by a fourth section on the ultimate goals involved: unity in faith and maturity in Christ (vv. 13–16).

1. Personal qualities in the unity of the Spirit

The crazy and unpredictable American humourist Groucho Marx is usually credited with the line, 'I wouldn't want to join any club that would have me as a member!' It was a dig at exclusive clubs made by someone who was prepared to admit that he did not always live up to the expected standards of behaviour. But of course, no-one does. Believers do not always live according to the Spirit and churches are certainly not clubs for perfect people. The church is for sinners who, after all, are the only kind of people there are. What ought to mark a community as Christian is not the fact that people never make mistakes or do wrong, but rather that when they do, repentance, grace and forgiveness permeate the situation to restore the wrongdoer and to rebuild the community. Thus what are essential for Christian community are those personal qualities which consider the other as more important than self (Matt. 20:26–27; Mark 10:44). The *unity of the Spirit* can only be maintained by those who appreciate Paul's advice to *be completely humble and gentle; be patient, bearing with one another in love* (v. 2). The three virtues mentioned (*bearing with one another in love* is an explication of patience)[6] are, in their general sense, not uniquely Christian as they had their place in first-century Jewish and secular society,[7] but in a Christian context they take on new dimensions as believers commit themselves to be humble, gentle and patient in the manner of Jesus Christ (Matt. 11:29). Humility, that is, not thinking more of self that another, gentleness with those around oneself and a patient bearing with one another's imperfections ('putting up with each other'[8]) are

[6] These are three of the five mentioned in Col. 3:12.
[7] Humility, however, was not generally considered a virtue in the Graeco-Roman world as it was associated with servility. E. Best, *Ephesians* (JSOT, 1993), 362, notes that it heads Epictetus's list (3:24.56) of qualities which cannot be commended.
[8] Snodgrass, *Ephesians*, 197.

293

qualities which make unity within a community possible[9] and, taken together, they exhibit love for one another. Unfortunately, while not completely neglected, these virtues are sometimes misinterpreted today. In a society where it is acceptable to proclaim the benefits of putting 'self' first, *humility* is sometimes confused with servility, poor self-esteem and personal inadequacy. At a time when personal, social, economic and sporting success and strength are highly valued, *gentleness* can seem like weakness and failure. When time is considered to be short and instant service and immediate gratification are highly regarded, then *patience* can appear to be a capitulation to incompetence, boredom and frustration. In personal relationships, though, they are qualities to be valued like gold because they take one's thoughts away from self to care of the other. Without them you will tend to think about your own needs and wants, and probably about how much better you are than others, about how much you deserve and how soon this ought to happen. If you want to be truly miserable then rid yourself of humility, gentleness and patience, for these things only lead to joy and contentment in love for others.

a. Keeping the unity

With these virtues it becomes possible to *keep the unity of the Spirit* (v. 3). It is clear that Christian unity is fundamentally spiritual – that is, of the Spirit – rather than something created by particular modes of organization. Verses 4–6 demonstrate the real nature of Christian unity in terms of seven 'ones': one body, one Spirit, one hope, one Lord, one faith, one baptism and one God and Father of all. Christian unity 'is not just a question of friendliness or fellowship, of good nature, or of desiring to do good together. It is something, once more which lifts us up into the realm of the blessed Holy Trinity, the Spirit, the Son, the Father!'[10] The instruction to *keep the unity* immediately points us towards two equally important facts concerning Christian unity. The first is that we are to *keep* the unity rather than to *create* it. It is the community's responsibility to maintain what already exists. It is a mistake to think that simply being together creates unity or that our human manipulations of form and structure create (or even destroy) Christian unity or the church. Unity cannot be 'created' where it does not exist and it cannot be destroyed where it does. On the other hand, it is clear from what Paul says about 'keeping the unity' that the spiritual,

---

[9] 1 Pet. 5:5; 2 Cor. 10:1; Gal. 5:23; 1 Thess. 5:14; 1 Cor. 13:4; 2 Cor. 6:6; Col. 1:11.
[10] Lloyd-Jones, *Christian Unity*, 26.

trinitarian foundation for Christian unity does not mean that believers have no responsibility in the way that they live together. As well as getting rid of the idea that we can create unity we must eliminate the notion that it is possible to ignore it or live as though unity did not matter. A number of local churches were arranging some interchurch activities, including youth outreach. The pastor of one of the larger churches in the area was asked why his church was not involved. The answer was, 'Oh, we don't need that. We're big enough to do it by ourselves,' which was not the motive for most of the others and it completely missed the point of the principle that Christian unity and cooperation do matter.

b. Growing up in love

Paul links the unity of the Spirit with the concept of a single body: *there is one body and one Spirit* (v. 4), and then later (in vv. 15–16) he continues the body image, saying that by speaking the truth in love, *we will in all things grow up into him who is the Head, that is, Christ. From him the whole body, joined and held together by every supporting ligament, grows and builds itself up in love, as each part does its work.* Body imagery is used differently in various parts of the New Testament. In Romans 6 – 7 it is used to contrast the body of sin which leads to death with life through participation in the body of Christ. In Romans 12:1–8 and 1 Corinthians 12:1–31 it is used to emphasize the mutuality, the equality and the importance of all members of the body and the need for them to *maintain contact with one another* to benefit from the gifts each part contributes to the church. In Colossians 1:18 – 2:19 and Ephesians 4:1–16 the focus is on the connection between the head and the rest of the body and the need for the body to *maintain contact with the head* which is the source of life (Col. 2:19; Eph. 4:15). Only through Christ can the body be nourished and remain healthy.

The image of the body is not just a way of saying 'you ought to behave like a body', but it is actually expressing a deeper and more significant truth which is a reality (and yet a mystical reality) that we are 'in' Christ and he is 'in' us. Other groups use the image of a body to express something about the nature of their organization, but it is necessary to claim that the Christian use of this image is fundamentally different. The Scout movement, or a service group like Rotary, or perhaps even a multinational business may use the image of the body as a metaphor of the way in which they are united despite being diverse and separated. They may extend the imagery to show that there are different parts of the 'body' with different functions and even that there is an underlying unity between the various parts by virtue of being one body. But the fact is that it remains a metaphor, a picture or an image which expresses a certain truth but which is held together only by an idea or a concept. The church, however, *is* a body in a different way and there is an underlying reality to its unity which is created by the real, actual presence of God. Members of the church *are* connected through the unity of the Spirit and the person of Christ: it is not just 'as though' they were connected or 'like' being united together, there is a spiritual reality involved which is unique and very real. Believers are brothers and sisters with responsibility and mutual accountability which extends beyond that which is required by the human structures we create. Other Christians and other churches are not opponents, enemies or competitors and any tendency to think that they are 'not quite right' (or worse) must be tempered with an honest recognition of our own deficiencies and of the fact that one cannot 'correct' others without first establishing a positive relationship with them. The three essential virtues referred to earlier, humility, gentleness and patience, need to be expressed not only in terms of individual relationships but also in terms of relationships between churches and other groups of Christians. This will mean honestly recognizing the values and strengths of other churches, dealing kindly and gently with them and always being patient. It will inevitably involve mutual support, prayer and encouragement. In this way the whole body *grows and builds itself up in love*.

2. Communal faith under one Lord Jesus

Having looked at unity from the perspective of the Spirit and the personal qualities essential for unity, Paul now turns to consider even more explicitly communal themes through considering the presence of the *one Lord* Jesus Christ which brings a unity of *one faith* and *one baptism* (v. 5).

One Lord: the reference to the church being united around *one Lord* clearly repudiates the idea that devotion to any other Lord will do. It was necessary in the first century to identify which 'Lord' one served, as there were many other gods in the religious marketplace. But as Peter said, 'there is no other name given under heaven by which we must be saved,' a theme reiterated by Paul: 'even if there are so-called gods, whether in heaven or on earth (as indeed there are many 'gods' and many 'lords'), yet for us there is but one Lord, Jesus Christ.'[11] It is no less necessary to reassert this truth today.

[11] Acts 4:12; 1 Cor. 8:5. Also see 1 Tim. 2:5.

One faith: 'faith' is a term which usually refers to an attitude of trust, given by God and exercised in Jesus Christ. While that sense is obviously included here, it is also possible that there is here one of the first uses of *faith* as 'the faith' – that is, the content which is to be believed. Because this content is focused on Jesus alone there can only be one faith, not multiple faiths.

One baptism: because there is *one Lord* and *one faith* there can be, in distinction to all other cultic initiations, religious rites and various washings, only *one baptism* for the forgiveness of sins: that undertaken in the name of Jesus marking union with God through participation in his death and resurrection.[12]

One Lord, one faith, one baptism all assert that there is a single truth, in itself a view which is seriously questioned in the present pluralist and relativist age, and that this truth is to be found in Jesus Christ, entered into through baptism and present in the life of the church. While there is one faith and one church, there are many congregations and believers today facing ever increasing choices concerning congregational ethos, worship styles and ministry models. Is the unity of the church in danger of being overwhelmed by the mutliplicity of forms? Not necessarily, but there are certainly issues of concern.

Whereas once congregational and denominational loyalty were highly valued, today people are much more comfortable with switching from one to another. The right to choose one's church is little more controversial than the right to choose one's car. The high level of choice generally exercised in our world today is a particularly modern phenomenon which has become characteristic of contemporary Western life. Wealth can be defined in terms of the ability to choose widely – including the location, style and size of one's home, the type of car, private or state education, quality of clothing and so forth – while poverty can be seen as restriction and the absence of such choices. In a way which contrasts dramatically with the level of choice of most previous generations and with much of the two-thirds world, the typical Western person makes an astonishing number of choices each day. We have become experts at choosing everything from breakfast cereal and what to wear, to which television programmes to watch, recreations to pursue and places to visit. In many previous generations, with the exception of the few wealthy ones, people ate what was grown locally and was in season (a diet that would seem incredibly repetitious by contemporary standards), were educated by their family, took up the occupation of their parents, travelled as far as they could walk and,

---

[12] Matt. 28:18–20; Acts 2:38; Rom. 6:5.

THE MESSAGE OF THE TRINITY

in many cases, married whoever they were told to. By contrast, we have become so used to choice that it has become an automatic and unconscious process, and for most people the only problem is if there is insufficient choice. It is hard to imagine the problem that too much choice presents to those not used to it, but missionaries to the majority world often report that the worst culture shock comes upon returning to the developed world and having to learn again to make choices about everything.

a. Church and choice

In a consumer society people are well trained in making choices and, by and large, the fundamental basis for making decisions is whatever we like best. Decisions are made within the bounds of our ability to pay and with consideration for other members of the family and so forth, but we do not normally choose a chocolate bar we do not like or a type of car we think is rubbish or wear clothes we do not think suit us. The fundamental aim is to choose what we prefer. Christians are as indoctrinated in this as anyone and the effect upon the church of this high level of choice is profound. The danger is of developing a community of consumers rather than of committed participants. The very fact that there is a choice presented to us makes us view the church in a different way than if there were none. It is now inevitable that churchgoers will make judgments, decide between, evaluate and measure churches against each other and, in so doing, will establish some criteria by which they determine attendance at one rather than another.

The process of deciding is easily influenced by the common day-to-day process of choosing that which seems best for us. But some people, particularly those questioning their faith, will be confused by the variety and may even decide that the differences seem to deny truth to any of them. Others will become church connoisseurs, moving from one congregation to another, tasting and testing what they find and then moving on. Some will do this constantly, others less frequently but sufficiently to undermine church stability. A few people will shut out the range of options and assert that there is no choice and that in fact only one variety is truth and the others are false. And whether they change church or not, virtually everyone will have in the back of their mind the idea that they *could* opt out of their particular church if they feel they want to. Previously, when the distance one could travel was restricted and the possibility of choosing another church was socially and geographically limited, there were high levels of incentive for people who had problems with their church to work them out. Indeed, there were probably far fewer perceived problems because there was not that constant process of comparison between churches which goes on today in people's minds. The problems created by choice are compounded by the fact that pastors are aware that changing church is very easy, and so the form and content of their ministry is inevitably (and often unconsciously) influenced by the awareness that the values people hold important in church selection need to be satisfied if they are going to stay. All of this presents the church with an unusual problem. We are more used to defending the value of variety than of observing the problems it presents, but in the case of the church the idea that choice is a good thing is something which needs to be challenged. Of course, alternatives are difficult and perhaps even less helpful. And so the question becomes, what principles ought to guide us so that commitment is not superseded by consumption?

b. Principles for choice

When choosing a church, whether from necessity (perhaps having moved home) or because of other changes in circumstances, there is a temptation to select purely on the basis of what best suits us and our family. Very appropriately, denominational association still has its place, but the reality is that size of congregation, style of worship, type of ministry, the kind of people attending, the availability of fellowship groups and so forth are often considered to be more important. The common factor in all of these is usually that they reflect some judgment with regard to what one will *receive* from a church. But it is also very valid to consider what one can *offer*. It may be better to consider attending a church where one is different, or where one's own gifts can be exercised and where there are opportunities for service. Much will depend on one's own maturity and gifting, but every choice does not have to be based on one's own needs: it can be based on one's abilities. It may even be possible to be part of a church where one might normally feel uncomfortable because of theological differences in order, for example, to provide a witness to the value of biblical theology in a congregation where that is not held in high regard. This is something which has to be considered carefully, along with all the other factors including the maturity of those involved, the need for fellowship and teaching and so forth.

One of the great problems that we have is that the English word 'church' is used in so many ways, most of which do not reflect any biblical precedent. There is, for example, only the most general biblical justification for defining church in terms of a denomination – in the sense that wherever believers gather together there is the

THE MESSAGE OF THE TRINITY

church. But the New Testament never deliberately defines church in such narrow terms, whereas, of course, the idea of there being *one* church in an area is definitely found (as in 'the church in Colossae', or Corinth, or Jerusalem) even when there is more than one place of meeting (as is likely with the church in Rome).[13] The whole church, in every expression, is called together and our human divisions must not be responsible for diminishing our common life or our future hope.

3. Universal purpose through the Father of all

From the unity of the one Lord Jesus, Paul moves on to consider unity from the perspective of *the one God and Father of all*, and here the concept is expanded to universal dimensions, for this is God *who is over all and through all and in all* (v. 6). The same associations of God, Fatherhood and universality are made in 1 Corinthians 8:6, 'For us there is but one God, the Father, from whom all things came and for whom we live,' which itself was probably a Christian adaptation of the Shema, 'The LORD our God, the LORD is one.'[14] In Corinthians Paul was stressing the contrast between Christian belief and those who believe in other 'so-called' gods, and while he is quite capable of shifting the emphasis it is possible that this parallel indicates that Ephesians 4:6 should be translated as a reference to God who is specifically Father of *us* all,[15] and thus as a recognition that it was only among Christians that God was known as Father.[16] God is only known in this way because he is revealed as the Father of the Lord Jesus Christ, which means that people need to know Jesus as Son of God in order to know the Father. He is, of course, potentially God and Father to all through the ministry of Jesus who died 'to bring us to God' (1 Pet. 3:18).

a. The Lord of the universe

The one God and Father who is *over all and through all and in all* is the source of the unity of the universe. He is the transcendent Lord of all, constantly at work in creation, in all people and in all things, guiding everything to its future destiny. At this point the unity of the church has given way to the unity of the whole cosmos and mere temporality has been overtaken by eschatology as the ultimate

[13] Col. 1:2; 1 Cor. 1:2; Rom. 1:7.
[14] Deut. 6:5; Matt. 22:37; Mark 12:30; Luke 10:27. Also see chapter 3.
[15] That is, taking *pantōn* as masculine rather than neuter.
[16] Mitton, *Ephesians*, 143. Also see Matt. 10:32; 11:27; 15:13; John 8:18, 49; 14:20; 20:17.

future of the universe in God is contemplated. The cosmos comes from God, is given life and sustained by him, is filled with the divine presence and is orientated towards God at the end of all things.[17] Scientific cosmologists – people who consider the ultimate physical origin and end of the whole universe – speculate on whether the universe will end, so to speak, with a bang or a whimper. There is debate as to what will happen to our expanding universe in the almost unimaginable future. Will the momentum of the various stars and constellations continue so that at some point it will be like a fire which has had its coals scattered all around, and so will it gradually suffer 'heat death' and fizzle out into a freezing and uninhabitable universe? Or will the accumulated gravitational forces within the universe eventually reverse this expansion so that it becomes a contraction, with a collapsing universe culminating in a 'big crunch' as everything comes together in a catastrophic implosion? In any event the earth will get swallowed up by the sun long before then. And what is even more certain is that other theories and projections will be made to join these ones. While science and theology make good companions, it is unwise to hitch one's theological wagon prematurely to speculative scientific trains. It is even inappropriate to let science always be the train, because while it has its role in assessing physical events and can make sensible projections, the future is unknown to science and it is certainly incapable of attributing reason, purpose and meaning to events. These are not found written into the nature of things. What we can know for certain is that *meaning* and *purpose* are found in theological reflection on God's revelation. Ephesians 4:6 is an assertion that there is meaning to the universe for God is its source, its sustainer and its future. We can be assured that there is a direction to events, there is a future, and whatever happens in physical terms, God is in control for he is *over all and through all and in all*.

b. The Father of all

What is the meaning and significance of the fact that God is *Father of [us] all*? Is it a metaphor indicating that God is a fatherly kind of figure? If so, then the direction of movement is from those characteristics ideally found in human fathers which are then applied to God, indicating that God's relationship to Jesus is like that of a human father to his son. The reality, then, is that fathers have certain characteristics and these are metaphorically applied to God. One then has to refer, of course, to characteristics 'ideally found in human

[17] See Acts 17:25; 1 Cor. 8:6; Col. 1:15–20; 1 Cor. 15:28; Rom. 11:36; Eph. 1:23.

fathers', because one would not want all actual characteristics found in human fathers to be applied to God! This is not too much of a problem, however, as the primary movement of the metaphor is actually in the other direction. That is, the notion of Fatherhood which is affirmed of God is not that general set of characteristics found in human fathers but more precisely those character-istics found in the relationship between God the Creator and Sustainer of the universe who is *over all and through all and in all* and the incarnate Jesus Christ. These can then be applied to the nature of relationship which ought to prevail between human fathers and their sons. God is not like a human father, but human fathers – and mothers – are to be like God the Father of Jesus who loved his son, worked with him to make the world, empowered him to minister, commissioned him to redeem the world, lived in complete intimacy with him, raised him from the dead and honoured him by seating him at his right hand.[18] Consistently throughout Ephesians relational metaphors operate in this direction, so, for example, in 3:14, 'every family in heaven and on earth' derives its name from the Father, and in 5:2 being a child of God means doing just as Christ has done. In 5:32 the bond of marriage is based on the relationship between Christ and his church. That is, the 'one flesh' mystery is really the relationship between Christ and the church, and human marriage relationships should be like that – rather than the relation-ship between Christ and the church being like a human marriage relationship.

(a) *Positive images for the family*: obviously, there is a sense in which any analogy works in both directions and so it is not inappropriate to draw out comparisons which work from human relationships in order to illuminate something of the divine nature, but the basic movement is in the other direction. No human father, however, can relate to his child in exactly the way that the Father related to Jesus. No-one can, for example, commission their son to save the world from sin. But there are important principles to be found in the Father's relationship to the Son, not least the love, the commitment, the care and support, the intimate relationship and the shared ministry. Note that the Father sends the Son to minister to the world. At a time when there are many pressures on families there is a tendency for Christian families to withdraw and focus on internal relationships to ensure that the family bonds remain strong. But they can actually grow weaker if this becomes too introverted and self-entertaining and does not involve ministry to others. A family does not live for itself any more than an individual does. The

[18] John 1:3; Matt. 3:13–17; John 3:16; 17:21; Acts 2:24, 36; Col. 3:1.

divine Father-Son relationship gives a good example of a family which is open to minister together to the world.

(b) *Negative images of God*: an approach which begins with those characteristics demonstrated by God the Father and Jesus the Son will be better equipped to overcome the all too common problems which occur with immature projections of imperfect human characteristics onto God. We all tend to model God on what we perceive in others and those who either have an immature understanding of God or have had difficulties in their own family relationships are especially liable to unhelpful projection. This applies especially to any unloving characteristics learnt from the people they love the most. Negative images of God often derive from emotional difficulties and relationships. Children, in particular, learn about God through their parents and a patient, loving, caring, involved parent is likely to enable a child to picture God in those terms and to feel worth God's time and concern. An uncaring, impersonal, demanding or domineering parent can cause a child to have an image of God who is the same. It often leads to a deep sense of unworthiness, failure or fear. Often this projection is unconscious, but at other times people may openly express their difficulty with the concept of God and be unable to pray to God as Father. Theologically, the answer lies in understanding that the divine relationships are the model for human life rather than the reverse. The teaching of the church should make this clear and should be orientated towards the positive development of images of God which reflect clearly and accurately the love, the grace, the compassion, the mercy and the care of God the Father. This, however, is unlikely to negate the need for specific counsel for some people.

4. Unity through maturity

Having moved through the three dimensions of trinitarian unity related to Spirit, Lord and Father, Paul moves on to consider the trinitarian diversity which produces the gifts that enhance the life and ministry of the church. 'For Paul the transition from the confession of God's oneness in 4:4–6 to the discussion of the many gifts, ministries, members given to the church in 4:7–8, 11, 12, 16, etc., is far from a logical *non-sequitur*. It is essential to both his doctrine of God and his doctrine of the church.'[19] These gifts are given to enable ministry and to build a church marked not by uniformity but by unity in diversity.[20] In verse 8 Paul uses Psalm

[19] M. Barth, *Ephesians 4 – 6*, 467.
[20] As is also expressed in 1 Cor. 12:25.

68:18 as scriptural confirmation for the idea of Christ giving gifts and comments on it in verses 9–10, before moving on to the argument that a diversity of gifts is not counterproductive to unity but actually the means for building it.[21] Then he comes to the goal of this: *unity in the faith* and *maturity in Christ*. These relate to the fact that there are always two things to do in response to the gospel: believe it and behave it. Both are expressed in trinitarian terms.

a. Unity in faith

Gifts of ministry, says Paul, are given *until we all reach unity in the faith and in the knowledge of the Son of God* (v. 13). The unity which comes from the presence of the Spirit, the Lord and the Father is thus expressed in a unity of *faith* and *knowledge*. It is not possible to argue that the *only* essential aspect of this unity of faith is that people have faith in Jesus Christ without any common doctrinal content. Not only does *the faith* referred to necessarily involve a level of objective doctrinal content (as in v. 5 and as stressed in v. 14), but separating personal faith in Jesus from essential doctrinal content would simply divide the person of Jesus from his ministry. He actually taught certain things, and to suggest that unity can be found in trust in Jesus without reference to theological content makes no more sense than troops affirming allegiance to their general while admitting that they will not be paying any attention to specific orders. Moreover, if *unity in the faith* only involved the presence of a subjective response rather than some objective content, it would be achieved now, whereas this dimension of unity will not be achieved perfectly *until* a later time.

But what *is* essential doctrine? This is a difficult question.

(a) According to the much discussed fifth-century formula of Vincent of Lerins, it is 'what has been believed everywhere, always, by all'. This points, usefully, to the need for both consensus and continuity of doctrine. But the degree of strictness with which the principle is applied is debatable (how literally do we take 'everyone' and 'everywhere' and 'always'?), and who is it that decides?

(b) One way of determining this is to utilize the ancient creeds of the church which did receive widespread approval and which are still accepted as standards of orthodoxy today. But helpful though they are, the creeds do not deal with every situation. People can agree on them and still be divided on issues which seem to go to the heart of the faith.

---

[21] For material on spiritual gifts see the discussion on 1 Corinthians 12 in chapter 13.

(c) Another economical approach to consensus is summed up in the well known principle 'in essentials unity; in non-essentials freedom; in all things love'.[22] It is a good reminder of the need to avoid the presumption of believing that everything we can believe is essential to faith, and it encourages love for all. But to some extent it still begs the question of precisely what is to be considered essential. The principle itself provides no guidance on that.

(d) Consequently, some groups have operated according to the maxim, 'We speak where the Bible speaks, and are silent where the Bible is silent.' Again that can be difficult to apply, especially when the point to be resolved hinges upon the right interpretation of Scripture, yet it is on the right track.

Overall, there is no quick or easy answer to this question as people attribute different values to the various sources: Scripture, tradition, reason and experience. *Scripture* will, of course, be treated as the primary authority and what contradicts it is not to be accepted. Nor is anything to be demanded as essential which is not found in Scripture. The *tradition* of the church is a valuable resource and anything which contradicts the fundamental creeds and confessions of the church should not be quickly adopted. But different traditions have different confessions of faith and some of them are in conflict, and consequently a decision about what is essential becomes a difficult matter for judgment. *Reason* and *experience* need to be treated as corporate sources – that is, the fact that one person reasons in such a way or has had a particular experience is not sufficient for it to be taken as necessarily right or essential. The fact that it is difficult to establish the parameters of the essential core of theology does not negate the validity, the helpfulness or even the necessity of seeking to do so. It is part of the church's responsibility to maintain sound doctrine (1 Tim. 1:3; 4:1, 13). At twilight it can be difficult to say whether it is day or night, but that does not mean we do not know the difference between the two. It is the same with establishing true and false doctrine and essential or non-essential theology: the fact that it can sometimes be difficult does not mean we do not know the difference for most of the time.

What does one do when there is a breach in the unity of the faith? This is an equally difficult question, but one which many people are finding they need to address. Many denominations are today facing difficulties over theological matters such as the divinity of Christ and ethical issues such as homosexuality. For some separation over essential matters of faith and practice is necessary to preserve

---

[22] Attributed to Rupertus Meldenius (pseudonym for Peter Meiderlin), although it is often associated with Puritan writer Richard Baxter who adopted it as his motto.

personal holiness and doctrinal purity, to protect the young and those easily influenced, and to mark out clearly and publicly that which is considered to be essential. For others it seems better to stay to witness to what they see as the truth, to continue showing love and to minister to those for whom leaving is not really an option. Richard Lovelace suggests that it is a mistake to think that leaving enhances one's purity or that staying diminishes someone else's. He warns that separation, like some divorces, may produce a sense of release which seems constructive in the short run, but it may be less helpful in the long term. Still, he concedes there are obviously situations in which the separation of a segment of the church may be either necessary or advisable. 'It can even be argued that in the deepest sense such separatist movements do not really violate Ephesians 4:13–16 if they maintain a stance of openness defined, not in terms of monolithic structure of polity, but rather as a network of Christian hearts creating fellowship and communication with one another.'[23]

Because Christian unity is not achieved or maintained by simply being together (or being separated) or by revised organizational structures, the question of whether to separate or to stay together is not really the fundamental issue and neither choice can really be said to be 'right'. Both are aiming to deal with a situation which ought not to have arisen in the first place and which will not be put right until the fundamental issue is resolved. All interim measures, even necessary ones, are therefore imperfect.

b. Maturity in Christ

The second part of the goal, closely associated with *unity in the faith*, is maturity in Christ: the aim is to *become mature, attaining to the whole measure of the fullness of Christ* (v. 13). This maturity is contrasted with being immature, changeable and deceived. *Teleios* can be translated as 'mature' or 'perfect'. While 'mature' is probably best here, 'perfect' is used in other places where it is required by the context.[24] The distinction in Greek is perhaps not as sharp as it is when using two different English words, and one ought not to use the present translation to diminish the expectation which Paul puts forward. Indeed, as he goes on, it is a maturity which involves nothing less than *attaining to the whole measure of the fullness of Christ*. If Christ is the measure of maturity, then it means having the same attitudes that he had (Phil. 2:5). Consequently, having a

[23] Richard F. Lovelace, *Dynamics of Spiritual Life* (IVP, 1979), 291, 311.
[24] E.g. Matt. 5:48, 19:21; Col. 1:28; Heb. 2:10.

mature faith means not viewing pain and disappointment as wrong, unhelpful or as a sign of God's rejection. A mature faith recognizes the difficult truth that God uses these things to strengthen us. Nor does a mature faith assume that the best or only thing for God to do is to make us happy. It understands that God wants to transform us into his own image and to use us to serve others. It is a sign of an immature faith to think that if we admit our weakness, helplessness and sinfulness it is a problem for God that will make him think less of us. A mature faith recognizes that God already knows these things and wants *us* to know them, confess them and be forgiven and changed. Those with a mature faith do not insist that God provide an immediate explanation for everything that happens, but instead trust in God's sovereignty.

Learning to have a mature faith is something which is grounded in prayer, Scripture and a love for Christ. Christians must become mature by growing up in every way into Christ, and they must not be like bonsai trees. It is fascinating to see a perfectly formed and complete tree which is usually taller than a house sitting inside on a table like a pot-plant, but that is what bonsai can do. Bonsai trees are genuine and complete, perfect in every way, except that they are unnaturally small in stature. They are grown in small containers and are unable to grow to maturity because their roots are constricted and cannot get the nourishment they need. Unfortunately, there are bonsai Christians who, like the trees, have been unable to grow to full maturity because they have roots which are incapable of providing proper spiritual nourishment. They look just the same, they are perfectly formed, but they are not of the right stature and are only of any use for decoration. They are stunted and permanently immature because they do not have the necessary roots to feed them. Maturity does not simply come with age, it must be fed and nurtured. It is vitally important to ensure that one's spiritual root system is in good order.

Those who are mature will not be *blown here and there by every wind of teaching*, but instead, *speaking the truth in love*, will *grow up into him who is the Head, that is, Christ* (v. 15). The reference to growing up into the head comes about as a result of the first-century conviction that it was the head which provided vitality and life to the body and enabled it to grow. It has been pointed out that the translation *speaking the truth in love* involves a certain assumption, because there is no reference to speech and the words literally mean 'truthing in love'. This is not a common way of speaking in English, however, and so it becomes *speaking the truth in love*. While this is certainly legitimate, given the discussion concerning heresy and correct doctrine (v. 14), a much broader meaning is also possible:

that truth is something we 'live' and 'do' in love as much as we 'speak' it. The concept of 'truthing in love' in all kinds of ways is an attractive one which has the virtue of expressing a valuable truth – that God does not want doctrinal correctness to be alienated from a life of practical ministry or humble service.

c. Conclusion

To sum up, we can say that Christian unity and maturity (or 'perfection') are found in these seven 'ones',[25] and especially in the three 'ones' of the Trinity: one Spirit, one Lord, one God and Father of all. They constitute a unity through diversity which has personal, communal and universal implications. This is nothing less than Paul's expansion on the ultimate aim of God's revelation of himself as Father, Son and Spirit, which was outlined in the first chapter of Ephesians. In it he draws all things together and shows how the Father's choosing, the Son's saving and the Spirit's indwelling overcome all sin, all fragmentation and division and bring 'all things in heaven and on earth together under one head, even Christ' (Eph. 1:10, NIV). This is the ultimate unity towards which God is taking the world.

---

[25] One body, one Spirit, one hope, one Lord, one faith, one baptism, and one God and Father of all.

Jude 20–21
16. The Day of the Lord

> But you, dear friends, by building yourselves up in your most
> holy faith and praying in the Holy Spirit, keep yourselves in
> God's love as you wait for the mercy of our Lord Jesus Christ to
> bring you to eternal life.

These words appear towards the end of the letter of Jude (vv. 20–
21). It is likely that this letter was intended to be read as part of a
service of worship[1] and he encourages his listeners to keep on
building yourselves up in your most holy faith. This means
(1) *praying in the Holy Spirit*, so that (2) they will be able to keep
themselves *in God's love*, while (3) they *wait for the mercy of our
Lord Jesus Christ* to bring them to eternal life. There is a clear
indication here of the trinitarian thinking which lies behind his
understanding of keeping the Christian faith. At the same time a
second, very common, Christian 'trinity' can also be discerned in
these verses, that of the three classic virtues of faith (*your most
holy faith*), hope (*waiting* for mercy and eternal life) and love (*keep
yourself in God's love*).[2] Can these verses, predicated as they are on
a trinitarian way of thinking about faith, help us consider again the
central question of this book: just how essential is the doctrine of
the Trinity? Does Jude, for example, view the Trinity in the same

---

[1] While the exact recipients cannot be known, the extensive use of the Hebrew
Bible and other Jewish literature and traditions (e.g., vv. 1, 5, 9, 11, 12, 14–15), its
apocalyptic character and its concern for antinomian teaching indicate that it is
almost certainly an early piece of writing aimed at building up Jewish Christians in
the faith. Vv. 21 and 22, which possibly reflect a catechetical formula, and the
doxology of vv. 24–25, indicate that it could have been read as a sermon within the
context of a service of worship.

[2] Compare with other places where these three are found together: Rom. 5:1–5;
1 Cor. 13:13; Phil. 1:9–10; Col. 1:4–5; Heb. 6:10–12; 1 Pet. 1:3–8.

way as the Athanasian creed?[3] This commences with the following claim:

> Whosoever will be saved, before all things it is necessary that he hold the catholic faith; Which faith except every one do keep whole and undefiled, without doubt he shall perish everlastingly. And the catholic faith is this: That we worship one God in Trinity, and Trinity in Unity; Neither confounding the persons nor dividing the substance.

The creed then sums up the results of the trinitarian and Christological controversies of the ancient church, expressing the doctrine so as to exclude those who hold to various heresies,[4] before concluding with the reminder, 'This is the catholic faith, which *except a man believe faithfully he cannot be saved.*' This approach has been subject to a number of criticisms.

(a) On the one hand, some have reservations about insisting on acceptance of words formulated in terms related very specifically to the world of the fourth and fifth centuries. On the other hand, although theology must be expressed freshly and appropriately for every place and context, the creed does cover theological issues concerning the nature of God as Father, Son and Spirit which can never become redundant without destroying Christian faith.

(b) Others have criticized it for approaching the question of salvation from the point of view of an intellectual understanding of faith. But while it is true that salvation is by the grace of God through faith in Christ rather than by correct doctrine, faith is a trust *in* something or someone and so there must be some specific content or focus for the faith of the believer.

(c) It has been suggested that the creed usurps the right of God to determine the status of people's salvation, but while God alone is the judge of people's hearts, the church does have a responsibility to outline its essential teaching positively and as best it can in order that others may come to saving faith themselves and not be mistaken or deceived about what is necessary for salvation.

The Athanasian creed may not be perfect, but it is a constant reminder of the need for trinitarian theology to be at the heart of

---

[3] The creed is named after the champion of trinitarian theology but was probably not written for at least a hundred years after his death (373 AD) and derives from other influences as well. It is accepted as an authoritative creed by the Roman Catholic, Anglican and many other Protestant churches.

[4] Including those who denied the true nature of either the three persons or the unity of God, the divinity of Christ or the Spirit, the incarnation, salvation through Christ, the resurrection, judgment and eternal life.

Christian faith and practice. In that sense it follows the practice of Jude, *a servant of Jesus Christ and a brother of James*,[5] who wrote to 'contend for the faith that the Lord has once for all entrusted to … his people' (v. 3) against 'ungodly people ' who denied the grace of God and the Lordship of Christ and who promoted immorality (v. 4). After demonstrating the inadequacy of their position, Jude's encouragement to his readers in verses 21 and 22 is an explicitly trinitarian appeal to the community to continue trusting in the faith of the Spirit, the love of God and the mercy of Christ. The absolute importance of holding to this faith is seen not only in the way it functions as the culmination of the argument against the heretics but also in the implications which follow from it. This trinitarian picture of salvation is what is needed for those who doubt (v. 22), for those who need to be snatched from the fire to be saved (v. 23), and for all believers who need to be kept from falling in order to be able to come into the presence of God without fault and with great joy (v. 24). The importance of the doctrine of the Trinity is thus seen in the way Jude relates it to the central biblical theme of salvation. All too often salvation is insufficiently related to the entire work of the Trinity. It is not enough to connect salvation with the work of Christ. A comprehensive view of salvation recognizes that there is a sense in which conversion is accomplished in three dimensions: in eternity by the predestining plan of God the Father, at the cross by the atoning death and resurrection of the Son, and at conversion by the converting work of God the Spirit. When understood in this way the doctrine of the Trinity can never be seen as superfluous, irrelevant or unbiblical. It is at the heart of faith.

1. Building yourselves up in faith

The term *dear friends* (literally 'beloved ones' – *agapētoi*) is very appropriate for those who are 'loved in God the Father' (v. 1). It also serves to contrast the listeners with the 'scoffers who will follow their own ungodly desires' (v. 18). The *dear friends* are told to keep on *building* themselves up in the *most holy faith*. Building imagery is used elsewhere in the New Testament and, as with most images of the church, it has a number of dimensions which, in this case, can be used to indicate the nature of spiritual growth. First, it is a dynamic image of the process of building rather than simply a comparison with a completed, static building. The community of the church is actually a building site where growth takes place

---

[5] Many identify Jude as the brother of Jesus. He was not a disciple during Jesus' lifetime (John 7:5; Mark 3:16–19) but became one after the resurrection. See Bauckham, *Jude and the Relatives of Jesus*, 178.

(1 Cor. 3:9–15) and those who are less mature need the help and example of those who are more mature. Secondly, the image is a corporate one. The building process, it should be noted, cannot be done individually. The instruction is not to build 'yourself' up but to build *yourselves* up in *your* most holy faith. There is only one building, not many individual ones, and so there is no competition to have the best building. The point is to help one another grow to maturity in Christ. Thirdly, the building is a holy one, often a temple (2 Cor. 6:16; Eph. 2:19–22), associated with the Holy Spirit (1 Cor. 3:16) or, in this case, *holy faith*. 'Holiness' refers fundamentally to the essential nature of anything which belongs to God or his activity, in distinction from all that is common or even opposed to God. In this context *holy faith* is clearly the opposite of ungodliness and immorality (vv. 4, 7, 16, 18). There can be no compromise with any form of immorality, as the consequences include 'the punishment of eternal fire' (vv. 7, 23). This leads to the final point, in which the building image indicates the importance of the need for correct teaching. Indeed, being built up in the faith is virtually synonymous with being properly taught and the most fundamental teaching is found in the trinitarian exhortation of verses 21 and 22.

Altogether, the image of being built up is a reminder of the importance of overcoming the sin and immorality which has become part of the teaching of 'the ungodly people', those who are dreamers, 'blemishes at your love feasts', 'shepherds who feed only themselves', 'clouds without rain', 'autumn trees, without fruit and uprooted', 'wild waves of the sea', 'wandering stars' and 'grumblers and faultfinders' (vv. 4, 8, 12, 13, 16). Edification, or being built up in the faith, is a continuous and vital process. There are many Christians who think that when Christ has enabled them to overcome one or two obvious sins this is enough, and who even secretly wish that he would now leave them alone. John Wesley's journal records the reasons for people in a particular area leaving the society of Methodists.[6] Some left of their own accord, five because people said such bad things about the society, three because they said they could not spare the time to come, and nine because they would not be laughed at. Others were expelled, some for committing serious sins, including seventeen for drunkenness, three for quarrelling, one for beating his wife and three for habitual, wilful lying. But by far the greatest number, twenty-nine, were dismissed for what is described as 'lightness and carelessness'. Here is recognized a lack of maturity, a failure to be grounded in the holy faith and, most

[6] March 1743.

importantly, an inability to recognize the importance of being holy which led to them not being concerned about the state of their spiritual life. But overcoming sin is a serious matter. The salvation which comes through Christ is by grace rather than works and thus is not based on the removal of this or that sin, but rather on the atoning work of Christ applied to our lives by faith through the Holy Spirit. Genuine salvation brings with it a process of sanctification by which we are transformed and any denial of that process is a denial of the work of God in our lives. Sin cannot be considered to be unimportant and it is unlikely that the godless men whom Jude opposes got to be like that in a single day. It is more likely that it was a process which involved false teaching on the one hand and the gradual deadening (or 'searing', as in 1 Tim. 4:2) of the conscience on the other. Having a good conscience is a result of a right, sincere conscience which has been taught the truth. Then it is possible to have the full assurance of faith and to be able to encourage one another on towards love and good deeds.[7] No Christian can be complacent about his or her spiritual life.

2. Praying in the Spirit

The first of the three instructions related to the Trinity is the call to keep on *praying in the Holy Spirit*. Prayer is, of course, not only associated with the Spirit. A common way of expressing the various biblical principles concerning prayer is to describe it as being *to* the Father, *through* Christ and *in* the Spirit. While this very useful summary should not be taken in too restrictive a manner (as though, for example, one could never address Christ or the Spirit in prayer), it does represent good practice and in verse 20 Jude is expressing the principle of prayer being *in the Holy Spirit*. The explicit reference to the Spirit is another way of marking off the true believers from the heretics, who are described in the previous verse as those who 'do not have the Spirit'. Believers are those who are in the Holy Spirit and so when they pray they 'pray in the Spirit'. The reminder to keep on praying is important because the battle against false teaching is not won without prayer. This is an encouragement to all to continue in prayer, for that unseen work is more important than any public disputation.

Some suggest that the instruction to 'pray in the Spirit' implies that believers can pray 'not in the Spirit' and that the former is a superior, better form of prayer. But Jude's contrast is not between 'super-prayer' and 'ordinary prayer' or between 'super-Christians'

[7] 1 Tim. 1:5-7; 3:8; Heb. 10:21-24.

and 'ordinary Christians', but between believers and heretics – that is, between those who are filled with the Spirit and those who are not. 'Prayer in the Spirit' stands in opposition to the prayer of the godless men who do not have the Spirit and who may even have given up on prayer, as is often the case with those whose doctrine is false. The fact is that, by definition, all Christians have the Spirit,[8] and in that sense it is impossible to pray 'not in the Spirit'. Yet, while all Christians have the Spirit of God's Son who prays on their behalf (Gal. 4:6), there is a sense in which believers need to bring all thoughts and prayers under the direct control of the Spirit. This means to be so inspired and guided that they are praying 'in the Spirit' in the sense that their mind and will are completely in accord with God's. There is no trick to this, no special technique, no secret or esoteric method. Believers can have confidence in the presence and power of the Spirit if they simply devote themselves to God and to prayer. Nothing is said here about prayer in some special format, whether extemporary or prepared, in tongues or in rational words, spoken words or silent adoration. Prayer and praise will be 'in Spirit and in truth' (John 4:23–24) and God will guide and lead (Rom. 8:9) all those who are devoted to prayer in his name, whatever method is used. In that sense prayer is the most ordinary of actions, yet it is at the same time most profound and important. The real tests of spiritual life do not often lie in supreme sacrifices or the more dramatic actions of life. They are more commonly found in the smaller habits and practices, including one's commitment to daily prayer. It is one's attitude to God in the quiet, routine and less active moments of life which is determinative of character and spirituality. These are the times that prepare us for more difficult situations and it is impossible to be at our spiritual best at critical moments if character and spirituality have been diminished by daily failure.

Praying, that is, praying in the Spirit, is to be a constant part of life.[9] There is no time when it is inappropriate to pray. As Paul said, 'pray in the Spirit on all occasions with all kinds of prayers and requests' (Eph. 6:18). Taking seriously the advice to 'pray continually' (1 Thess. 5:17) does not mean that we have to live ignoring all other activities which demand our time or attention. It is possible to make a distinction between 'praying continually' and 'saying prayers'. The latter refers to those focused times of prayer when one prays with the active mind,[10] while the former is a reference to an ongoing and constant attitude towards life in which everything is

---

[8] Those who confess Jesus as Lord do so by the Spirit (1 Cor. 12:3) and so they are led by the Spirit (Gal. 5:18) and have the Spirit of sonship (Rom. 8:15).

[9] Acts 1:14; 2 Thess. 1:11; 2 Tim. 1:3.

[10] A distinction found, albeit in a somewhat different context, in 1 Cor. 14:15.

perceived as being done in the presence of God and for his glory. In other words, in addition to specific times of intercession for others there needs to be a recognition that the whole of life is a celebration of God, for Christians are convinced that God is always everywhere and so should rejoice and give thanks in all circumstances while carrying on with all life's occupations.

There are actually three attitudes, like concentric circles, which should permeate Christians' approach towards life and continually take them into the presence of God. The first is an attitude of thanksgiving. Saying 'thank you' is a mark of appreciation. We thank people for what they have done, especially when they have shown some extra kindness to us. It is good to be the kind of person who says 'thank you', and most people do so because it is a matter of common courtesy. But there are some who find it hard to say 'thank you', and it is usually a sign that they are focused on themselves and not really able to see the good in others. It has been said, perhaps rather cuttingly but with an element of truth, that 'people who are all wrapped up in themselves make very small parcels'. Spiritual maturity means opening up and recognizing what God has done and giving thanks to him as well as to others.[11] As we do so our attention is directed away from ourselves and towards God. Believers should give thanks for all that God has done in creation, for his providential care, redemption, guidance and involvement in their life.

The second attitude, like a second circle which is closer to the centre of things, is praise. If anything will take the believer deeper into relationship with God, it is this. Praise is different from thanksgiving, and more personal. We praise people not so much for specific things that they have done but for the kind of person they are. We praise people for being honest or kind, for having a particular characteristic or personality. It involves looking at the person as a whole. We thank people for what they have done but praise them for who they are, and doing so builds them up and strengthens them. Just as in human relationships there are more who are comfortable with saying 'thank you' than there are with giving praise, so too in the spiritual realm there are probably more people who are thankful to God than there are who really praise him. Praise is more personally committing and involving. Believers should praise God for being the God he is and for his divine character of love, grace, mercy, forgiveness, humility and patience.[12]

[11] Eph. 5:20; Col. 1:12; 1 Thess. 5:18; Rev. 4:9.
[12] 2 Cor. 1:3; Eph. 1:3; 1 Pet. 1:3, 7; Rev. 5:13.

Praise thus takes one closer into the presence of God than thanksgiving, but the third circle, adoration, gets even closer to the heart of things and brings the believer very close to God. Thanksgiving is appreciation for what a person has done and praise is the outward recognition of a person for who they are, but adoration is the fundamental, internal attitude which individuals have towards one they love. While thanksgiving and praise necessarily involve words, adoration is more likely to be an almost silent contemplation, as when lovers gaze into one another's eyes. Praise without adoration is an empty shell, meaningless words, form without content, style without substance. Adoration is the heart of worship. Continually being filled with, living in (Eph. 5:18; Rom. 8) and praying in the Spirit (v. 20) means developing a profound intimacy with God.

3. Keeping in God's love

The encouragement for believers to *keep yourselves in God's love* parallels the first verse of the letter, which reminds the readers that it is only possible to keep themselves in God's love because of the fact that first of all they 'are loved in God the Father and kept by Jesus Christ'. The focus here is on God's love for his people and so, while it is possible to translate it as 'keep yourself in *your love for God*' (in the sense that believers are elsewhere exhorted to love God[13]), it is better understood as 'keep yourself in *God's love for you*'.[14] The security of the Father's love and the Son's keeping means that it is possible for believers to keep themselves in God's love. It is, after all, God the Saviour through Jesus Christ the Lord 'who is able to keep you from stumbling and to present you before his glorious presence without fault and with great joy'. Nonetheless, it is clear that although the relationship is not symmetrical (God's love for us is more fundamental than our love for God) it is reciprocal – God's love calls for a response in love and a commitment by Christians to *keep yourselves* within that love.

This love comes from the Father through the Son, who is 'the reflection of God's glory', and the Holy Spirit, who is 'the Spirit of glory',[15] and it calls for a corresponding response of love because of the way this shows that God is glorious and beautiful. 'Glory' is one way to speak of God's unique, immense and profound beauty and the dynamic for the believers' love for God emerges when they

[13] As in Luke 11:42; John 5:42; 1 John 2:5, 15.
[14] In the same way *the mercy of the Lord Jesus* refers to the mercy which God has for believers. Also see passages such as John 15:9 and Rom. 5:5; 8:39.
[15] Heb. 1:1–3; 2 Cor. 4:4; 1 Pet. 4:14.

become aware that God is indeed beautiful beyond description (Ps. 27:4; Isa. 4:2). It is the sense of beauty which leads us into love. A genuine falling in love is a capitulation to beauty. Everyone who falls in love believes that their beloved is most beautiful, in personality or appearance or both, and they are always right! Their love shows that they have perceived the beauty which is to be found in that person because they are made in the image of the beautiful God. Falling in love is not superficial infatuation but is 'selfless commitment to the fascinating beloved'.[16] The fact of God as Trinity, existing in love, freely creating all things, redeeming through grace and calling the world into a communion of joy and peace is simply beautiful. And we are instinctively persuaded that the beautiful is true because God is the source and origin of the beauty for which our inner spirit searches. In mathematics and science as well as in art and culture it is the compelling power of beauty which points to the truth. In this sense all works of art have a spiritual dimension and whoever rejects genuine beauty 'can no longer pray and will soon no longer be able to love'.[17] Beauty triggers wonder in the human heart and is essential for spiritual growth. By loving we are made beautiful. 'Therefore, if you wish to love anything, love Jesus Christ, who is the fairest, richest and most wise of lovers, and whose love lasts forever in eternal joy.'[18]

4. Waiting for the mercy of Christ

While it is likely that most people reckon some days to be more important than others, it is certain that everyone needs to understand that the final 'Day of the Lord' is the most important of all. This is the day Jude wants believers to look forward to as they *wait for the mercy of our Lord Jesus Christ to bring you to eternal life.*[19] This is the day when the implications of one's life and actions are revealed. Although not specifically Christian in orientation, the comedy film *Groundhog Day* explores the importance of various days and the implications of how they are lived. Phil, a self-centred and obnoxious television weather presenter, finds himself trapped in the worst day of his year, unable to escape from the day and the implications of his behaviour – until he learns genuinely to love another rather than himself. Each year Phil has to make a report from the Groundhog Day Festival in Punxsutawney, Pennsylvania, something he hates doing. To his amazement he finds himself

[16] Dubay, *Beauty*, 20.
[17] Ibid., 47.
[18] Rolle, 'The Law of Love', 156.
[19] As described in 2 Tim. 1:18; also see 1 Cor. 1:8; 2 Cor. 1:14.

trapped in that terrible day again and again. As soon as the day finishes it restarts at 6am to the sound of the radio playing Sonny and Cher's 'I Got You Babe', and the day proceeds with everyone else apparently unaware that it is repeated. As he goes through the same day time and again, what changes is Phil's behaviour as he explores the possibilities of various attitudes to people. His frustration with the day turns to amusement and then anger as he experiments with overeating, robbery, seduction and eventually suicide. But as soon as the day ends, in one way or another, it starts all over again. He has a unique chance to get it right. It is clear that Phil's actions affect him even more than they affect others and his selfishness condemns him to being trapped in a temporal 'eternity' which is more like hell than anything else. His escape from this endless day into a genuinely different tomorrow comes with his transformation from self-centredness to a focus on others. Serious issues are presented by this comedy which asks viewers to consider the ultimate implications of their own behaviour, and this is something which every person should do because there is a day, the Day of the Lord, on which all human actions and attitudes will be judged by God.

Biblically, the idea of the Day of the Lord has its background in the preaching of the Old Testament prophets, who referred to any 'day'[20] on which God intervened in history in some dramatic way as 'the day of the Lord'.[21] Eventually it came to refer more specifically to the time of God's final judgment and the return of Christ.[22] On that final day all people will be judged[23] according to the deeds they have done and the words they have spoken,[24] for these demonstrate the attitude of the heart. It is possible to have complete confidence in God's judgment in this regard, for he is able to judge even the secret things and the most fundamental motives.[25] God's love is such that he has made salvation possible through Jesus Christ (Matt. 1:21; 1 Pet. 1:18–19) and on that day, although no-one lives without sin (1 Cor. 3:11–15; 1 John 1:8), believers will be kept strong and blameless (1 Cor. 1:8; 2 Cor. 1:14) not because they have become intrinsically better than others but because of *the mercy of our Lord Jesus Christ* (2 Tim. 1:18). Believers therefore wait with hope and confidence, but not without frequent consideration of the

---

[20] It could refer to any specific event or period of time; it did not have to be a single twenty-four-hour day.

[21] Isa. 11:10; Ezek. 7:7; Hos. 1:9; Joel 2:28 – 3:21; Zeph. 2:2; Zech. 14:1–21.

[22] 1 Thess. 5:2; 2 Thess. 2:2; 2 Pet. 3:10.

[23] 1 Tim. 4:5; 2 Tim. 4:1; Heb. 12:23.

[24] Matt. 12:36; 25:31–46; Rev. 21:12.

[25] Rom. 2:16; 1 Cor. 4:5; 1 Pet. 1:17.

implications of their actions not only on others but on themselves and of the kind of person they are becoming because of them. While there is a transformation of our lives on that final day and all sin and corruption are removed, the *eternal life* of the believer is connected with the character and personality of the believer here and now. We cannot imagine the nature of the changes that will take place, but we do not become someone else in eternity. The self who lives with the Lord is a transformed self but nonetheless the self that lives now, and there is a real sense in which we are preparing ourselves now for eternity. Who we are now affects who we are in the future, both immediate and eternal, and so it is important for us to reflect continually on the significance of our thoughts and actions.

It is appropriate that the last words relate to the importance of Christians maintaining a clear view of the final Day of the Lord. 'Waiting' for it, whenever it is mentioned,[26] does not 'indicate a merely passive attitude, but an orientation of the whole life toward the eschatological hope'.[27] The one who has no vision of eternity will never get a true understanding of the significance of time. The present is transformed by our understanding of the future. This means having an awareness of the significance of one's actions not only for oneself, but also for others. The one who has a clear vision of the return of the Lord Jesus and God's desires for the trans-formation of the world can never be entirely satisfied with the status quo. Faithfulness in carrying out present responsibilities is the best preparation for the future. The one who is faithful in small things will become faithful in much (Matt. 25:21, 23).

If we return to the question asked at the start – 'How important is it to believe in the Trinity?' – the answer has to be that it is of absolute importance. But even more important than *believing* in the Trinity is *living* in and through the life of the Trinity. If, as Paul affirms, 'in him we live and move and have our being' (Acts 17:21), then it is only in and through the trinitarian God that we live at all. The doctrine of the Trinity is not a piece of abstract theology, it is the foundation of all that is truly Christian and it is essential for Christian faith and life. It is for this reason that Jude reminds Christians to pray in the Holy Spirit, to keep themselves in the love of God and to wait for the mercy of the Lord Jesus Christ.

[26] Rom. 8:23; 1 Cor. 1:7; 4:5; 1 Thess. 1:10; Titus 2:3.
[27] Bauckham, *Jude*, 114.

Study guide

The aim of this study guide is to help you get to the heart of what Brian has written and challenge you to apply what you learn to your own life. The questions have been designed for use by individuals or by small groups of Christians meeting, perhaps for an hour or two each week, to study, discuss and pray together.

The guide provides material for each of the sections in the book. When used by a group with limited time, the leader should decide beforehand which questions are most appropriate for the group to discuss during the meeting and which should perhaps be left for group members to work through by themselves or in smaller groups during the week.

In order to be able to contribute fully and learn from the group meetings, each member of the group needs to read through the section or sections under discussion, together with the Bible passages to which they refer.

It's important not to let these studies become merely academic exercises. Guard against this by making time to think through and discuss how what you discover *works out in practice* for you. Make sure you begin and end each study by focusing on God in praise and prayer. Ask the Holy Spirit to speak to you through your discussion together.

Introduction (pp. 20–22)

1 Since the word 'Trinity' does not appear in the Bible, what grounds are there for using it?
2 Why do people tend to shy away from the doctrine of the Trinity? How about you? What makes it difficult to understand?
3 How does a right understanding of the Trinity help us when thinking about worship?

'… *the doctrine of the Trinity is a practical, grace-filled doctrine which will take us into the heart and life of God*' (pp. 23–24).

---

4 What difficulties have some modern theologians had with the doctrine of the Trinity?
5 In what ways is the doctrine of the Trinity 'essential'?
6 Why is it so important to hold the 'inner life' and the 'outer

work' (p. 25) of the Trinity together? What happens when either one is emphasized at the expense of the other?

7 Can you give some examples of the way in which the doctrine of the Trinity 'provides a biblical pattern or model for the development of all other doctrines' (p. 28)?

8 What are the 'two main approaches to the process of discerning the Trinity in Scripture' (pp. 30–31)? Why is neither 'entirely satisfactory'?

PART 1. THE TRINITY OF LOVE

2 Corinthians 13:14
1. The God of grace, love and fellowship (pp. 35–51)

1 'It is a problem today that many Christians do not think or speak in terms of the Trinity' (p. 36). Can you think of any examples of this?

2 Is the phrase 'the grace of the Lord Jesus Christ' a prayer or a declaration? Why?

3 What does the word 'grace' mean to you? How does what the author says here enlarge your understanding of what the Bible has to say about this?

'Nothing in the Christian life is outside the orbit of God's grace' (p. 38).

---

4 'One cannot overestimate the significance of this amazing fact' (p. 39). What is the author referring to?

5 In what ways is the name 'The Lord Jesus Christ' trinitarian? Why is this so important?

6 What is 'a challenge to every human way of looking at things' (p. 41)? How does it challenge you?

7 What four characteristics of the 'love of God' does the author draw out here?

8 What is distinctive about Christian love as opposed to romantic love?

9 'It is fairly easy to believe in God's love in general, but it is very difficult to believe in God's love for me personally' (Peter Van Breemen, quoted on p. 45). Why is this the case? How does what the author says help?

10 What 'three interlocking relationships' (p. 47) does the word *koinonia* refer to?

11 In what ways is the Holy Spirit 'the go-between God' (p. 48)? Is this how you think of him?
12 What is 'often neglected' (p. 49)? What does this mean in practice?
13 'The role of the community is critical ...' (p. 50). For what? Why is this important?
14 Why is it important to 'balance the presence of the Spirit in the life of the individual and the life of the community' (p. 50)? How do you think we can best do this?

'We cannot do any better than to let this trinitarian prayer sum up our worship and become the theology at the foundation of our Christian lives' (p. 51).

Ephesians 1:1–14
2. A trinitarian blessing (pp. 52–66)

1 In what ways does this passage reveal Paul's understanding of God as divine Trinity?
2 How do 'worship and Trinity' (p. 54) go together?
3 'God's interaction with the world is expressed in trinitarian fashion' (p. 54). How does Paul draw this out?
4 'The outsider who comes into worship knowing nothing about God should be able to deduce something of God's trinitarian nature from the worship that is offered' (p. 54). In what ways is this true in your experience? How do you think this could be improved?
5 What 'distinctively Christian attitude towards God' (p. 55) does Paul express here? What is so special about it?
6 How would you sum up what Paul means by 'mystery' (p. 57) here?
7 What are the 'three pictures of God's grace which reveal the extent of divine love' (p. 58) here?
8 Why is it so important to stress that 'before we chose God, he chose us' (p. 58)? How is this reflected in your experience?
9 What aspects of the fact that God chose us does Paul emphasize here?
10 How does an understanding of Roman adoption customs help us to understand what God has done for us? How does Paul draw this out?
11 Why is God's forgiveness 'so costly' (p. 62)? How does Paul emphasize this?

12 How does the doctrine of the Trinity help us when thinking about the mystery that 'God should die' (p. 63)?

'In the alienation of the beloved Son from the loving Father, God knows death in all its horror' (p. 64).

---

13 In what ways is Paul's teaching about the Holy Spirit 'in perfect *continuity* and profound *contrast* with Old Testament teaching' (p. 64)?
14 How does Paul express 'the close connection between Jesus and the Spirit' (p. 64)? In what ways is this true in your experience?
15 What does the phrase 'marked with a seal' (pp. 64–65) emphasize about the work of the Holy Spirit?
16 What differences are there between the fruit and the gifts of the Spirit?
17 'God is essentially a God of love, and love is best known and responded to not by mind but by love' (p. 66). How exactly do we do this?

PART 2. THE TRINITY IN THE OLD TESTAMENT

Deuteronomy 6:4–9
3. The Lord our God is one (pp. 69–84)

1 Why does the oneness of God mean that we should love him?
2 What is 'the Shema' (p. 70). Why is it so 'profoundly important for understanding God' (p. 71)?
3 When we say that God is 'one', what exactly do we mean?
4 What was 'the greatest danger that the children of Israel faced' (p. 73)? In what ways do we face a similar danger today?
5 How does the assertion that 'God is the universal ruler' (p. 74) challenge the way many people think about faith today? How would you answer someone who said 'It doesn't matter, we all worship the same God'?
6 What is the significance for us today of the claim that God is 'unique' (p. 75)?

'Evil must be seen for what it is: a temporary aberration ... which will one day cease to exist as God becomes all in all' (p. 76).

---

7 How does New Testament trinitarianism develop out of Old Testament monotheism?

8 What are Christians 'in danger of overlooking' (p. 78) in relation to the command to love God? Why is this so important?

9 'Only a fully trinitarian model of God can provide a complete theology of love ...' (p. 79). Why?

10 Why does the Great Commandment specify that we are to love God with heart and soul and strength? Why do we need to hold these together?

11 How does the command to 'love your neighbour as yourself' (p. 81) relate to the command to love God? Why can't we have one without the other?

12 What were the children of Israel to do 'in order to ensure that these important truths remain a priority for the community' (p. 82)? How do they apply to us today?

Proverbs 8:22–31
4. The wisdom of God (pp. 85–102)

1 In what ways is the wisdom that comes from God 'in conflict with the so-called wisdom of the world' (p. 85)?

2 What is the difference between intelligence and wisdom?

3 What consequences of wise behaviour are highlighted in Proverbs?

4 Since 'there is no unconditional guarantee that the wise person will never suffer' (p. 89), why bother with 'being good'?

5 What different approaches have there been to considering the relationship between Wisdom and God?

6 What 'new and challenging dimensions to the understanding of Wisdom' (p. 91) emerge from Proverbs 8:22–31?

7 How did ideas about the divine personification of Wisdom help early Christians in their thinking about 'the origin of Christ and his unique relationship with God' (p. 94)?

8 In what ways are the life and ministry of Jesus connected with Wisdom? How does Paul develop these ideas?

'That which was hinted at in Proverbs is revealed in Christ. A mere personification has become an actual incarnation, and in Christ the Wisdom of God is revealed fully and is really present' (p. 96).

---

9 In what ways is Proverbs 8:22–31 'an anticipation of the doctrine of incarnation as described in John 1' (p. 97)?

10 'The role of Christ in salvation can tend to overshadow his work in creation' (p. 98). What consequences of this distortion can you think of?
11 How does Paul's teaching about the crucifixion of Jesus dramatically underline the contrast between God's wisdom and the wisdom of the world?

'The completely contrary nature of human and divine wisdom means that each seems as foolishness to the other' (p. 100).

---

12 'People can "murder" God ...' (p. 101). How?
13 In what ways can Christians misunderstand the wisdom of God? How is this reflected in the life and message of the church?

Ezekiel 37:1–14
5. The Spirit of God (pp. 103–118)

1 '... the best measure of one's true spirituality is ...' (p. 103). What? Why is it so important to get this right?
2 What was Ezekiel's role? What grain of hope did his message contain?
3 What does Ezekiel's vision of the valley of dry bones tell us about God and his ways of working?
4 What 'four characteristics of the Spirit' (p. 108) does this vision demonstrate?
5 In what ways have you found rationality to 'get in the way' (p. 110)? How can this be resisted?
6 What do we mean when we describe the Spirit of God as 'personal'? What 'two opposite errors' (p. 111) can people fall into when reflecting on this?
7 What is the difference between the Old and New Testament views of the Spirit?
8 What exactly are 'the implications of Ezekiel's vision for today' (p. 114)? How do they apply to you?

'... God specializes in bringing people and situations back from the dead' (p. 115).

---

9 Do you think that this vision 'constitutes biblical evidence for ... belief in the resurrection of the body' (p. 116)?
10 As you reflect on the way the author has unpacked this vision, in what ways does it speak into your situation today?

PART 3. THE TRINITY IN THE EXPERIENCE AND TEACHING OF JESUS

Luke 1:26–56
6. Incarnation: divine coming (pp. 121–136)

1 What do you think about angels? How does what the Bible says about them clarify your thinking?
2 Who do you know who might be seen as 'the most unlikely of people to be bearers of divine grace' (p. 123)? What is your attitude to them?
3 What are 'perhaps the most profound words that can ever be said to God' (p. 124)? Why?
4 Was the so-called 'virgin birth' real history or a literary construction by the early church (p. 126)? Does it matter? Why?
5 What is 'the primary theological point of the biblical account of the conception of Christ through the Spirit' (p. 127)?

'We are children [of God] by adoption rather than by nature; Jesus is Son of God by nature and was so from conception' (p. 128).

---

6 What does the author suggest is 'the real beginning of the doctrine of the Trinity' (p. 128)? Why is this?
7 What else does the conception of Jesus by the Spirit tell us?
8 In the light of what the author writes here, how might you modify the way you celebrate Christmas?

'Once touched by the grace of God, life can never be the same again' (p. 132).

---

9 What does Mary's song reveal about her understanding of God? In what ways are you able to share her perspective?

Mark 1:1–14
7. Baptism: heavenly empowering (pp. 137–152)

1 How exactly does John the Baptist 'prepare the way for the Lord'? How does this apply to us today?
2 Why is it important to stress that 'repentance is *preparatory*, but it is not everything' (p. 140)?
3 What would people at the time have made of John's baptism? How is this relevant for us today?

4 How is the baptism of Jesus linked to the doctrine of the Trinity?

5 Mark records that Jesus 'saw heaven being torn open'. Would it help us to see the same thing? Why don't we?

6 Why does Jesus insist on being baptized by John?

'It has been said that a Christian is someone who shares the sufferings of God in the world' (p. 144).

7 Why is the dove 'suitable as a symbol for the Holy Spirit' (p. 145)?

8 Do you find the imagery of the dove 'surprising' (p. 146)? What does this underline about the way in which God works?

9 In what ways was the ministry of Jesus 'characterized as a life lived with and through the Spirit of God' (p. 146)?

10 'The aim of the Christian life is not to have an easy life ...' (p. 147). What is it then? In what ways does your life reflect this?

11 What does God's declaration of the Sonship of Jesus at his baptism reveal about him?

12 'In Jesus alone is there the possibility of salvation' (p. 150). Why?

'The true measure of a spiritual life is not ecstasy but obedience' (Oswald Chambers, quoted on p. 150).

13 What implications of Jesus' complete humanity and complete deity does the author highlight here?

'The Trinity is not an "add-on", it is not an "extra", it is the gospel' (p. 152).

Matthew 12:15–32
8. Mission: spiritual encounter (pp. 153–168)

1 What do you make of the statement that mission is 'the mother of theology' (p. 153)?

2 Why was Jesus 'reluctant to have too much attention paid to what he was doing' (p. 154)?

3 'God can use the most unlikely people to achieve his purposes' (p. 155). What examples of this can you think of?

4 How is the mission of Jesus 'bound up together' (p. 156) with the trinitarian nature of God?

5 What modern applications of the call not to break a bruised reed or snuff out a smouldering wick can you think of?

6 What 'trappings … which the world values and believes to be essential' (p. 158) can you think of in relation to Christian ministry? Are they useful or distracting?

7 What is the difference between miracles in general and the miracles of Jesus in particular?

8 'One cannot remain neutral in the presence of Jesus' (p. 160). Why not?

9 What questions are raised by the claim that Jesus 'could simultaneously be God and man in body and, especially, mind and soul' (p. 161)? What are the Lutheran and Reformed views to which the author draws attention? How do they help?

10 Do you agree with any of the various ways the idea of Christ's 'self-emptying' has been expressed? Why? What do you make of the proposed alternative?

'While we tend to think of humanity and divinity as opposed, God does not' (p. 165).

---

11 Why is blasphemy against the Holy Spirit different from blasphemy against Jesus? Why is one forgivable and the other not?

John 14:15–31
9. Teaching: knowledge of God (pp. 169–190)

1 In what ways does this passage underline 'the trinitarian character of [Jesus'] teaching' (p. 169)?

2 'Love and obedience go hand in hand' (p. 171). Why does God's love demand our obedience like this?

3 '… whether it is immediately apparent or not, God's commands are for our good' (p. 171). What examples of this can you think of?

4 How would you answer someone who suggested that rules are obsolete because 'all you need is love'?

5 What does 'perichoresis' mean? How does it apply to us?

6 What approaches have there been to exploring the 'social relationships of the Trinity' (p. 178)? How does the author suggest assessing their validity?

7 What does John 14 say about the relationships within the Trinity?

8 If all the persons of the Trinity are divine, what does Jesus mean by saying that the Father is *greater than I* (p. 181)?
9 What do you think is the best way of understanding the role of the Spirit as 'paraclete' (p. 184)? Why?
10 What can we say about 'the peace which Jesus leaves with his disciples' (p. 186)?

'In Christ there is a perfect peace which is greater than any problem we can have. His peace should permeate our lives' (pp. 186–187).

11 What four characteristics of divine love does John record Jesus talking about in these verses?
12 How would you answer someone who said that God the Father was 'cruel, even monstrous, in sending his Son to die for the sake of the world' (p. 189)?

Matthew 28:16–20
10. Resurrection: commissioned to discipleship (pp. 191–209)

1 How does Matthew emphasize the 'utmost importance' (p. 192) of what Jesus says at the end of the Gospel?
2 'The Great Commission is not a problem to be faced, nor an obligation to be fulfilled' (p. 193). Is this how you see it? If not these, what is it?
3 How would you answer someone who suggested that the trinitarian baptismal formula was 'a later insertion reflecting the theology and the baptismal practices of a later age' (pp. 193–194)?
4 How should mission be related to Trinity and church? Why does this relationship need to be 'carefully defined' (p. 194)?
5 What problems can arise when the 'theological and trinitarian dimensions of mission' (p. 196) are neglected?
6 What would happen to theology generally 'if there were no theology of mission' (p. 198)?

'Where a part of the church neglects the theology of mission and its relationship to the Trinity it is in danger of ending up with a diluted and irrelevant theology' (p. 198).

7 What is 'the most important message of the church' (p. 199)? Why?
8 What parallels are there between the Great Commission and 2 Chronicles 36:22–23? Why is this significant?
9 Why is it important to insist that the Great Commission 'has only one main verb' (p. 202) rather than two? What difference does this make?
10 Why is teaching 'an important part of evangelism' (p. 204)?
11 '... it is very important to note that Jesus calls his disciples to obey everything he had taught them' (p. 205). Why is this?
12 What significance is there in the fact that some of Jesus' disciples are recorded as doubting him earlier in Matthew chapter 28? How does this help us?

'What makes mission possible is not self-confidence but confidence in Jesus' (p. 207).

13 How can we come to see mission as 'more of a joy and a privilege' (p. 208)?

PART 4. THE TRINITY IN THE EXPERIENCE AND TEACHING OF THE EARLY CHURCH

Acts 2:1–47
11. The day of Pentecost (pp. 213–231)

1 Why is Acts chapter 2 'critically important' (p. 213)?
2 What is the significance of the fact that the Spirit came on the day of Pentecost?
3 How does the account of the building of the Tower of Babel in Genesis 11 illuminate the significance of Pentecost? What specific application does the author suggest for us today?
4 What do wind and fire teach us about the filling of the Holy Spirit?
5 What was it that made Pentecost 'completely new' (p. 219)? How is this change related to the Trinity?

'A church that is always boring, always under complete control and unable to explode at times with joy and spontaneity is not a church which reflects the dynamic presence of the Holy Spirit' (p. 222).

6 How are we to 'discern rightly the difference between the genuine work of God in renewal and the fanciful imagination of some of his followers' (p. 222)?

7 What can we learn from the way in which the crowd reacted to the events of Pentecost?

8 'If we spend our time trying to be normal and aiming not to stand out then we may miss something of what it means to be a Christian' (p. 223). To what extent is this true of you?

9 In what ways was Peter's preaching 'very theological' (p. 225)? How does what he said point to the Trinity?

10 How does Peter respond to the crowd's distress? Can you trace the way this is 'expressed in trinitarian terms' (p. 226)?

11 What are the 'four essential characteristics' (p. 228) of the healthy church that emerge from this passage? What is it that makes them essential?

12 The author goes on to describe five typical features which 'provide us with an outline of the life of a healthy church' (p. 230). What are these? In what ways do you think your church could become healthier?

13 Why does Luke specify that 'the Lord added to their numbers daily' (p. 231)? Why is this so important?

'Before Christ sent the church into the world he sent the Spirit into the church and the same order of things must be followed today' (p. 231).

Romans 8:1–17
12. Christian experience (pp. 232–249)

1 What is 'the only way to deal with the effects of sin' (p. 232)? Why?

'There is no doubt that authentic Christianity is not merely theoretical, nor only cerebral, nor solely moral, but also definitely and clearly experiential' (p. 233).

---

2 '... the best form of balance is not necessarily achieved simply by being moderate in everything' (p. 233). To what is the author referring? In what ways does this speak to you?

3 What are the 'four aspects of trinitarian salvation' which the author highlights in Romans 8:1–17?

4 What is 'the greatest miracle possible' (p. 236)? What hinders people from seeing this?
5 What misconceptions does Paul's 'careful description of the nature of the incarnation' (p. 237) avoid? In what ways is this issue important for us today?
6 Do you 'dare to be a sinner' (p. 239)? How is this possible? Why is it necessary?
7 What three things are true of 'those who live *according to the sinful nature*' (p. 240)?
8 How would you answer someone who suggested that God is 'a divine killjoy who makes up rules just to spoil people's fun' (p. 241)?
9 How exactly does the Spirit help us to overcome sin?
10 Why would 'Coffin Cheaters' (p. 244) be a suitable name for Christians?
11 What things can you think of in your life which, although not wrong in themselves, 'nonetheless need to be put away or left behind for the sake of a life lived under the guidance of the Spirit' (p. 244)?
12 What truths follow from 'the adoption of believers by God the Father' (p. 244)?
13 What 'positive dimension' (p. 246) of Christian suffering does the author highlight?
14 Why are some Christians in danger of becoming 'slaves again to fear' (p. 247)? In what sense then should we 'fear' God?

1 Corinthians 12:1–11
13. Christian community (pp. 250–269)

1 Why doesn't Paul seem to be concerned about 'establishing a comprehensive list of gifts and determining the right form of categorization for them' (p. 250)? What matters more to him?
2 What was the 'basic Corinthian problem' (p. 251)? In what ways are we prone to a similar situation?
3 What is 'striking' and 'impressive' (p. 253) about what Paul says here?
4 What kinds of diversity in the church are unhealthy? How do we know?
5 What does the term 'gift' (p. 254) mean?
6 How would you seek to help a Christian who has become 'discouraged because they cannot find their spiritual gift' (p. 254)?

7 Why is it important to maintain a clear distinction between 'the doctrine of the priesthood of all believers and the doctrine of the ministry of all believers' (p. 256)?

8 Why is the connection of 'service' with the Lord Jesus 'entirely appropriate' (p. 257)? What difference does this make to the way we understand and use spiritual gifts?

9 Why can no-one say, 'Jesus is Lord', except by the Holy Spirit?

10 What differences are there between a natural ability and a spiritual gift? Which of your natural abilities are also spiritual gifts? And which are not? Why do you think this is?

11 What problems with church leadership does the author identify here? How does this passage help?

'Every Christian is a leader ... because every Christian is gifted' (p. 262).

---

12 What attitudes to his own leadership does Paul demonstrate? What is there here for us to learn from?

13 Why has God given us 'the privilege of sharing with him in his work' (p. 264)? Is this how you see your spiritual gifts?

14 'The gifts of God must be used with discernment' (p. 265). Why is this? How do we do it?

15 Why is it important for us to see our gifts 'as gifts of the body rather than of the individual' (p. 267)? What happens when we don't do this?

16 'A right character is more important than intellect, training, position, status and even gifting or ability' (p. 268). Why is this the case?

Galatians 3:26 – 4:7
14. Christian security (pp. 270–288)

1 In what ways have you experienced the truth that the basic principles of religion 'enslave people but ... cannot bring salvation' (p. 271)?

2 What was 'both unremarkable and shocking' (p. 271) about the claim that the Galatians were all 'sons of God'?

3 What does the doctrine of the Trinity contribute to the way we understand ourselves as the 'sons of God'?

4 What differences between sons and servants are highlighted here?

5 What does it mean to be 'all one in Christ Jesus' (p. 274)?

THE MESSAGE OF THE TRINITY

'Paul is speaking about the experience of intimacy with Christ, the deepest religious experience of God that anyone can have' (p. 276).

6 What is at issue in the controversy over the *filioque* clause in the Nicene creed? What do you think about it?
7 How would you help someone who wanted to know that they really have been saved?

'All those who recognize that they love the Lord a little and who would like to love him more are children of God' (p. 279).

8 What has led to the description of Galatians 3:28 as 'the Magna Carta of humanity' (p. 280)?
9 What does the author mean by 'a social dimension to salvation' (p. 281)? Why has this sometimes been ignored? Where does the doctrine of the Trinity fit in here?
10 What divisions in our world parallel those that Paul mentions here? What practical steps can we take to break down such barriers?
11 Do you think that the 'restrictions that are placed on the ministry of women' (p. 287) relate to the specific, cultural situation in Paul's time? Or are they general principles which apply to us as well? Why?
12 What has happened as a result of the fact that 'modern Western society [has] lost its understanding of the importance of the doctrine of the Trinity' (p. 287)?

Ephesians 4:1–16
15. Christian unity (pp. 289–308)

1 'There are many things that individuals can do on their own, but being a Christian is not one of them' (p. 290). Why not?
2 How does the Trinity provide 'a model for the structure, the unity and the mission of the church' (p. 290)? What do you make of the different perspectives the author sets out here?
3 Is the diversity of the church 'like a garden of many coloured flowers' or like 'a broken glass or vase' (p. 292)?
4 What examples of 'unedifying dissension, failure to communicate and unnecessary duplication' (p. 292) are you aware of in the life of the church?
5 'The true unity of the church is grounded in the triunity of God ...' (p. 292). How does Paul bring this out in this chapter?

6 What 'ought to mark out a community that is Christian' (p. 293)? Why are these features so important?

'If you want to be truly miserable then rid yourself of humility, gentleness and patience, for these things only lead to joy and contentment in love for others' (p. 294).

---

7 What 'two equally important facts' (p. 294) follow from the instruction to *keep the unity of the Spirit*?
8 What is 'fundamentally different' (p. 295) about the Christian use of the image of the body when compared with secular groups? What does this mean in practice?
9 What dangers for the unity of the church are there in the fact that we have such 'a high level of choice' (p. 297) in our culture today?
10 How did you choose the church to which you belong? 'What principles ought to guide so that commitment is not superseded by consumption' (p. 299)?
11 What does Paul mean when he says that 'God is *Father of [us] all'* (p. 301)? What can human families learn from the way in which God the Father and God the Son relate to each other?
12 How would you seek to help someone who had difficulty with praying to God as Father?
13 What *is* essential doctrine? Why is this 'a difficult question' (p. 304)? Which do you find to be the most satisfactory answer?
14 What principles are there to guide us when thinking about leaving or staying in a situation where 'there is a breach in the unity of the faith' (p. 305)?
15 What are the characteristics of Christian maturity? How can they be developed?
16 Are you a 'bonsai Christian'? What does the author mean by this? How can it be avoided?

'Maturity does not simply come with age, it must be fed and nurtured' (p. 307).

Jude 20–21
16. The Day of the Lord (pp. 309–319)

1 Can a person be saved without believing the doctrine of the Trinity?

THE MESSAGE OF THE TRINITY

 2 'It is not enough to connect salvation with the work of Christ'
   (p. 311). Why not?
 3 In what ways does the imagery of building 'indicate the nature
   of spiritual growth' (p. 311)?
 4 What does it mean in practice to affirm that 'being built up in the
   faith is a continuous and vital process' (p. 312)?

'No Christian can be complacent about his or her spiritual life'
(p. 313).

---

 5 Why does Jude specify that prayer should be 'in the Holy
   Spirit'? What does this mean?
 6 What does the author identify as 'the real tests of spiritual life'
   (p. 314)? How do you measure up?
 7 What is the difference between 'praying continually' and 'saying
   prayers' (p. 314)?
 8 What 'three attitudes' (p. 315) does the author suggest should
   permeate our approach to life? What is distinctive about each of
   them?
 9 What does 'keeping ourselves in God's love' mean? How do we
   do it?

'Beauty triggers wonder in the human heart and is essential for
spiritual growth' (p. 317).

---

10 In what sense are we 'waiting for the mercy of Christ' (p. 318)?
   What does this 'waiting' actually involve?
11 What is 'even more important than believing in the Trinity'
   (p. 319)?

'The doctrine of the Trinity is not a piece of abstract theology, it is
the foundation of all that is truly Christian and it is essential for
Christian faith and life' (p. 319).
